EXPLORE
EUROPE
ON FOOT

EXPLORE EUROPE ON FOOT

YOUR COMPLETE GUIDE TO PLANNING A CULTURAL HIKING ADVENTURE

CASSANDRA OVERBY

MOUNTAINEERS
BOOKS

For Mac, my knight in shining armor, my favorite travel companion
and the one who works an office job so I don't have to

 MOUNTAINEERS BOOKS is the publishing division of
The Mountaineers, an organization founded in 1906 and dedicated to the
exploration, preservation, and enjoyment of outdoor and wilderness areas.

1001 SW Klickitat Way, Suite 201, Seattle, WA 98134
800-553-4453, www.mountaineersbooks.org

Printed in China
Distributed in the United Kingdom by Cordee, www.cordee.co.uk
First edition: first printing 2018, second printing 2019

Copyeditor: Kris Fulsaas
Cover & book design: Jen Grable
Cartographer: Lohnes+Wright
All photographs by the author unless otherwise noted
Cover photographs (clockwise from top left): *In England's Lake District, you'll walk past charming old build-
ings and hardy sheep.* (Photo © John Hodgson) | *On Portugal's Rota Vicentina Fishermen's Trail, the weather
is typically warm, so a chilled glass of local wine makes for an excellent post-hike snack.* | *In Cinque Terre,
you'll wander through a series of vibrant seaside towns.* | *On Iceland's Laugavegur Trek, stunning scenery takes
center stage.* (Photo © Thomas Fick).
Back cover photographs (from top): *Bachalpsee Lake, near Switzerland's Alpine Pass Route* | *A must-do in
Turkey: tea time with locals* | *Enjoy the wonderful variety of castles on walks in France and Germany.*
Frontispiece: *Switzerland's Alpine Pass Route is at its best midsummer, when the wildflowers are in bloom.*
Page 27: *The big draw of Croatia's Plitvice Lakes National Park is the network of cascading waterfalls that flow
through the park.* | Page 40: *Getting married on the steps of the Cathedral of Santiago de Compostela* | Page
149: *Lake Windermere, in England's Lake District, is the country's largest natural lake.* (Photo © John
Hodgson) |Pages 202–208: Exercise model, Elizabeth Wyosnick | Page 239: *Even in late summer, the Tour
du Mont Blanc is often embellished with vibrant wildflowers.* | Page 249: *A trail outfit for an inclement day*
(Photo by Mitzi Sugar) | Page 287: *One of my favorite trail views is the snow-covered Alps in the spring.* |
Page 298: *Clock* (Photo by EuroVizion/Flickr) | Page 299, top: *Thermometer* (Photo by Acid Pix/Flickr) |
Page 299, bottom: *Metric route signs*

Library of Congress Cataloging-in-Publication Data is on file at https://lccn.loc.gov/2018005759.

Mountaineers Books titles may be purchased for corporate, educational, or other promotional sales, and our
authors are available for a wide range of events. For information on special discounts or booking an author,
contact our customer service at 800-553-4453 or mbooks@mountaineersbooks.org.

Printed on FSC®-certified materials

ISBN (paperback): 978-1-68051-107-9
ISBN (ebook): 978-1-68051-108-6

CONTENTS

PART 2 PLANNING 149

PART 3 PACKING 239

PART 4 TRAVELING 287

INTRODUCTION: START HERE

Once upon a time, when I was in my early twenties, I saved up $18,000 to fulfill one of my all-time biggest life goals: a trip around the world. I decided to kick things off in Guatemala by volunteering at an orphanage and then bouncing around to different cities. Here's the part I've always been embarrassed about: after three months in Guatemala, I called it quits and went back home with all but $1,000 still in my bank account. I felt like the biggest (and weirdest) failure: Who saves up for a bucket-list trip like that and then decides they'd rather be at home?

At first, I couldn't explain it to myself, let alone anyone else. A lot of my identity was wrapped up in traveling—I'd lived abroad twice in college and traveled extensively beyond that. It was what I thought about, dreamed about, worked multiple jobs at a time to save up for. So what gave?

The answer didn't bode well for my future as a traveler: I no longer found fulfillment in sightseeing. I was tired of long lines, loud tourists, bus exhaust and expensive attractions. I was fed up with how inauthentic—and global, not local—international travel had become; it seemed like no matter what city I was visiting, it was American pop music that played on the radio and french fries that were the side dish of choice.

Figuring my time as a gypsy was over, I threw all of my extra money and enthusiasm in the opposite direction: home. I focused on my community and got an office job. I bought a car. As determined as I had been to travel the world, I was now determined to stay in one place—and enjoy it.

Flash forward three years and just imagine my surprise—and, yes, dismay—when I met the man I'd eventually marry, and he told me that his big dream was to do a months-long grand tour of Europe. Oh, and he wanted me to go with him.

I knew at the time that it was a make-or-break-the-relationship kind of request. What I didn't know was that my eventual decision to join him would lead to an epiphany on trail in Switzerland, the healing of my rift with travel and a new life calling to spread the word that there is a better, more authentic way to travel.

A Better Way to Travel

In 2015 my then-boyfriend and now-husband, Mac, and I launched out on our grand tour of Europe. Because we planned on traveling for five months, we wanted to pace ourselves; because of my disillusionment with travel, we also wanted to live like locals instead of tourists. So we started taking long walks wherever we were; it was about the slowest and most local way we could think of to explore not only the cities but the countryside we were passing through.

We didn't expect these long walks to become the most enjoyable part of our trip, but they soon did. After a series of outstanding one-day wanders through the likes of the Loire Valley of France and Cinque Terre of Italy, we excitedly planned a multiday walk along the Alpine Pass Route that runs from east to west across Switzerland.

I thought I was ready for the APR. After all, I'm from the Pacific Northwest, where we have our share of skyscraping mountains, remote alpine passes and glacier-fed rivers. I've hiked extensively in Montana and Colorado. But nothing could have prepared me for the exquisiteness of the Alps. It was the most incredible place I'd ever been—enchanting and magical, like *The Sound of Music* come to life.

There was nothing subtle about its beauty; it held nothing back. And for six days, we discovered deep valleys with lush grass and lazy rivers as well as windswept peaks where patches of snow stubbornly refused to melt in the hot sun and fat marmots played hide-and-seek. Our favorite part was the endless pastures of impossible green that clung to the sides of the mountains like a lover. Here, small farms nestled in the folds of the hills and thousands of cows dotted the landscape, filling our ears with the constant soft tinkling of cowbells. Wildflowers crept up to the edge of our footpath, swaying provocatively in the slightest breeze and freely giving up their intoxicating scent so that even if I closed my eyes, there was no doubt about where we were.

The walking itself was as good as the landscape we were passing through. For six days, we

From lush meadows to dramatic mountains, Switzerland's Alpine Pass Route has it all.

got up early each morning, eager to hit the trail while the air was still brisk and breakfast warmed our bellies. By noon, we'd been walking—and exploring—for hours: small farms selling milk and cheese on the honor system, tiny chapels offering generations-old art and the promise of a short rest, quaint villages showcasing the best of rustic Alpine architecture, with its wooden buildings and overflowing boxes of fire poker–red geraniums.

Lunch was always a highlight, a long, drawn-out affair. Some days, we'd find a cool alpine lake to dip our feet in while we devoured a picnic of local delicacies. Other days, we'd stop at a small mountain hut for cold beers and hot sausages. Sometimes we'd read our books; other times we'd take a short nap in the sun.

We were never in a hurry; we enjoyed everything, especially hoisting our packs onto our backs once again and continuing our walk. I came to understand that each afternoon we weren't just walking to the next guesthouse— we were going back in time. One evening, we were almost to our destination when we spotted an old man in worn lederhosen coming down the trail carrying the longest instrument I'd ever seen. His wife was beside him with her picnic basket on her arm, holding their small granddaughter's hand. I'd never heard an alpenhorn before, so I asked the man (in German) if he would play us a note. Better than that, he played us an entire song from memory, a haunting melody that floated over the hills and gave me goose bumps before it settled peacefully in the valley.

Most nights, we stayed at working farms along the trail. They were nothing like the farms we knew from back home; everything was done by hand as it had always been done, in part because there was still no electricity in these remote hamlets. It was fascinating, and

There are many charming restaurants that make excellent rest stops along the Tour du Mont Blanc. (Photo by Cheryl Nilson)

we spent hours talking to the families we stayed with about everything from farm life to local politics as the animals were brought in for the night, dinner was prepared and day turned to dusk. We saw firsthand the process of making milk and cheese; we learned how to feed hogs and take care of goats.

As darkness gathered outside, the farm would flicker to life one last time with the light of a dozen long candles and gas lamps. Dinner—some of the best comfort food we'd ever tasted—was served. Several courses and a couple of hours later, we'd push back from the table, satisfied beyond belief. And so, so tired.

Every night of that trip, I dutifully took a candle to our bedroom and attempted to put down on paper the essence of everything we were experiencing, from gorgeous landscapes

When hiking in Turkey, one of the must-sees is a whirling dervish performance.

to unimaginable walking, to a totally different way of life. But as I snuffed out the candle and climbed into bed for another long night of sleep, my mind would always come back to one thought: there was, in fact, a better, more authentic way to travel—and this was it.

I call it exploring on foot, this new kind of travel. We loved it so much—and found such value in it—that long walks became our favorite way to discover foreign lands. In every country we visited, from Ireland in the west to Croatia in the east, we set out on country roads and bike paths, forest trails and cliff walks with the goal of discovering the best natural beauty and most authentic culture a region had to offer. And it worked. By simply taking advantage of what the trail put in our path—from ancient ruins in Turkey to harvest festivals in Bavaria— we found each day filled with more interesting experiences and Rick-Steves-eat-your-heart-out, only-tourists-around moments than we'd ever experienced through traditional tourism. And we were having fun! So much fun, actually,

that our five-month grand tour of Europe became a nine-month twenty-six-country trip around the world.

I knew my rift with travel was healed when we eventually returned home and all I could think about was leaving once again. I could hardly wait for my next chance to explore on foot. Tens of trails and thousands of miles later, I still haven't lost my craving for more.

Exploring Europe on Foot: This Guide

It's no secret that exploring on foot has become not just my favorite thing to do but also my favorite thing to talk about. So I was thrilled when family, friends and friends of friends started asking for my advice on how to do it. I loved helping them prepare for their trips and hearing their stories once they were back. But the most exciting thing to me was that people who started exploring on foot didn't want to stop—just like me! Even before they finished their first trail, they were already thinking about the next.

And it wasn't just people who loved to walk. I witnessed grudging exercisers and those who had to dig deep because they'd never walked that far in their lives become excited about walking for days at a time. I saw trip after trip reignite the passion of experienced travelers who felt like they'd seen—and done—it all. For those new to travel, it became the gold standard that they measured all other trips against. It was amazing.

Watching other people become as enthusiastic as I was about exploring on foot was a game changer for me. I realized it wasn't just the solution to *my* problem with travel—it was the answer a lot of other people were looking for as well. And that's when spreading the word about this better, more authentic way to travel became my life calling—and I started writing this book.

WHY EXPLORE ON FOOT

And that brings me to you. I'm so glad you're here, because I'm not just convinced that exploring on foot works for me and those I know who have tried and loved it—I'm confident it will work for you too. Here's why:

You Find Your Way to the Best Small Towns

If you want to truly experience a foreign culture, the best place to look is a small town. That's because cities are hotbeds of globalization and more a reflection of the greater world than the country they're a part of. While globalization comes in handy when you're in London and craving sushi or Thai food, it's not so great when you want to discover authentic British culture. I'm not saying it doesn't exist in London—it's just harder to find.

If you want to experience pure foreign culture, your best bet is in rural outposts where people primarily speak the local language, cook local food, listen to local music and have real communities with a flavor all their own. Now, I know what you're thinking—if the aim is to simply get to small towns, you don't need to walk. You could just sit down with a map, point

In many small European towns, you'll feel like you've gone back in time to a simpler—and infinitely more charming—era.

to a small town and drive there in your rental car. And you might get really lucky and have an amazing travel adventure. But most likely you wouldn't, because not every small town is equipped for visitors. Some are too small to have the basic services that travelers need; others are too industrial to have anything cultural on tap.

It's a fine balance of finding a small town that's not too small. But it's a balance that's easy to strike when you're walking. And that's because long trails are typically divided into daily stages that end where you can find accommodations, food and interesting things to do, taking the guesswork out of discovering the best small towns.

You Catch a More Authentic Glimpse of the Culture

Walking into one of these villages is an amazing way to drop in on a culture and see it for what it really is and how it really functions. As travel host Samantha Brown said in a speech in Washington, DC, "Authentic travel is never in the must-sees, always in the mundane." That's exactly what you have to look forward to. You'll learn about the rhythm of everyday life, about when people get up, what they do for work, how they spend their free time, when they go to bed and what they believe. But I guarantee it won't be mundane—it'll be magical.

Just as when we were in Switzerland and had the opportunity to help with chores on the farm, many times you won't just observe the local culture—you'll also be invited to experience it. You may be asked to share a meal with a family in Germany or get a lesson on regional politics from a French B and B host who loves to talk as much as he loves to host. You may be included in an after-hours sing-along in

an Irish pub. All of these things happened to Mac and me as we walked around Europe for months.

There's something about traveling on foot that makes you more accessible to local people and thus more likely to be brought into the fold. There's nothing to hide behind—no throng of peers, no fancy clothing, no rolling luggage. With just a backpack and a map, you appear far more relatable and approachable. For Mac and me, it opened the door to trail magic. Locals helped us with everything from car rides to language questions. When we were in Spain to walk the English Way, a kind stranger stood with us for an entire *Semana Santa* (Holy Week) procession of more than two hours to explain all of the traditions and practices of the event, patiently narrating as each float went by so that we would really understand what we were seeing.

Walking is a natural way to practice slow travel, which emphasizes slowing down and enjoying every moment rather than rushing around and seeing as many sights as possible. Want to learn more about slow travel? A good place to start is Nicky Gardner's "A Manifesto for Slow Travel" at online travel magazine *hidden europe* (see Resources at the back of this book for details).

You Have Historical Wonders All to Yourself

Exploring on foot not only takes you to intriguing small towns where you can discover the most authentic culture, it also leads you to important places that don't get visited as often because they're not as convenient to get to or are downright inaccessible by car or coach.

When I was walking France's Grande Randonée 34, the route passed nearly on top of several eerie, crumbling bunkers of the Nazis'

Atlantic Wall. I didn't just get to see these relics; I got to climb down into them. Surrounded by heavy concrete, I looked out a narrow slit in the rocks to the same view the Germans had during World War II—endless coast, sunlight glinting off the water, fishing boats bobbing on the horizon. I imagined nervous sentries incessantly scanning the English Channel, waiting for the invasion that Hitler was convinced would happen—and did, on June 6, 1944. It was a unique experience, even more amazing because not a single other person (other than my two walking companions) was around.

It's something I've discovered time and time again—when you're on foot, you don't need to beat the crowds to these places; most of the time, you'll have them all to yourself. Another bonus: You can experience these gems on your own time, whether that means spending an hour in contemplation or giving them a quick nod of appreciation before moving on.

You Gain a Greater Appreciation for the Landscape

Besides coming across the best small towns and most interesting sights when you're exploring on foot, you'll also gain a far greater appreciation for the land and scenery you're traveling through. This is something that can't be experienced in three minutes as you drive along a road or from the air-conditioned interior of a museum. It needs to be processed by your body—and every sense you have. That's easy to do when you're walking. As Robert and Martha Manning, authors of *Walking Distance*, say, "The deliberate pace of walking allows us to more fully sense the world, to see its richness of detail, to touch, hear, smell and even taste it."

It's one thing to learn that the world's steepest vineyard is the Calmont on the Moselle River in Germany; it's another to experience the shocking pitch of the vineyard as you climb ladders and steady yourself with metal cables among the vines. You can know intellectually that parts of Turkey are incredibly arid; you only really understand what that means when you accidentally kick the bone-dry ground with your feet and have to rush to cover your mouth before the swirling dust chokes you. You can read that Iceland is one of the most volcanically active landscapes in the world; it takes on new meaning when you have to watch your step because you're surrounded by hissing and boiling sulfurous mud.

You Have a Better Experience for Less Money

It's almost hard to believe, but when you explore on foot, you visit more interesting towns, experience culture more vividly, see undiscovered sights and gain a better appreciation for the landscape, all for *less* money than you would spend on traditional sightseeing. One of the reasons is that your main activity each day is walking—not purchasing admission into expensive attractions or paying for spendy tours—so you don't have a lot of costs beyond gear, food and accommodations.

Gear doesn't have to cost you a ton—athletic clothes, a backpack and comfortable shoes will get you where you need to go. Food and accommodations in rural areas cost less than they do in metropolitan areas. Combined with the fact that the cost of living in Europe can be significantly cheaper than in the United States (an average double room will cost you €50 a night, and two people can eat a good dinner—with wine—for €25–€50), a walking holiday can be downright affordable. If you walk in Eastern rather than Western Europe, it can actually be cheap. No matter where in Europe you walk, your most significant outlay of money will be for airfare, and you can usually find great deals

One of the best things about exploring on foot is the ability to unplug and live in the moment.

on flights during the shoulder seasons, when the walking is also good.

You Have the Restorative Experience That Vacation Is Meant to Be

I'm convinced that exploring on foot isn't just the best way to travel; it's also the best way to get back to basics. Modern life can be so complicated. Between electronic screens and urban schedules, it can feel like you're always on, always connected and always busy. Exploring on foot can help you unplug, focus on your body and find your own pace.

It's easy to unplug when you're on trail, especially if you're visiting a remote region that doesn't have good cellular service or Wi-Fi. (Or electricity, as I experienced in the Swiss Alps!) After all, there's not much you can do for the people back home when you're in the middle of nowhere. You might as well turn your phone off if you don't need it for navigational purposes.

It's amazingly freeing to know that you won't be disturbed by news alerts, Facebook notifications or work email. I always sleep better when I'm off the grid, and I'm sure you will too.

Disconnecting from technology will help you shift your attention from your mind to your body. You might be surprised by what you don't know about it—and what it starts to show you. You'll get a feel for how much water, food and sleep you really need to function at your best. You'll feel sensations in places you didn't even know could have sensations, such as in between your toes or under the knob of your kneecap. And you'll feel yourself getting physically stronger—your back, your legs, even your core. Once you shake off the cobwebs of sitting at a desk all day, your body will probably feel better than it ever has before.

Walking won't just get you out of your head and into your body; it will also help you find your own pace. That's because it forces you to

There's a lot to look forward to when it comes to exploring on foot. Here are some of my favorites:

- Eat whatever you want because you know you'll burn it all off.
- Sleep like a baby because you've exhausted your body and your mind.
- Be an explorer—a rare treat in a world that feels completely mapped and known.
- Experience the incredible camaraderie that exists among walkers.
- Feel the high that comes with achieving a challenging physical goal.

travel at the speed of you. For most people, that's only 2 miles (3.2 km) an hour. If you cover 10 miles (16 km) or so a day, that equates to five hours of putting one foot in front of the other, looking around, taking pictures, contemplating and taking breaks whenever you feel like it. There's no pressure to go faster or squeeze more in, because walking is your main activity for the day. You may find yourself slowing down and indulging in things you would never make time for at home: a trailside nap, a reading break next to a small stream or a midday yoga session. The result: Vacation becomes the restorative experience it was meant to be instead of a whirlwind that leaves you more exhausted than when you left home.

WHY EUROPE

There's so much to look forward to when it comes to exploring on foot—and there's no better place to do it than Europe. I've explored a lot of places around the world, from Central America to Southeast Asia, but I keep coming back to Europe time and time again. From world-class trails that suit every kind of interest

and walker to impressive public transportation, plenty of on-trail accommodations and a variety of services that make tackling a long walk easy, Europe has everything it takes to be your favorite place to walk.

World-Class Trails

One of the best reasons to explore Europe on foot is that it's home to some of the greatest trails in the world. Many of them pass through remnants of the most significant times in Western civilization, including the rise and fall of the Roman Empire, the Renaissance, the French Revolution, and WWI and WWII. Others are bucket-list walks and sights that you'll remember and talk about for years. All of them blend

When you're walking the Tour du Mont Blanc, flat sections of trail are hard to come by—and much appreciated.

In France and Germany, you'll see plenty of romantic castles and abbeys perched on cliffs in the distance.

the best of the wilderness with the best of civilization in unique ways so that walking becomes the cultural exploration you want it to be.

Imagine walking through Germany on a chilly autumn day and seeing Neuschwanstein—the fanciful castle that inspired Walt Disney's creation of the iconic *Sleeping Beauty* one—hanging from a cliff in the distance (Walk 9, King Ludwig's Way). How about pounding the trail in Italy as the Alps turn pink and orange with alpenglow (Walk 8, Alpine Pass Route). (And did you notice that? *Alp*englow?) Picture yourself walking the same steps an ancient Celtic warrior did hundreds of years ago through the Highlands of Scotland (Walk 13, West Highland Way). There's a reason these trails have inspired everything from pop culture to language to hundreds of years of repeated use. They're that good. And no matter what kind of walker you are, there's something for everyone, whether you want a steep alpine trail that will challenge you or an easy, flat trail

with plenty of opportunities to stop and smell the roses.

The sad fact is terrorism has become a relatively common occurrence, not just in Europe but around the world. And it (understandably) makes travelers nervous. But don't worry about exploring Europe on foot. Because of its emphasis on small towns and nature—the unflashy things that terrorists have no interest in destroying—it's one of the safest ways to travel in Europe.

Impressive Public Transportation

Thanks to the amazing infrastructure of Europe, you'll have not only incredible trails to choose from but also an easy time making those long walks a reality. Europe is a traveler's paradise, whether you're new to globe-trotting or you've been around the world a few times. One reason: It has a lot of different cultures in a really small area. And because it's brilliantly connected by public transportation, it's easy to be somewhere totally new—and totally different—in a short amount of time. You can be admiring Moorish architecture in southern Spain one day and the very next be drinking Guinness with an Irishman in Dublin.

That accessibility extends to trails. Unlike North America, where most trailheads are in the wilderness and require a car to get to, most European trailheads are in towns that are served by buses, trains and even cheap hopper flights (see Chapter 7, Get There). That's great when you're walking just one long trail, but it's especially helpful when you're trying to tackle two or more long trails in one trip. Want to see the Alps and the ocean but have only a week to explore them both? Totally doable.

Another reason public transportation makes walking in Europe a breeze? It's easy to shorten long or challenging stages by taking everything from a gondola to a taxi.

Plenty of On-Trail Accommodations

One of my favorite things about walking in Europe is that you don't have to camp. There are plenty of on-trail accommodations, which means that you can look forward to sleeping in a real bed (usually in a supercharming spot) and eating food that someone else has prepared

MORE REASONS TO EXPLORE EUROPE ON FOOT

Here are five more reasons why Europe's a delightful place to explore on foot:

1. **Many people speak English.** Many Europeans, especially those in the tourism industry—guesthouse owners, restaurateurs, train stewards—speak English, so you can be confident that you'll be able to communicate with them, even if you don't speak a foreign language. (That said, you'll have the best interactions if you learn at least a few phrases in the local language wherever you go, so study up! Check out Chapter 11, Make Your Walk a Cultural Experience, for tips.)

2. **It's safe.** Unlike some places around the world where you have to worry about carjackings or kidnappings, small European towns like the ones you'll find on trail are very safe; crime, especially violent crime, is uncommon. Even when I'm traveling on my own, I feel safer walking around a small village in Portugal or Germany after dark than I do walking around some neighborhoods of Seattle midday.

3. **It's not too remote.** In Europe, you will never be too far from civilization—on all but the remotest trails, you'll see at least a few people each day and walk past everything from farms to villages—so if you need help, from resupplies to medical attention, it can be there quickly. The response time gets even faster when you have a mobile phone, because most of the time you'll have cellular service.

4. **There are few scary animals.** Thanks to a mild climate and overhunting in the eighteenth and nineteenth centuries, there aren't many large animals in the wilderness of Europe to be afraid of. According to the official website of the Via Alpina trail system (see Resources), there are fewer than fifty bears and wolves and about a hundred lynxes in all of the Alps—and most of these are incredibly shy. The animal you're most likely to encounter in Europe? A wild boar.

5. **Few permits or passes are required.** Most European trails don't require permits or passes, and I've never encountered a trail that limits the number of visitors. If you do need a pass, for a national park or other protected land, you'll usually be able to buy it once you arrive, easy as pie.

For dramatic, wide-open views, there's no better trail than Iceland's Laugavegur Trek. (Photo by Thomas Fick)

for you (often the best food you've ever tasted). And you'll have a light load, because you won't need to pack a tent, sleeping bag, sleeping pad, pillow, water purifier, camp stove, dishes, backpacking food or any of the other (bulky, if not heavy) things you'd need to sleep outside. Score!

It's not just having a place to stay that's great about walking in Europe—it's the variety of accommodations that are available. And that applies to both how much or how little luxury you want and the kind of experience you're looking for. On a budget? Try a hut, a hostel or a guesthouse. Interested in seeing what foreign family life is like? Rent a room from locals. Want to stay in a fitness hotel and enjoy a sauna and massage every day when you get off trail? You can have that too. And if you're like me and want to try something different each night, that's also an option.

It's not just accommodations that you'll find on trail. Most routes also feature a selection of cafes, pubs and restaurants, which means that you can enjoy a hot meal and a cold beverage at lunchtime instead of a squished sandwich.

A Variety of Services That Make Tackling a Long Walk Easy

Beyond amazing trails, great public transportation and a variety of accommodations, Europe has an abundance of services to support walkers and make your trip easier. Of course, if you want to do everything yourself—from planning your stages to booking your hotels—you can do that. (It's what I always do, and this book will show you how.) But if you'd like some help, from one-off services like ordering packed lunches from your hotel to having your luggage transported to the next spot so you can walk with only a day pack, there are many companies that would love to assist you. Some are even full-service, meaning that all you have to do is get yourself to the airport. They'll take care of everything else, from getting you to the trailhead to providing you with a guide who can explain what you're seeing as you walk. (For more information on hiring any or all of these services, check out Chapter 6, Walk Independently or Hire Help.)

WHY YOU

At this point, I hope that you're beginning to picture yourself exploring Europe on foot. Whether you're looking for a better, more authentic way to travel or you just want to try a new kind of adventure, I'm certain that this kind of travel is for you. Still not 100 percent positive? Below are the three most common concerns I hear about exploring on foot—and how we're going to overcome them together.

What If I'm Not a Superathlete?

The most common worry I hear from people about exploring on foot is that it sounds too physically challenging. Maybe you are even saying to

yourself right now, "Yeah, all of this sounds great, but I'm no superathlete." So let's get this out of the way before we go any further: you don't have to be a superathlete to explore on foot.

You don't have to have the magazine-worthy body of a fitness model or the extraordinary strength of a mountain climber or the outsized endurance of a runner. There's a reason I often use the word "walk" in this book instead of "hike"—this is not about exercise. Walking and hiking, for the purposes of this book, are one and the same—a form of travel and exploration. Yes, you'll have a better experience if you're physically ready for the challenge of walking longer distances than you probably do in your daily life, and I'll help you get your body ready for the trail, but exploring on foot is not about walking the fastest or climbing the biggest hill. If you are a superathlete and whip through these trails, you'll miss the point, which is to enjoy *everything*. You're encouraged to stop and take a break or slow down. This is vacation. Remember, it's supposed to be fun!

Even if you're not in the best shape of your life, I promise that exploring on foot is far more

A NOTE ABOUT SAFETY

Safety is an important concern in all outdoor activities. No guidebook can alert you to every hazard or anticipate the limitations of every reader. Therefore, the descriptions of roads, trails, routes and natural features in this book are not representations that a particular place or excursion will be safe for your party. When you follow any of the routes described in this book, you assume responsibility for your own safety. Under normal conditions, such excursions require the usual attention to traffic, road and trail conditions, weather, terrain, the capabilities of your party and other factors. Keeping informed on current conditions and exercising common sense are the keys to a safe, enjoyable outing.

Political conditions may add to the risks of travel in ways that this book cannot predict. When you travel, you assume this risk, and should keep informed of political developments that may make safe travel difficult or impossible.

—*Mountaineers Books*

Europe boasts an incredible wealth of mountaintop huts that are perfect for admiring nature in relative comfort.

accessible than it may seem. While the prospect of walking 100 miles (160 km) can be downright intimidating, you'll be surprised what you can accomplish when you break things up into daily goals. Suddenly a 100-mile trail means only 10 days of walking 10 miles (16 km) a day—totally doable! That's true even if you have an imperfect body—and let's face it, most of us do. Maybe for you it's weak ankles or a bad back or creaky knees. We'll tackle all of these things in turn (check out Chapter 9, Train for the Trail, for more information on getting your body in trail shape); for now, just know that these minor limitations are not showstoppers.

Plus, because of the variety of trails in Europe, the ability to shorten long walking days with public transportation, and the abundance of services you'll typically find on each route, it's easy to find a trail experience that matches your comfort level and ability. This is true whether you're an experienced walker or just a beginner.

What If I'm Not Outdoorsy?

You also don't need to be superoutdoorsy to explore on foot. That's because with a little planning, you can explore Europe on foot in a way that allows you to neutralize the top three

While traveling, the most ordinary things—like laundry on the line—can seem extraordinarily beautiful.

reasons most people don't enjoy being outside: having to rough it, being unprepared for the elements and feeling afraid of remote wilderness.

The most common reason nonoutdoorsy people don't like being outdoors is that they don't like roughing it. It's true—the outdoors is not always the most comfortable place to take care of daily business: going to the bathroom, taking a shower, eating and sleeping. But based on the European trail you choose and the amenities it offers, you can feasibly avoid doing all of these things outside, even going to the bathroom on trail.

Maybe you don't like being outside because it's too wet, cold or hot. I get that—being unprepared for the elements can be quite uncomfortable; I've been there. You forget your rain shell and a surprise spring shower leaves you wet and shivering. Your shoes are worn out and have lost their traction, so you slip and skin your knee. It snows and you don't have enough layers, so you're colder than you've ever been in your life. The solution to these problems isn't staying inside—it's making better gear choices. Once you do, you'll understand the popular Norwegian adage: "There is no bad weather, only bad clothes."

A lot of people avoid spending time in the outdoors—especially in remote areas—because they're scared of being alone. It's probably more common today than ever before; so many of us live in cities, constantly surrounded by the comforting presence of other people. We may not want to interact with them, but we like to know they're there. They make us feel safe. You can have that same feeling when you're exploring Europe on foot because you'll pass in and out of villages, walk through farms and make your way down country roads. You'll even occasionally see other walkers on trail. And it

makes a difference. I know I always feel reassured by the occasional presence of civilization; I bet you will too.

At the very least, exploring on foot will expand your comfort zone when it comes to recreating outside. The more likely scenario is that it will turn you into an outdoorsy person. You might find that you like feeling the cool breeze on your face in the morning and how clean and fresh the air is outside. You may soon fall in love with seeing firsthand the changing seasons or even the path of the sun as it winds its way through the sky. You could find yourself hitting the trail extra early in the morning, just to catch the sunrise. And that's when you'll know—you've caught the outdoor bug.

What If I've Never Done This Before?

To get to that amazing spot of being on trail and in love with the experience, you may have to fight through some nervous feelings about trying something new—especially if you've never considered yourself a walker. I remember the first time I went paragliding. It looked so fun from afar, but as we took the chairlift higher and higher up the mountain, I wasn't sure I could do it. I wasn't a fan of heights and I sure wasn't a bird—what was I doing? Somehow, I jumped off the mountain in faith. (It definitely had something to do with the fact that I'd already paid the €100—an awful lot of money for a poor college student.) But when the parachute filled with cold alpine air and we were gliding gently down to the valley below, I was so darn happy I'd pushed through my trepidation. Because I found what was on the other side of my fear: the pure bliss of doing something new and exciting—and finding a new love. It can be the same for you with exploring on foot.

There's nothing more satisfying than tackling a challenging trail like Iceland's Laugavegur Trek and proving to yourself that you can do it.

You and I Are a Team

Regardless of how in shape, outdoorsy or confident you are, I'm here to be your guide, your inspiration and your cheerleader. We're going to navigate this journey together. I promise that even if you've never walked or traveled much, by the end of this book, you'll be ready to make your dream trip a reality. So let's get to work.

WHY THIS BOOK

This book isn't just a collection of travel and walking wisdom, although I've gained a lot of that as a professional travel and outdoor writer and an avid hiker. It's a distilled version of the most important things I've learned from living in Europe for more than two years, walking every trail that's featured in this book (and more) and learning things the hard way.

It also contains the advice of those who joined me on my book research trips, a variety of novice and expert walkers who gave me their unique perspectives on the common problems and experiences that we all have on trail. Teaching them the art of exploring on foot, in advance of our walks and while traveling, helped tease out knowledge that had become so ingrained in me that I took it for granted—little-known exercises to prepare for

IF YOU:	THEN:
Want to design your own independent adventure . . .	Tackle all of the chapters, in order.
Like the concept of exploring Europe on foot but want some help with the execution (hiring luggage transfer, a guide, etc.) . . .	Pay particular attention to Chapter 6, Walk Independently or Hire Help.
Are already booked on a guided walking tour of Europe and the company is doing the majority of the logistics work for you . . .	Focus on Part 2, Planning; Part 3, Packing; and Part 4, Traveling.
Are already an experienced walker-traveler . . .	Skim the how-to information for tips that improve on your own existing methods and flip to Chapter 3, Get a Recommendation, for inspiration and new trail ideas.

steep downhill sections, unconventional blister-care techniques, even map-reading skills. You can be confident in knowing that the advice in this book is time-tested and walker-approved.

What This Book Covers

As much as I was my walking companions' coach, I will be yours as well. This book is designed to teach you everything I know about exploring Europe on foot in the order you need it as you dream up, plan and live the trip of a lifetime.

The first two chapters in Part 1, Dreaming, guide you in envisioning your European walking adventure; Chapter 3, Get a Recommendation, will help you pick a trail that's not just great but a great fit for you. I've included fifteen handpicked suggestions, walks that will wow you with their good information and accessibility, stunning natural beauty and fascinating cultural offerings. I've narrowed down these iconic trails to their most iconic sections—perfect for the one to two weeks most people have for a European trip.

Once you've chosen your dream destination, Part 2, Planning, shows you how to get to work on figuring out all of the details of your trip, including who to travel with, how to hire help of many different kinds, how to get to the trailhead, where to stay, how to train and how to prepare for a cultural experience, not just a vacation.

Part 3, Packing, helps you decide what to bring, from clothes and shoes to documents and electronic devices. To make sure you don't get lost in the details, I include the high-level planning timelines and checklists that I use whenever I organize this kind of walking trip.

Finally, Part 4, Traveling, covers all of my tips and tricks for settling into Europe, adjusting to life on trail and making each walking day as successful as possible.

Throughout this book, you'll find side-bars with perspectives and asides on the main text, as well as boxes with tips and tidbits I've gleaned from my own experiences of exploring on foot. Charts, illustrations and photographs, as well as overview maps of the fifteen hand-picked walks, further enrich the information you'll find here. A Resources section at the back of the book pulls together in one place all the organizations and publications mentioned throughout the book.

I've always erred on the side of giving more information rather than less. I'm the kind of person who likes to geek out in the months before a trip. I love planning my itinerary and

The author exploring Mont Saint-Michel

perfecting my gear—to me, it's really fun. Your preparations don't have to be as optimized or extensive as mine. You're welcome to skim the information and use whatever is most helpful to you. This is your book and your trip!

How to Apply This Book to Your Situation

So where should you start? It depends on what you're looking for; see the chart on page 25.

GET OUT THERE AND DO IT

No matter how you go about your planning or which trail you choose, there's so much to look forward to—food, music, wine, people and, of course, amazing walking!

My hope is that you won't use this book just to explore Europe on foot but that it will change the way you travel everywhere, one mountain, village and authentic B and B at a time. I hope it will not only deepen your love of the outdoors but also widen your experience of the world and connect you with everything from foreign cultures to people who are nothing like you—and yet just the same. I hope that it will help you slow down, to see foreign marvels at a pace they were designed for. I hope you savor a glass of wine in a vineyard as the melody of foreign sounds washes over you. More than anything, I hope your trip is everything you imagine it will be, that you take away from these walks more memories than you know what to do with and that you tell others about exploring Europe on foot.

Let's create a revolution of more authentic and immersive travel, one trail at a time.

—*Cass*

P.S. Don't be a stranger! Share your stories and adventures of exploring Europe on foot with me at **exploreonfoot@gmail.com**. And find even more helpful resources at **explore-on -foot.com**.

PART 1
DREAMING

The highlight of England's Lake District is exploring the region's many "meres" or "waters."
(Photo © Andrew Locking)

This section is where the rubber meets the road. From this point on, I won't be talking about "if" you'll explore Europe on foot. Everything will focus on "when." In a matter of weeks or months, you'll be on trail in some incredible foreign country, having the time of your life. In order to get there, you and I have some work to do. In time, we'll tackle everything you need to plan your perfect trip. But first things first: You have to figure out what your perfect trip looks like. And for that, you have some dreaming and deciding to do.

Chapter 1, Understand What's Ideal for You, starts by leading you through a series of questions that will help you figure out not just the perfect trail experience but the perfect trail experience *for you*—that way, you'll be more likely to recognize the right trail when you

come across it. I'll also give you suggestions on how to modify routes that aren't quite ideal but could be with a little creativity. Then Chapter 2, See What's Possible, helps you figure out the European trail system and cycling routes, plus guides your brainstorming and inspiration with a list of great resources. To top it all off, Chapter 3, Get a Recommendation, gives you fifteen handpicked suggestions—the trails I love more than any others for exploring Europe on foot.

Once you know what you're looking for and what's out there, you can start narrowing down the field. Chapter 4, Make a Final Decision, ensures you have all the information you need to select your destination. Just think: you're only a few chapters away from choosing your trail!

UNDERSTAND WHAT'S IDEAL FOR YOU

There are so many amazing trails in Europe and so many different experiences. (If you haven't already paged through the next few chapters, you're in for a treat!) Just how are you supposed to choose between them?

To get to the answer—and help you decide on your ideal trail—let's talk about dating for a moment. Think back on all of your relationships that didn't work out. Chances are, most of the people you've dated—and broken up with—are fine folks in their own right. And they probably went on to be excellent partners for other people. They just weren't the right fit *for you*.

There's a similar compatibility aspect when it comes to trails. So the question to ask yourself is not "What's the perfect trail?" but, rather, "What's the perfect trail *for me*?" And that's what we'll tackle first. You'll be in a much better position to know what you're looking for—and to recognize the perfect trail when you find it—once you've reflected on your preferences, abilities and interests and learned how easy it can be to modify trails that aren't quite perfect right out of the gate. Let's start with a few questions.

HOW LONG DO YOU WANT TO WALK EACH DAY?

One of the things that will inform your trail choice the most is knowing how long you want to walk each day. There's no right answer here. Some people enjoy half a day's worth of walking; they spend their remaining time doing other activities: napping, reading, exploring town. Others want to see as much as they can each day and walk from nearly dawn till dusk.

I've walked everything from two hours a day to eleven, and I've found that my personal sweet spot—and the sweet spot for most of the people I talk to—is between five and seven hours. In my

When you explore areas like Tuscany on foot, you have more time to take in everything from charming old buildings to bucolic farmland.

experience, if you walk less than five hours, you have too much time on your hands, especially if you're walking to very small towns where there isn't a lot to do at night. And if you walk more than seven hours, you end up feeling like you don't have very much time left in the evening for other things, including relaxing.

Three main things influence walking time: distance, elevation gain and pace. The farther you have to go, and the more elevation gain you have on your route, the longer it will take you to walk it. And that's not even counting how quickly—or slowly—you walk. The average person, walking a trail that has a little up and down but nothing dramatic, walks 2 miles (3.2 km) an hour. So if you want to walk between five and seven hours a day, daily stages of 10–14 miles (16–22 km) are perfect.

Modify it: There are many ways to modify a trail that has daily stages that are longer—and steeper—than what you're comfortable with. Check out the accommodations and food available en route to see if you can simply cut the distance of the daily stages down a bit. I've done that several times, sometimes going so far as to spend two days walking what was recommended for one day. Below are some other ways you can shorten your walking time; for information on what services are available on different trails and how to hire help, check out Chapter 6, Walk Independently or Hire Help.

- Hop on public transportation to a point farther down the trail; this works really well when you're going through a series of small towns.

- Arrange a ride with a taxi or helpful guesthouse proprietor; some guesthouses even offer this as a regular service.
- Hire someone to transport your luggage for you; you can walk a lot faster when you're not weighed down.

Trail mileage and elevation numbers can seem like just that—numbers—until you get familiar with how different ones actually make your body feel. Contemplating a walk that has daily stages of 12 miles (19 km) with 1,500 feet (457 m) of elevation gain? Find a walk at home that has similar stats and see what that's like before you commit to it.

DO YOU WANT A LONG TRAIL OR A SERIES OF DAY HIKES?

There are two main ways to explore on foot. You can either plan your trip around a long trail and walk a different section each day, or you can find a town or region you'd like to visit and piece together several shorter one-day walks in the area. Both have advantages.

With town-to-town or hut-to-hut walking on a long route, you'll see something new every day. You'll be exposed to more scenic variety as well, because you'll be traveling beyond one small area. And you'll have less work to do when it comes to choosing your trails; as long as you stay on your long trail, you're set.

With basing yourself in one town and going on a series of one-day wanders from there, you can walk with less on your back. Take a day pack with everything you need on trail during the day and leave everything else at the hotel. Other benefits? You'll have more time in your home base, so you'll be able to explore it more fully. You'll also have a better chance of forming long-term relationships with locals you meet, since you won't be just passing through.

Modify it: If you'd like to get even more creative than either of these two main ways of exploring, consider planning your own amble through the countryside. Pick a few towns you want to visit that are relatively close together—8 to 10 miles (13 to 16 km) apart—and connected by smaller roads than highways, then look on maps or search Google Maps for a walking route (quiet country lanes, sidewalked streets through town) that brings them all together.

IS IT OK TO CHOOSE A "STRETCH" TRAIL?

If you're using your walking trip as an incentive to make healthy changes in your life, you may be tempted to choose a trail that's more challenging than what you're currently capable of. It seems fine in theory—surely by the time your trip rolls around, you'll be fantastically fit and ready for anything, right?

Unfortunately, life is rarely that predictable. Even if you have the best of intentions, things can go wrong. All of a sudden work gets hectic or your dad gets sick and the next thing you know, you complete only half of your training walks.

Save yourself from this scenario by hedging your bets. Choose a trail that's a little out of your reach but not completely undoable with your current level of fitness. If you can comfortably walk 7 miles at a time right now, it's probably OK to aim for a trail with daily stages of up to 10 miles. But don't commit to anything more strenuous than that until you've increased your base level of fitness (see Chapter 9, Train for the Trail).

Walking in loose sand can make Portugal's Rota Vicentina Fishermen's Trail challenging at times but the views are more than worth it. (Photo by Kelsey Overby)

WHEN DO YOU WANT TO WALK?

If the timing of your walk is important to you, it's crucial to know that from the beginning, since not all trails can be walked year-round. Some trails, such as high alpine routes, can be accessed only in high summer, after the snowpack has melted and the trail is free of ice and before fall storms bring new snow. Other trails, such as desert paths, are best walked in the shoulder seasons, because they're too hot during summer and too cold during winter. For most European trails, the walking season kicks off in late March or early April and goes through mid-September. Even though a trail might be physically walkable before and after these months, accommodations are typically closed for the winter. That means most

European trails are available in three seasons: spring, summer and fall.

The main season, of course, is summer: July and August. This is when the weather is best, which is why summer is so popular. Because it's the favorite time of year to travel, it's also the most expensive. If you don't mind seeing other walkers and paying a little more than you would in the shoulder seasons, this is a great time to walk. You'll have the best chance of warm days, a lot of daylight and plenty of services (restaurants, et cetera) on trail.

If you have some flexibility in your schedule, I suggest walking in the shoulder seasons: spring and fall. These are my favorite times to travel. You'll see fewer people on trail and will usually find better deals (even on airfare)

that will bring down the cost of your trip. And you'll get a different perspective on the natural beauty of the area you're exploring on foot. In spring, you'll be treated to heaps of green foliage and colorful wildflowers! In the fall, you'll be spellbound by more shades of red, yellow and orange than you ever thought possible.

Modify it: If you're more of a cold-weather person, consider exploring on foot in the winter. This isn't possible for all trails (for example, high alpine routes), but for more than you'd think, especially near small mountain towns. It might mean expanding your definition of exploring on foot to include cross-country skiing, snowshoeing or even walking with traction devices, but winter can be one of the most enchanting times of year to travel and explore.

HOW LONG DO YOU HAVE TO TRAVEL?

The number of days you have to travel will affect how many days you're available to walk—and that can help you choose the right trail. The two sample itineraries in this section are based on a one-week and a two-week vacation, building in travel days (flying to and from Europe, as well as traveling within Europe between walking tours) and walking days.

Sample Itinerary: Nine-Day Trip

Because of the long flights involved in getting to Europe from North America, most people choose trips that are at least nine days long. If you're trying to maximize your trip time and minimize the days you're taking off from work, that can be done with two weekends and the five weekdays in between. When you account for travel days and a rest day in the middle of your walk to take a break from walking and explore other facets of the local culture (for instance, museums), a trek that can be done

in four daily stages is perfect for a nine-day European trip. Here's a sample itinerary:

> **Saturday:** Travel day—fly to Europe
> **Sunday:** Travel day—arrive in Europe (because of the time change) and travel to the trailhead
> **Monday:** Walk day 1
> **Tuesday:** Walk day 2
> **Wednesday:** Rest day—explore, take a break, et cetera
> **Thursday:** Walk day 3
> **Friday:** Walk day 4
> **Saturday:** Travel day—make your way back to the major city you flew into
> **Sunday:** Travel day—fly back home

Rest days are really important. Especially if you're not used to walking multiple hours a day (and who is?), your body—especially your legs—will likely need the break. I like to plan a rest day after every two to three walking days. It's a nice change of pace; I wake up a little later, take things easy and explore something I wouldn't have made time for otherwise. By the next morning, I'm rested up and itching to get back out on trail.

Sample Itinerary: Sixteen-Day Trip

If you have more time, you're in luck: you have even more choices for what kind of walk you can fit into your travel plans. If you're planning on taking two weeks off from work and using the weekends that bookend those weeks (a total of sixteen vacation days), you can more than double your walking days: from four to ten. You could spend those ten days walking a single trail and get a very in-depth experience in one country or region, or you could even chain a few shorter trails together for a broader experience by using your rest days to travel to the next trail. For example, the itinerary below could be a six-day and a four-day walk, two three-day walks and a four-day walk, or a three-day walk and a seven-day walk. If you have two weeks in Europe, your itinerary could look more like this:

> **Saturday:** Travel day—fly to Europe
> **Sunday:** Travel day—arrive in Europe (because of the time change) and travel to the trailhead
> **Monday:** Walk day 1
> **Tuesday:** Walk day 2
> **Wednesday:** Walk day 3
> **Thursday:** Rest day—explore and take a break, or travel to the next trailhead
> **Friday:** Walk day 4
> **Saturday:** Walk day 5
> **Sunday:** Walk day 6
> **Monday:** Rest day—explore and take a break, or travel to the next trailhead
> **Tuesday:** Walk day 7
> **Wednesday:** Walk day 8
> **Thursday:** Walk day 9
> **Friday:** Walk day 10
> **Saturday:** Travel day—make your way back to the major city you flew into
> **Sunday:** Travel day—fly back home

Modify it: If you don't have time to tackle your dream trail in its entirety, it's fine not to walk an entire route at one time. Maybe this is something you want to come back to and finish later. Or maybe you'll never finish it—you'll just move on to a different trail the next time you explore Europe on foot. That's OK too! You don't always need to walk a long trail in its entirety to get the essence of the local area.

WHAT'S YOUR COMFORT ZONE?

When you're choosing a trail, it's important to consider your comfort zone as it applies to the wilderness, creature comforts and culture shock.

First, how comfortable are you in the wilderness? While long European trails tend to pass through more civilization—small towns, farms and the like—than ones in North America, the amount of civilization does vary depending on the trail you choose. If you get nervous when you haven't seen people in a few hours (I have to admit, this is me) or you're simply not comfortable being in a remote area or dense forest, it's best to choose a trail that minimizes wilderness and maximizes civilization, at least for your first trip. This is especially true if you're planning on walking solo, since you won't have anyone there to boost your confidence or give you a pep talk.

Next, what creature comforts do you need and not need on trail, especially with regard to accommodations? There's a lot to think about: Would you enjoy sharing a room with other people (dormitory style), or would you sleep better in a room by yourself? Does the prospect of sharing a bathroom fill you with dread or not bother you a bit? Do you want to share

THE ART OF CHAINING TRAILS TOGETHER

If you have two weeks or more to explore Europe on foot and you want more than one trail experience, you'll need to chain at least two trails together—maybe even several. Unless you have unlimited time to travel, it's best to choose trails that are close together (I aim for no more than half a day apart by train); that way, you can simply convert one of your rest days to a travel day to avoid extra downtime.

When I chain trails together, I look for very different experiences that will complement each other. I'll pair a mountain trail with an ocean trail or an urban walk with a countryside amble. It's a great way to feel like you've gone deeper in your explorations without investing a lot of extra travel time.

When you explore Europe on foot, you'll typically stay in cozy accommodations in villages along the trail.

family-style meals with other walkers, or are you more interested in having quality dinner conversation with your walking companion(s)? Are you on a budget, or do you have money to burn? There's no right answer to any of these questions, but your answers will inform your choice of accommodations—and sometimes your choice of a trail. If you are a light sleeper and know you won't get any shut-eye in a dormitory surrounded by ten snoring walkers, a hut-to-hut route is probably not for you—you'll be happier (and better rested) if you choose a trail with a wider variety of accommodations, including private rooms. (For information on what creature comforts different types of accommodations entail, turn to Chapter 8, Find a Place to Stay.)

Finally, what is your comfort zone relative to culture shock and how open are you to foreign experiences? This question might seem odd—after all, you're going to Europe to have a foreign experience, right? Well, yes and no.

Traveling means putting yourself in the middle of cultures that do things differently—sometimes very differently—than what you're used to. That's exhilarating up to a point—and after that point, it can be stressful to be in a place that's so completely different from what you're used to. Think about what you're ready for. Want to start off exploring in a place where you're guaranteed to understand the language and the customs? Try a trail in the United Kingdom or Ireland. Want to immerse yourself in a completely different way of life, something that feels incredibly exotic? A trail on the opposite side of the spectrum—in Eastern Europe, Turkey or Morocco—might be more your speed.

Modify it: If you want to walk somewhere that's a bit outside your comfort zone, consider walking with a group or hiring a guide. Learn how to find good people to travel with in Chapter 5, Find (the Right) Adventure Companions, and companies to partner with in Chapter 6, Walk Independently or Hire Help.

Going for trail experiences that are on the exotic side of the foreignness spectrum can make for a more memorable trip, but it can also mean a little more work up front and on trail. You might have trouble finding good trail information and maps in English. It could also be more challenging for you to assimilate into the local culture—and communicate with locals—while you're walking. Don't let the extra work scare you away; walking in a place that's completely different from anything you've known can take your trip from enriching to life changing.

WHAT LIGHTS YOU UP?

It's important to choose a trail that matches what you're physically capable of, gives you the freedom and home base you're looking for, fits into your vacation time slot and is within your comfort zone. But there's still one more thing the right trail should do: give you an experience you're really excited about. So start thinking about what you want to learn, see and do. Choose something that lights you up, so your trail choice can eventually do the same. Here are some ideas:

History walks. A trail that emphasizes history can be just as intellectually stimulating as it is physically invigorating. There are many options. You could chain together a series of important historical sights, walk a path or road that was important at one point in history, or even create a pilgrimage to a historically significant site. The at-home preparation for a history walk can be incredibly rewarding, as you read books, watch documentaries, listen to music and visit museums that prepare you for your journey.

Nature walks. If you're excited about experiencing scenery—from harsh volcanic landscapes to snowy summits—that can't be found where you live, a nature walk might be right for you. Focusing your trail time on nature can give you a different perspective on the foreign culture you're experiencing, because to a certain extent geography influences how people live and, thus, their culture.

Food and wine walks. If you're passionate about food, wine or beer, a walk that highlights a region's local specialties could be the experience of a lifetime. There are so many options.

Vineyards make excellent spots for scenic picnics when you're walking through wine country.

No matter what your preferences are for the perfect trail experience, five things that aren't negotiable are what I call my trail deal breakers:

1. **Doable daily sections:** Modify a trail to your heart's content, but if its daily stages can't be made doable for you, look elsewhere.
2. **Sufficient services en route:** At the bare minimum, you'll need food, water and a place to sleep every day you're walking; if a route doesn't have these, keep looking.
3. **Detailed route information:** It's important to have sufficient instructions on trail junctions, hazards, et cetera, similar to what you can find in a good guidebook. If information is scant, look elsewhere.
4. **Paper map or GPX tracks (preferably both):** Even if the trail description says there's no way you can get lost, it's important to always have a paper map or GPX tracks of the trail you want to walk. If you haven't walked with GPX tracks yet, I highly recommend them (see Chapter 15, Trail and Travel Tools). It's really nice to be able to automatically see your location on a map, especially if you're not very good at traditional map reading. If there are no maps available, find another route.
5. **Quality trail signage:** Not only should the route have signage, you also need to be able to understand it. But it doesn't need to be in English for it to be understandable. For example, Swiss signs utilize only town names, arrows and the time it will take you to get there—easy for anyone to understand. It's almost impossible to relax on an unmarked trail because you're always wondering if you're lost, so if the signage is poor or missing, choose another route.

Chain together several vineyards or breweries, make a tour of a region's top restaurants, explore the fields that produce an area's top ingredients. Want to bring foreign cooking back with you? Take a cooking class on one of your days off.

Culture walks. Focusing on culture while you walk can open your eyes to whole new worlds: music, art, tradition, attitudes. It can widen your perspective on what's considered "normal" in foreign cultures—and maybe even show you some things you can bring into your own life. A culture walk can be very different depending on what you focus on. You could organize a walk around music, literature or art. You could even adopt a foreign tradition and make a pilgrimage on a culturally significant route. Or expand your horizons by walking through a region with a culture that's very different from yours.

Milestone walks. One of my favorite categories is milestone walks. These trails are chosen primarily for their challenging nature. They're meant to stretch you, force you to dig deep and do something more impressive than you ever thought possible. A good milestone walk can involve significant elevation gain or a significant period of time. These are great for celebrating a major birthday, anniversary, graduation or other major life event.

Modify it: What if you can't find a trail to match what you're most interested in? Create it. Having a focus for your trip is all about emphasizing the things that matter to you, so seek out opportunities on trail that excite you. For example, you don't have to be on a bona fide food and wine walk to learn about local delicacies. You can treat each meal as an exploration and each conversation with a guesthouse owner, shopkeeper or restaurateur as a learning opportunity. So get intentional—and get creative.

CHAPTER

2

SEE WHAT'S POSSIBLE

Once you have a general idea of what you're looking for, you can explore your trail options and see what fits. It helps to have an overview of the European trail system and cycling routes, so I'll cover that first. This general knowledge serves as a good starting point as you identify the kinds of trails that are out there and the kinds of trails that you're most interested in. It will also help you identify all the possible trails that match your specifications and figure out where to go for more information.

After covering the basic structure of the European trail system and cycling routes, I'll introduce you to a selection of one-day wanders that show you how easy it is to add a walk—especially a short walk—to a European vacation. I'll wrap things up by sharing some of my favorite resources for uncovering trails that are perfect for exploring on foot.

THE EUROPEAN TRAIL SYSTEM

When I first started exploring Europe on foot, I had a lot of trouble finding good trails to walk. It wasn't that there was a lack of trails; I just couldn't seem to find them. I scoured roundups—tantalizing lists of summary information on a variety of spots; I paged through magazines. Occasionally I would land on something that appealed to me, but it wasn't an easy process. Then I discovered, by talking to other walkers and doing a lot of research, that there is a hierarchy of routes in the European trail system. And once you know what's what, it's a lot easier to find what you're looking for. Understanding the different kinds of trails in the European trail system is the magic key that can unlock thousands of trails—and the perfect experience. Let's examine the categories in turn, starting with the most helpful.

Leading Quality Trails

Leading Quality Trails (LQT) are some of my favorites to walk because they have everything a walker-traveler is looking for, from beautiful natural sights to cultural attractions, good signage,

These trail categories are not entirely separate; some overlap. Different trail-sponsoring organizations—for example, government offices and tourism boards—are known to collaborate. Some trails physically overlap; for instance, E-paths are made up of many Grand Route (GR), national, regional and local trails. And a few trails fall under more than one category: for example, Portugal's Rota Vicentina is a GR but also a Leading Quality Trail (LQT).

public transportation and walker services en route. They are usually very well maintained and easy to follow. Why are they so amazing? Because they have to be. Trails are designated as LQT only if they pass a lengthy and rigorous certification process that's administered by the European Ramblers' Association (see Resources). Because LQTs are so predictably good, they're a natural choice for those exploring Europe on foot.

Example: Germany's Moselsteig Trail (See Walk 10, The Moselle, for information on a three-day section of the Moselsteig.)

More information: Check out the European Ramblers' Association's website (see Resources) for a listing of LQTs and links to more information on individual trails.

I've included several Leading Quality Trails in my handpicked suggestions in Chapter 3, Get a Recommendation. To identify them, look for the LQT symbol: (★)

Tourism Trails

While most trails in Europe got their start as military roads, trading routes, village connectors or pilgrims' paths, trails built for the express purpose of tourism have sprung up in the past twenty-five years. The aim of these routes is to promote a region via trail tourism, so they're constructed to show off the best a region has to offer—and typically in a responsible and sustainable manner, since they're very modern. Because they're meant to serve tourists, they usually have great information (even in English!) and many support services available. Many also have educational signage about the local area, conservation issues and important sights.

Example: The Via Alpina (Check out Walk 8, Alpine Pass Route, for information on a fifteen-day section of the Via Alpina.)

More information: Tourism trails aren't branded as such, so it's hard to find information on the group as a whole. That said, once you come across one (an official trail website is a key indicator), you'll often be treated to lots and lots of additional resources, from maps to downloadable GPX tracks to an official (and many times free) guidebook.

Pilgrims' Paths

Long before people thought to walk long distances for leisure, they were doing it for religion. Since the peak of its popularity in the Middle Ages, the pilgrimage has been an important part of European spiritual life, especially for Roman Catholics, for nearly two thousand years. Most pilgrims either follow in the steps of a saint or walk to a place of purported miracles or reliquaries. Traditionally, pilgrims started walking from their homes. Over time, common routes emerged. Those routes are now used not just by modern-day pilgrims but also by recreational walkers.

Example: The Camino de Santiago (Check out Walk 2, English Way, for information on a weeklong section of the Camino.)

Key advice: A pilgrimage means the most when one of your main goals is introspection. You don't have to be religious or spiritual, however. You can design a pilgrimage that suits your own needs exactly. Maybe you want to contemplate a big life change or finally break free of a technology-centered existence in favor of something simpler. Just remember, a pilgrimage isn't about the walk—it's about the *way* you walk. So give yourself plenty of time to stare at the clouds, think and journal. Also, remember that you don't have to walk a pilgrims' route all at once—it's something that can be tackled in sections over time.

More information: There's an amazing amount of information online and in print about pilgrims' paths. One reason is that once many pilgrims return home from the trail, they want to help others have the same kind of experience they did. To find the right pilgrimage route for you, research top routes online, then drill down into travel blogs, travel forums, guidebooks and pilgrims' associations for more information.

Protected Land

Protected lands—including national parks, nature reserves and United Nations Educational, Scientific and Cultural Organization (UNESCO) World Heritage Sites—can be found all around Europe. While their designation is in part intended to protect them from development and destruction, it is also meant to put whatever impressive thing they offer—from rare birds to unique geology to evidence of some of the most influential (and rapidly fading) cultures in world history—on display. Because walking usually has a low impact on the environment, most of these protected places feature footpaths and are accessible to walkers. Trail length varies; some are an hour long, while others can be walked over several days.

Example: Italy's Cinque Terre (Walk 6)

More information: Plenty of information is available online for national parks and nature reserves in Europe. Looking for inspiration? A good roundup article will have a lot of ideas— try searching online for "best national parks in

THE PILGRIMAGE WEDDING

When it came time to plan our wedding, Mac and I wanted to do something epic. So we walked the English Way, using the pilgrimage to reflect on the vows we were going to make before we got married in a pop-up ceremony on the steps of the Cathedral of Santiago de Compostela. Our officiant was a pilgrim we had befriended on the route; our guests were more than two hundred enthusiastic locals and travelers who gathered round to witness the ceremony—and catch the bouquet. It was a dream come true, and it's a great example of how an ancient pilgrimage can have modern significance.

Italy's Cinque Terre is both a protected national park and a UNESCO World Heritage Site.

Europe" or "best national parks in (insert country name)." To find a UNESCO World Heritage Site that interests you, check out the organization's website (see Resources).

> I've included several UNESCO World Heritage Sites and Geoparks in my handpicked suggestions and One-day Wanders. To identify them, look for this symbol: ⛰

E-paths

European long-distance walking trails, known as E-paths, are typically thousands of miles long, much like the Pacific Crest Trail or the Appalachian Trail in the United States. Unlike the PCT or the AT, however, these epic trails are not commonly thru-hiked; it's more typical for people to hike them in sections. The trails each cross a minimum of three European countries, and they're intended to be samplers that serve up the best of each country. There are currently twelve E-paths in existence, which together contribute more than 37,000 miles (60,000 km) of trails to Europe.

Example: The E-4 (Cool fact: The E-4 is not just the longest E-path but also the longest trail in Europe.)

Key advice: If you don't have time to walk an entire E-path, consider walking the section that most appeals to you. Don't know where to start? Search for travel blogs that are written by people who have walked the E-path you're interested in and see what sections they walked.

More information: Even though E-paths are maintained by members of the European Ramblers' Association (see Resources), there's no official source of information on walking them. I've had the most luck running an Internet search for the particular path I'm interested in and piecing together information from many different sources, including Traildino (which also occasionally has GPX tracks and

Many trails in Europe, including the Tour du Mont Blanc, are waymarked with painted stripes of white and red.

map and book suggestions; see Resources), travel forums and travel blogs.

Grand Route Footpaths

This network of trails goes by several names: Grande Randonée in France, Grote Routepaden or Lange-Afstand-Wandelpaden in the Netherlands, Grande Rota in Portugal or Gran Recorrido in Spain—all shortened to GR. While there are currently more than seventy-five GR footpaths in existence—mainly in France, Belgium, the Netherlands, Spain and Switzerland—you'll see their signage (a white stripe above a red stripe) nearly everywhere in Europe. Because they're shorter and more plentiful than E-paths, they're much more popular. A typical trail is hundreds of miles long and can span part of a single country or a couple of countries. They vary widely in difficulty; some are incredibly flat while others are very mountainous.

Example: France's GR 34, which features Mont Saint-Michel (Walk 3)

Key advice: In their entirety, GR footpaths make good longer trips that can really allow

you to dive into a particular region you're interested in. They can also be done in shorter increments. For a long-term travel goal, consider walking a different section of a GR footpath every year, until you finish it.

More information: Because proper guidebooks are available for these trails—and more people have walked them and written about them—they're much easier than E-paths to research. To find GR footpaths you may be interested in, check out Traildino (see Resources) and Wikipedia; for a great site with information on French GR footpaths and their daily stages, visit gr-infos.com.

Want to do a local trail in the United Kingdom? Britain on Foot (see Resources) has a great routefinder tool called OS Maps.

National, Regional and Local Trails

The network of national, regional and local trails in Europe is extensive. These trails, traditionally built and maintained by the local government, can be anywhere from hundreds of miles long for a national trail (perfect for a sabbatical-length vacation) to a couple of miles long for a local one (great when all you have is an afternoon). Like the GR footpaths, these trails let you dive into a particular region you're interested in—on a smaller scale. They cover, at maximum, one country.

Example: Germany's King Ludwig's Way (Walk 9)

Key advice: These paths, especially the shorter ones, are most often used by locals and local walking groups. Want to join a local walking group on trail? Check out Meetup.com (search by your destination and "walking" or "hiking") or the local chapter of the European Ramblers' Association or the Internationaler Volkssportverband to find people to walk with (see Resources).

More information: To find out more about national trails, start with a search on your intended destination's official national tourism website, where you can drill down to trails and hiking opportunities within that country. (A great example is Germany's germany.travel/en.) The best way to learn about regional and local trails is usually regional guidebooks or local tourist information offices, which typically have a website in addition to physical locations. Want an easy way to find these resources and more? Run an Internet search for "walking/hiking trails in (insert the name of your destination)." For maps and route information while you're traveling, stop by tourist information offices, which are universally signed with a white *i* (for "information") superimposed on a blue background.

CYCLING ROUTES

It may seem odd to suggest a cycling path to walkers, but these routes are excellent options for those who are looking for flat paved routes through Europe.

CYCLING TRAIL ETIQUETTE

Use good manners when you're walking on a cycling trail. What does that mean specifically? Always keep your eyes out for cyclists, and move to the side of the trail when they come by. At busy times, avoid walking two or three abreast; if it's busy, walk in line (one person in front of the other). Where you walk is dictated by which side of the road people drive on in that location. If they drive on the right side of the road (most countries in Europe), walk on the right side of the cycling route. If they drive on the left side of the road (the United Kingdom and Ireland), walk on the left side of the cycling trail. And remember, cyclists aren't encroaching on your walking path; you're encroaching on their cycling path.

Germany's King Ludwig's Way is at its best in the fall, when the changing leaves are shockingly vivid.

A great option for shortening a long trail is doing part of it on a bike—you'll just need to be a little creative with your backpack. (Photo by Cheryl Nilson)

EuroVelo Cycling Routes

Just like E-paths, EuroVelo trails are thousands of miles long in their entirety. The whole network, which comprises more than fifteen trails and 28,000 miles (45,000 km), is expected to ultimately swell to 43,000 miles (69,000 km). Just like official walking trails, these paths each have a slightly different focus, from the Iron Curtain Trail (EuroVelo 13), which traces the former border between Eastern and Western Europe, to the Capitals Route (EuroVelo 2), which takes you through some of Europe's most captivating capitals for plenty of urban time, drinking, dancing and entertainment.

Example: France's Alsace Wine Route (Walk 4)

Key advice: Like E-paths, EuroVelo cycling routes are very long; choose the section you're most interested in, and modify any information you can find on daily stages for walking (instead of cycling).

More information: A good place to start researching EuroVelo routes is EuroVelo.com. Another great resource is Cycling Europe (see Resources), which has a great breakdown of official websites, blogs, books, forums and maps for each of the EuroVelo routes.

Europeans use "cycle" and "cycling" more than "bike" and "biking." Try varying your search terms to unearth even more information online.

National, Regional and Local Cycling Routes

Europe has an incredibly large network of national, regional and local cycling routes that can also be walked. The national routes are known by different names in different places— the Germans have D routes, the Dutch have LF routes, the British have a National Cycle Network (NCN). Regional and local trails go by other monikers entirely. But they all have something in common: just like EuroVelo routes, these trails are generally flat and paved, perfect for walkers with mobility issues, families walking with kids or walkers who just don't like huffing and puffing up hills. These cycling routes vary in mileage; some are hundreds of miles long in their entirety, while others span only a handful of miles. The shorter local trails, especially, can make for great one-day walks.

Example: England's Lake District National Park (See Walk 12, The Lake District, for more information.)

Key advice: Just as with EuroVelo cycling routes, you'll need to modify the daily stages of these cycling trails for walking.

More information: One of the best places to look for cycling routes is at the national level. Once you choose the country you'd like to visit, check out their official tourism website and drill down to more specific information on individual trails. Regional tourism websites are also great sources of information on cycling paths that go through their area. Another easy way to find these resources and more? Run an Internet search for "cycling trails" and the name of your destination. For maps and route information while you're traveling, stop by tourist information offices, which are universally signed with a white *i* (for "information") superimposed on a blue background.

STARTING SIMPLY: ONE-DAY WANDERS

While planning your European trip around a several-day walk is ideal, don't panic if you don't have time for a long trail or if you already have a sightseeing trip planned. Any time spent exploring on foot is better than none. Even a single one-day wander worked into your

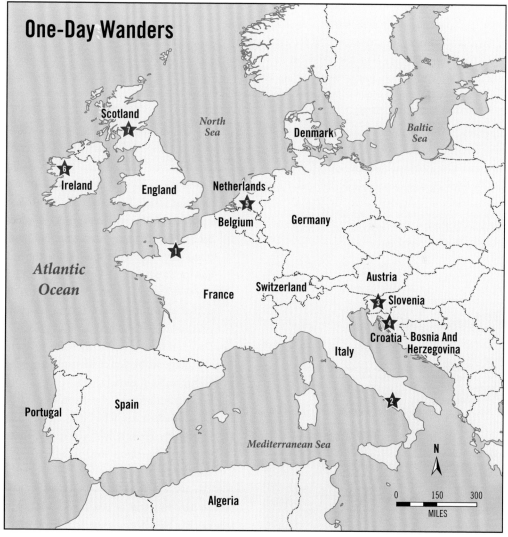

One-Day Wanders

1. Omaha Beach, France 2. Mount Vesuvius, Italy 3. Lake Bled, Slovenia 4. Plitvice Lakes National Park, Croatia
5. Kinderdijk, The Netherlands 6. Cliffs of Moher, Ireland 7. Arthur's Seat and Holyrood Park, Scotland

LOADING YOUR DAY PACK

Depending on the weather conditions and the difficulty of the trail you're keen on walking, you don't need a lot for a half-day or daylong walk. But at a minimum, these five key items should make it in your day pack:

1. **Food and water:** enough for the length of time you'll be gone—plus a little extra, in case you're gone longer than expected.
2. **A map or GPX tracks:** see Chapter 16, Electronic Tools, for information on Gaia, a GPS app for your smartphone.
3. **Cash in the form of local currency:** for the rural farm stands and restaurants that don't take credit cards.
4. **A lightweight rain jacket:** in case of surprise sprinkles.
5. **Sunscreen and sunglasses:** helpful not only for sunny days but cloudy ones as well.

You don't need to bring a bona fide hiking day pack with you if you're planning on walking only a half-day or daylong route. Instead, I recommend putting your walking essentials in a comfy cross-body bag or a lightweight drawstring backpack (for more on day packs, check out Chapter 17, Packs).

itinerary can hugely enrich your trip. It can help you experience a different facet of the local culture, give you a new perspective on what you're seeing, provide a welcome outdoor break from all of those indoor activities (like visiting museums) and even help counteract all of the heavy restaurant food you'll be eating. Here are some tips for adding a daylong walk to your trip:

- Do your research in advance so you have a plan and know where to go. If you wake up late one morning and go about your planning from there, you risk leaving too late for an all-day adventure.
- Know the ways to shorten your route with public transportation or taxi in case you get tired or need to turn around early.
- Dress in layers, as the weather is likely to change while you're on trail, and wear comfortable walking shoes.
- Let someone know where you'll be walking and when you'll be back.
- Start early, especially if you're not completely certain how long your walk will take.

Look for the (TTT) symbol for One-day Wanders that have earned a UNESCO designation for being of particular cultural or geographical importance.

Although most European trails are well signed, I recommend always walking with a paper map and GPX tracks for backup.

Omaha Beach is at its best after the crowds have departed for the day. (Photo by Archangel 12/Flickr)

ONE-DAY WANDER #1: OMAHA BEACH, FRANCE

LOCATION: Normandy, northwestern France
DAY-HIKE FROM: Paris, Rouen, Caen, Bayeux
TYPE: Out and back

DISTANCE: Up to 10 miles (16 km) round-trip
MORE INFO: en.normandie-tourisme.fr

There's no better way to immerse yourself in World War II history than with a walk at Omaha Beach, the largest of the D-Day assault areas. And there's no better time to visit Omaha Beach than after a full day of museum hopping in Colleville-sur-Mer and Bayeux, as the sun sinks lower on the horizon and the tour vans of somber visitors clear out.

A good place to start your walk is the Les Braves memorial, about halfway down Omaha Beach, near the town of Vierville-sur-Mer. Walk east, and you'll have the beach nearly to yourself, which is perfect: this is a contemplative walk, ideal for helping you process everything you've seen and heard about the suffering and death that took place here on June 6, 1944,

when it was a place of carnage, the air filled with bullets and explosions and the sand littered with bodies. On that day alone, 2,400 American soldiers lost their lives.

Remember them as you walk and experience for yourself just how long and exposed Omaha Beach is. Despite its violent past, the beach is once again the most peaceful of places, a haven of endless sand, calmly lapping water and children playing joyously. When you reach the end of the beach, turn around and return the way you came. If you're still content meandering, walk past the memorial where you started and all the way to the western edge of the beach before making your way back to your starting location.

From the crater at Mount Vesuvius, you can see all the way to the Gulf of Naples.

ONE-DAY WANDER #2: MOUNT VESUVIUS, ITALY

LOCATION: Vesuvio National Park, southwestern Italy
DAY-HIKE FROM: Rome, the Amalfi Coast, Naples, Pompeii

TYPE: Loop
DISTANCE: 2.5 miles (4 km) round-trip
MORE INFO: parconazionaledelvesuvio.it

In AD 79, a fast-moving current of hot gas and volcanic matter roared down the steep flanks of Mount Vesuvius toward a series of bustling villages at the base of the once-sleeping giant. In a matter of moments, several of them, including Pompeii, were covered in ash, their inhabitants mummified and permanently frozen in time. While most visitors to southern Italy stop by Pompeii for an up-close view of the destruction, some of the best views of the area are actually from above. And it's all accessible with a visit to Vesuvio National Park, a short bus ride from Pompeii.

It's difficult to find up-to-date information and timetables online for the public and private buses that run from Pompeii to the top of Mount Vesuvius. Your best bet for planning your adventure: stop by the information center in Pompeii for details. The bus to and from Vesuvius takes approximately an hour each way. Once you reach the park, walk along the rim of the still-steaming crater of Mount Vesuvius, along Route 5, Gran Cono.

Want to see even more of Mount Vesuvius? Check out the other—and longer—trails in the national park.

Peer into the mouth of the monster before looking out toward the Gulf of Naples and the very flat land in between the gleaming blue water and the base of the volcano—it's not hard to see why the destruction from the eruption was so complete. This is a short walk, but take your time; there's no better place in the area to enjoy panoramic views or a glass of wine—plenty of idyllic benches are perfect for photography and contemplation.

ONE-DAY WANDER #3: LAKE BLED, SLOVENIA

LOCATION: Bled, northwestern Slovenia
DAY-HIKE FROM: Ljubljana, Triglav National Park, Bled

TYPE: Loop
DISTANCE: 4 miles (6.5 km) round-trip
MORE INFO: bled.si/en

Lake Bled is one of the most photographed spots in Europe for a reason. Its charms extend past the calm, deep lake, the romantic island that floats in the middle and the ancient castle (more than 1,000 years old) that dangles from a cliff over its placid waters. You'll feel it especially in the fall, when the air crisps up, the leaves turn electric hues and the fog rolls in, nearly obscuring the island—there's just something mysterious, even moody, about the lake.

From the small town of Bled (population 7,000), it's an easy walk through town to the shores of Lake Bled and its pretty lakeside path. Although this walk can be done in as few as ninety minutes, give yourself plenty of time. It's possible to spend an entire afternoon walking around the lake—it's that good.

Iconic Bled Island is a peaceful, ten-minute boat ride from Lake Bled's shores.

Soak in the ambiance—and take those amazing photos—on a flat loop walk around the lakeshore. Along the way, you'll wander past plenty of waterside cafes that are perfect for savoring a bite of Slovenian food. You can detour to explore that spooky castle—and some of the best up-high views of the lake in the area. You'll also find plenty of opportunities to journey to the iconic island (a short, serene meander in its own right) by skiff.

ONE-DAY WANDER #4: PLITVICE LAKES NATIONAL PARK, CROATIA

LOCATION: East-central Croatia
DAY-HIKE FROM: Split, Zagreb, Zadar
TYPE: Multiple loops

DISTANCE: 2.2 to 11.4 miles (3.5 to 18.3 km)
MORE INFO: np-plitvicka-jezera.hr/en

Plitvice Lakes National Park, widely known as the gem of Europe, is so beautiful that you could spend days taking in its allure. If you're short on time, however, a day is perfect for exploring the park and its sixteen terraced lakes, which are connected by cascading waterfalls of the prettiest aquamarine. Located in the mountains east of Croatia's Adriatic coast, this park is a natural paradise, with more than 160 species of birds, 321 different kinds of butterflies and 90 waterfalls.

The loop trails that crisscross the park are accessible from both of the park entrances, which are within walking distance of each other. The best way to get a detailed look at the trail system is to purchase a trail map at one of the entrances. Not sure which loop to walk? Ask park staff—they can give a recommendation based on what you'd most like to see and how much time you have available.

Not only is Plitvice Lakes National Park one of the oldest national parks in southeast Europe, it's also the largest national park in Croatia and a UNESCO World Heritage Site.

As you make your way through the park on the series of relatively short, well-trodden loop trails, you'll be as close to the enchanting water as possible, in many places suspended just

If you're lucky, you may just see a water snake from the main path that meanders through Plitvice Lakes National Park.

Plitvice Lakes National Park is home to a series of boardwalks that are perfect for exploring the lush park from the lakes' shores.

inches above the water on sturdy boardwalks that meander past sleepy trout. The paths take you up through limestone caves and reward you with incredible panoramas of the whole area.

Keep your eyes out for wildlife as you walk. If you make it out to one of the wooded paths that take in the local hills rather than the water, you might even see wolves, owls and brown bears.

ONE-DAY WANDER #5: KINDERDIJK, THE NETHERLANDS

LOCATION: Southwestern Netherlands
DAY-HIKE FROM: Amsterdam, The Hague, Delft, Rotterdam

TYPE: Out and back
DISTANCE: 4.4 miles (7 km) round-trip
MORE INFO: kinderdijk.com

For a flat, easy path that showcases the best of old-time Netherlands, you don't have to look farther than a walk through Kinderdijk, a UNESCO World Heritage Site that features nineteen iconic eighteenth-century windmills and 740 years of Dutch water-management history. Don't forget your camera—this is one daylong wander that will

have you reaching for your viewfinder over and over.

Getting to Kinderdijk from Rotterdam is easy: you can drive, take the bus or bicycle—there are several convenient places to rent bikes in the city. I recommend cycling; it's not only fun and the best way to see the peaceful Dutch countryside, it's also a good way to avoid the

steep parking fee (and crowded parking lot) at the entrance to Kinderdijk.

Once you're there, a slow meander shows you everything in turn. Most of the windmills have their date of origin posted on them and are still in working order, doing what they were designed to do: pump water out of drainage ditches and into canals. From the path or a well-placed bench, watch the windmill tender changing the direction of the blades in response to changing winds. Want to know more about the process? Ask one of the tenders or stop by Museum Windmill Blokweer, Museum Windmill Nederwaard or the visitor center at the Wisboom Pump Station to learn about the inner workings of the windmills.

The windmills of Kinderdijk may be old (they're from the eighteenth century), but they're still in good working order.

ONE-DAY WANDER #6: CLIFFS OF MOHER, IRELAND

LOCATION: West-central Ireland
DAY-HIKE FROM: Galway, Limerick, Doolin
TYPE: Out and back

DISTANCE: 6.2 miles (10 km) round-trip
MORE INFO: cliffsofmoher.ie

The Cliffs of Moher, which stretch for 5 miles (8 km) along the Atlantic Coast, are where Ireland drops off into the ocean in spectacular fashion—it's all jutting cliffs and the most verdant of rolling hills in every shade of green: lime, emerald, shamrock. Walk along the cliffs and enjoy spectacular views of both land and sea, including Galway Bay and the Aran Islands, to the peaceful sound of waves crashing below you.

To get to the Cliffs of Moher from Galway, you can either drive or take a bus; from Doolin, you can drive, take a bus, bicycle or walk. I don't

recommend driving to the Cliffs of Moher; parking is expensive, and it can be stressful to find a parking spot in the very crowded lots.

Want to walk farther? Start the Cliffs Coastal Walk in Doolin, rather than at the Cliffs of Moher Visitor Center, for an additional 5 miles (8 km) one way of trail to Hags Head. For a hop-on, hop-off shuttle bus that services multiple stops along the Cliffs Coastal Walk, check out cliffsofmohercoastalwalk.ie.

Once you're there, if you want to enjoy the splendor of the cliffs without the crowds that stick to the core paved paths, head south from the visitor center on the Cliffs Coastal Walk to Hags Head, the most southerly point of the Cliffs of Moher.

Along the way, you'll wander through wide grasslands and get up close and personal with the cliff edge—this isn't a trail for those who are afraid of heights. Eventually you come upon an abandoned ruin of a first-century BC fort that stood where the Moher Tower now stands. It's perfect for exploring and imagining what Ireland was like 2,000 years ago, back when this area first earned its name from the old Irish word *mothar,* which means "ruined fort."

The Cliffs Coastal Walk weaves you through the most breathtaking sections of the Cliffs of Moher.

There's no better view of Edinburgh and Holyrood Park than the one from Arthur's Seat.

ONE-DAY WANDER #7: ARTHUR'S SEAT AND HOLYROOD PARK, SCOTLAND

LOCATION: Edinburgh, southeastern Scotland
DAY-HIKE FROM: Glasgow, Edinburgh
TYPE: Loop

DISTANCE: 3 miles (4.75 km) round-trip
MORE INFO: walkhighlands.co.uk/lothian/arthurs-seat.shtml

Scotland's capital city, Edinburgh, is one of the best places in the United Kingdom for urban exploration on foot. The heart of the city is a UNESCO World Heritage Site. Edinburgh, dubbed the "Athens of the North," has the largest concentration of Georgian buildings in the world. See it all from another angle—up high—with a walk through Holyrood Park to Arthur's Seat, the highest of a set of hills that were formed from the remains of an ancient volcano.

One more daylong walk you should consider is Italy's Cinque Terre. Although the route I recommend in Chapter 3, Get a Recommendation, is a longer version of the iconic route (see Walk 6, Cinque Terre 2.0), many people walk Cinque Terre in a day.

Arthur's Seat and Holyrood Park are very accessible from Edinburgh. You can drive (there's a parking lot near Holyrood Palace), take a bus (there's a bus stop there as well) or simply walk from the Old Town. Although you'll still be in the city, you'll feel like you're smack-dab in the middle of the wilderness, surrounded by scrubby bushes, rolling hills of golden grasslands and birds riding channels of wind. At very nearly the last moment, you climb up a small rocky summit for a dramatic view of the city far below you. Don't head back down quite yet—this is the perfect spot for a memorable picnic.

> These one-day wanders might just inspire you to fit even more walking into your trip schedule. If that's the case, simply search for other walks around the one-day wander you're interested in (those regional and local trails described in the section above come in really handy here)—there are plenty out there to explore!—and piece together a longer itinerary.

FIND EVEN MORE INSPIRATION

The trail categories and one-day wanders covered in this chapter are an excellent starting point for identifying a good trail, the backbone of exploring on foot. But I also recommend opening yourself up to inspiration in other places as well. After all, you never know where the perfect trail experience may be hiding—for you it might be in a good roundup article or even a friend's travel blog. The following are some of the resources I typically frequent in my search for trails that are worthy of exploring on foot.

> To start exploring Europe on foot with a trail that's already been vetted, turn to Chapter 3, Get a Recommendation, for fifteen of my favorites.

Extensive grasslands and delicate wildflowers adorn the cliffs of France's seaside GR 34.

You'll get the most expansive views from walking, rather than boating, along Germany's Moselle River.

Through Your Network

One of the most powerful resources you have is those you know—and who know you. Chances are, these folks have a good idea of the kind of trail you'd enjoy. So do yourself a favor and seek out the advice of people like those listed below.

Friends and family: If they're walkers, pick their brains about their favorite places in Europe to walk. If they're not walkers, ask about their all-time favorite destinations and research trails around those spots.

Social media: Pinterest and Instagram are great for discovering drool-worthy photos of trails you might like to walk. Need to expand your network to include walkers? Consider following walking organizations, guidebook authors and walking magazines. Facebook is great for personal recommendations; simply post on your wall that you're looking for a great trail in either Europe or a specific country and see what people suggest.

Guesthouse owner or hotel concierge: If you've already booked a sightseeing trip to Europe and want to add some exploring on foot, reach out to the tour company or your accommodations host. Because they are in the tourism industry (and may even be avid walkers themselves), they should have a good idea of what trails are in the area—and which ones shouldn't be missed.

Online Resources

There's so much information available on the Internet—with a few clicks, you could have enough trail inspiration to last you for years and years. Here's where I've had success:

Tour companies' websites: Look for companies that offer guided walking tours in Europe and see what trails they're exploring. Many of these companies also have their own online travel magazines that you can subscribe to—you'll have trail ideas regularly delivered to your in-box. (For more suggestions on finding

(Photo by Andy Offinger)

companies that offer these services, check out Chapter 6, Walk Independently or Hire Help.)

Travel roundups: These lists are a personal favorite of mine because they get to the point really quickly. Find them by searching online for things like "top ten trails to hike in Europe" or whatever country you're interested in.

Online travel agents and bookers: Travel companies like Expedia, Orbitz and Booking .com often have destination guides with ideas for exploring nature wherever you're heading.

Traildino: This is advertised as the world's largest walking-trail database, and you can search by continent, country and even region for the perfect trail (see Resources).

Wikiloc: This website has more than six million trail listings from around the world and country-specific search functionality; it also allows you to search trails by mileage and difficulty (see Resources).

National, regional and local tourism websites: Most of these have an activity tab for walking or cycling, and from there you can drill down to more information. To find a specific tourism website, search online for "visit (insert destination name)" or "tourist information (insert destination name)."

Travel blogs: See what trails other people have done and read whether they enjoyed the experience—or not. There are blogs for every kind of walker-traveler, including pilgrims, solo travelers, overweight adventurers and families with kids.

Travel forums: These sites, like the ones offered by Rick Steves, Lonely Planet and TripAdvisor, allow you to see what trails and experiences other people have enjoyed. Looking for a recommendation? You can typically post a question.

Online travel and walking magazines: Some niche European travel publications like *Route Notes*, the online adventure magazine of tour company Macs Adventure (see Resources), are available exclusively online. Others have

One of the prettiest lakes in Europe, the Bachalpsee, is a short trail detour from Switzerland's Alpine Pass Route.

expanded online issues. All around, they tend to be a great source of trail inspiration and tips for making your walk a success.

In Print

It's always fun to turn the pages of a physical book or magazine when you're brainstorming. While I love simply making my way to the travel section of the local bookstore and browsing the shelves for inspiration, here are some specific ideas for print resources that can help you in your search for the right trail.

Magazines: Many magazines, typically those devoted to general travel, active travel or adventure, feature stories on walking. But you'll get the most bang for your buck by choosing one that is devoted to the activity, like *Country Walking* (a UK publication; see Resources). For magazines that focus on Europe but are written in English,

choose those that are published in English-speaking Europe (Ireland and the United Kingdom). Speak a foreign language? Most countries have walking magazines—one of my favorites is Germany's *Wanderbares Deutschland* (see Resources). Can't find these magazines at the bookstore or get them to ship internationally? See if you can sign up for an online subscription instead. If nothing else, most walking magazines also have free online content.

Guidebooks: These are a great source of trail information and inspiration, especially ones that cover entire regions, and also for the practical details of making your walk happen. Check your local bookstore or search for them online before you travel, or find them at bookstores once you arrive at your destination.

Walking Distance by Robert and Martha Manning: I like flipping through this book to get an idea of what trails the authors personally enjoyed. While the book covers the whole world, it does have several good choices for Europe.

Fifty Places to Hike Before You Die by Chris Santella: Not all of these walks are in Europe, but some are. The rest can serve as inspiration for another trip.

On Location

If you're walking a long trail, you need to decide which one when you're still at home. (How else would you know where to fly to or what to pack?) But if you're looking to just add a one-day wander to your European trip or you're doing trail reconnaissance for future trips, there are several resources you can tap once you're in Europe.

Locals: Those in the tourism industry, especially, will know what the walking options are for a particular area—it's part of their job. So ask your hotel concierge or the owner of your guesthouse for a suggestion. But don't limit yourself to people in the tourism industry. Ask anyone and everyone you meet who could be a walker—the clerk at the local outdoor store, the couple with backpacks and walking shoes, even the cashier at the corner store. Their favorite trail might just become yours as well.

Tourist information offices: I love visiting tourist information offices because they have so much information—racks of brochures (including those that list the best walks in the area), stacks of maps (including walking maps and cycling maps of the local area) and so many partners (from companies that run walking tours to guides for hire). If you can't find what you're looking for, ask a staff member. They're there to help. If they don't know the answer to your question, they usually know someone

who will—and they'll point you in that direction. Tourist information offices are universally signed with a white *i* (for "information") superimposed on a blue background.

Brochure racks: Brochures don't live at just the tourist information offices. You'll find them everywhere—at the airport, in the lobby of your hotel and even in the train station. Most of these brochures advertise companies that run tours, including afternoon-long walking tours of the city, countryside, et cetera. Some of them have really cool themes—I've done everything from a ghost tour to a Communist walking tour. They're a fun way to get in a walk without having to research anything.

Regional and city parks: Most parks are great for walking. So stop by a park that's on your city map and check out what trails are available. If there is an extensive trail system, there is usually a big map in the main parking lot. Want to gather a little information before you arrive? Zoom in on the park in Google Maps—you should be able to see the paths.

SO MUCH INSPIRATION!

You may be on the hunt for one particular trail for your trip, but don't let all of the other great trails fall by the wayside. Keep those ideas for the future. I have two separate files for trail inspiration: one is an online folder that lives in my favorite browser; the other is a paper folder that sits on my bookshelf. Whenever I find information on a trail I want to consider for the future, I add it to the appropriate file. That way, the next time I want to travel (or when I need to remember why I'm saving money or working so hard), I can page through the ideas and get inspired.

CHAPTER

3

GET A RECOMMENDATION:
FIFTEEN HANDPICKED WALKS

Some people get a real kick out of researching and finding their own travel gems that no one else knows about. If that's you, I hope you now have a great understanding of where to start when it comes to researching and finding your own incredible trail experiences. But if you prefer personal recommendations rather than searching out your own walks, get excited, because I'm about to let you in on my favorite fifteen trails for exploring Europe on foot (see Walks at a Glance for a summary). I think you'll love them as well. Here's why:

They're impressive: I've done a lot of exploring on foot, so the bar I have for great trails is pretty darn high. These walks are the cream of the crop—they have amazing natural beauty, are a joy to walk and showcase really fascinating aspects of local culture.

They're rightsized: Most long trails, including several that I recommend, are simply too long for the average one- to two-week vacation. That's why I've rightsized them—cut them down to their most iconic sections—so you can be confident that you're experiencing the best that a long trail has to offer, even if you don't have time to walk the whole thing.

They're accessible: I've chosen only routes that you can replicate yourself. That means they are reachable with public transportation, they have good information available in English (from trail descriptions to maps) and they're well signed.

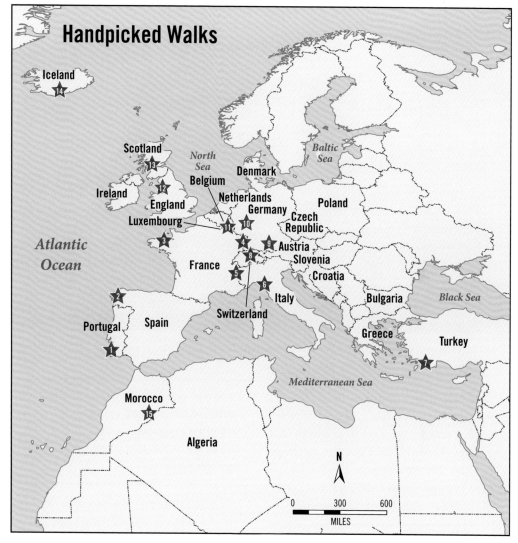

Handpicked Walks

1. Rota Vicentina, Portugal 2. English Way, Spain 3. Mont Saint-Michel, France 4. Alsace Wine Route, France
5. Tour du Mont Blanc, France and Italy, 6. Cinque Terre 2.0, Italy 7. Lycian Way, Turkey 8. Alpine Pass Route,
Switzerland 9. King Ludwig's Way, Germany 10. The Moselle, Germany 11. The Ardennes, Luxembourg and Belgium
12. The Lake District, England, UK 13. West Highland Way, Scotland, UK 14. Laugavegur Trek, Iceland 15. The Sahara
Desert, Morocco

How to Use the Walk Write-Ups

For each of the fifteen recommended walks in this chapter, I've included a variety of information to introduce you to the trail, show you the kind of experience it offers and help you determine if it's a good fit for you.

Each walk starts with an **overview map** to give you a general idea of where the trail is located (but refer to text for exact distances as scales are approximate) and an **"At a Glance"** section that includes a summary of important details such as the trail's location, information

Italy's Cinque Terre treats walkers to quaint seaside towns, ocean views and steep vineyards.

on how easy it is to explore the area as an English speaker, and a listing of the trail's biggest selling points when it comes to scenery and cultural experiences. Then I describe the flavor of each trail and what to expect—what it's like to walk, what your senses will experience, what you'll remember most, why it's worth doing.

You'll notice that not every trail that I've recommended is actually in Europe. A couple are in nearby Turkey and Morocco. Both of these countries—and the walks there that I recommend—are very easy to get to from Europe. In fact, with the profusion of hopper flights (see Chapter 7, Get There), traveling to these two countries can even be quicker and cheaper than finding your way to one of the more remote European trails. And if you're walking with the intent of seeing a completely different way of life, there's nowhere better to visit than Turkey or Morocco!

I've written route guides on walking several of my handpicked trails. How will you know which ones? Look for the Explore on Foot icon 🚶 next to the write-up and see the "More Information" section of those trail summaries.

Next you'll find a section called **"On the Trail"** that will help you plan your walk. A short information summary includes the trail's official name, how long the route is in miles (and kilometers), how much elevation gain and/or loss you'll experience, the average number of days it takes to walk, the season(s) the route is walkable, how difficult the trail is and where you should start and end your walk. I've also provided tips on getting to and from the trailhead, information on how well signed the trail is, suggested stages and pointers on making the daily stages shorter, as well as information on

WALKS AT A GLANCE

WALK NO.	TRAIL NAME	LOCATION	DISTANCE	ELEVATION GAIN/LOSS	TIME	SEASON	DIFFICULTY
1	Rota Vicentina	Portugal	47 mi (75 km)	+2,365/-2,431 ft (+721/-741 m)	4 days	Sept–June	Moderate to challenging
2	English Way	Spain	73 mi (118 km)	+6,572/-5,788 ft (+2,003/-1,764 m)	5 days	Year-round	Moderate
3	Mont Saint-Michel	France	45 mi (72 km)	+2,288/-2,265 ft (+697/-690 m)	4 days	Mar–Sept	Easy to moderate
4	Alsace Wine Route	France	40 mi (64 km)	+2,300/-2,462 ft (+701/-750 m)	4 days	Apr–Oct	Easy
5	Tour du Mont Blanc	France and Italy	43 mi (69 km)	+13,970/ -13,337 ft (+4,258/-4,065 m)	4 days	Mid-June to mid-Sept	Challenging
6	Cinque Terre 2.0	Italy	10.5 mi (17 km)	+2,575/-2,590 ft (+785/-789 m)	1–5 days	Apr–Oct	Moderate
7	Lycian Way	Turkey	115 mi (185 km)	+26,575/ -26,657 ft (+8,100/-8,125 m)	13 days	Feb–May; Sept–Nov	Moderate to challenging
8	Alpine Pass Route	Switzerland	202 mi (326 km)	+59,242/-58,868 ft (+18,057/ -17,943 m)	15 days	Late June– early Oct	Challenging
9	King Ludwig's Way	Germany	72 mi (115 km)	+7,006/-6,438 ft (+2,135/-1,962 m)	5 days	May–Sept	Moderate
10	The Moselle	Germany	24 mi (39 km)	+4,871/-4,965 ft (+1,485/-1,513 m)	3 days	Year-round	Moderate
11	The Ardennes	Luxembourg & Belgium	65 mi (105 km)	+8,312/-8,267 ft (+2,533/-2,520 m)	5 days	Year-round	Moderate
12	The Lake District	England, UK	1.2–9.6 mi (1.9–15.4 km)	(see route description)	3–5 days	Year-round	Easy to moderate
13	West Highland Way	Scotland, UK	37 mi (59 km)	+4,334/-4,864 ft (+1,321/-1,483 m)	3 days	Mar–Oct	Moderate
14	Laugavegur Trek	Iceland	36 mi (58 km)	+6,004/-7,218 ft (+1,830/-2,200 m)	4 days	Late June– late Aug	Moderate to challenging
15	The Sahara Desert	Morocco	1 mi (1.6 km)	+/-493 ft (+/-150 m)	3 days for trip; 2 hours for night walk	Mid-Sept to mid- May	Moderate

Walking a cycling trail such as France's Alsace Wine Route is perfect for those who love flat, paved paths.

Season refers to the main months a trail is walkable. Some of these trails can be enjoyed outside of their main season (for example, you could snowshoe parts of Walk 9, King Ludwig's Way, in the winter and it would be lovely) and others can't (for example, high alpine routes like Walk 5, Tour du Mont Blanc). If you're interested in exploring outside of a trail's main season, check out more-detailed trail resources to see if it's possible or recommended.

Difficulty refers to how physically challenging a trail is for someone of average walking ability, which I define as someone who can easily walk six hours in a day, traveling an average of 2 miles (3.2 km) an hour over moderate terrain with 1,000 feet (305 m) of elevation gain. My rating also takes into consideration any special challenges a trail may present, such as extreme weather, that could make things more difficult for someone who's new to exploring on foot. In each walk write-up, I include a box with the walk's difficulty rating and a short explanation of why I've categorized the trail as easy, moderate, challenging or a combination of those.

Finally, each walk concludes with a **"More Information"** section that lists additional resources for continuing your trail research. Although I provide a lot of information in my walk write-ups, they're meant to be helpful summaries, not ubercomplete guidebook entries. So before you lace up your hiking boots, seek out more-detailed resources like trail-specific guidebooks and topographical maps. They're essential to planning a safe and fun trip.

accommodations and things to do in the surrounding area. Here are some important things to keep in mind as you read that section:

Distance and **elevation gain/loss** numbers are grand totals for the route as I've described it. Also, because there are slight differences in how individual GPS devices record tracks and how individual map programs interpret GPS data, distances and elevation figures are approximations.

Average time is how long the route takes to walk when you stick to the suggested stages. That said, I encourage you to modify these walks. I've included trail-specific suggestions for making the daily stages shorter and easier as you see fit; break them up to spend more days on trail.

KEY TO WALK SYMBOLS

⍟ Leading Quality Trail

ⓜ UNESCO World Heritage Site or Geopark

⍟ Separate Explore on Foot route guide available

ROTA VICENTINA, PORTUGAL

Unspoiled dune wilderness and beautiful beach towns on Portugal's southwestern coast

---

At a Glance

LOCATION: Southwest Alentejo and Vicentine Coast Natural Park, southwestern Portugal

LOCAL LANGUAGE: Portuguese

USE OF ENGLISH: Widely understood and used

SCENERY: Extensive sand dunes, Atlantic Ocean, isolated beaches, pine forests

DON'T MISS: Beach bars, coastal towns, delectable seafood, *vinho verde*

If there's one incredibly photogenic trail that's even more beautiful in real life, it's Portugal's Rota Vicentina Fishermen's Trail, a stunning cliff-side route through unspoiled dune wilderness and beautiful beach towns on the southwestern coast of the country—and the best-preserved coastline in Europe. Although the Fishermen's Trail is a path that was originally created by locals to reach their favorite beaches and fishing holes, nowadays everything around you is protected, part of the Southwest Alentejo and Vicentine Coast Natural Park, a magical place that's replete with not only breathtaking views but unique species of plants and animals that aren't found anywhere else in the world. It's a biologist's dream—many from around the world come here to study the local flora and fauna—and you can see it all for yourself in four days.

Just don't make the mistake of thinking it's going to be easy. The land makes you work for its treasures. As you wind your way through the largest succession of consolidated dunes in Portugal, you'll trudge through loose sand that's famous for the toe blisters it causes. (Be smarter than the sand—wear toesocks. Check out Chapter 12, Clothing, for more information.) But you won't even mind once you see the

views, especially between March and June, when the dunes spring to life with fragrant herbs and wildflowers, like the buttery yellow *Biscutella vicentina*, so named because its fruit is shaped like a little biscuit. The bright colors of the wildflowers—hot pink, fire-poker red, majestic purple—stand out in gorgeous contrast to the orange-red of the sand, the emerald of the foliage that carpets the dunes and the azure of the water beyond. The flowers perfume the air,

---

The Southwest Alentejo and Vicentine Coast Natural Park is protected for a reason—the land and its rare plants and animals are delicate, so be especially careful to tread lightly. Always follow Leave No Trace principles (see Chapter 10, Be Prepared for Anything, for the full list of guidelines). That means staying on trail so you don't trample sensitive vegetation or cause greater erosion of the dunes. It also means packing out all of your trash—including any toilet paper—and disposing of it in town. The only way this landscape will stay as gorgeous and unspoiled as it is today is if we all do our part to keep it that way. So take only memories, leave only footprints. For other points of interest in the Southwest Alentejo and Vicentine Coast Natural Park, including fascinating old ruins, check out the park's website (see Resources).

Portugal's Rota Vicentina Fishermen's Trail closely follows the country's rugged and beautiful southwestern coast.

mixing with the fresh, salty aroma of the ocean to create a scent that's as distinctive as the trail.

Always, to your right, is the limitless ocean. In some places, you'll see fishing boats bobbing on the surface or surfers riding the waves (this is some of the best surfing not only in Portugal but in the world), but for the most part it's a solitary trail. The sound of the sea crashing on the shore calls to you incessantly. At times, you'll heed the call and dip your toes—or submerge your whole body—in its cold waters on a secluded, sandy *praia* (beach). This is the perfect way to cool off during the often-hot Portuguese afternoons.

You won't always be close to the water; in some places, the trail heads heavenward along jagged cliffs peppered with lithified sand tubes and *palheirões*, jet-black rocks that have been forced out of the earth in interesting formations. These cliffs aren't just beautiful—they're important, at least for the more than twenty species of birds (many of them rare) that nest here, including peregrine falcons, rock doves (the original species from which all feral pigeons in the world descend), fishing eagles and the pièce de résistance, white storks—this is the only place in the world where they build their nests on ocean-side cliffs.

Occasionally the path retreats from the ocean even farther, heading toward the flat interior of the country, with its bucolic farmland, green tunnels of bamboo, peaceful pine forests and impressive stands of acacia trees. (Don't be deceived by their beauty—these aggressive acacias are on a mission to dominate the landscape, wiping out many endemic species in the process.) The change of scenery—and smells—will reset your senses

so that when you make your way back to the coast, you will be properly impressed all over again.

Although the main highlight of the Fishermen's Trail is its natural beauty, the route also takes you to nature-inspired civilization. During the day, you'll typically pass by at least a couple of remote beach bars or small rural outposts with cliff-side cafes that will tempt you to take a break and refuel. But that's nothing compared to the evenings, when you'll be led to a series of beautiful coastal villages that make delightful temporary homes. It's hard to believe from the number of picturesque white buildings that now colonize them all, but thirty years ago, these towns were tiny fishing and agricultural hamlets without electricity or cars; most of their residents lived a subsistence life and couldn't read or write.

Development was slow to come to southwestern Portugal—it still feels relatively undiscovered—but nowadays, you'll find a variety of services to make you comfortable: Bed-and-breakfasts will give you not only a comfortable bed for the night but a giant breakfast in the morning, and mom-and-pop seafood restaurants offer up a fresh-caught dinner cooked to order as the sun goes down over the ocean.

The seafood isn't just fresh here, it's also mouthwatering. And there's so much to choose from: sea bream, sea bass, shrimp, mussels, clams, octopus, gooseneck barnacles. The platters are served alongside other local specialties, from olives and cheese to fresh-baked bread and salad. You can wash it all down with a glass of *vinho verde* (green wine) that tastes a bit salty, just like the sea. And did I mention that such gluttony won't set you

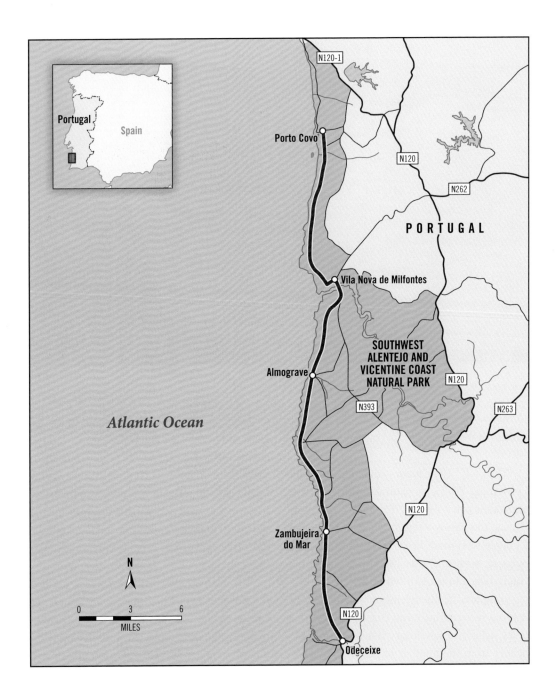

back much at all? Portugal is one of the most affordable places to travel in Europe; it's not uncommon to pay €1 for a glass of wine or €20 for a whole feast.

At night, you'll fall asleep to the sound of the waves crashing against the shore. It's a siren call, beckoning you to return to the trail and the dunes, beaches and beauty that make this incredibly photogenic landscape so alluring. At night you'll dream; there's plenty of time the next day to give in to temptation, at least until you finish your walk on day four.

On the Trail

ROUTE: Rota Vicentina Fishermen's Trail

DISTANCE: 47 miles (75 km)

ELEVATION GAIN/LOSS: +2,365/-2,431 feet (+721/-741 m)

AVERAGE TIME: 4 days

SEASON: September to June

DIFFICULTY: Moderate to challenging

START: Porto Covo, Portugal

END: Odeceixe, Portugal

Moderately Difficult to Challenging: The Fishermen's Trail combines moderate beachside and countryside walking with challenging stretches of trekking up and down sand dunes—and through loose sand. For ideas on making the walk easier, check out "Make it shorter."

Although the entire Fishermen's Trail consists of 75 miles (120 km) of coastal walking, you don't need nine days to experience the best of the route. Instead, I recommend the four-day 47-mile (75 km) section from Porto Covo to Odeceixe ("ode-SAYSH"), which is undoubtedly the most iconic. The most convenient airport for accessing the Fishermen's Trail is in Lisbon, and no exploration of coastal Portugal is complete without a visit to beautiful Lisbon. Build a couple of days into your trip for walking tours, relaxing at ocean-side cafes and dancing in the streets—yes, it happens there at night, and it's quite romantic.

Start: To get from Lisbon to Porto Covo and the start of the trail, take one of the frequent and relatively cushy buses offered by Rede Expressos

(see Resources). Porto Covo is a small town built on an even smaller bay of the Atlantic Ocean, but it doesn't take long before the streets of town peter out into the sandy single-track that leads you into the wilderness.

Suggested stages:

Day 1: Porto Covo to Vila Nova de Milfontes, 12.4 miles (20 km)

Day 2: Vila Nova de Milfontes to Almograve, 9.3 miles (15 km)

Day 3: Almograve to Zambujeira do Mar, 13.7 miles (22 km)

Day 4: Zambujeira do Mar to Odeceixe, 11.2 miles (18 km)

Signage: The official trail sign of the Fishermen's Trail is a lime-green stripe above a sky-blue stripe. Although there is plentiful signage on trail, sometimes the signs for important junctions are low to the ground and easy to overlook if you're not paying close attention. I recommend using both a detailed paper map and GPX tracks, which are available on the trail website (see More Information below).

Accommodations: There are plenty of accommodations on the Fishermen's Trail, most typically family-run small hotels and guesthouses. If you'd like to experience the idyllic Portuguese countryside, consider booking at a guesthouse that's located just outside one of the towns, where oftentimes you can rest up among beautiful fruit trees and cool off with a dip in a swimming pool. These facilities often offer a free pickup from town or can help you arrange a cheap taxi.

Tip: Get out into the ocean you've admired so much from the shore—and experience some of the best surfing in the world—with a surfing class. Several beach bars along the Fishermen's Trail offer intro lessons on a walk-up basis. To lock down your lessons in advance, search

Spring (March–June) is the best time to see the incredible array of wildflowers that pop up along Portugal's Rota Vicentina Fishermen's Trail.

online for "Vicentine Coast surf schools" and "surf schools Costa Vicentina."

Make it shorter: You can shorten one or more of the suggested stages by arranging a taxi in advance. Just remember that you'll need to arrange pickup near a road—your best bet for the more remote stretches of trail is to check local maps for rural hamlets and beach bars with road access.

Return: Once you've finished the trail, the easiest way to get back to Lisbon is to taxi from Odeceixe to Santa Clara-Sabóia (approximately forty-five minutes) and take the train from there.

Other Activities Nearby

If you have more time to enjoy the coast of southwestern Portugal, check out the rest of the Rota Vicentina trail system.

In addition to the main Fishermen's Trail, there are five complementary circuits on the route (all can be done in a day or less) with a combined total of 28 more miles (45 km) of trail to explore.

And if you'd like to spend some time discovering the inland part of this region, don't miss the 143-mile (230 km) Historical Way.

More Information

For more information on all of these trails, including accommodations along the way, check out the official website of the Rota Vicentina trail system (see Resources).

2 ENGLISH WAY, SPAIN

In search of Saint James on the Camino de Santiago

At a Glance

LOCATION: Galicia, northwestern Spain

LOCAL LANGUAGE: Spanish, Galician

USE OF ENGLISH: Not common in most small towns; brush up on your Spanish

SCENERY: Sandy coastline, gently rolling farmland, orange and lemon trees

DON'T MISS: *Semana Santa* (Holy Week), pilgrims' meals, *albergues* (pilgrims' accommodations), Cathedral of Santiago de Compostela and its giant *Botafumeiro* (censer)

Since the Middle Ages, Europe's Camino de Santiago—a trek to the remains of Saint James—has been one of the most popular pilgrimage routes in the entire world. And although its original draw was religion, specifically for the Catholics of Europe, these days it attracts a diverse group of spiritual and non-spiritual walkers from all over the globe. Modern pilgrims walk the Camino for a variety of reasons. Some are looking to mourn or celebrate a major life event; others seek the physical and mental challenge of walking for days—or weeks—on end; yet others are searching for something that's increasingly rare in our modern world: a deep sense of interpersonal connection. Whatever you're looking for, it seems, you can find it on the Camino.

Although the route sounds like a single trail, it's actually a spiderweb network of weeks- and months-long paths that start as far away as Norway and coalesce at the Cathedral of Santiago de Compostela, the most famous of which is the 478-mile (769 km) French Way.

Just as the name implies, the English Way is the route that English pilgrims took to the cathedral for hundreds of years, after traveling to Spain by boat and disembarking in one of

two port cities, A Coruña or Ferrol. Today, you can follow in their footsteps on a hilly route that takes you from the sandy beaches and deep-blue waters of the Atlantic Ocean through the beautiful farmland of rural Galicia before delivering you to the ancient stone edifice of the Cathedral of Santiago de Compostela.

You can walk the English Way year-round, but there's no better time to kick off your pilgrimage than during Spain's *Semana Santa*, or Holy Week (the week before Easter), when the streets of Ferrol are transformed by large processions celebrating the Passion of Christ. It's an incredible sight: massive metal floats and wax statues so tall that special attendants are needed to lift up powerlines as they pass and so heavy that the only way the large groups of men who carry them on their shoulders can move them forward is by slowly rocking from one foot to the other in complete synchronicity, gaining only inches of pavement at a time. The processions dominate the town from morning till (very late at) night, filling the streets with not only floats but military and church bands, colorful hooded penitents and small robed children passing out holy cards of their favorite saints. It's a deeply moving sight; it's also a

You'll walk through extensive agricultural land on the Spanish section of the Camino de Santiago. (Photo by Staffan Andersson/Flickr)

gigantic weeklong party, one that's televised all over the country.

Get even more out of your pilgrimage by using it as an opportunity for walking meditation, a practice in which you bring all of your attention to the simple act of putting one foot in front of the other. For more information, check out the variety of resources that are available online by searching "walking meditation."

Once you've had a couple of days to take in the processions and all that is *Semana Santa*, it's time to start your trek. Although there's so much to see around you—small inlets where sailboats get stuck in the mud at low tide, lemons and oranges hanging enticingly from chartreuse trees, vines that create natural leafy arbors above your head—this is a peaceful route that's perfect for contemplation; the constant sound of your walking shoes may just put you in a reverie that's broken only by a local or a fellow pilgrim calling out the heartwarming words you'll come to cherish, *buen Camino!* (This translates directly to "good way!" but means something more like "good luck!")

Each day, the English Way passes through a series of small Galician towns and rural outposts where you can find food and a bed. You'll have some time to kill before dinner—the Spanish don't eat until the sun goes down, around 8:00 p.m.—so grab a snack as you check in to your room for the night. Most pilgrims stay in *albergues*, cheap dormitory-style accommodations that are first-come, first-served. You don't have to stay in *albergues*—there are a variety of private rooms, guesthouses and hotels available on trail for those who prefer a little more comfort (and like making reservations in advance). But the *albergues* offer the best opportunity to meet and talk with other pilgrims from all over the world, many of whom are utterly fascinating and have really amazing stories—indeed, befriending your fellow walkers is often one of the most enjoyable parts of walking the Camino.

Oftentimes, you'll share a meal together, either at the *albergue* or at a restaurant in town. Keep your eyes out for pilgrims' meals, which are set meals of two to three courses . . . and usually include a generous serving of *vino tinto* (red wine). I also recommend trying as many different *pinchos* or *tapas* (small plates typical to this region) as you can find, from gooseneck barnacles to Spanish-style *bruschetta* (grilled bread with a variety of toppings) to Galician octopus. Several *tapas* together make a great meal.

All too soon, you'll be walking the cobblestone streets of Santiago de Compostela and making your way to the famous cathedral. For

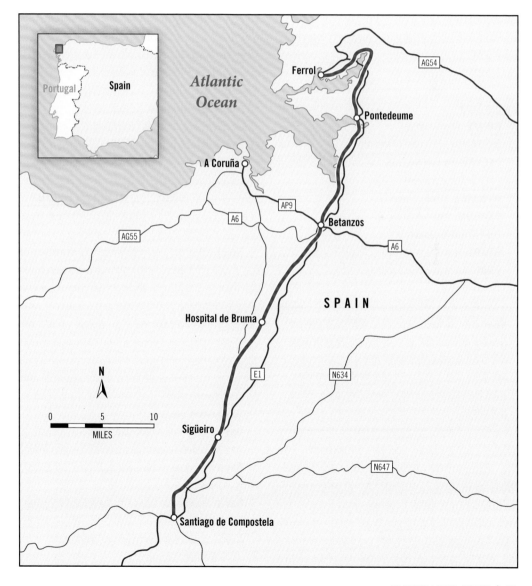

a fitting end to your walk, hug the statue of the apostle, head down to the crypt for a look at the remains of Saint James and attend a pilgrims' mass (several are offered each day). As the priest confers blessings in Spanish and the giant *Botafumeiro* (a famous censer) saturates the room in heavy incense, glance around— you're surrounded by thousands of dirty, exhausted and exultant walkers who, just like you, are at the end of their journey. It's a powerful experience, one that can make you feel like you found whatever it was you were searching for—and can kindle a deep desire to embark on yet another pilgrimage.

On the Trail

ROUTE: English Way
DISTANCE: 73 miles (118 km)
ELEVATION GAIN/LOSS: +6,572/-5,788 feet (+2,003/-1,764 m)
AVERAGE TIME: 5 days
SEASON: Year-round
DIFFICULTY: Moderate
START: Ferrol, Spain
END: Santiago de Compostela, Spain

Moderately Difficult: Because there's a decent amount of elevation gain along the English Way, and the recommended daily stages as prescribed are quite long, this is a moderately difficult walk. Want the walk to be easier? Read the tips in "Make it shorter."

There's no reason to be intimidated by the Camino de Santiago—you don't need thirty-plus days or hundreds of pilgrims on your route to walk it. I recommend the shorter and less crowded English Way, which requires only five days and 73 miles (118 km) of walking. While you can begin the route in either

Ferrol or A Coruña (the two paths eventually meet up and become one), you'll be eligible for a *compostela*—a certificate from the Pilgrim's Office certifying you've walked the last 63 miles (100 km) of the Camino—only if you start your walk in farther-away Ferrol.

In order to prove you walked those miles of the Camino and are eligible for a *compostela*, you'll need to collect at least two stamps a day from local businesses like restaurants and *albergues* along the route. The document that will hold your stamps is called a credential or a pilgrim's passport. To obtain your credential in advance of your trip (which I recommend), visit the website of the American Pilgrims on the Camino (see Resources), which provides free credentials to North Americans. Credentials are also available in person from several Ferrol-area Catholic churches and municipal *albergues*. To find out when *Semana Santa* is happening in Ferrol and see a calendar of events to plan your time, check out the organizing body's website (see Resources).

Start: The easiest way to reach the start of the route in Ferrol is by flying into nearby A Coruña and taking a short train ride (approximately an hour) to Ferrol. Alternatively, you can fly into Santiago de Compostela and take the train or bus to Ferrol. Over the next several days, you'll weave your way ever southward, spending most of your time in rolling hills and verdant farmland.

Suggested stages:
Day 1: Ferrol to Pontedeume, 18 miles (29 km)
Day 2: Pontedeume to Betanzos, 12.4 miles (20 km)
Day 3: Betanzos to Hospital de Bruma, 18 miles (29 km)
Day 4: Hospital de Bruma to Sigüeiro, 14.9 miles (24 km)
Day 5: Sigüeiro to Santiago de Compostela, 9.9 miles (16 km)

Signage: The signage on the English Way is plentiful: at every junction (and sometimes even in between), you'll see a cockleshell with an arrow pointing you in the right direction.

Accommodations: There are plenty of accommodations on the English Way, whether you're on a budget or are prepared to pamper yourself, walking alone or with a partner. For budget- and group-friendly accommodations, the *albergues* are your best bet (you will need valid credentials and will need to bring along a sleeping bag for most). If you're walking with a partner, I suggest staying in the variety of guesthouses that are available on the route; a standard one is only a little more expensive than paying for two people to stay in an *albergue*—well worth the small splurge if you like comfort and privacy. Most accommodations along the English Way don't provide a hearty breakfast, surprisingly, so have some calorie-dense food on hand for when you wake up hungry and want to set out on your walk.

Tips: Once you reach Santiago de Compostela, don't forget to head to the Pilgrim's Office to redeem your credential for a *compostela*. More information on directions, office hours, et cetera, can be found at the Pilgrim's Office website (see Resources). For a great end to your walk, head inside the cathedral for a pilgrims' mass. Most of the time it's delivered in Spanish, so don't count on understanding much of it, but it is an incredible opportunity to share a spiritual moment—one that transcends words—with thousands of other walkers. For a schedule of masses (including those in other languages), check out the website of the cathedral (see Resources).

Make it shorter: It's possible to shorten individual daily stages by staying in the variety of rural accommodations that have popped up in the last few years and are available on the route, not just in the towns mentioned above.

Spain's Camino de Santiago routes are incredibly well signed. At junctions, you'll see a cockle shell and an arrow. (Photo by M a n v e l/Flickr)

The best way to shorten the English Way is by taking a private taxi for some of the way. If you are pressed for time and don't mind missing out on your *compostela*, you can also shave some miles off the trail by starting your walk in A Coruña rather than Ferrol.

Return: Once you've reached Santiago de Compostela and finished your walk, simply fly out of the airport in town.

Other Activities Nearby

The Camino is famous for making lifelong fans of those who walk it, and many return, year after year, to walk new routes to the Cathedral of Santiago de Compostela. To find new routes starting in different spots all over Europe, check out Wikipedia's Camino page (see Resources).

More Information

For detailed guidebooks on several of the Camino routes (including the English Way), I recommend those published by the Confraternity of Saint James (see Resources).

You'll walk on sandy paths through sheep-filled grasslands on your way to the abbey island of Mont Saint-Michel.

3 MONT SAINT-MICHEL, FRANCE

Journey to an eighth-century abbey along France's Emerald Coast

At a Glance

LOCATION: Brittany, northwestern France
LOCAL LANGUAGE: French
USE OF ENGLISH: Widely understood and used
SCENERY: Wide headlands, rugged cliffs, Atlantic Ocean, extensive oyster beds

DON'T MISS: Idyllic beachside promenades, WWII relics, fresh oysters, *agneau de pré-salé*, Mont Saint-Michel

 There's nothing more motivating during a long walk than seeing your destination—at first just a slight smudge on the horizon—come ever closer. This is especially true when what you're walking to is a magnificent eighth-century abbey that rises majestically from a jagged rock island just off France's Emerald Coast. It may sound like a dream, but this can be your reality on France's Grande Randonée 34. Along the way, not only will you be enticed by views of the ever-nearing abbey, you'll also be treated to ocean-side walking, cute French seaside towns and even well-preserved relics from World War II.

Your route starts in Saint-Malo, a walled city that originally made a name for itself hundreds of years ago because of its merchant ships and government-sanctioned privateers (pirates). Nowadays, with its charming outdoor cafes, walkable ramparts and extensive sandy beaches, the town caters to wealthy Parisians, who can be in the weekend hideaway in as few as three hours thanks to the TGV (high-speed train).

Leaving town on a paved beach-side path, you meander past a string of bed-and-breakfasts with breezy balconies overlooking the turquoise water. Within just a couple of miles, though, the path turns to hardpacked sand and the buildings are replaced with hardy dune grass and pretty wildflowers. Wide headlands, rugged cliffs and limitless views of the horizon dominate the first two days of your walk. The shore you're walking on is subject to some of the greatest tidal changes on earth, and the land that has been torn open and scattered by erosion is now being rehabilitated.

You'll also come across something far more exciting—evidence of World War II. The route you're walking was once part of the Atlantic Wall, a series of fortresses, gun emplacements, tank traps and obstacles that Hitler commissioned in 1942 to protect more than 2,000 miles (3,200 km) of northern European coastline from invasion. You'll see several old bunkers on trail—big, empty concrete blocks hunkered down in the sand with narrow slits for machine guns. You can even climb down into several of them and look out to the same view the Germans had all those years ago.

Two days into your walk, you'll emerge in the town of Cancale, a picturesque strip of small restaurants and shops on the shore of Mont Saint-Michel Bay. This is the perfect place to catch a glimpse of the distant silhouette of Mont Saint-Michel, seemingly floating in the middle of the bay. It's also a great spot to explore one of the best-loved features of the French coast: the seafood. It's the specialty of nearly every restaurant in town; prepare to gorge on platters of crab, shrimp, clams, whelk, sole, snails and *langouste* (spiny lobster). But no matter how full you are, don't miss the oysters— Cancale is famous for them. In fact, King Louis XIV is rumored to have loved them so much that he had them hand-delivered to Versailles every day.

After Cancale, the landscape changes, and for the next two days, your walk takes you past myriad oyster farms and roadside stands where you can get a fresh snack to top off your tank. Eventually you'll come to a series of high dikes that overlook extensive marshland filled with grazing black-faced downy sheep. They look quite ordinary, but they're not—they're a world-famous variety known as *agneau de pré-salé* (salt-marsh lamb) that feed on special plants that have evolved to tolerate the high salt concentration of the soil. (Remember those incredible tidal changes I mentioned earlier?) Because of the salt, the meat of these sheep takes on a unique flavor and tenderness—it's a prized local delicacy that you'll see on the menu of nearly every nice restaurant in the area.

From these dikes, Mont Saint-Michel is tantalizingly close. And for hours, it will seem as though you're very nearly there. Until suddenly you are. The final approach to the rock outcropping is by a bridge that offers incredible photo opportunities of the island, with its narrow, winding cobblestone streets that lead up, up, up, past hole-in-the-wall restaurants and small shops hawking postcards and photo

WHAT IS MONT SAINT-MICHEL?

The rocky island now known as Mont Saint-Michel was home to strategic fortifications in ancient times, although it wasn't until AD 708 that its true destiny was set in motion. That's when, according to legend, the archangel Michael appeared to the bishop of nearby Avranches and instructed him to build a church on the site. It took centuries to build, but Mont Saint-Michel eventually became a monastery—and one of the most important pilgrimage sites in all Christendom. It's now a UNESCO World Heritage Site.

books, to the massive stone abbey that crowns it all. For even dreamier photos, come back at night, when everything is lit up and silhouetted against the black backdrop of the night sky.

It's a view that has tantalized travelers for centuries—one that's all the sweeter because you earned it. So step in and explore. Walk the uneven cobblestone steps; listen to a poetry reading or a concert echo out in the high chapel of the abbey; circle the bay (with a licensed guide) to see every spire, every rampart, every half-timbered building from every angle. And soak it all in—the physical manifestation of a dream turned reality.

France's GR 34 traces the stunning coastline of Brittany for more than a thousand miles (1,600 km). (Photo by Sofia Gaiaschi)

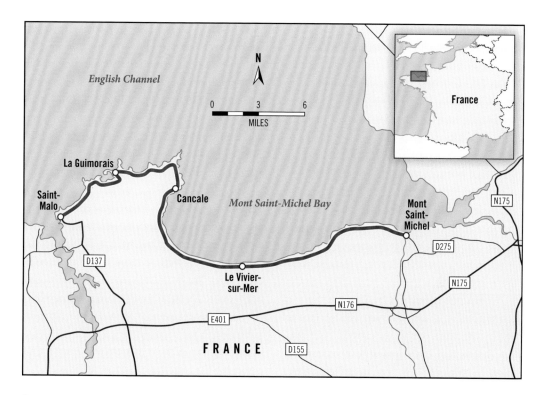

On the Trail

ROUTES: GR 34, Alternate GR 34
DISTANCE: 45 miles (72 km)
ELEVATION GAIN/LOSS: +2,288/-2,265 feet (+697/-690 m)
AVERAGE TIME: 4 days
SEASON: March to September
DIFFICULTY: Easy to moderate
START: Saint-Malo, France
END: Mont Saint-Michel, France

Easy to Moderate: The GR 34 from Saint-Malo to Mont Saint-Michel is a combination of very flat, easy walking along the beaches and steeper trekking along the rocky cliffs. For ideas on modifying the trail to make it easier, see "Make it shorter."

Although the GR 34 runs for 1,118 miles (1,800 km) along the coast of Brittany, you don't need to walk the whole thing for stunning views of Mont Saint-Michel. Instead, I recommend a four-day 45-mile (72 km) walk around the rim of Mont Saint-Michel Bay, starting in the town of Saint-Malo and ending at the abbey itself.

Start: Saint-Malo (and Mont Saint-Michel) is incredibly accessible from Paris by TGV (high-speed train). For the best rates, reserve your spot on the TGV—which requires reservations—at least three months in advance. Keep your eyes out for special discounts on the route; the French national rail carrier SNCF runs them often, especially in the spring and summer. When you're in Saint-Malo, don't miss a walk on the city's ramparts. It's an excellent way to see the city—and the ocean—from above. And it's free!

Begin your GR 34 walk on the paved beachside promenade that starts at Porte Saint-Vincent, one of the eastern town gates.

Suggested stages:

Day 1: Saint-Malo to La Guimorais, 8.3 miles (13.4 km)

Day 2: La Guimorais to Cancale, 13.8 miles (22.2 km)

Day 3: Cancale to Le Vivier-sur-Mer, 8.5 miles (13.7 km)

Day 4: Le Vivier-sur-Mer to Mont Saint-Michel, 14.3 miles (23 km)

Signage: The official marking for the GR 34 is a white stripe above a red stripe. The signage can be hit or miss (it's better near populated areas), so be sure to pack a paper map and GPX tracks.

Accommodations: There is a plethora of accommodations available on this stretch of the GR 34, most commonly strand-side boutique hotels and cozy bed-and-breakfasts. To make the most of your time in the area when you're walking, I recommend choosing accommodations with a view of the ocean—there's nothing better than going to sleep listening to the sound of the powerful Atlantic.

At Mont Saint-Michel, there are two main options for accommodations: on the abbey island or just beyond the access bridge in a small tourist enclave with views of the island, about 1 mile (1.6 km) away. Staying on the island is an excellent opportunity to explore it after all of the visitors have left for the day, but that said, the accommodations on the island are typically very expensive. If you stay in the tourist enclave just beyond Mont Saint-Michel, you'll still be able to walk to the abbey at night—or take the free shuttle between the two, which runs every few minutes, even after dark. You'll also benefit from amazing views of the lit-up abbey and score a more affordable place to stay.

Tip: Once you reach Mont Saint-Michel, discover it the most fun way possible: sign up for a barefoot walk in the bay with a certified guide. It is dangerous to explore the bay on your own because of rapidly changing water levels. Of the many tours that are offered, some trek across the entire bay like pilgrimages of old; others offer family-friendly short jaunts that circle the abbey. Information on guides and itineraries can be found at the official website for the island (see More Information, below).

Make it shorter: Local bus service connects Saint-Malo, Cancale, Le Vivier-sur-Mer and Mont Saint-Michel, which is helpful for shortening the route (taxis in the area are quite expensive). For bus details, including schedules, reach out to the local tourist information office. You can also experience Mont Saint-Michel in a day—without walking to it via the GR 34—by taking the TGV to Mont Saint-Michel and exploring the muddy bay at low tide.

Return: From Mont Saint-Michel, take the TGV (high-speed train) back to Paris. (This involves a short bus connection that's included with your train ticket.) Or, if you have more time to explore Normandy, take the train to Bayeux for an in-depth exploration of WWII history and relics that you'll never forget. Sure to top your list: the American and Canadian cemeteries and memorials, the Memorial Museum of the Battle of Normandy, and Omaha Beach—for a memorable daylong walk, see One-Day Wander #1: Omaha Beach in Chapter 2.

More Information

For more-detailed information on walking this section of the GR 34, check out my route guide *Explore France's GR 34 on Foot: Saint-Malo to Mont Saint-Michel.* For more information on visiting Mont Saint-Michel, visit the official website for the island and the official website for tourism in France (see Resources).

4 ALSACE WINE ROUTE, FRANCE

A medieval wine crawl through northeastern France

At a Glance

LOCATION: Northeastern France near Strasbourg

LOCAL LANGUAGE: French

USE OF ENGLISH: Widely understood and used

SCENERY: Colorful vineyards, pretty picnic spots, foothills of the Vosges Mountains to the west and Rhine River to the east

DON'T MISS: Charming medieval villages, half-timbered houses, mingling of German and French cultures, incredible local wine

There's nothing better than a quiet stroll through romantic wine country, especially when you're in one of the most famous wine-producing regions of the world—and you have the trail all to yourself. Welcome to the hidden gem of France, the Alsace Wine Route. Although Alsace retains an undiscovered feel (it is only starting to become popular with travelers), this narrow north-south corridor of fertile land in the very northeast of the country, bordered by the foothills of the Vosges Mountains in the west and the Rhine River in the east, is one of the oldest wine-producing regions of France, with roots

Every 3 miles (5 km) or so along France's Alsace Wine Route, you'll reach an inviting village.

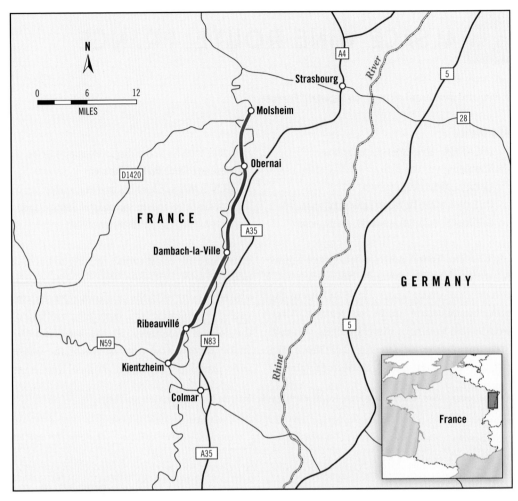

that go back to Roman times. It's also one of the most productive, boasting more than seventy wine-growing villages and 1,000 producers.

It's the very things that make the region so hospitable to wine production—a dry, sunny climate and mostly flat landscape—that also make it an excellent place to explore on foot. And there's no better path than the Alsace Wine Route, where you'll pass through a series of peaceful vineyards that are perfect for a long repose in the shade with a cold glass of dry wine, as well as charming medieval towns that will make you feel like you're in the Middle Ages.

Your route starts just outside of Kientzheim up one of the only hills you'll climb on trail, providing an intimate look at the leafy vines and ripening grapes that will be your constant companions on trail. They stretch arm to arm and in rows that number in the thousands for miles in every direction, a mass of life that's occasionally tempered by the prettiest of picnic spots and small wooden crucifixes.

Despite just this one type of plant dominating the landscape, there's so much to see. And the view changes all the time. In spring, when the vines are young and small, the rich brown soil carpeting the earth peeks out from between the plants. In summer, there's nothing but bright green leaves and the currant and mint hues of fat grapes as far as the eye can see. But nothing, perhaps, compares to fall, when a magnificent display of oranges and reds turns the land around you into a harvest paradise.

No matter the season, the vineyards hum with activity. As you walk, you'll come across farmers buzzing around the vines like bees around a flower, busily trimming vines here and tying them there—work that never seems to stop. Above them, hanging from cliffs in the distance, are old stone castles (many from the thirteenth century) that stand guard over everything.

It's a scene so beautiful you'll want to stop, over and over again, to take it all in. And I encourage you to do just that. Don't just pass by those picnic spots you see along the trail; take a seat on one of the many worn benches in the shade and stay for a while. If you've brought wine with you (see Chapter 15, Trail and Travel Tools, for the best way to do so) or a sweet, confectionary-dusted *kugelhopf* (a yeasted light marble cake), this is the perfect place to enjoy it—and a moment of quiet contemplation—before you continue on. (It's rare to find a tasting room in the countryside of Alsace, so if you want to drink local wine while you walk, pack it with you or enjoy it in town.)

Every few miles, you're in for a different kind of treat—a walled medieval village. This is the stuff of fairy tales and storybooks: gingerbread-like half-timbered houses painted in cheerful pastels, fountain-decorated public squares that are home to a throng of outdoor cafes, quaint shops passed down for generations and flowery lanes that connect everything. Don't forget to look up or you might miss the most whimsical thing of all—storks nesting in tall towers high above you. These storks are the unofficial mascot of Alsace, and you'll see their image everywhere, from murals that decorate the sides of buildings to figurines that adorn the local window boxes.

After wandering around town (don't miss the back alleys—they're charming), it's time to taste the vineyards that you'll spend each day walking through. There are a variety of places to do this—independent cafes, fancy restaurants, winery-run tasting rooms. Regardless of where you choose to sip, there's a lot to look forward to. Alsace is known for its white wine, from dry Riesling (unique because most Riesling is sweet) to pinot blanc, pinot gris, gewürztraminer and *crémant* (sparkling wine). If you're a wine connoisseur, you'll notice a distinctly Germanic influence on the wine, thanks to the fact that not only is Germany just across the Rhine River but this area has, over the centuries, been caught in a long-term tug of war between the two countries.

My favorite way to enjoy the wine of Alsace is to pair it with one of the three-hour dinners that the French are famous for, complete with white linens, real china, candlelight and good conversation. It's also the perfect way to end a long, satisfying day on trail. Work your way slowly through the local specialties and fully savor them in turn, just as you've done with every vineyard you've passed. There are so many to choose from—*tarte flambée*, an oven-baked thin-crust pizza with cream, onions and chopped bacon; *spätzle*, handmade Alsatian pasta; *bäcköffe*, a casserole of pork, lamb, beef and sliced potatoes that's slow-cooked all day in a white-wine sauce; and *choucroute garnie*, sauerkraut crowned by sausages and pork. As you let the rich French ingredients linger on your tongue and mingle with the dry white wine, you're literally tasting the fertile landscape around you. Tomorrow, do it all over again—until, at last, you arrive at Molsheim, the end of your journey back in time through vineyards and villages.

On the Trail

ROUTES: Cycle routes VV 111, VV 11, EuroVelo 5
DISTANCE: 40 miles (64 km)
ELEVATION GAIN/LOSS: +2,300/-2,462 feet (+701/-750 m)
AVERAGE TIME: 4 days
SEASON: April to October
DIFFICULTY: Easy
START: Kientzheim, France
END: Molsheim, France

Easy: Thanks to the paved bike routes it utilizes, the Alsace Wine Route is very flat and easy to walk. Still want to make things a little easier or cut down on the mileage of the daily stages? Check out "Make it shorter."

While the complete Alsace Wine Route runs for 106 miles (170 km), I recommend the 40-mile (64 km) stretch from Kientzheim to Molsheim, which is arguably the most iconic. An extensive series of country roads and paved cycle paths knit the region's vineyards and villages together.

Start: To get to Kientzheim, I suggest flying into the Strasbourg Airport and taking the train to Colmar. If you'd rather fly into Paris, a TGV (high-speed train) connects to Strasbourg as well; reserve your TGV spot at least three months in advance for the best rate. In Colmar, take a bus or private taxi (around twenty minutes) to Kientzheim.

But before you take that ride to begin your walk, spend a day exploring Colmar—it's not only a gorgeous town but a treasure trove of

sidewalk cafes, the most peaceful of places to linger over a hot espresso and a melt-in-your-mouth pastry while you watch the world go by. When you're ready, head to Kientzheim and find the trailhead just outside of town. Your walk starts on a narrow, winding path that curves gently up a hillside. Every 3 miles (5 km) or so, you'll reach another appealing town.

You'll pass through two similarly named towns on the Alsace Wine Route: Kientzheim (the start of Day 1) and Kintzheim (encountered on Day 2). Even map programs get the two confused. If you're having trouble locating Kientzheim on the map, search for nearby Kayserberg and Sigolsheim; Kientzheim is between the two. (Although be aware that Google Maps may confuse you even more by incorrectly labeling it Kintzheim.)

Suggested stages:
Day 1: Kientzheim to Ribeauvillé, 5.4 miles (8.7 km) via VV 111
Day 2: Ribeauvillé to Dambach-la-Ville, 13.2 miles (21.2 km) via VV 11 to Bergheim, then via EuroVelo 5
Day 3: Dambach-la-Ville to Obernai, 13.5 miles (21.7 km) via EuroVelo 5
Day 4: Obernai to Molsheim, 7.8 miles (12.6 km) via EuroVelo 5

Signage: You'll see plenty of trail signs as you walk—the signage along the route is excellent. Some are confidence markers, letting you know you're on the right track. Others (typically those at junctions) note the distance to the next town. Regardless, keep your eyes out for two different kinds of trail signs: (1) the green letters and white background of the VV signs, which plainly state "VV 111" or "VV 11"; (2) the white number five surrounded by yellow stars, all inside a blue box, that is the official marking of the EuroVelo 5.

Colorful squares and flower-bedecked buildings are par for the course along France's Alsace Wine Route.

Accommodations: The selection of accommodations along the Alsace Wine Route is dominated by cute half-timbered guesthouses that have been providing shelter since the Middle Ages. Most have been retrofitted with gorgeous modern bathrooms and comfy beds but still retain all the charm of the hundreds of years they've been in use. Breakfast is typically included in your stay.

Tips: For a day off while on trail, there's no better village than Obernai. You could spend a whole day just meandering through the little shops, snacking at one of the many pastry stands and taking photos of this stunning gem. For even more of a medieval flair, visit during one of the region's many festivals, which include a fiddlers' fair, a festival of ancient music and a Middle Ages–style Christmas market.

Make it shorter: There is the possibility of cutting the length of the daily stages on the Alsace Wine Route by overnighting more frequently in the many towns along the route. Although bus and train service connects several of the towns along the route (contact the local tourist information office for more information), the easiest way to shorten the daily stages is by private taxi or bike rental. If you're interested in renting a bike for part of your trip, check out Bike Air (see Resources); for a fee, they'll deliver your rental bike and pick it up again—anywhere in the greater Colmar area.

Return: From the end of the trail in Molsheim, it's a quick fifteen-minute train ride back to Strasbourg.

More Information

For more information on the Alsace Wine Route, including how to walk this iconic section of it and what to do in the surrounding area, check out my route guide for the trail, *Explore France's Alsace Wine Route on Foot: Kientzheim to Molsheim*. Other good information sources include the websites of the Alsace Wine Route and the local tourism authority (see Resources).

5 TOUR DU MONT BLANC, FRANCE AND ITALY

Jaw-dropping alpine scenery and cozy mountain huts on Europe's most famous long-distance path

At a Glance

LOCATION: Eastern France near Chamonix and northwestern Italy

LOCAL LANGUAGE: French, Italian

USE OF ENGLISH: Widely understood and used

SCENERY: Tallest peak in Europe, deep valleys, colorful wildflower meadows, grazing sheep and cows

DON'T MISS: Alpine culture, comfy mountaintop refuges, family-style dinners, local delicacies like *tartiflette*

The Tour du Mont Blanc winds its way through lush, green valleys and up steep mountainsides as it encircles Western Europe's tallest peak.

If there's one European route that shows up on nearly every walker's bucket list, it's the Tour du Mont Blanc. It's popular for a reason: from jaw-dropping alpine scenery to cozy mountain huts, the trail showcases the very best of the Alps, long considered one of the most beautiful mountain ranges in the world, by circumnavigating 15,782-foot (4,810 m) Mont Blanc, the tallest peak in Western Europe.

There's no better place to become acquainted with the mountains you're going to walk through than in the village of Chamonix, not only the birthplace but also the world capital of mountaineering. The town in the shadow of the impressive Mont Blanc massif is a geranium-bedecked hamlet in the heart of a green valley that's the year-round playground of a variety of outdoor enthusiasts.

It's also home to several facilities that will give you a good premountain education: the mountaineering museum where you can learn about the changing nature of mountaineering (before it was a sport, it was done for scientific research) and the gondola up the 12,605-foot (3,842 m) Aiguille du Midi, where you'll get a racing heart from the high elevation and the best up-close-and-personal views of the Alps that are possible without strapping on climbing gear. But perhaps the best spot of all is the Maison de la Montagne (Mountain House), housed in a tufa building that was a priory for Benedictine monks in the 1200s. Nowadays, it's the center of mountain life in town, and it'll complete your education with a variety of free resources for exploring these mountains safely, from weather forecasts to maps to office-hour consultations with local experts.

Once you know a little about these mountains, it's time to enter their realm and explore them in person. Your route starts in the nearby village of Les Houches, and it doesn't take long for you to feel like you're a million miles away from everything except snowcapped mountains, cold glacial rivers and colorful alpine meadows. And almost immediately, you get a sense of what this route will be like for the next four days: steep. As you huff and puff your way up one craggy mountain pass only to lose all of your hard-won elevation going down the other side, you'll feel a little masochistic, especially when you see the network of roads that you could be walking in the valley floors below.

But you can't get to know these mountains by skirting their bases, and the more you get to know them, the more you can't imagine it any other way. There's so much to fall in love with: the patches of heather and alpine wildflowers that perfume the air, the hardy sheep sauntering over to nibble on your backpack when you're taking a break, the unbelievable 360-degree views that lead you on despite your aching legs and, of course, the occasional spectacle of Mont Blanc itself.

It's a paradise, and you'll stop over and over to appreciate it (and catch your breath). At many of these viewpoints, you'll run into people you've been leapfrogging all day. Sometimes you'll enjoy a hot meal or cold beer together at one of the many cozy Alpine huts you pass along the way. Because the Tour du Mont Blanc is walked in daily stages, you'll see these same folks every day. And by the time you're done walking (if not by the end of the first day), they won't be strangers—they'll be friends.

You have plenty of time to visit, especially at night, when you sit down for a family-style meal at one of the picturesque mountain huts like Rifugio Elisabetta that will be your temporary home. These family-style dinners are one of the best parts of walking the Tour du Mont Blanc, and they usually happen at the most beautiful time of day, when the Alps are turning deep orange and golden yellow from the setting sun.

Although you'll be hungry enough to eat anything, you'll be served incredible local delicacies that will have you reaching for not only seconds but thirds. In France you'll swoon over *tartiflette* (a potato casserole with *reblochon* cheese, pork fat and onions) and *raclette* (melted cheese spooned over potatoes, meats, salads and pickles). In Italy you'll go nuts for *risotto alla valdostana* (a rice dish made with fontina, tomatoes and parmesan) and *carbonada* (stewed meat with white wine, onions and spices). Even in the remotest of huts, you can wash everything down with some of the best wines you've ever tasted. And they're local—Italy's Aosta Valley, where you end your walk, is particularly well known for its wine.

The Aosta Valley is also home to Courmayeur, the perfect place to rest up and relax after a strenuous four days of Alpine walking. Make yourself at home at one of the many sidewalk cafes—in the afternoon and evening, when you order a drink, you'll often get a free appetizer. (And the people-watching is amazing.) There are plenty of other opportunities for pampering yourself as well, from luxurious spas to candlelit restaurants. Just don't be surprised if you'd trade all that pampering for one more night in those rugged mountains.

On the Trail

ROUTE: Tour du Mont Blanc
DISTANCE: 43 miles (69 km)
ELEVATION GAIN/LOSS: +13,970/
  -13,337 feet (+4,258/-4,065 m)
AVERAGE TIME: 4 days
SEASON: Mid-June to mid-September
DIFFICULTY: Challenging
START: Les Houches, France
END: Courmayeur, Italy

Challenging: The Tour du Mont Blanc as prescribed involves significant elevation gain (and loss!) and plenty of mileage, making it a challenging walk. To make the trail easier, check out "Make it shorter."

Although the entire Tour du Mont Blanc is a 105-mile (170 km) loop that passes through three countries—France, Italy and Switzerland—you don't need twelve days to experience the best of the trail. Instead, I recommend the first third of the route, a four-day iconic trek through France and Italy that will leave you with plenty of time to explore the charming villages that bookend the trail.

Start: The easiest way to access this section of the Tour du Mont Blanc is to fly into Geneva Airport (Switzerland) and take a long-distance bus (approximately two hours) to Chamonix. Build in at least a day (or two or three) to explore this beautiful little town—there's so much to do, from hiking to biking to paragliding to sipping an espresso at a sidewalk cafe.

From Chamonix, local buses can take you to the trailhead at the village Les Houches, just 4.5 miles (7 km) from Chamonix. Or, better yet, take the chairlift from Les Houches to Bellevue and start your walk there—most people do, to avoid the steep and scenically unrewarding initial part of the trail. Overall, you'll tackle nearly 14,000 feet (4,267 m) of elevation gain and 13,500 feet (4,115 m) of loss during your four-day trek!

Suggested stages:
Day 1: Les Houches to Les Contamines-Montjoie,
  11.2 miles (18 km)
Day 2: Les Contamines-Montjoie to Les Chapieux,
  11.2 miles (18 km)
Day 3: Les Chapieux to Rifugio Elisabetta,
  9.3 miles (15 km)
Day 4: Rifugio Elisabetta to Courmayeur,
  11.2 miles (18 km)

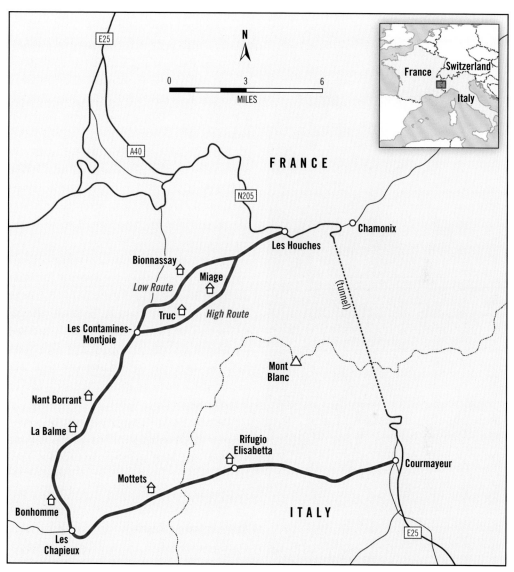

Signage: Keep your eyes out for a white stripe painted above a red stripe; you'll also see many more-detailed signs at junctions that list the upcoming towns or refuges and how far away they are (typically in minutes, not miles or kilometers). There is very good signage along the Tour du Mont Blanc, but because it can be obstructed in inclement weather, I recommend also walking with a paper map and GPX tracks.

In bad weather, it's safer to take Day 1's low route, which starts out at the same trailhead in Les Houches but passes through Bionnassay and La Gruvaz instead of Col du Tricot on its way to Les Contamines-Montjoie.

Accommodations: Along the Tour du Mont Blanc, there is a wide variety of accommodations to choose from. That said, most of the variety tends to be found in villages, which

At times, it feels like the Tour du Mont Blanc goes only one direction—up. Trekking poles can make the route a little easier.

are full of hostels and guesthouses and hotels. Up in the mountains, you're more limited in your choice of accommodations. On remote sections of trail, you'll typically stay in a hut or refuge, which you'll pass along the way every 0.5 mile to 5 miles (0.8–8 km). For the best

chance of getting a private room in one of these (or even just a bed in the busy summer season), I recommend booking your accommodations at least six months in advance. Because very few of the huts have Wi-Fi, plan on calling for a reservation. (This is where Skype comes in handy.)

Tip: Just before you get into Courmayeur on the last day, you'll walk through the little village of Dolonne. This is a great place to stop, meander and take some photos—all of the buildings are ancient and charming. You'll want to stay there for hours.

Make it shorter: There aren't many opportunities to shorten the daily stages of the Tour du Mont Blanc because the trail often utilizes high alpine routes. You can, however, keep to low routes whenever possible (see a detailed guidebook for specific routes) and take buses between some of the villages en route (for routes and schedules, contact the local tourist information office).

Return: From Courmayeur, take the chairlift over the mountain (only available in good weather) or a local bus to make your way back to Chamonix, then retrace your travels to Geneva Airport.

Other Activities Nearby

Once you reach Courmayeur, it's easy to launch an exploration of local wine on the Aosta Valley Wine Route (see Resources), which winds through vineyards and wine cellars with some pretty incredible wine.

More Information

For more information on walking the Tour du Mont Blanc, including accommodations along the way, check out the official website of the trail, as well as my favorite guidebook for the route, Kev Reynolds's *Tour of Mont Blanc*.

6 CINQUE TERRE 2.0, ITALY

Seaside towns and sky-high vineyards on Italy's breathtaking Ligurian Coast

At a Glance

LOCATION: Cinque Terre National Park, northwestern Italy

LOCAL LANGUAGE: Italian

USE OF ENGLISH: Widely understood and used

SCENERY: Endless ocean, rocky cliffs, dusty groves of olive trees, shockingly steep vineyards

DON'T MISS: Photogenic coastal towns, long and lingering meals as the sun goes down, the best of Italian comfort food, local *limoncino*

Of all of the walks in Europe, Cinque Terre is perhaps the most iconic. With sweeping views of the Ligurian Sea, a series of romantic small villages clinging to the shoreline like pearls on a necklace and forays into lush vineyards that are some of the steepest in the world, it's not hard to see why.

Although Cinque Terre, which means "five lands," was made popular by the American travel writer Rick Steves, who visited in the 1970s, most of the route is much, much older—it goes back to Roman times. But it wasn't until the eleventh century, when a group of forward-thinking inhabitants started turning

As you walk Italy's Cinque Terre, you'll make your way through some of the steepest—and most scenic—vineyards in the world.

the coastline's forests and steep slopes into cultivated terraces of grapevines, that the region started to take on its now-famous look, and its destiny as one of the most photographed places in the world was set in motion. As the centuries passed, the vines weren't the only things that grew. As the region became more prosperous, small villages sprang from the earth, along with humble dirt paths that connected them all.

Cinque Terre was chosen as a UNESCO World Heritage Site for being a distinguished example of the way in which humans have been able to model and transform the environment without altering the beauty of the landscape. The area is also a protected national park and marine area.

It is along these dirt paths, now paved in parts, that the splendor of Cinque Terre is revealed to visitors. Although the most typical way to walk Cinque Terre is to start at either end of the five main villages and visit them in a north-to-south or south-to-north sequence, I recommend starting your walk one town north of the main villages, in Levanto, and walking ever southward toward Riomaggiore.

Because you see more than just the standard Cinque Terre on this route, I call it Cinque Terre 2.0. In addition to introducing you to more of the region, this route leads you to one of the most gorgeous photo opportunities you could ever hope for on that first section of walking: a view of all five of the main villages—Monterosso al Mare, Vernazza, Corniglia, Manarola and Riomaggiore—strung out alongside the azure water. And it lets you tackle the most challenging sections of the trail while your legs are still fresh.

That's important, because this isn't an easy route. Over and over, you wind your way up and down steep paths, from the villages at sea level to the vineyards on the clifftops high above them, and then back again. Along the way, you'll enjoy astounding views of villages, vineyards and sea that will make all of the elevation gain worth it.

After leaving Levanto, the first of the five core towns you'll pass through on the route is Monterosso al Mare, the most developed of the five and the only one with a swimming beach. The prevalence of charming hotels and restaurants that spill out of the walls of the old town and down toward the water make this an easy choice for those seeking a home base for their time in Cinque Terre. You won't even have to dodge cars, since none are allowed in the villages; the towns are connected by trains that run all day long.

As you keep walking, the beauty not only leads you on, it surrounds you: venerable olive trees reach over the trail to shade you from the hot sun, bright lemons shine like jewels against the backdrop of the cerulean sky, plump grapes weigh heavily on their delicate-looking vines and sway slightly in the lazy Mediterranean breeze. At times, you'll be so lost in the scenery that you'll forget you are walking with a purpose: to reach the next town.

Although the villages are often referred to collectively and have a similar aesthetic—ancient-looking and delightfully crooked stone buildings, warm pastels that bring to mind the different hues of the setting sun, porches full of little old ladies hanging their laundry—they each have their own personality. After the first of the Cinque Terre villages, you'll come upon the quieter, more local villages: Vernazza, known for its colorful fishing boats and fresh seafood; Corniglia, the only one built on a cliff instead of next to the sea; Manarola, the oldest of the five towns; and Riomaggiore, a romantic village that draws in walkers with a castle and the promise of sweet kisses along

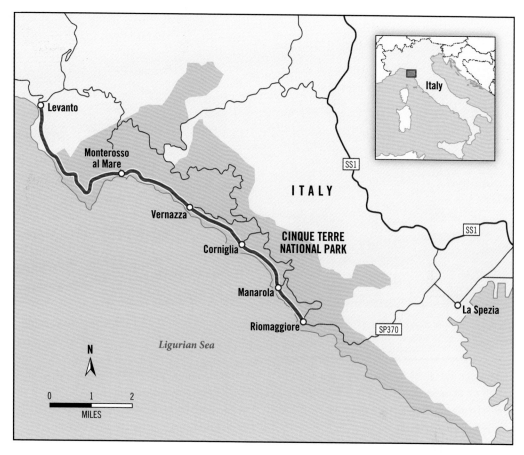

the last section of the trail, known as the Via dell'Amore, or Lover's Lane.

Just outside of Vernazza, you'll reach the highest point on trail, the hamlet of Prevo, at 682 feet (208 m) above sea level. Watch your footing but do look down—there's a great view of the famous Guvano Beach.

Wander the village streets in turn, but when you're ready to delve deeper into Italian culture, let your taste buds be your guide. Cinque Terre is a mecca for foodies intent on experiencing the best of Italian comfort food: *pasta carbonara* served tangy and dry; *trenette* noodles coated in avocado-colored pesto; salty *acciughe* (anchovies) fresh from the ocean; fragrant *pane* (bread) dipped in local olive oil. But that's not all. Wherever you dine, you can look forward to incredible house wine and *limoncino*, a sweet liqueur the color and flavor of lemons, both sourced from the verdant land that towers above you—and which you've gotten to know intimately on your breathtaking walk through Cinque Terre.

On the Trail

ROUTES: Trail 591, Trail 590, Blue Trail/Trail 2
DISTANCE: 10.5 miles (17 km)
ELEVATION GAIN/LOSS: +2,575/-2,590 feet (+785/-789 m)
AVERAGE TIME: 1–5 days
SEASON: April to October
DIFFICULTY: Moderate
START: Levanto, Italy
END: Riomaggiore, Italy

The main paths of Italy's Cinque Terre are steeper and longer than most tourists anticipate. Wear comfy shoes and pack plenty of water.

Moderate: For all of its popularity, Cinque Terre isn't a walk in the park. The route is actually quite steep in places. Plan on some significant elevation gain between towns and the vineyards high above them—and moderate difficulty. To make the trail easier, check out "Make it shorter."

Although the Cinque Terre route isn't long, at just shy of 11 miles (17 km) in total, it's a breathtaking journey that's best undertaken—and savored—a few miles at a time. It will take only a day for Cinque Terre to seduce you, but I recommend spending at least four to five days exploring the region.

Start: While the closest airports to Cinque Terre are in Pisa, Genoa and Milan (with Pisa Airport being the easiest), Cinque Terre is well connected to the rest of Italy—and Europe—by train. Simply take a main line to La Spezia, the main train station closest to Cinque Terre, and connect to one of the smaller trains that service its individual villages. I don't recommend

renting a car and driving to Cinque Terre, since the villages are inaccessible to cars and you'll need to park up in the hills, but if that's what you choose, there are several car parks in the area.

After leaving the more modern and suburban Levanto, you'll wind up and down steep dirt paths, some now paved—sometimes on extensive staircases, sometimes on narrow ledges that are large enough for only one person—as you reach first Monterosso al Mare, then Vernazza, Corniglia, Manarola and Riomaggiore.

Suggested stages:

Day 1: Levanto to Monterosso al Mare, 3.6 miles (5.8 km) via Trails 591 and 590

Day 2: Monterosso al Mare to Vernazza, 2.3 miles (3.7 km) via Blue Trail/Trail 2

Day 3: Vernazza to Corniglia, 2.5 miles (4.1 km) via Blue Trail/Trail 2

Day 4: Corniglia to Manarola, 1.4 miles (2.2 km) via Blue Trail/Trail 2

Day 5: Manarola to Riomaggiore, 0.7 mile (1.1 km) via Blue Trail/Trail 2

Want to shorten your walk in Cinque Terre but not blast through in one day? Take three. Here's how to break up the walking to maximize your enjoyment of the trail:

Day 1: Walk Levanto to Monterosso al Mare, 3.6 miles (5.8 km)

Day 2: Walk Monterosso al Mare to Vernazza, 2.3 miles (3.7 km); have lunch, then walk Vernazza to Corniglia, 2.5 miles (4.1 km), for 4.8 miles (7.8 km) total

Day 3: Walk Corniglia to Manarola, 1.4 miles (2.2 km); have lunch, then walk Manarola to Riomaggiore, 0.7 mile (1.1 km), for 2.1 miles (3.3 km) total.

Signage: Cinque Terre has very good signage, especially the major routes mentioned here. Most junctions are signed with the name of and distance to the next town, and you'll also occasionally see confidence markers. If you explore beyond the main route through the villages, you'll need a paper map—the less-traveled paths through the hills aren't signed as well.

Accommodations: While there is a wide variety of accommodations in the villages of Cinque Terre, from chain hotels to boutique hotels to guesthouses, I recommend renting a room from a local family. The first time I was in Cinque Terre, I rented a charming room with a window that opened to the ocean from an old Italian woman who didn't speak any English. I only spoke a few words of Italian, but I had the best time visiting with her (we did a lot of pantomiming) and learning about Italy—it was a really memorable experience. For help finding a private room to rent, contact the local tourist information office. In summer, Cinque Terre fills up quickly, so make your reservations at least three to six months in advance.

Tip: Each town in Cinque Terre has its own sanctuary, usually in the hills above town, and you can walk to them for a quiet place to reflect. These are places of worship and devotion for locals; you can find more information on them online (see Resources).

Make it shorter: The best way to shorten the length of the individual daily stages of Cinque Terre is to tackle only one town at a time. You can also choose from a couple of alternate forms of transportation—train and boat; you'll find both in each town. You could bypass the crowds on the train one day and commute back to your home base by boat—you'll see the cliffs and towns from a completely different perspective.

If you're in a hurry, you can always do this walk as a daylong wander; you'll just have less time to explore the villages along the way. For another daylong wander in Italy, see One-Day Wander #2: Mount Vesuvius (Chapter 2, See What's Possible), near Pompeii and farther south along Italy's Mediterranean coast.

Return: Take the train or boat back to La Spezia and train back to the city you flew into.

Other Activities Nearby

If you have more time, there are plenty of other walks in the area, including several in the hills above the villages that are equally as amazing and yet far less traveled; see the Cinque Terre National Park website for details (see Resources).

One possibility is to get more Ligurian flavor with a one-hour boat ride—or five-hour walk—to Portovenere, a nearby town that's off the beaten path and well known for its outstanding local food products such as olives, olive oil, pesto and fresh pasta.

More Information

For more information on Cinque Terre, visit the official website of the towns (see Resources).

7 LYCIAN WAY, TURKEY

Small rural villages and ancient ruins along Turkey's Turquoise Coast

At a Glance

LOCATION: Southwestern Turkey on the Mediterranean coast

LOCAL LANGUAGE: Turkish

USE OF ENGLISH: Not common in most small towns; brush up on your Turkish

SCENERY: Beautiful Mediterranean coast, orange-red soil, rocky cliffs, amber grasslands, sandy beaches

DON'T MISS: Goats, the call to prayer, ancient ruins, ghost town of Kayaköy, small-town Turkish life

If there's one trail that will capture your imagination, entice you with the exotic and lead you into a sojourn among a completely different way of life, it's the Lycian Way along Turkey's southwestern Mediterranean coast, where the water is so blue that the area is often called the Turquoise Coast. As the route takes you deeper into the countryside, it also takes you back in time, and traces of ancient people are everywhere.

Your route begins in the modern port town of Fethiye, the largest town you'll see on your walk, but it doesn't take long before you leave it behind for the Turkish countryside. Nearly every day on this trail, as you make your way past sandy beaches and head up the coastal cliffs through pine forests to finally reach the agricultural plateaus at the top—then head back down to the turquoise water for a much-needed dip—heat will be your constant companion in this arid land.

Chartreuse lizards scamper across the trail as though their feet have been burned; lumbering big turtles couldn't seem to care less. As you head deeper into the countryside, you'll likely meet them both, along with more scraggly goats than you've ever seen in your life. Goats are everywhere in southern Turkey, picking their way carefully up steep slopes, grazing on patches of grass scorched to amber by the sun and blocking traffic on country lanes as they're slowly herded en masse by a lone farmer who seems to have nowhere else to be.

Unless, that is, it's one of the five times of day when the *ezan*, or call to prayer, goes out and thousands of devout Muslims unfurl their prayer mats, turn to Mecca and talk to God. Even if you're not religious, there's something moving about the soulful chant that echoes through the land. The sound reaches your ears even when you're on trail in the middle of nowhere, from towering minarets so far away they're not even visible on the horizon. If your walk had a sound track, this would be it. It's incredible to have such a different way of life filter through your ears and surround you as you walk. It's enchanting.

As you walk the trail, it gives you an education on the centuries of proud civilizations—Romans, Greeks and, most important to this area, Lycians—that it took to make this path. Don't forget to look up, or you may miss the countless elaborate rock tombs carved into the limestone cliffsides you skirt—although most

Turkey's southwestern Mediterranean coast is often referred to as the Turquoise Coast.

have now been raided and stand empty, they were once the final resting places of the honored Lycian dead, who were entombed as close to the sky as possible to aid their transfer to the afterlife by magic winged creatures. In other places, the ruins aren't high above you but down below, poking up through the hot sand. They'll trip you up if you don't watch your feet.

But my favorite ruins of all aren't above or below the trail—you can actually walk through them on the trail. One of the two most notable on this stretch of the Lycian Way is the more recent ruins of Kayaköy (which you pass through on Day 1), a ghost town of slowly disintegrating houses and churches that was created in 1923, when the multinational Ottoman Empire crumbled and a population exchange occurred between now-separate Greece and Turkey. The other is the major ruins of the ancient naval and trading port of Patara (encountered on Day 8), where enough of the stone architecture has been reconstructed to reveal a 5,000-seat theater, a stately parliament building and a colonnaded street that was once the city's grandest boulevard. Both ruins are open-air museums where you can wander at your leisure, soaking in their stories and secrets before moving on.

It's not just ancient or abandoned civilizations that are revealed to you on the Lycian Way. You'll also make your way through a medley of exotic-sounding villages that are perfect

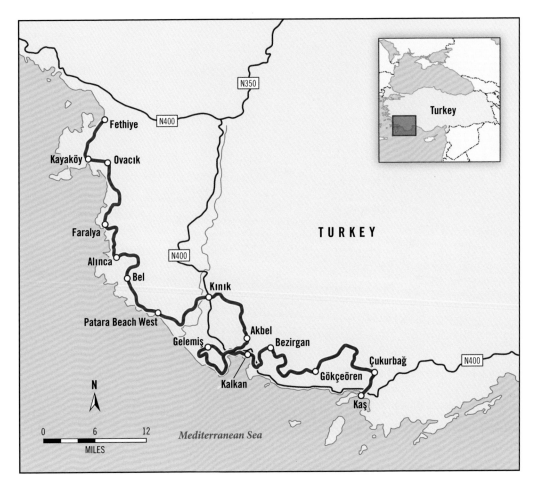

for discovering present-day rural Turkish life—and a variety of smaller hamlets in between. In most of these towns, you'll pantomime conversations with locals who don't speak a word of English but whose warm smiles and heartfelt hospitality will communicate everything you need to know. You may not look or dress anything like these people, but they will happily take you into their homes, rent you a room and cook you a meal that will have your stomach growling long before it's served: thick and tangy homemade yogurt with a dollop of local honey, cold and hot *meze* (small plates of various salads and appetizers), grilled fish fresh from the ocean, and as much brewed black tea as you can drink. Small Turkish towns are vibrant places, full of old men playing heated games of backgammon, children kicking up dust in the street and mothers in colorful head scarves assembling the next family meal in their kitchens, doors open and radios on.

When you reach the end of your route at the bustling coastal village of Kaş, take it all in as you sip strong Turkish tea and watch the sun sink below the horizon, until the first notes of the final call to prayer float through the night sky. Then you'll know: this far-flung land, full of foreignness and the unfamiliar, can give you the opposite of what you thought you'd find—a deep sense of belonging.

On the Trail

ROUTE: Lycian Way
DISTANCE: 115 miles (185 km)
ELEVATION GAIN/LOSS: +26,575/
-26,657 feet (+8,100/-8,125 m)
AVERAGE TIME: 13 days
SEASONS: February to May, September to November
DIFFICULTY: Moderate to challenging
START: Fethiye, Turkey
END: Kaş, Turkey

Moderately Difficult to Challenging: Although the Lycian Way is a moderate trail in terms of distance and elevation gain, intense heat (depending on when you visit) and often-confusing routefinding can make the trail a challenge for inexperienced walkers. Want to make the trail easier? Consider walking with a tour group (see Chapter 6, Walk Independently or Hire Help) or check out "Make it shorter."

The Lycian Way, Turkey's first long-distance walking path, in its entirety runs for 335 miles (540 km). Although the full route takes twenty-nine days to explore, the essence of the trail can be gleaned from a shorter walk of 115 miles (185 km) and thirteen days along its most iconic section, from Fethiye to Kaş.

Start: The closest airport to the start of the Lycian Way is Dalaman Airport, which has frequent flights to and from Istanbul. No exploration of Turkey is complete without at least two or three days in Istanbul. Adventures that should top your bucket list: hit the spice market, visit the Blue Mosque and Hagia Sophia, grab lunch at the tippy boats down by the water and walk across the Galata Bridge (don't miss the shops and cafes below the car deck). From Dalaman, take a mini-bus ride (approximately forty-five minutes) to the trailhead in Fethiye.

From Fethiye, soon the black pavement of civilization turns to the rich orange-red dirt paths of the countryside. In the bright glare of the ever-present sun, your path seems molten, a flame of dirt that reflects the heat of the day back at you through the soles of your hot feet. The trail passes through a series of villages and towns, past farms and amazing coastline on its journey south to Kaş.

Suggested stages:

Day 1: Fethiye to Ovacık, via Kayaköy, 7.5 miles (12 km)
Day 2: Ovacık to Faralya, 7.8 miles (12.5 km)
Day 3: Faralya to Alınca, 7 miles (11.3 km)
Day 4: Alınca to Bel, 10.5 miles (16.9 km)
Day 5: Bel to Patara Beach West, 8.3 miles (13.3 km)
Day 6: Patara Beach West to Kınık, 8 miles (13 km)
Day 7: Kınık to Akbel, 11.9 miles (19.2 km)
Day 8: Akbel to Gelemiş, 9.3 miles (15 km)
Day 9: Gelemiş to Kalkan, 11.8 miles (19 km)
Day 10: Kalkan to Bezirgan, 6.2 miles (9.9 km)
Day 11: Bezirgan to Gökçeören, 9.6 miles (15.5 km)
Day 12: Gökçeören to Çukurbağ, 12.9 miles (20.7 km)
Day 13: Çukurbağ to Kaş, 4.2 miles (6.7 km)

Signage: Keep your eyes out on trail for the official markings; you'll see yellow and green signs with town names and arrows, as well as confidence markers (a white stripe above a red stripe) painted on rocks, tree trunks, et cetera. The signage on the Lycian Way isn't always reliable, so I recommend walking with not only a detailed paper map but GPX tracks as well.

Accommodations: The Lycian Way has a wide assortment of accommodations en route, and the options vary according to the size of the town or village. Medium-size places like Fethiye and Patara boast the biggest selection, everything from nicer hotels to hostels. In smaller towns (the majority of towns on the route), you'll typically stay in private rooms

Along Turkey's Lycian Way, goats far outnumber people. You'll see them in fields, on roads and up trees.

and family-owned guesthouses—the perfect way to get to know the locals.

Make it shorter: Turkey has plenty of mini-buses that run short routes all over the country, including between several of the towns on the Lycian Way. It's also possible in many of the more medium-size towns to hire a private taxi. On the Lycian Way, you can down the length of the daily stages by staying more frequently in rural accommodations along the route (not just in the towns recommended above).

Return: From Kaş, there is frequent mini-bus service (approximately two hours) back to Dalaman Airport, where you can fly back to Istanbul.

Other Activities Nearby

For a different view of the scenery you're walking through, go paragliding at the ocean-side cliffs just outside of Ölüdeniz, a short mini-bus or taxi ride from Ovacık (Day 1's endpoint).

If you're not afraid of heights—and you have some extra time on trail—don't miss the half-day (there and back) trek from Faralya (Day 2's endpoint) into Butterfly Valley. You'll see goats climbing the canyon walls, huge plants, a waterfall—and, of course, butterflies. There's even a beach to cool off at in the heat of the day.

More Information

For more information on this trail, look for its only print guidebook, Kate Clow's *The Lycian Way* (the guidebook has a companion app with the same name). Or check out Trekopedia's TrailSmart app: you can access digital maps and comprehensive walking directions for each stage of the Lycian Way.

8 ALPINE PASS ROUTE, SWITZERLAND

East to west across rural Switzerland

At a Glance

LOCATION: The Swiss Alps

LOCAL LANGUAGE: German, French

USE OF ENGLISH: Widely understood and used

SCENERY: Rugged mountains, colorful wild-

flowers, scenic overlooks, bucolic farmland

DON'T MISS: Mountaintop huts, quaint villages, trailside fresh milk dispensers, alpenhorns, lederhosen

For a bucket-list trail that you'll yearn to walk over and over again, look no further than the Alpine Pass Route. This east-to-west traverse of Switzerland offers an intimate look at Swiss life and the startling beauty of the Alps. It's also considered among the best walking in the world.

Although the route covers only one country, it begins at the intersection of three—

Switzerland, Liechtenstein and Austria—in the ancient eastern city of Sargans. Over the course of more than 200 miles (325 km), it winds its way ever westward, traveling over rugged mountain passes and through pastoral meadows to deliver lucky walkers to the azure shores of Lake Geneva and the border of France.

Switzerland's Alpine Pass Route has many self-service farm stands that are perfect for a mid-walk snack.

At first glance, the Alpine Pass Route can seem intimidating. After all, there are sixteen mountain passes and nearly 12 miles (19,000 m) of elevation gain (and an almost equal amount of elevation loss) to tackle. But even with its heavy reliance on mountain passes, this is one trail that doesn't require any technical mountaineering skills. And once the route is broken up into its fifteen recommended stages, each one the equivalent of eight to ten hours of walking, it becomes quite doable for even the average walker, especially when the trip is tempered with alternative transportation options (from chairlifts to gondolas) and the most restful of rest days in rustic Swiss villages.

Although the Alpine Pass Route can be enjoyed by all, it is first and foremost a trail for those who love mountains. In Sargans you become acquainted with the towering, snow-covered giants almost immediately as they stand in profile in the distance and you prepare to enter their territory. Although they seem far off here, you'll come to know them intimately in turn. The smaller gatekeeper mountains you start out with have a beauty of their own and an important function: they'll warm up your legs and introduce you to the land of the larger, more esteemed peaks that await.

Your introduction doesn't last long before the route reaches heavenward to incorporate more challenging climbs and dramatic peaks. If you have any knowledge of German, you'll marvel at the mountains' evocative names: the Große Scheidegg, the Wetterhorn. And of course the most famous of them all, the trio of the Eiger, Mönch and Jungfrau. These icy castles of rock and snow will awe you in turn, as will the tens of other peaks that are lesser known but no less magnificent, until you trade in isolated peaks for Montreux on the busy shores of Lake Geneva, blue water as far as you can see.

It's not just the beauty of the mountains that draws you in and makes the Alpine Pass Route better for their presence, it's the path they lead you through as you walk along their spine and dip into the folds of their hidden valleys. There is always something different to look at and discover, from gushing waterfalls to towering timber to jagged cliffs.

As you walk, you'll enter valleys like the Lauterbrunnen that cut so deeply into the rocks and are so carpeted in lush green grass that you won't be able to look away, unless it's to take a picture. You'll pass through high alpine meadows that cling perilously to the sides of imposing mountains, especially near the Seinenfurke, where the grass has been almost completely replaced by colorful wildflowers including gentians, monkshood and lady's slipper orchids. You'll spot fat marmots lazing on hot rocks in the sun and watch chamois pick their way expertly through scree as buzzards and eagles circle overhead. Every valley, every meadow, every day, you'll feel like you've been dropped into *The Sound of Music*.

On the Alpine Pass Route, the mountains entice you forward and lead you into some of the most incredible nature you'll ever experience. It seems fitting, then, that they also lead you into the best of nature-inspired civilization. Like each valley you experience on this trail, each village along the way has something distinct to offer. Engstlenalp's old wooden buildings, nearly concealed by tremendous window boxes of colorful geraniums, are perfect places to watch the alpenglow light up the mountains in time

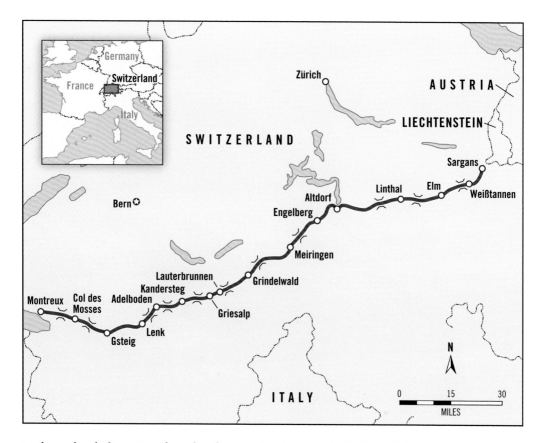

to the melancholic notes of an alpenhorn and the distant tinkling of cowbells. The mountain ski resort of First, a worthy short detour from the trail, caters to walkers in the summer with lodge-style accommodations, ice-cold beer and calorie-filled comfort food, from *Schweizer schnitzel* (Swiss-style breaded pork cutlets) to *rösti* (hashbrown pancakes), served at the brink of the very mountains you've worked so hard to climb. Bustling Grindelwald is a perfect stepping-off point for exploring the region's main attraction, the Kleine Scheidegg, by antique steam train before soaking your sore muscles at the spa during a welcome day off.

Evenings are the most magical time on the Alpine Pass Route, especially if you're staying in rustic accommodations just outside of town, where many farms rent out rooms for extra income. As the light fades, wine is poured and dinner is served, it's easy to feel transported to a simpler time, to imagine yourself living before the age of Internet and cell phones and cars. It helps that most farms don't have electricity and you'll eat—and later read—by candlelight. But it's not just the simplicity of your accommodations that will clear modern life from your mind; it's the authentic, rural and distinctly old-fashioned Swiss way of life.

There's more than nature-inspired civilization in villages at the end of each walking day—the Alpine Pass Route is dotted with mountainside huts, Swiss-style pubs and small farms; you'll pass through several each day. Most are staffed; some are run on the honor system. But all are great for taking a break, talking to other walkers or restocking your food supplies. Most days, you

The Jungfrau region of Switzerland, viewable from the Alpine Pass Route, is often considered one of the most jaw-dropping places in the world.

won't need to carry a lunch with you because of the many options for getting food on trail.

But don't rule out picnics. Along the Alpine Pass Route, meadows and mountains often collide at alpine lakes where you can take off your shoes and cool your heels in water that's as icy as it is blue. These are natural picnic spots where you can enjoy the local delicacies you've picked up along the way and will dream about when you're back at home: cold, fresh milk straight from the cow, sparkling Rivella in the bottle, tangy goat cheese from a family pet, rich chocolate that melts in your mouth. With lunches like these, you'll be glad to have a full afternoon of hiking to burn them off.

It doesn't take very many days of hiking the Alpine Pass Route for the mountains, valleys and villages to combine into a cadence that your body—and mind—will learn to savor and anticipate. Before long, your legs will ache to climb in the morning and descend in the afternoon. Your stomach will growl at the mere thought of a farm stand or mountainside pub. And your mind will crave—all day—the unexpected pleasure of reading by candlelight. Because it's not just the breathtaking scenery that will keep you coming back to the Alpine Pass Route again and again, as people have been known to do, it's the Swiss way of life.

On the Trail

ROUTE: Alpine Pass Route
DISTANCE: 202 miles (326 km)
ELEVATION GAIN/LOSS: +59,242/-58,868
    feet (+18,057/-17,943 m)
AVERAGE TIME: 15 days
SEASON: Late June to early October
DIFFICULTY: Challenging
START: Sargans, Switzerland
END: Montreux, Switzerland

Challenging: Based on elevation gain and the distance recommended in the daily stages, the Alpine Pass Route as prescribed is a challenging trail. But it doesn't need to be—downgrade the trail to moderate with the help of alternative transportation options in "Make it shorter."

The Alpine Pass Route winds its way west from Sargans for 202 miles (326 km) over sixteen mountain passes and through pastoral meadows to Montreux near Lake Geneva. It boasts 59,242 feet (18,057 m) of elevation gain—and nearly as much elevation loss—over the course of fifteen recommended daily stages.

Start: The two international airports closest to the Alpine Pass Route are in Geneva and Zürich. Although there are excellent connections by rail to Sargans, Montreux or almost any other city you'd like to reach from either airport, Zürich is closer to the start of the route in Sargans. If you will be traveling in Switzerland before or after you hike the Alpine Pass Route, consider purchasing a Swiss Travel Card, which entitles you to discounts on Swiss trains, which can otherwise be quite expensive.

Lucky for you, in Sargans your journey begins with a series of smaller training peaks that build your stamina for the giants to come. Leading you on are the Tödi and the Titlis—and, almost before you know it, the Bernese Alps, known around the world for their ragged splendor. The scenic diversity in the valleys between the peaks, especially in the most iconic part of the walk, from Days 6 through 13, is unmatched. Engstlenalp, which you'll pass through on Day 6, is considered by many to be one of the most charming spots in the Alps, and Grindelwald, Day 7's endpoint, has plenty to offer for a rest day.

Suggested stages:
Day 1: Sargans to Weißtannen, 8.7 miles (14 km)
Day 2: Weißtannen to Elm, 13 miles (21 km)
Day 3: Elm to Linthal, 13.7 miles (22 km)
Day 4: Linthal to Altdorf, 19.9 miles (32 km)
Day 5: Altdorf to Engelberg, 17.4 miles (28 km)
Day 6: Engelberg to Meiringen, 19.3 miles (31 km)
Day 7: Meiringen to Grindelwald, 13 miles (21 km)
Day 8: Grindelwald to Lauterbrunnen, 11.8 miles (19 km)
Day 9: Lauterbrunnen to Griesalp, 13 miles (21 km)
Day 10: Griesalp to Kandersteg, 9.3 miles (15 km)
Day 11: Kandersteg to Adelboden, 10 miles (16 km)
Day 12: Adelboden to Lenk, 8.1 miles (13 km)
Day 13: Lenk to Gsteig, 13.7 miles (22 km)
Day 14: Gsteig to Col des Mosses, 14.3 miles (23 km)
Day 15: Col des Mosses to Montreux, 17.4 miles (28 km)

Signage: Trail signage throughout Switzerland is enviably reliable and meticulous, and that includes the signage on the Alpine Pass Route. In many places, the Alpine Pass Route is signed with a red stripe between two white stripes (for itself) or the green square of its more official alias, the Via Alpina. It is important to note, though, that the most common signs on the route are bright yellow with black writing—signed for individual towns and in hiking hours and minutes instead of distance.

Because of the generous attitude toward land use in Switzerland, much of the land you'll traverse on the Alpine Pass Route is privately owned pastureland. When passing through fields, always be sure to close and latch gates behind you. If you don't, you could have hundreds of cows—and an angry farmer—on your heels.

Accommodations: There are plenty of accommodations on the Alpine Pass Route, from mountain huts to guesthouses to boutique hotels—and everything in between. Options are available in the villages you pass through but also on the outskirts of town, deep in farm country or on mountaintops. Several villages and rural resorts also have campsites, but note that dispersed camping (which is known in Europe as wild camping) is not permitted along the route.

Most guesthouses, hotels and huts on the Alpine Pass Route have a *ruhetag*, a rest day when they are closed for twenty-four hours. And not every place has the same *ruhetag*. When making plans for accommodations, it's important to either look on the Internet or call in advance to make sure the place where you want to stay will indeed be open.

I recommend staying at one of the working farms along the way, where the room rate also includes dinner and breakfast. Those interested in doing the Alpine Pass Route on a budget should look for *massenlagers* or *matratzenlagers*, which are like hostel dorm rooms but filled with mattresses instead of bunk beds. Rooms are usually single sex, and guests have access to bathrooms down the hall. Half-pension is normally available, which means that dinner and breakfast are included in the room rate—the cheapest you'll find on trail.

During summertime, accommodations can fill up quickly. To avoid a headache—and guarantee yourself a spot for the night—make reservations in advance, even if you only book two or three days ahead.

Make it shorter: There are plenty of opportunities on this route for using alternative methods of transportation, from train to PostBus to cable car, to shorten individual stages. These options can be found in a more detailed trail guide, on local maps or by contacting the local tourist information office. On the Alpine Pass Route, there is also the possibility of cutting down the length of the daily stages by staying more frequently in rural accommodations along the route. If you don't have time to hike every section of the Alpine Pass Route, the central section, Days 6 through 13, from Engelberg to Gsteig, is the most iconic and scenically rewarding, making for a great alternate itinerary of eight to ten days covering 98.2 miles (158 km).

For a daylong walk near the Julian Alps southeast of Switzerland, see One-Day Wander #3: Lake Bled, in Slovenia (Chapter 2, See What's Possible).

Return: West of Kandersteg, the mountains lose their intensity, becoming more muted as you enter the Vaudois Alps and then finally reach Montreux. Once you leave the trail at Montreux, Geneva is more convenient to fly out of than Zürich.

Other Activities Nearby

Spend a night in First, outside of Grindelwald, where you'll be surrounded by more stars than you've probably ever seen in your life. Take the resort trail up to Bachalpsee, a small nearby lake, for a charming picnic spot and one of the most picturesque views of the Jungfrau region of Switzerland. (It's so pretty that Gmail used it as its mountain theme background!)

Don't bother with the Glacier Express, one of Switzerland's most famous scenic train rides.

While it's worth doing if you *haven't* hiked through Switzerland and seen the gorgeous scenery up close and personal, it's just a repeat—and a very expensive one at that—of what you'll see on the Alpine Pass Route.

Do, however, take the train to Zermatt for a great dose of Swiss mountaineering culture. Watch climbers coming back from the mountains each afternoon, loaded down with all of their ropes and ice axes as the sun goes down and alpenglow lights up the Matterhorn.

Other things that should be on your Zermatt bucket list: Take the chairlift up to the glacier and the Ice Palace, visit the Matterh Museum and the Mountaineers' Cemetery and spend an evening people watching at a sidewalk cafe on Bahnhofstrasse.

More Information

For more information on the Alpine Pass Route, my favorite guidebook is *Trekking the Swiss Alpine Pass Route—Via Alpina Route 1,* by Kev Reynolds; it's considered the definitive guide to the route with details on logistics, each stage of the hike and towns and accommodations along the way.

9 KING LUDWIG'S WAY, GERMANY

Into the heart of Mad King Ludwig's Bavaria

At a Glance

LOCATION: Bavaria, southern Germany
LOCAL LANGUAGE: German
USE OF ENGLISH: Widely understood and used in the cities, not common in most rural enclaves
SCENERY: Storybook forests and farmland, foothills of snow-covered Alps, swan-filled lakes
DON'T MISS: Monasteries and churches hundreds of years old, rural Bavarian life, geranium-bedecked guesthouses, German beer, Neuschwanstein Castle

 There's nothing like a good murder mystery on trail, especially when the victim in question was known as the Mad King and he was a strong swimmer whose body was found floating in a lake beside that of his physician just days after he was declared insane and dethroned. Intrigued? The best way to unravel the mystery—and the madness—is with a five-day walk on Germany's King Ludwig's Way, a trail through what used to be known as the Kingdom of Bavaria—and the stomping grounds of the Mad King himself, Ludwig II.

It seems only fitting to honor a Mad King with a walk that's done backward, and that's exactly how most people approach King Ludwig's Way, starting at the spot where he died and walking south toward the region where he spent his childhood. It's a walk through the romantic storybook landscape that Ludwig (an avid walker) loved so much, along with old-world towns and, finally, Neuschwanstein, the beloved castle that was the crowning glory of Ludwig's life. Even today, it's not hard to see why Ludwig loved Bavaria so. The landscape is just as romantic and whimsical as any Wagnerian

JUST WHO WAS LUDWIG II?

King Ludwig II

Ludwig II (commonly referred to as Ludwig) ascended the throne of Bavaria in 1864, when he was only eighteen years old, and ruled erratically for twenty-two years, until his suspicious death at the age of forty. He was a highly creative recluse who loved Wagnerian opera and the Bavarian landscape, and these sounds and sights inspired the whimsical and elaborate castles that he spent most of his reign building. In the process, he ignored what many considered to be more essential issues of state, thoroughly frustrated his ministers and threatened to bankrupt the royal family. By 1886 his cabinet had had enough. They had Ludwig declared insane and removed him from power; his uncle, Prince Luitpold, took over the Bavarian government. Three days later, Ludwig was dead.

opera, a bounty of swan-filled lakes, endless pastoral fields and snowcapped Alps that you come to know intimately over these five days. Although the countryside is picturesque at any time of year, it's at its best in the fall, when the changing of the leaves turns everything bright shades of scarlet, flaxen and apricot and the homey savor of wood fires flavors the air.

Old-world attractions hide treasures that have been around since before King Ludwig was even born. On Bavaria's Holy Mountain, just outside of the village of Andechs, you'll discover a fifteenth-century abbey that's famous for the beer its monks have been brewing for hundreds of years. Near Hohenpeißenberg, you'll trek past a weather station originally founded in 1781 by monks from the nearby Rottenbuch monastery, the first and oldest observatory in the world. (It's also home to the best view in all of Bavaria.) And just outside of Unterhäusern, you'll come across the Pilgrimage Church of Wies, a sumptuous rococo masterpiece of ornate gold statues and vivid murals that was

commissioned in 1745 and is now a UNESCO World Heritage Site.

Just as charming are the old-world rural outposts like Unterhäusern that you pass through, where life looks a lot like it did in the 1800s. Colorful maypoles adorn the entrances to these villages, advertising all of the services that are available in town, from logging to farming to baking. On special days like Sundays and holidays, everyone dresses in their best, always the traditional dirndls and lederhosen that Bavarians have worn for centuries. And most of the flower- and mural-bedecked large houses also double as barns.

In these places, you won't find a lot of people who speak English. What you will find is a gregarious group of small-town folks who are eager to make you feel at home, whether that's fetching you a large doughy *brezel* (pretzel) and a bottle of König Ludwig Dunkel (a popular local dark beer) when you wander into their pub for a midwalk snack or whipping you up a homemade feast of *krautschupfnudeln* (a casserole of noodles, sauerkraut, bacon and cheese), *apfelstrüdel* (apple strudel) and *glühwein* (hot spiced wine) when you check into their guesthouse for the night. As you'll discover over and over again on King Ludwig's Way, there's nothing quite like small-town Bavarian hospitality.

By the time you catch your first glimpse of Ludwig's Neuschwanstein on your last day of walking, you'll be as entranced with Bavaria as he was. And as you explore the still-unfinished castle whimsically nestled in the mountains like a sleeping swan, its rooms alive with the romantic old-world scenes you've walked through, you'll be in love—and it won't seem quite so mad that after living in the midst of such beauty for years, Ludwig was driven to neglect his royal duties and build fanciful castles. One thing that still won't make sense: just how or why he died; to this day, the official cause of Ludwig's death is inconclusive, although drowning was ruled out. Like the long-lasting splendor of Neuschwanstein, the mystery endures.

On the Trail

ROUTE: King Ludwig's Way
DISTANCE: 72 miles (115 km)
ELEVATION GAIN/LOSS: +7,006/-6,438 feet (+2,135/-1,962 m)
AVERAGE TIME: 5 days
SEASON: May to September
DIFFICULTY: Moderate
START: Berg, Germany
END: Füssen, Germany

On the last stage of Germany's King Ludwig's Way, you'll reach Ludwig's beloved Neuschwanstein Castle. (Photo by Jiuguang Wang/Flickr)

If you hike through Rottenbuch, along Germany's King Ludwig's Way, on May 1, you may see a traditional maypole-raising ceremony.

Moderate: Although King Ludwig's Way is mainly flat, the distance of the suggested daily stages ups the challenge level, making it a moderate trail. For ideas on making the trail easier, check out "Make it shorter."

The 72-mile (115 km) King Ludwig's Way is mainly level, though the countryside around you undulates gently. The route takes you back in time, through old-world towns that look much like they did in the 1800s.

Start: It's very easy to get to and from King Ludwig's Way. Simply fly into Munich Airport and take the S-Bahn to Lake Starnberg (*Starnberger See*). From there, take a short bus ride (approximately five minutes) or a taxi to Berg and the trailhead.

Most people start from a small chapel on Lake Starnberg and walk south toward the Allgäu. On your last day, you reach Mad King Ludwig's master creation, Neuschwanstein Castle, near Füssen.

If you plan to travel by train on the weekend, check out Germany's *Schönes Wochenende* (Happy Weekend) discount ticket, which allows you to take unlimited local and regional trains on Saturdays and Sundays for a reduced rate. The base fare is €40 for the first person and €4 for each additional person; the maximum number of people who can be covered by a ticket is five.

Suggested stages:

Day 1: Berg to Dießen, 16 miles (25.7 km) (Does not include 4-mile [6.4 km] ferry from Herrsching to Dießen.)

Day 2: Dießen to Paterzell, 10.8 miles (17.4 km)

Day 3: Paterzell to Rottenbuch, 15.9 miles (25.6 km)

Day 4: Rottenbuch to Prem, 13.5 miles (21.7 km)

Day 5: Prem to Füssen, 15.4 miles (24.8 km)

Signage: The signage along King Ludwig's Way is excellent. The official marking of the trail is a blue *K* topped by a blue crown—you'll see this mark not only at important junctions but often as a confidence marker on long, straight sections as well.

Accommodations: Cozy guesthouses and family-owned small hotels are the most common accommodations on King Ludwig's Way, although you can also find a variety of vacation rentals and private rooms. I recommend

Most guesthouses, hotels and huts on King Ludwig's Way have a *ruhetag*, a rest day when they are closed for twenty-four hours. And not every place has the same *ruhetag*. When making plans for accommodations, it's important to either look on the Internet or call in advance to make sure the place where you want to stay will indeed be open.

staying in the guesthouses; most of them have great restaurants on-site that serve delicious food—perfect for when you're already tired

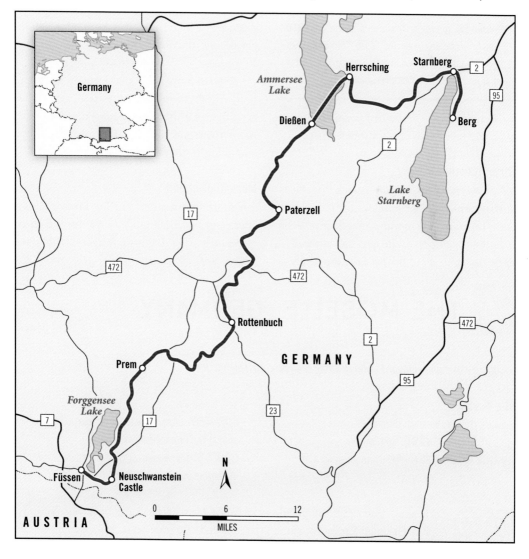

from walking all day. Most of these guesthouses also include a hearty German breakfast.

Make it shorter: Buses and trains connect several of the towns along King Ludwig's Way; private taxis are also available to shorten individual daily stages. For more information, contact the local tourist information office. On King Ludwig's Way, there is also the possibility of cutting down the length of the daily stages by staying more frequently in rural accommodations along the route.

If you'd like to explore this area of Bavaria but you have only one day, walk the route from Füssen to Neuschwanstein—you can bus back to town after an afternoon of exploring the castle.

Return: Once you're in Füssen, a regional train will take you back to Munich.

Other Activities Nearby

Be sure to reserve your tickets for Neuschwanstein and Hohenschwangau castles at least three to six months in advance—only a limited number of people are allowed in each day and spots fill up fast, especially in

the busy season. You can buy tickets for both at the Hohenschwangau Castle website (see Resources). And if you visit on a chilly day, track down some *glühwein* at the convenience store connected to the ticket office or in the cluster of stands just outside of Neuschwanstein (up on the hill)—it's amazing!

If you have more time to explore Bavaria, drive the Romantic Road, which winds for 255 miles (410 km) from Füssen to Würzburg, passing through forests, mountains and small towns. There's also a long-distance walking route and a bike route. For more information, check out the Romantic Road website (see Resources).

To learn more about the Germany of yesteryear, visit Freilichtmuseum Hessenpark, a 150-acre open-air museum near Frankfurt with more than one hundred historical buildings and living-history exhibits (see Resources).

More Information

For more information on King Ludwig's Way, check out my route guide to the trail, *Explore Germany's King Ludwig's Way on Foot* (see Resources).

10 THE MOSELLE, GERMANY

Stunning views and vineyard walking along the romantic Moselle River

At a Glance

LOCATION: Western Germany
LOCAL LANGUAGE: German
USE OF ENGLISH: Widely understood and used

SCENERY: Steep vineyards, dramatic river bends, the romantic Moselle River
DON'T MISS: Medieval castles, a *via ferrata*, incredible local wine, candlelit *weinstubes*

 Each year, thousands of people explore Germany's most romantic

river, the Moselle, by cruise boat. But the ships are packed, the waterways are busy and there's no opportunity for getting higher than the upper deck for a grand look at the majestic scenery that's all around. There's a better way to see the Moselle, and it's on trail—from a path that's been voted Germany's Most Beautiful Trail by *Wandermagazin* (*Walking Magazine*), one that winds from river to ridge and swoops along every stunning curve that makes this body of water so remarkable. It's called the Moselsteig.

Along the way, you'll pass through the vineyards of Germany's oldest wine-growing region, walk to scenic overlooks designed to show off the panorama-worthy curves of the river and spend your evenings in cozy *weinstubes* (wine pubs) in a series of quaint German if that weren't enough, on the last also have the opportunity to walk a *klettersteig*, better known as a *via ferrata* (a steep, narrow route equipped with cables, ropes and ladders), through the world's steepest vineyard. It doesn't get much better than that.

The extensive rows of grapevines that give these river walls their contour will eventually become Riesling. In some sections, the vineyards are pitched at such a steep angle that the soil is held in place by hardy-looking stone walls centuries old, whose quality craftsmanship the local farmers still rely on. Although the ancient walls proudly stand, the ground

The dramatic bends in the Moselle River are best seen from up high along Germany's Moselsteig Trail.

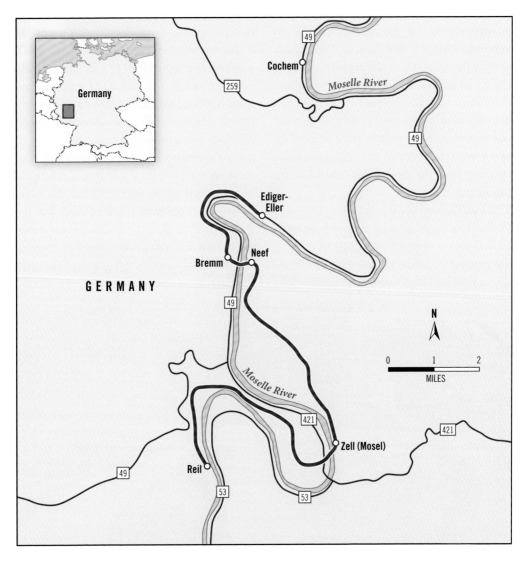

around them is littered with crumbly red and gray slate that's torn up in places from food-seeking wild boars. It's this slate—and its high mineral content—that seeps into the vines and gives the local wine its distinctive flavor.

While the sides of the river walls are bedecked with vineyards, the tops of them are home to extensive woodlands of box tree and oak. The ground levels out as you enter their territory, a welcome change from the incline

you've ascended. It's an easy walk through these trees, and you might find your mind wandering as cheerful-sounding chaffinches and rock buntings trill their calls and hares hop energetically through the underbrush. Until, that is, the trees suddenly open up to a ridgetop viewpoint with jaw-dropping views of the slow-moving river down below.

The beauty of it will catch you by surprise. It's a million little things: the deep blue water that stands out so starkly against the terraced bright green vineyards that contain it; the Lilliputian towns lining the river's shores like jewels in a crown; the crumbly ancient castles that lord over everything from rocky precipices high above. But nothing compares to the beauty of the sensuous big curves that the water carves into the land. The river is a tease, coming directly toward you, only to turn away at the last moment, swinging a full 180 degrees in the opposite direction. The scene is so wide and full of details that the only way to capture it is with a long, lingering panorama.

You may not want to leave your first viewpoint—I didn't—but there are plenty more to enjoy on your route. Some are as inconspicuous as small benches in a clearing; others are as elaborate as high viewing platforms hundreds of stairs above the trail. Together, they'll give you an intimate view—and so many photo opportunities—of everything that makes the Moselle unforgettable.

After viewing the river from up above each day, you'll head down to its banks in the evening, to the small towns that suddenly don't seem so small. Here, you'll find a variety of charming restaurants that will woo you with local delicacies, many of them made with the region's wine, from *rieslingsuppe* (Riesling soup) to *tresterfleisch* (pork marinated in wine spirits). And there's no better way to end a long day of walking than with a couple of hours spent trying different Moselle wines at a cozy, candlelit *weinstube*. (This is a great place to find friendly locals to talk to, as well.) When it's time to sleep, you'll have your choice of small inns that line the riverfront, where you can watch the boats go by from your own personal balcony.

Too soon, it will be your last day on trail. But this is, perhaps, the very best day, because you have the opportunity to walk the Calmont Klettersteig, a unique trail equipped with cables, ropes and ladders that runs parallel to the Moselsteig—and through the world's steepest vineyard. (If you're afraid of heights, continue on the Moselsteig to Ediger-Eller.) If you've never attempted a *via ferrata* before, this is a great one to start with because it's not too challenging. There's no special equipment required—just a sense of adventure. As you climb and pull your way along the route, you'll get great views not only of the special equipment that's required to maintain and harvest a working vineyard that's just too steep for growers to walk (they'd need a trail like the one you're on for every row) but also of the river down below and the impressive Roman ruins that stand proudly on the opposite side of the bank. From up here, you can see in all directions, including down to where the cruise ships drift by, their passengers unaware that what they're missing is a walk—and the very best of the Moselle.

On the Trail

ROUTES: Moselsteig, Calmont Klettersteig (optional)
DISTANCE: 24 miles (39 km)
ELEVATION GAIN/LOSS: +4,871/-4,965 feet (+1,485/-1,513 m)
AVERAGE TIME: 3 days
SEASON: Year-round
DIFFICULTY: Moderate
START: Reil, Germany
END: Ediger-Eller, Germany

Moderate: Because there's a decent amount of elevation gain on the Moselsteig and the Calmont Klettersteig and because the second walking day as prescribed is pretty long, this is rated as a moderately difficult walk. For ideas on how to make the route easier, check out "Make it shorter."

Germany's Moselsteig Trail puts the country's oldest wine-growing region on perfect display. (Photo by Andy Offinger)

The entire Moselsteig runs for 226 miles (365 km), from the German-French-Luxembourg border near Perl in the south to where the Moselle flows into the Rhine near Koblenz in the north—but you need only three days to experience the most iconic section of the trail, from Reil to Ediger-Eller.

Start: The closest airport to this stretch of the Moselsteig Trail is Frankfurt Airport, but Germany is so brilliantly connected by train that it's easy to get to both Reil and Ediger-Eller from almost anywhere in Europe. I recommend buying your train tickets at least three months in advance for the best rate.

Although your route starts in Reil, it doesn't take long for the trail to turn rural as you start winding your way up into the hills and vineyards. After enjoying the Moselle River from up high each day, you'll wander down to its shores in the evenings, to the little towns of Zell, Neef and Ediger-Eller.

If you plan to travel by train on the weekend, check out Germany's *Schönes Wochenende* (Happy Weekend) discount ticket, which allows you to take unlimited local and regional trains on Saturdays and Sundays for a reduced rate. The base fare is €40 for the first person and €4 for each additional person; the maximum number of people who can be covered by a ticket is five.

Suggested stages:
Day 1: Reil to Zell, 7.8 miles (12.5 km) via the Moselsteig

Day 2: Zell to Neef, 12.4 miles (20 km) via the Moselsteig

Day 3: Neef to Ediger-Eller, 4 miles (6.4 km) via the Moselsteig to Bremm, then via the Calmont Klettersteig (optional)

Signage: Keep your eyes out for the official route marking—five horizontal yellow lines stacked on top of the word "Moselsteig"; the signage along the Moselsteig Trail is reliable and accurate. The signage along the Calmont Klettersteig isn't as prevalent but because you're on an open hillside with views in every direction, it's hard to get lost.

Accommodations: On the Moselsteig Trail, you'll find plenty of places to spend the night, both in the towns the trail leads you to each evening and many places in between. There's a lot of variety as well, from wellness hotels to boutique hotels to family-owned guesthouses. For more information on accommodations on the route, including descriptions of specifically what's available in each town and any available package deals, check out the official website of the trail (see Resources).

Tip: Time your trip during one of the many festivals in the area. From wine and music festivals to folk festivals, there's a really impressive array, especially in September. Find a schedule at the website of the local tourist information office (see Resources, Tourism in Germany).

Make it shorter: Trains connect many of the towns along the Moselsteig Trail, including a few on this stretch. For more information, including schedules and tickets, check out the website of the German national rail carrier, Deutsche Bahn (see Resources). Private taxis are also available to help shorten individual daily stages. On the Moselsteig, there is also the possibility of cutting down the length of the daily stages by staying more frequently in accommodations scattered along the route (not just in the towns recommended).

Return: Take the train from Ediger-Eller to Frankfurt Airport or wherever you're flying out of.

Other Activities Nearby

If you're still up for some more exploring after you've finished your walk in Ediger-Eller, take the short (five-minute) train ride to Cochem for an enchanting visit to what many call the most romantic town on the Moselle. And definitely walk up to the castle!

From Cochem, you can also take to the water; several companies, including Moselle Tours (see Resources), offer daylong boat cruises leaving from Cochem. You'll see the curves of the river and the landscape you've just walked through from a totally different perspective.

More Information

For more information on walking the Moselsteig, visit the official website of the trail, and for more-detailed information on the Calmont Klettersteig, visit its website (see Resources) available only in German. Or search online for one of the many English write-ups on the trail.

11 THE ARDENNES, LUXEMBOURG AND BELGIUM

Timeless woodlands, ancient history and old-world towns in the Ardennes Forest

At a Glance

LOCATION: Northern Luxembourg and south-eastern Belgium

LOCAL LANGUAGE: Luxembourgish, French

USE OF ENGLISH: Widely understood and used

SCENERY: Extensive forests, babbling brooks, scenic overlooks, pastoral countryside

DON'T MISS: An ancient Celtic fortress, WWII relics, the pearl of the Ardennes, Blanc Bleu Belge steaks

★ If you're a forest lover, there's no better place to explore on foot than the Ardennes, one giant forest that's split between four different countries: Germany, Luxembourg, Belgium and France. It's not just the woodlands that will enchant you; it's the history that's concealed behind the many trunks and vines and the old-world towns that have

Luxembourg and Belgium's Escapardenne Eisleck Trail is ideal for those who love forests. (Photo © Escapardenne Eisleck Trail)

sprouted in the forest's shadows. And you can experience it all with a five-day walk on the Escapardenne Eisleck Trail, which winds through one of the most iconic sections of the forest from Luxembourg to Belgium.

Although your route starts in a bijou town with a smattering of modest houses and one very cozy inn, it doesn't take long before you leave civilization behind and immerse yourself in the trees. You'll get to know them all in turn: the oaks, beeches, birches, Douglas firs, spruces and larches that line the trail. But look closer—or, as they say, you'll miss the forest for the trees.

There's so much to take in: sunlight filters down through viridescent leaves; small deer, foxes and roe scamper shyly through the underbrush; wood pigeons, Turkish doves and thrushes flit about; bubbling brooks gently break the silence. The farther you walk, the more there is to admire, especially once the diversity of the forest begins to flaunt itself. The Ardennes is far from a uniform blanket of trees; instead, it covers the land in a unique tapestry of woods, heaths, wetlands and farmland. The trail doesn't just take you through this landscape—it highlights it; over the next five days, you'll enjoy forty-four impressive panoramas, most of them replete with benches and picnic tables to give you not just a second look but a momentary break from the often-hilly terrain.

But there's much more to discover in the forest than just natural beauty. There's also a significant amount of history, some of it ancient. There are a variety of castles to explore, like the imposing one in Clervaux, Luxembourg, that dates back to the twelfth century. Near the town of Bérismenil, Belgium, you'll walk past the partially reconstructed remains of Cheslé, a Celtic fortress that was inhabited between the eighth and sixth centuries BC, the most extensive fortress of its kind in Belgium.

And then there's WWII. Because the Allies didn't think mass troops could get through the dense Ardennes, they left it relatively unguarded during the war. But where the Allies saw improbability, the Germans saw opportunity, and during two important battles—the Battle of France (1940) and the Battle of the Bulge (1944–1945)—they tried to use the forest as a secret back door to France and Belgium.

Although the towns and bridges that were destroyed in the intense fighting have been rebuilt, the landscape of the Ardennes still bears the scars of these battles—and occasionally coughs up its secrets. Those who walk through the forest with metal detectors routinely find gas masks and guns; occasionally when excavating for a new house, construction workers will come across unexploded grenades; in the winter, it's a common practice for local residents to check their firewood for old bullets. Some of the relics are more obvious. You'll see them on trail—old tanks and anti-aircraft guns frozen in time, tree trunks punctured by bullets, even the wreckage of a plane shot down in 1945 during a covert mission to drop three Belgian secret agents behind enemy lines.

To learn more about the World War II history of the Ardennes, check out the nearby Bastogne War Museum and the La Roche Museum of the Battle of the Ardennes (see Resources for both).

The Escapardenne Eisleck Trail doesn't just lead you to enchanting woodlands and fascinating history; it also drops you into charming old-world towns where you can take a load off, put up your feet and contemplate what you've seen while enjoying a thick steak from a Blanc Bleu Belge (a local type of cow that looks more like a bodybuilder than a farm animal) and a

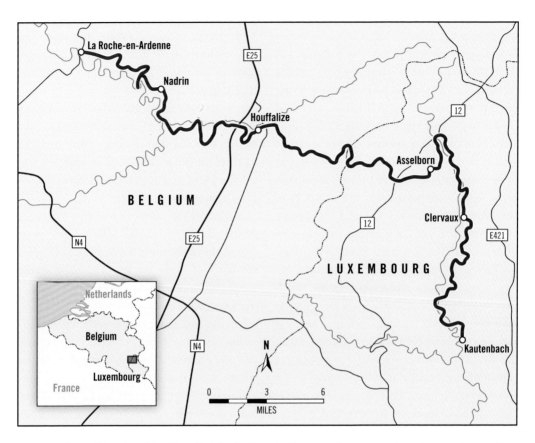

gnome-adorned bottle of La Chouffe (ale that's brewed in nearby Achouffe, Belgium).

Although there are three cities and nineteen villages on the route, you'll stay in just four of them as you walk (and because the starting and ending towns are so far from anything else, you'll likely stay in those too, for a grand total of six). They all showcase something different about the local area. Stylish Clervaux gives you a window into modern small-town-Ardenne life. Asselborn, with its thousand-year-old mill, transports you back in time. Houffalize and Nadrin show you how the old and the new often coexist in the very same town.

But none will impress you like La Roche-en-Ardenne, also known as the pearl of the Ardennes. The last town on your route, it's by far the most beautiful: a picturesque stone city

built around a serpentine river and set off to perfection by the dense forest that rises from the tall walls of the valley in every direction. It's a pairing that makes sense—only civilization like this could ever tempt you to leave a forest like the Ardennes.

On the Trail
ROUTE: Escapardenne Eisleck Trail
DISTANCE: 65 miles (105 km)
ELEVATION GAIN/LOSS: +8,312/-8,267 feet (+2,533/-2,520 m)
AVERAGE TIME: 5 days
SEASON: Year-round
DIFFICULTY: Moderate
START: Kautenbach, Luxembourg
END: La Roche-en-Ardenne, Belgium

The Escapardenne Eisleck Trail winds for 65 miles (105 km) through the Ardennes Forest from Kautenbach, Luxembourg, to La Roche-en-Ardenne, Belgium.

Start: The closest airports for accessing the trail are Luxembourg Airport and Brussels Airport. From either, you can jump on a train and be at the trailhead in Kautenbach in a few short hours. I recommend purchasing your train tickets at least three months in advance for the best deal. Before you head to the trailhead, though, check out Naturpark Öewersauer (see Resources), just south of Kautenbach: it's great for swimming, sailing, surfing, fishing— and has more than 435 miles (700 km) of trails

You'll come across many charming old farm buildings on Luxembourg and Belgium's Escapardenne Eisleck Trail.

to warm up your legs for the Escapardenne Eisleck Trail.

Although your route starts in Kautenbach, it doesn't take long before you leave civilization behind and head into the forest, where you spend the majority of your walk. Along the way you'll pass through a series of picturesque towns.

Suggested stages:

Day 1: Kautenbach to Clervaux, 15.8 miles (25.5 km)

Day 2: Clervaux to Asselborn, 11.7 miles (18.8 km)

Day 3: Asselborn to Houffalize, 13.5 miles (21.7 km)

Day 4: Houffalize to Nadrin, 13.3 miles (21.4 km)

Day 5: Nadrin to La Roche-en-Ardenne, 10.8 miles (17.4 km)

Signage: You'll recognize the official trail sign by its white wavy line inside of a blue rectangle. (Signs at key junctions also list the distances to upcoming towns.) For the most part, there is good signage along the Escapardenne Eisleck Trail. There are some areas of the trail where logging has had a negative effect, in part destroying some of the trail signs—and confusing walkers in the process. I recommend ordering a paper map and downloading the free GPX tracks from the official website of the trail (see Resources).

Accommodations: Although there are a variety of accommodations on the Escapardenne Eisleck Trail, including chain hotels and boutique hotels, I recommend staying somewhere old and charming. You'll have your pick of cool spots—for example, in Asselborn, you could stay in a mill that dates from the eleventh century, when it was part of an abbey! Just remember to be a little patient with these older buildings. Although most of them have undergone serious renovation, they can still have a few

quirks, from creaks to low doorways. So duck your head and remember, it's part of the charm!

Make it shorter: It's possible to occasionally shorten the stages of the Escapardenne Eisleck Trail with trains. Private taxis are also available, although they must be arranged in advance. For details, contact the local tourist information office.

If you'd like to explore the Ardennes but have only a day, check out one of the many daylong walks around La Roche-en-Ardenne.

Return: Once you've finished your walk in La Roche-en-Ardenne, take a short bus ride to the train and ride it back to either airport.

For a daylong walk in the Netherlands north of Belgium, see One-Day Wander #5: Kinderdijk in Chapter 2, See What's Possible.

Other Activities Nearby

After your walk, plan to spend at least a couple of days meandering through and discovering La Roche-en-Ardenne. (Hint: The city is especially photogenic in the fall!)

If you have more time to explore the Ardennes, check out the rest of the Escapardenne trail system. In addition to the Eisleck Trail, there are six smaller loop trails to discover (each can be done in a day or less), as well as the 33-mile (53 km) Lee Trail, which connects with the Escapardenne Eisleck Trail in Kautenbach.

More Information

For more information on all of these trails, including descriptions of the daily stages and free downloadable GPX tracks, visit the official website of the Escapardenne trail system (see Resources).

It's often drizzly in England's Lake District, but that only adds to the moody and romantic ambiance of the area. (Photo © Andrew Locking)

12 THE LAKE DISTRICT, ENGLAND, UK

Poetry and puddles in one of England's most beautiful national parks

At a Glance

LOCATION: Lake District National Park, northwestern England
LOCAL LANGUAGE: English
SCENERY: Rolling hills, hidden meres (lakes),
romantic vistas, billowy clouds
DON'T MISS: Charming inns, reading poetry by the fire, tea time

Walking village to village isn't the only way to explore Europe on foot; having a home base in a town and tackling a series of daylong walks can also be really wonderful. There are plenty of benefits: you'll get to know the town you're staying in more intimately, you'll have more opportunities to befriend the locals and you'll be able to leave your main pack behind each day and walk with just a light day pack. There's no better place for this kind of walking than England's Lake District, where you can choose from an abundance of quaint towns, diverse scenery and peaceful walking trails.

Although the Lake District was originally made famous by the poet William Wordsworth, who loved it so much that he penned a guidebook for the area in 1810, it didn't become a national park until 1951. While some of the most impressive sights in England are found within its borders, from the country's tallest mountain to its longest lake and even a mysterious stone circle that's more than 5,000 years old, it's not the kind of national park you'd expect—there's no main gate, it's rare to see a ranger walking around and you don't have to pay for admission. And it's home to real people—nearly 42,000 of them—who live in a collection of countryside villages that are so charming they could've been lifted from the pages of a Beatrix Potter book. (Apparently she thought so too, since she made the Lake District her home.)

Windermere is the gateway town to the Lake District, and it's easy to get between all of the small towns in the park via the Lake District bus line, which runs several times a day. There are so many quaint villages that you won't have trouble finding a comfortable home base. Indeed, your main difficulty will be choosing just one.

My favorite is Grasmere, a picturesque town where hole-in-the-wall tea shops, romantic stone cottages, cozy pubs and peekaboo views of the eponymous lake abound. These were the stomping grounds of Wordsworth—and the inspiration for much of his poetry—and you can visit his beloved Dove Cottage in the middle of town. If you have several days to explore, don't just home-base in one town—pick two or three. I also recommend Ambleside and Keswick.

There's more to these towns than just civilization. Each one also has a collection of daylong walks that are perfect for exploring the local landscape, with something for everyone. Some trails are challenging high-ridge walks; others are easy lakeside ambles. A variety of guided walks are offered by the park (most of which are free) for those who would like some company or narration of the route. And there are accessible routes called Miles Without Stiles for those walking with a wheelchair or stroller. Regardless of the specific trails you choose, there's a lot to look forward to: billowy clouds, babbling brooks, rolling hills, bucolic countryside, golden eagles, black-and-white spotted sheep and, of course, more lakes (called "meres" or "waters")—some big, some small—than you'll see anywhere else.

This is the stuff of picnics and poetry, so take your time and stop often. Wordsworth did. He was known to meander with his notebook and pencil for hours at a time, going nowhere fast, just letting the scenery wash over him until it became verse that he put on paper.

During your walks, you'll become acquainted with the very thing that makes this landscape so stunning: water—and not just in the form of puddles, lakes and waterfalls. Chances are, even if you travel to the Lake District in summer, you'll experience some rain. Because it's typically more of a drizzle or a mist than a driving, send-you-running-for-your-guesthouse kind of shower, it doesn't need to spoil your walks. Instead, it can add another dimension to them. You'll love the pungent and fresh smells that suddenly swirl around you. It may sound odd, but rain is part of the appeal of the Lake District. It adds something moody and romantic to the ambiance of the whole area.

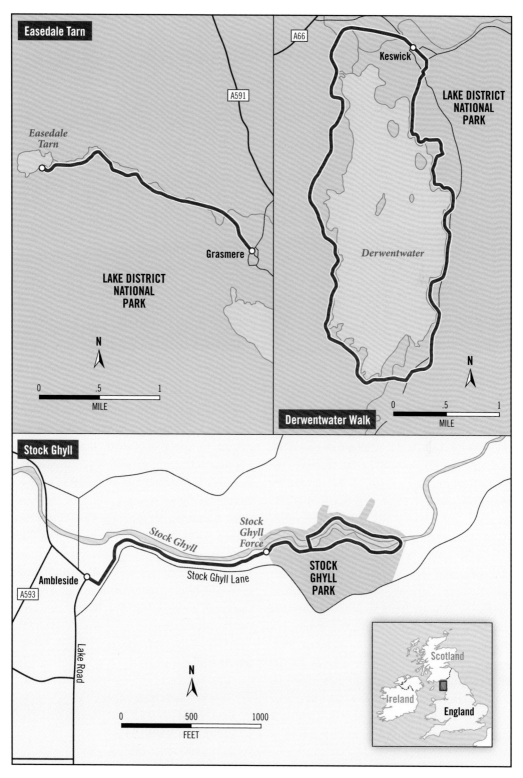

Easedale Tarn

Easedale Tarn

A591

LAKE DISTRICT
NATIONAL
PARK

Grasmere

N

0   .5   1
MILE

A66

Keswick

LAKE DISTRICT
NATIONAL
PARK

Derwentwater

N

0   .5   1
MILE

Derwentwater Walk

Stock Ghyll

Stock Ghyll

Stock Ghyll
Force

STOCK
GHYLL
PARK

Ambleside

A593

Stock Ghyll Lane

Lake Road

N

0   500   1000
FEET

Scotland

Ireland

England

Grasmere, the old haunt of poet William Wordsworth, is my favorite home base in England's Lake District. (Photo © Son of Groucho)

There are plenty of places to dry out after your walks, from old-world cafes to homey pubs. My favorite ritual is to warm up with a steaming-hot mug of tea. Really, there's never a bad time for tea in England. It's enjoyed by locals around the clock and no matter the weather, to the tune of 165 million cups a day! Although drinking tea can be a simple affair—you can order it à la carte—it's most fun when enjoyed as part of the larger experience of "high tea." This can easily take the place of lunch and should be done well in advance of dinner lest you spoil your appetite; the food is dainty, but there's a lot of it: crustless sandwiches, fresh scones, clotted cream and several kinds of cake, all served on beautiful tiered dishes. If hearty, stick-to-your-ribs comfort food is more your style, pop into a local pub and try the Herdwick lamb cobbler or Cumberland tattie pie, both of which are local specialties.

Other than a heaping plate of food, there's no more welcome sight after a good long day of walking than that of a cozy inn, smoke puffing cheerfully from an ancient chimney, sunset turning the thatched roof all shades of gold. It's the kind of sight that makes you long for everything accommodations in the Lake District are known for: sitting rooms with roaring fires, libraries and old phonographs playing classical music, white-lace bedrooms with delicate carved furniture, roomy bathtubs that overlook the green countryside. And it may just bring out the poet in you.

On the Trail
ROUTES: Stock Ghyll, Easedale Tarn, Derwentwater Walk

DISTANCE: 1.2–9.6 miles (1.9–15.4 km)

ELEVATION GAIN/LOSS:
Stock Ghyll: +280/-285 feet (+85/-87 m);

Easedale Tarn: +779/-778 feet (+237/-237 m);
Derwentwater: +691/-691 feet (+211/-211 m)
AVERAGE TIME: 3–5 days
SEASON: Year-round
DIFFICULTY: Easy to moderate
START: Windermere, England
END: Grasmere, Ambleside and Keswick,
England

Easy to Moderate: The three walks I recommend range from short with a bit of steepness to longer and mostly flat—but these are just a sampling of the many options in the Lake District, which also features some challenging walks.

Although the Lake District, with its plethora of short trails and villages that are never very far apart, can be sampled in as little as a day, I suggest spending at least three to five days exploring the area. Choose a town—or three—as a home base, and take daylong walks from there.

Start: The closest airports to the Lake District are in Manchester, England, and Glasgow, Scotland, but the park is also accessible by train from many other spots in England and Scotland. I recommend taking the west coast main line, which runs from London to Glasgow, to Oxenholme, the gateway station to the Lake District. A smaller local train will then take you to Windermere, the town most people enter the national park through. Renting a car is also an excellent—and oftentimes much more convenient—option than public transportation for getting around the Lake District.

Windermere's Information Centre is a good resource: you can book accommodations, purchase maps and guidebooks of the area, and get information on local buses. The Lake District bus line runs several times a day—you can hop on a bus that threads its way through the park to

many of its villages. For a tour of easy to moderate walks that showcase several villages—and the beautiful water near them—I recommend choosing three home bases.

Suggested stages:
Day 1: From Ambleside, the Stock Ghyll path (moderate), 1.2 miles (1.9 km)
Day 2: From Grasmere, the Easedale Tarn trail (moderate), 4.1 miles (6.6 km)
Day 3: From Keswick, the Derwentwater Walk (easy), 9.6 miles (15.4 km)

Signage: The trail signage in the Lake District varies considerably. It's better the more accessible (i.e., flat and/or near town) the trail is but can be spotty on longer or more remote trails. I recommend walking with a good paper map to help keep yourself on track.

The Stock Ghyll walk in Ambleside is a short, occasionally steep route that winds from the village and up through the forest to the Stock Ghyll Force, an impressive seventy-foot waterfall (and an excellent picnic spot). In Grasmere the Easedale Tarn path is a countryside jaunt that takes you past stone bridges and bucolic farmland before eventually leading you up a hillside to a hidden lake. The Derwentwater Walk in Keswick is a peaceful and flat meander on a pretty lakeside path around Derwentwater, known locally as the queen of the lakes.

Accommodations: Because most of the villages in the Lake District are small, much of the accommodations on tap are also quite local, such as family-owned bed-and-breakfasts and boutique hotels. I heartily recommend staying in a B and B; there's no better way to start off a long day of walking than with a huge, delicious breakfast served in a cozy English sitting room. Give yourself the best chance of finding a good deal by reserving your room at least three to six months in advance.

Tip: Even if you make afternoon tea a habit, experience high tea, complete with the endless platters of finger sandwiches, scones and dainty desserts, at least once. It's amazing.

Make it shorter: There are many trails sprinkled throughout the Lake District that can be done in a day, a half day or an hour. There are also many trails that are relatively flat or even wheelchair and stroller accessible. Rather than shortening long or difficult trails, guarantee yourself a great experience by handpicking trails that suit your needs perfectly.

For a short excursion on nearby Ireland's central-west coast near Galway, see One-Day Wander #6: Cliffs of Moher in Chapter 2, See What's Possible.

Return: From your home-base village, take the local bus back to Windermere, and from there take trains back to Glasgow, Manchester or London (or wherever you came from).

For even more culture (and one of the coolest, cheapest things you can do in England), take the train to London and be a groundling at Shakespeare's Globe Theater. It'll only set you back £5 (about $7).

Other Activities Nearby

To enhance your cultural education, take in a play at the Theatre by the Lake in Keswick. For a schedule of events, check out the theater website (see Resources).

More Information

For more information, check out the websites of the Lake District National Park, National Trust and Lake District (see Resources).

13 WEST HIGHLAND WAY, SCOTLAND, UK

Desolate beinns and cozy pubs on Scotland's most famous long-distance trek

At a Glance

LOCATION: West Highlands, western Scotland
LOCAL LANGUAGE: English
SCENERY: Golden hills, gray *lochs*, rivers frothy with peat, near-constant drizzle

DON'T MISS: Cozy pubs, legends and storytelling, ancient ruins, gigantic Scottish breakfasts

There's no better way to discover the real Scotland—remote, rolling *beinns* (mountains); ever-drizzly rain; warm, cozy pubs—than with a walk on the country's most famous long-distance route, the West Highland Way. Although the entire route runs from a town called Milngavie on the outskirts of Scotland's second-largest city, Glasgow, north to the capital of the West Highlands, Fort William, the very best of the trail can be experienced in only three days on its iconic final section.

You'll start to fall in love with the West Highland Way even before you set foot on trail, and that's because of the gigantic Scottish breakfast your guesthouse will serve you the morning you start your walk—and every morning after that. There's nothing quite like a Scottish breakfast; it's heavy enough to keep you full long into the afternoon, sometimes even to dinner. There are typically two courses to the meal. The first is from a buffet, where you serve yourself yogurt, cereal, fruit and juice. Don't make the rookie mistake of getting too full, because the best is yet to come: eggs made to order, bacon, sausage, buttered toast, baked beans and fresh tea or coffee delivered to your table.

Once you've eaten your fill, it's time to hit the trail, a series of paths that go back hundreds of years: cobblestone streets built by the military to help control the Jacobite clans, old coach routes, abandoned railway lines, dirt roads along which farmers herded their cattle and sheep to market in the lowlands. It's a mainly flat walk that takes you deep into the most remote—and beautiful—areas of the West Highlands.

You can look forward to one significant climb: the Devil's Staircase, the top of which is the highest point on trail, at 1,797 feet (548 m). But don't worry—the climb sounds far worse than it is. There is only 850 feet (259 m) of elevation gain to reckon with.

This is the land of gray *lochs* (lakes) and golden *beinns*, dark brown rivers frothy with peat that look like Guinness pouring from the ground, vibrant purple thistles that add a spot of color to the otherwise earthy palette. You'll notice all of these in turn, but the thing you'll be struck with most is a sense of vastness. Nothing here is close and contained; it's as if the scenery decided to stretch itself out and get comfortable, with gently rolling hills that extend for

Along Scotland's West Highland Way, colorful heather stands out in vivid contrast to the main gold-and-straw palette of the surrounding landscape.

miles in every direction, broken only occasionally by scattered herds of fluffy sheep and hairy "coos" (cows, in the local dialect). Even the sky, with its ever-shifting shades of gray, feels more expansive than anywhere else.

In places the landscape is desolate and eerie, almost supernatural. The route takes you to two ancient ruins—Tigh-na-sleubhaich and Lairigmor—that contribute to the ambiance and give you the feeling that something else is out there, you just can't see it. When I was at the ruins, no matter how I tried taking a photo of one specific area that was very well lit, part of the frame kept mysteriously turning out dark. As empty as the landscape is in some areas, it's shockingly lush in others, from immense fern forests where thousands of bright green plants look like they're climbing on top of each other, to dense pockets of timber where moss drips from every surface.

You'll have plenty of time to enjoy the scenery, because, with the exception of Kinlochleven, there's not much in the way of civilization on trail. Instead, you'll pass an inn here and there and a few houses—if that. There's no better place to take a short break from the trail and warm up on a chilly, drizzly Scottish day than these inns, especially one with a roaring peat fire, a cozy sitting room and the opportunity to order what the locals call a "cuppa" (cup of tea) before you move along to finish your walk for the day.

In the evenings, once you've checked into your accommodations, you'll usually eat in the on-site pub or restaurant, filling your belly with Scottish comfort food that is so strange sounding you'll swear it's not even in English: mince and tatties (minced beef and mashed potatoes), haggis (a mixture of sheep innards, oatmeal and spices), cullen skink (a thick soup of smoked haddock, potatoes and onions). Wash

everything down with a pint of Scottish ale, a dark, sweet malted brew with a smoky taste, or a glass of the national drink of choice, Scotch whisky.

As the sun goes down and the first chords of live music hit the air, locals drift into the pub. Especially in remote areas like the West Highlands, inn pubs aren't just for travelers—they also play a large role in the social scene of nearby residents, who don't have anywhere else to go to meet neighbors or get out of the house. They're a friendly bunch, eager to laugh and tell stories, and it won't take much convincing to get them talking about local history and the Scottish way of life. Snuggle a little closer to the fire, kick your boots up and listen to their singsong voices and centuries-old stories of clans that ruled the land, massacres that wiped out entire families and ghosts that continue to haunt the villages. When at last you reach Fort William, there will be no doubt in your mind— you have seen the *real* Scotland.

On the Trail

ROUTE: West Highland Way
DISTANCE: 37 miles (59 km)
ELEVATION GAIN/LOSS: +4,334/-4,864 feet (+1,321/-1,483 m)
AVERAGE TIME: 3 days
SEASON: March to October
DIFFICULTY: Moderate
START: Bridge of Orchy, Scotland
END: Fort William, Scotland

Moderate: Although a lot of the West Highland Way is flat and easy, there is a moderate amount of elevation gain—and a couple of long daily stages—on this stretch. To make the trail easier, check out "Make it shorter."

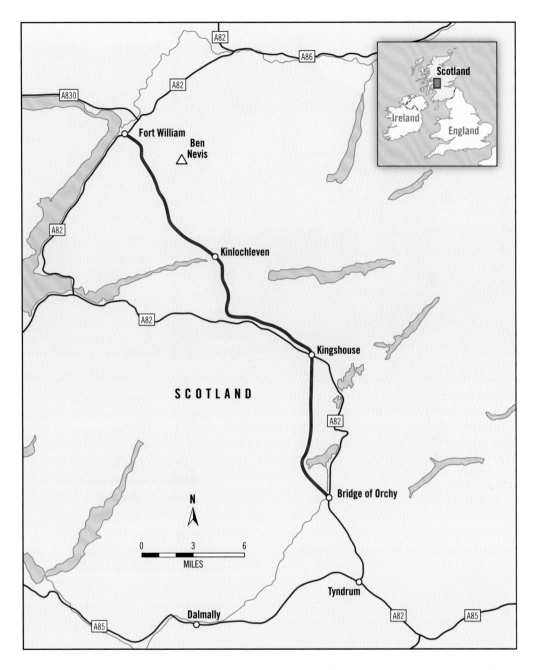

The entire route runs for 96 miles (154 km), but you don't need thirteen days to explore the West Highland Way. In fact, the very best of the trail can be experienced in only three days from Bridge of Orchy to Fort William.

Start: The best way to get to the trailhead is to fly into Glasgow Airport and take the bus or train to Bridge of Orchy. (I recommend the bus, which runs more frequently than the train.) As you leave Bridge of Orchy, a hamlet

The Kings House Hotel, just outside of Glencoe on Scotland's West Highland Way, has been giving walkers a good night's sleep for nearly 400 years.

with a smattering of modest houses and one very nice hotel, you walk a series of paths that pass through small rural outposts.

Suggested stages:

Day 1: Bridge of Orchy to Kingshouse, 13 miles (21 km)

Day 2: Kingshouse to Kinlochleven, 8.5 miles (14 km)

Day 3: Kinlochleven to Fort William, 15 miles (24 km)

Signage: You'll see markings—the official one for the trail looks like a geometric thistle—at important junctions, as well as confidence markers on many straightaways. The signage along the West Highland Way is excellent, but in adverse weather conditions (rain or fog) you'll need to be extra vigilant about spotting trail signs. For the most part, though, it's hard to get lost on the West Highland Way.

For a great side trip, take the bus from Kingshouse to Glencoe. The drive alone is worth the excursion, filled with craggy cliffs and enchanting green. It's like nothing else you'll see in Scotland.

Accommodations: Bed-and-breakfasts are the most common type of accommodations on the West Highland Way. They offer exactly what you'd expect: a cozy bed for the night and a huge breakfast the next morning. Many also give you the option to order a packed lunch to go.

These are wonderful, comfortable places to stay. There's only one drawback: they fill up fast. Book them at least six months to a year in advance—or chance not having anywhere to stay. There are a few hostels, Airbnbs and campgrounds located near the trail, but I suggest using these as a last resort—they're often difficult to get to, unless you want to add hitchhiking to your itinerary.

Tip: Don't miss the best panoramic photo opportunity of the trip. It's on the first day's stretch from Bridge of Orchy to Kingshouse, at the big rock cairn overlooking Loch Tulla and Inveroran, approximately 1.5 miles (2.4 km) from Bridge of Orchy.

Make it shorter: Buses and trains connect many of the towns on the West Highland Way, including several along this stretch, which can help shorten the individual daily stages. Private taxis are also available. If you're looking to make things a little easier on your legs, I suggest opting for luggage transfer instead—it's cheap, and you can use it exclusively for the more challenging days, like the stretch from Kinlochleven to Fort William.

Return: Once you're in Fort William, hop a bus or train back to Glasgow.

Other Activities Nearby

If you have more time for exploring at the end of your trip, take the bus from Fort William to Edinburgh, one of the most gorgeous (and history-filled) cities in Europe. If you time it just right, you can even make the city's biggest event, the Royal Edinburgh Military Tattoo, which is held every August. (Picture more bagpipes than you've ever seen in your life!) For a day hike in Edinburgh, see One-day Wander #7: Arthur's Seat and Holyrood Park in Chapter 2, See What's Possible.

More Information

For more information on the West Highland Way, check out the official website of the trail. I also recommend Charlie Loram's guidebook *West Highland Way*. For an incredible map of the trail, one of the most user-friendly ones I've ever walked with, check out Footprint Maps; you can find the West Highland Way map under "Long Distance Paths" (see Resources).

14 LAUGAVEGUR TREK, ICELAND

At the foot of active volcanoes in the land of fire and ice

At a Glance

LOCATION: Southern Iceland
LOCAL LANGUAGE: Icelandic
USE OF ENGLISH: Widely understood and used
SCENERY: Active volcanoes, vast glaciers, gushing waterfalls, dramatic colors
DON'T MISS: Swimmable hot springs, northern lights, rustic huts, fresh seafood

There's a reason the Laugavegur Trek is not only Iceland's most famous long-distance trail but one of the most lusted-after walks in the world: from belching volcanoes and swelling lava fields to gushing rivers and advancing glaciers, the route takes you through some of the most active—and photogenic—landscapes on earth, all in the span of only four days.

The trail is situated in the highlands of Iceland, and if it feels like the middle of nowhere,

Snow can stick around well into late August on Iceland's Laugavegur Trek.

that's because it is. Don't even bother looking for a grocery store, restaurant or hotel nearby. Civilization isn't on the docket here; nature is. And you'll see plenty of it. In four days, as you walk south on this sometimes-rolling, sometimes-flat trail from Landmannalaugar to Thórsmörk, you'll pass through two different nature reserves and the just-as-scenic land in between.

Your walk starts in Landmannalaugar, a remote outpost run by the Icelandic Forest Service that has the look and feel of a Himalayan base camp, with backpacking tents scattered everywhere, colorful towels and wet clothes fluttering in the strong breeze, and half-geared-up walkers milling about at all hours of the day. The complex also has the only swimmable hot springs on the Laugavegur Trek, so

give yourself enough time for a prewalk soak. (Icelanders aren't like most Scandinavians; they do wear swimsuits. So pack yours, unless you want to be the only one swimming naked—you don't want to learn that lesson the hard way!)

As you crest a short, steep ridge, you get a preview of the geologically active landscape you'll be walking through for the first three days—cool black lava as far as the eye can see. It's not apparent from this vantage point, but this 500-year-old lava flow still gives off enough heat to warm the hot springs you just bathed in. And it's just one sign that the ground under your feet is far from static—it's in the middle of explosive re-creation.

This landscape is so alive that it's practically barren. Save for a few hardy sheep and scraggly bushes, all of the accoutrement you've been taught to expect from nature has been stripped away. At first, and especially when the reek of sulfur starts to overwhelm your nose as you pass hissing vents in the earth, it can seem like a bitter and inhospitable place. A hell, you could even say. When the dense fog moves in, as it's often known to do, it smothers the landscape in an eeriness that's hard to shake.

Until, that is, the fog lifts and you finally start to notice the beauty all around you. At first it's subtle, then shockingly overt: braided hills of neon algae and black volcanic ash, lavish waterfalls hidden in the folds of otherwise naked canyons, intricate designs swirled into the earth by crawling and cooling lava, brave wildflowers that don't mind a challenge. And lording over everything: a line of imposing volcanic cones, their shoulders draped in majestic mantles of ice.

One thing you won't notice on trail—even next to potentially hazardous spots such as steaming vents or boiling puddles—is a sign saying "Danger" or "Stand back." That's because Icelanders are really into common sense—and they trust that you will be too.

There's so much to see that you won't want to be anywhere else—until you see a rustic hut on the horizon, a shining beacon of warmth and camaraderie. You'll stay at four of these during your time on the Laugavegur Trek; run by the Icelandic Forest Service, they're strategically placed one day's walk apart. While the huts aren't anything fancy (it's like camping inside), there's nowhere cozier when the sun goes down, the air chills and the fire is lit. If you're walking with a local guide, they'll regale you with stories of their people and their culture as they expertly prepare your dinner. You can look forward to a variety of local specialties: lamb, potatoes, salmon and haddock, to name

a few. Everything is fresh; it's been transported to the hut that day by adventurous drivers in snorkel-outfitted beefy all-terrain vehicles.

If you win a free shower at a hut, make sure to collect your prize—for the sake of your fellow walkers. This is the warden's polite way of telling you that although you can't seem to smell yourself, you're stinky.

As you grow full and sleepy, the tale of this island's few but mighty people will become a bedtime story of sorts. It's the tale of Viking descendants who wear thick wool sweaters as an unspoken uniform and believe in all manner of things they can't see—elves and trolls, to name a few. (You might, too, after witnessing how otherworldly the landscape is.) And it's the story of those who haven't just learned to peacefully coexist with 130 volcanoes (30 of which are active), but who have come to embrace their presence, even going so far as to build their economy (through tourism) around them.

As the stories turn to conversation and laughter, you'll stay up later than you thought you could, passing spirits like Brennivín ("burning wine," also known as Black Death) back and forth with other walkers as you talk long into the night. When you're finally ready for bed, don't forget to peek outside for a glimpse of the northern lights. They can be hard to see with the naked eye, but if you spot something akin to faint green goblins shape-shifting across the sky, that's probably them. If you want to know for sure, just take a picture: your camera sensor is much more sensitive to light than your eyes, and oftentimes those faint green goblins will appear as huge swaths of brilliant color on the screen.

Before you know it, it'll be your last day of walking—and you're in for a treat. This final trail section is as lush as the others are barren, replete with fragrant pockets of heather and wild blueberry that morph into an actual birch forest near Thórsmörk, which means "Thor's Forest." Although by global standards it's small, by Icelandic standards it's colossal. (There aren't a lot of trees in Iceland, which was deforested for longships in the tenth century.) And after the last few days, this section of trail will feel like a rebirth. It's no wonder that this area is regarded not only as land fit for a god (Thor) but one of the most beautiful places in all of Iceland—and the perfect end to an incredible walk.

On the Trail

ROUTE: Laugavegur Trek
DISTANCE: 36 miles (58 km)
ELEVATION GAIN/LOSS: +6,004/-7,218 feet (+1,830/-2,200 m)
AVERAGE TIME: 4 days
SEASON: Late June to late August
DIFFICULTY: Moderate to challenging
START: Landmannalaugar, Iceland
END: Thórsmörk, Iceland

Moderately Difficult to Challenging: Although the Laugavegur Trek is of moderate difficulty from a physical perspective, the ever-changing and intense nature of the local weather, along with the fact that there are several rivers to ford, can make it challenging—or even dangerous—for inexperienced walkers. This is the ideal trail to tackle with the help of a professional guide. I recommend Icelandic Mountain Guides (see Resources).

The start of the Laugavegur trail is a four-hour drive—via four-wheel-drive vehicle—from Reykjavik. As you walk south from Landmannalaugar for four days, you'll pass through two nature reserves on the way to Thórsmörk.

For a good sound track to your walk, download a few songs by Björk—by far the most famous Icelander and the most popular music on the island.

Start: First fly into Reykjavik, where most tours rendezvous downtown for the four-hour 4WD drive to the trailhead. If you're traveling independently, you can take a bus from Reykjavik to Landmannalaugar; check out the Sterna buses (see Resources)—reservations are recommended. I don't suggest renting a car and driving to the trailhead—or Thórsmörk; the route is best suited to four-wheel-drive vehicles and experienced off-road drivers. Also, near Thórsmörk the road passes through (yes, through) several rivers and you'll likely lose your vehicle or get it stuck.

You start walking from Landmannalaugar up a short, steep ridge with a vista of the volcanic landscape you'll walk through for three days. The last day brings you through heathery plains to Thor's Forest.

Suggested stages:
Day 1: Landmannalaugar to Hrafntinnusker, 7.5 miles (12 km)
Day 2: Hrafntinnusker to Álftavatn, 8 miles (13 km)
Day 3: Álftavatn to Emstrur, 9.9 miles (16 km)
Day 4: Emstrur to Thórsmörk, 10.6 miles (17 km)

Signage: There is no official trail sign to be on the lookout for; instead, keep your eyes out for a combination of rock cairns, plastic poles in the ground and wooden signs that list the name and direction of the next hut. The signage along the Laugavegur Trek isn't always reliable, and in foggy or rainy conditions, it's even more difficult to spot. Make sure you walk with a guide or bring along a paper map and GPX tracks to stay on track.

Accommodations: The only accommodations on the Laugavegur Trek are rustic huts spaced one day's walk apart and the camping spots that are available outside of them. Reservations (made at least six months to a year in advance) are essential. To reserve the huts, email the dates you need beds at each hut and the number of people in your party to the Iceland Touring Association at fi@fi.is. If you're traveling with a tour group, your beds will be reserved for you.

Make it shorter: Because this area is quite remote, there are no public transportation services, private taxis or alternate accommodations en route—with the exception of one more hut, Hvanngil, that's located on trail about an

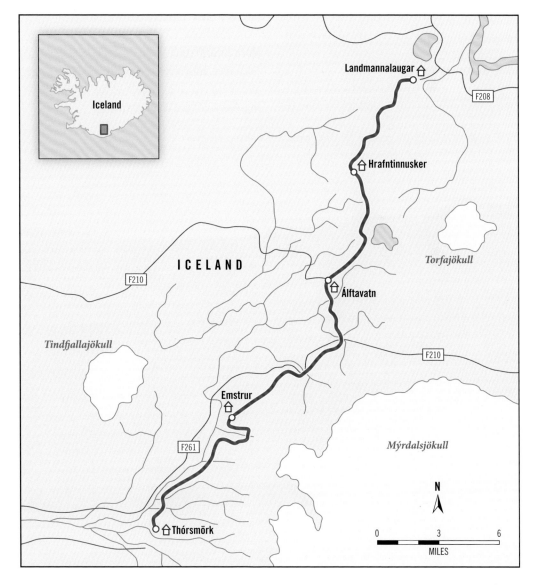

hour beyond Álftavatn—to shorten the daily stages of the Laugavegur Trek.

To shorten your time on trail, consider getting an early start and combining the first two stages for a three-day walk. If you're interested in experiencing the highlands of Iceland and you have only one day, check out the day-tour packages of Landmannalaugar or Thórsmörk that are offered by several of the local tour companies.

Return: If you're traveling independently, take a bus from Thórsmörk back to Reykjavik.

Other Activities Nearby

If you have more time to explore the highlands, I recommend spending it in the Thórsmörk area—it's amazing. Among several nice daylong walks in the area is an iconic 15.5-mile (25 km) route from Thórsmörk to Skógar.

If you don't have time to enjoy the geothermal baths in Landmannalaugar, search out a public bath when you're back in Reykjavik. For a less expensive and less crowded alternative to the Blue Lagoon, try one of the baths that locals frequent. Vesturbæjarlaug and Laugardalslaug are both good choices (see Resources).

More Information

For more information on walking the Laugavegur Trek, visit the website of the Iceland Touring Association (see Resources).

The huts along Iceland's Laugavegur Trek are spaced one walking day apart.

15 THE SAHARA DESERT, MOROCCO

In the footsteps of nomads in the world's largest desert

At a Glance

LOCATION: Erg Chebbi dunes, east-central Morocco

LOCAL LANGUAGE: Arabic

USE OF ENGLISH: Widely understood and used in large cities; not common in most small towns—brush up on your Arabic

SCENERY: Africa's largest mountain range, verdant oases, towering sand dunes as far as the eye can see

DON'T MISS: *Tajine*, nomadic Berber lifestyle, camel rides through the desert, a fire circle with traditional instruments, stargazing

If you've read Paulo Coelho's book *The Alchemist*, you've probably heard the siren cry of the Sahara Desert and dreamed of crossing its expanse. It's a romantic vision—nothing but sand as far as you can see, deep silence that's broken only by the snort of a camel, the shockingly green oases that appear in the heat waves on the horizon and promise welcome relief from the relentless sun. It's a life nomads have lived for thousands of years, and it's an experience that you can have with a desert walk just outside of Merzouga, Morocco, in the impressive dunes of Erg Chebbi.

Your adventure starts far from the dunes, in the city of Marrakesh, where you'll barter for a spot on a private or group tour with the countless companies that hawk their experiences alongside snake charmers and monkey handlers in the Aladdin-like *souks* (markets) near the famous main square, Jemaa el-Fna. Bartering is part of the culture in Morocco, so don't expect to pay the first price that's offered. At the time I was there, it was $75 per person (including lodging and two dinners) for a three-day group tour—and it will be more if you want a private guide. Your choice of a company doesn't make much difference, since everyone follows the same route to the Sahara, like a modern-day caravan.

As sandy and hot as it is in Marrakesh, it's farther than you think to the edge of the Sahara. You'll be picked up from your guesthouse while it's still dark out because you have a full day of driving ahead of you. Along the way, plenty of stops for stretching your legs will add to your Moroccan education.

Your first stop is in Africa's largest mountain range, the Atlas Mountains, where you'll wind your way heavenward on narrow highways folded into tree-lined valleys of evergreen, oak, cedar and pine that feel completely out of place in this flat and barren land. You'll follow the curves of cool rivers, so shallow in areas that popular outdoor restaurants set their tables and chairs midstream and locals dangle their feet in the flowing water. Occasionally you'll come out of the trees to gorgeous panoramas of modest peaks that stretch as far as you can see.

Once you pass through the extensive mountains, the sights come more quickly: impossibly deep gorges cut like angry gashes into the red desert rock, mud-castle-like kasbahs (fortified buildings) that lord over small settlements,

A night walk in the Erg Chebbi dunes of Morocco's Sahara Desert is a magical experience.

verdant oases where crops spill from the earth in great heaps.

One of the kasbahs you can look forward to visiting is the UNESCO World Heritage Site of Aït Benhaddou; several well-known films have been shot there, including *The Mummy* (1999), *Gladiator* (2000) and *Prince of Persia* (2014).

It's enough to make you forget that you have a final destination in mind: the dunes of the Sahara Desert. Although you've been driving all day, you have farther to go. But first, you'll stop for the night in one of several small rural outposts in the Dadès Valley, where you can enjoy a hot meal, a comfy bed and a break from the road before resuming your caravan ride to the desert the next morning. After another half

day of driving, you'll know you're almost there when the signs of civilization start sputtering out around you, replaced by larger and larger tracts of billowy sand.

Your real journey begins at the edge of the largest dunes, just outside of Merzouga. From here on out, you'll be on camel and on foot. The excitement is palpable as you cover your head and body from the blistering sun in preparation for your trek, your guides teaching you the art of making a turban from a scarf. When the camels are brought around and loaded, their soft grunts and groans fill the air as they heave themselves, rider and all, six feet or more into the air on sinewy long legs.

You'll trek in a long line toward your camp, making photo-worthy shadows on the sand as the sun begins its slow descent, lighting up the dunes with bright shades of titian and scarlet. If you look closely enough at the sand around you, you'll see evidence of life: bugs that skitter here and there, prints of foxes and feral cats that come out at night. As the final drops of color fade from the evening light, you'll arrive at your camp: a circle of canvas tents around a fire pit.

As nomads have known for centuries, camp is one of the best things about the desert. Even for a night, it's home. This is where you'll eat delicious *tajine* (comfort food, named for the earthenware pot it's made in, that is the staple of Moroccan cooking), smoke pungent flavored tobacco from a hookah—a contraption that's straight out of *Alice in Wonderland*—and dance around a fire to the beating of drums and the clanging of hand cymbals meant to imitate the shackles that once held the Gnawa people captive.

You may never want to leave the circle, but you won't want to miss what's waiting for you on the other side of it: a night walk into the dunes for some of the best stargazing you've ever seen in your life. As your guides lead you up the steep sand, they'll regale you with tales of what it's like to be a modern nomad, which most of them are.

As the light of the campfire gets farther and farther away, the stars get closer and closer, until they're so big and bright you're positive you could reach out and touch them. There's nothing for miles save camels, bugs, cats, foxes and scattered camps. Sit down in the rapidly cooling sand at the top of the dunes and take it all in. (Most guides will give you at least half an hour to lose yourself in your surroundings.) When the incessant beating of a far-off drum reaches your ears, you'll swear that you're a thousand years in the past, just another nomad setting out to traverse the largest desert in the world, ready for the journey of a lifetime instead of the next day's long drive back to Marrakesh.

On the Trail

ROUTE: Varies

DISTANCE: About 700 miles (1,125 km) by vehicle; 5 miles (8 km) by camel; 1 mile (1.6 km) on foot—all round-trip

ELEVATION GAIN/LOSS: +/-493 feet (+/-150 m) or so for the night walk

AVERAGE TIME: 3 days for the trip, 2 hours for the night walk

SEASON: Mid-September to mid-May

DIFFICULTY: Moderate

START: Marrakesh, Morocco, for the trip; Erg Chebbi dunes, Morocco, for the night walk

END: Erg Chebbi dunes, Morocco, for the night walk; Marrakesh, Morocco, for the trip

---

Moderate: Although the Sahara Desert night walk isn't very long—typically 1 mile (1.6 km) round-trip—walking up steep sand dunes in loose sand can be relatively strenuous. Stop often for breaks to catch your breath and to take in everything around you.

A day-and-a-half drive from Marrakesh through the Dadès Valley takes you to the edge of the Sahara at Merzouga. From there, a camel ride brings you to a camp at the Erg Chebbi dunes, where you make a night walk into the star-filled desert.

Start: The closest airport is Marrakesh Menara Airport, just outside the city. To save yourself the chaos of the taxi stand, as well as the confusion of trying to navigate the maze-like streets, I recommend arranging an airport transfer in advance through your accommodations. Then visit the city center and settle on a tour company.

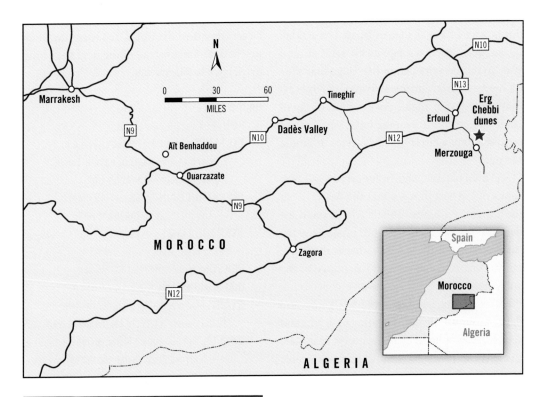

If the busyness and chaos of Marrakesh starts to get to you, escape to the Jardin Majorelle (see Resources), an urban oasis of calm. This two-and-a-half-acre botanical garden is as peaceful as can be—the perfect spot to meander, read a book and relax.

The morning of your trip, you can expect to be picked up (and dropped off again) from your accommodations. Although the Sahara Desert night walk can be done in one night, the full three-day trip itinerary looks like what's shown in the suggested stages below.

Suggested stages:

Day 1: Drive from Marrakesh to Dadès Valley, sightseeing along the way and staying overnight in Dadès Valley, about 230 miles (370 km)

Day 2: Drive from Dadès Valley to Merzouga, about 120 miles (190 km), sightseeing along the way; ride a camel to Erg Chebbi desert camp, 2.5 miles (4 km); embark on night walk in Erg Chebbi dunes, 1 mile (1.6 km) round-trip; stay overnight in desert camp

Day 3: Ride a camel from Erg Chebbi desert camp to Merzouga, 2.5 miles (4 km); drive from Merzouga to Marrakesh, about 350 miles (560 km)

Is it worth three days and 700 miles (1,125 km) of driving to experience the Sahara Desert by camel and on foot at night, even briefly? Yes! This is one of the coolest walks I've ever done, and I know you'll love it too. If you're not on a tight schedule, check out "Tip" for ideas on extending your time in the desert.

Signage: There is no signage in the desert, so always walk with an experienced guide.

Accommodations: When you're on a tour, you'll likely stay in a family-owned hotel in the Dadès Valley the first night and a canvas tent in the desert the second night; your tour company will make all of the arrangements.

If you spend more time exploring Morocco, you'll also have the opportunity to stay in a *riad*, a family-owned small guesthouse that's built around an open-air courtyard—the most common type of accommodations in Morocco. There are hundreds to choose from in Marrakesh alone. It can be a tough choice because they all seem about the same: simple and cheap. This is where reviews come in really handy. If you're arranging your accommodations through Booking.com, I recommend looking only at places that have been rated nine stars and above. You'll still find good deals, but you'll also be more likely to find a few luxuries (comfier beds, quieter rooms) that will be well worth the money. And it's worth it to splurge for a good location—Marrakesh can be a very confusing city to navigate on foot, so staying somewhere central and easy to find is really important.

Tip: It's hard to relax into desert life when you're on a tight schedule, so do what I did: Book yourself a three-day tour so you have transportation to the desert—with stops at all of the best places along the way—and a night at the desert camp with your group. But when your group loads up in the van for the ride back to Marrakesh, stay in Merzouga and transfer to other accommodations. There are several luxury camps in the area—I loved Moda Camp (see Resources)—where you can stay for an additional few days. You'll travel to these camps from Merzouga by camel. Whenever you're ready to head back to Marrakesh, take an intercity bus from Merzouga.

Make it shorter: For more control over your time in the desert, consider hiring a private guide instead of going with a group. A private guide can customize the trip to your specifications and provide modifications such as a night camel ride instead of a walk. Because

The huts you can rent in the Erg Chebbi dunes of Morocco's Sahara Desert range from very basic to downright luxurious.

travel is relatively cheap in Morocco, it won't even set you back much.

Return: The three-day tour includes transportation back to Marrakesh with a drop-off at your accommodations. If you stay longer in Merzouga, you can take an intercity bus from Merzouga to Marrakesh without transfers.

Other Activities Nearby

There are also tours of the Erg Chebbi dunes, with variations in the sightseeing along the way, that leave from Fez, Morocco.

To see a completely different side of Morocco—the ocean—take a trip to the town of Essaouira. This calm coastal village is very relaxed—picture long walks on the beach, watching the sun go down from a rooftop deck and eating all the fresh seafood you can stomach. Bonus: The locals here are also relaxed, so you'll get to wander through the markets to your heart's content without being given the hard sell.

More Information

For a good firsthand account of a Sahara Desert tour, check out Lauren Juliff's helpful article at *Never Ending Footsteps* (see Resources), which also gives suggestions on how to book a good tour (either in advance or once you arrive).

CHAPTER 4

MAKE A FINAL DECISION

Knowing what experience you're going for and what trails are out there is half the battle in choosing the right trail. The other half is gathering enough information on individual trails to be able to decide if there's a match and if there are enough resources (for instance, detailed route information or maps) to make walking that dream trail a reality for you.

But the value of good information doesn't stop there. The information and resources you unearth will also inform all of your planning, everything from arranging transportation to the trailhead to making reservations at accommodations along the way. Chapters 2 and 3 provide resources for finding good trails. Now it's time to learn how to find more-detailed information on individual trails you're interested in walking.

DO YOUR RESEARCH

For a lot of trails—especially popular ones—it's not difficult to find good information. You'll be treated to everything from detailed trip reports to downloadable GPX tracks to full guidebooks. A good example is the Camino de Santiago—Walk 2, English Way. When it comes to researching the Camino, there's so much free information available online that the challenge actually becomes sifting through it all.

The farther off the beaten path you want to walk, the more creative you'll need to be in your research. Bavaria's King Ludwig's Way (Walk 9) now has a lot of great information available online and in English nonetheless, but when I originally walked it, all I had to go by were two rudimentary websites of incomplete (and oftentimes contradictory) information. And did I mention that everything was in German?

Putting some good effort into this information-gathering step will pay off. I promise. The more you know about a particular trail up front, the more likely you are to have a good experience walking it.

For peaceful forest walking with a good dose of WWII history, look no further than Luxembourg and Belgium's Escapardenne Eisleck Trail. (Photo © Escapardenne Eisleck Trail)

The opposite is also true. I can attest to that—I regularly scout European trails that not much has been published about in the hopes of revealing these hidden treasures to walkers everywhere and making them more accessible. One time I scouted a trail that I had discovered in a decades-old British newspaper article. The write-up was pretty bare-bones but it mentioned two daily stages of 11 and 13 miles (18 and 21 km). When I walked the trail, those daily stages ballooned to 22 and 26 miles (35 and 42 km), respectively, which made for two very long days—and a couple of very (understandably) grumpy walking companions.

Don't let my double-mileage trail debacle happen to you. Whenever possible, verify the trail information you come across by cross-referencing it with other materials.

The next two sections cover the types of resources I recommend for researching trails.

General Resources

Internet search: The best way to start your search for good trail information is with a general Internet search. Plug the trail name, such as "King Ludwig's Way," into your favorite search engine. I also recommend searching "walking/hiking (insert the name of the trail)." The results of your search are important for a couple of different reasons. They will inform you about the extent of the resources that are available for that specific trail—a good indication of whether you're going to have an easy or a hard time with your research. They will also reveal individual resources that you can dive into for more information.

Official trail website: If the trail you want to walk has a website, you're in luck, because this is often one of the best sources of trail information out there. You'll likely have access to everything from detailed descriptions of the daily stages to photos of what you'll see on trail to links to more information. Have a question that's not answered on the website? Oftentimes an email address will be provided for queries.

Guidebooks: If you can get your hands on a good guidebook for the trail you're interested in, do it. A good guidebook is worth its weight in gold—it's one of the best purchases you'll make for your trip. It will help you with everything from understanding what each day on trail will look like—including detailed descriptions, maps and elevation profiles—to what to keep in mind while planning for that specific route: packing suggestions, weather information and even phone numbers for accommodations that can't be found online. The most comprehensive guidebooks also contain cultural and language basics.

To find a guidebook, do an Internet search or check your favorite travel store, bookstore or online retailer. I really enjoy Cicerone guidebooks—although they cover a wide variety of European trails, they're published in the United Kingdom, so they're written in English and the quality is very good. Here's my top advice for buying a guidebook:

Choose the right one: Guidebooks are written for different audiences and experiences, so make sure you get one that suits what you're trying to do. Whenever possible, look for a walking-specific book. Also aim for a book that goes into sufficient depth to be helpful.

Always buy the most up-to-date version: Old guidebooks are cheaper but may lack crucial updates that could make or break your trip.

Go light: I love paging through paper guidebooks—they make really good trip mementos—but they're hard to pack around. You can cut down your pack weight if you carry only photocopies or tear-outs of applicable sections that you'll need on trail, take photos of your guidebook and store them on your cell phone, or buy an e-book.

Want to carry *Explore Europe on Foot* with you while you travel? Check out the e-book version (see Resources). I've also written (e-book) route guides for several of my handpicked trails—see Resources for details.

Tourist information offices: Just as the helpful folks at your destination's tourist information office can help you find out what trails are available, they can often point you to local brochures and publications with more-detailed information about individual trails—and will often send or email them to you free of charge. To find a particular tourist information office online, search the Internet for "visit (insert destination name)" or "tourist information (insert destination name)."

Tour companies' websites: For information on daily stages, route descriptions and sample itineraries, tour companies' websites can be really helpful. Sometimes these sites also offer informational brochures on trails that they feature, either free of charge or for a small fee that will be credited back to your account if you book a tour at a later date.

Blogs and personal websites: Reading about a trail from someone who's hiked it is very beneficial—it can give you all sorts of important details on what the trail is really like. Also, bloggers tend to give more personal and less whitewashed advice than organizations officially trying to promote a trail. Bonus: You can often ask these people specific questions via the comments section or an email.

Friends and family: Ask around to see if any of your friends or family have done the trail you're interested in. When I was researching the Tour du Mont Blanc, I knew a former coworker of mine had done it a few years before, so I was able to ask for her overall impressions and recommendations.

Hiking or walking clubs: The odds of finding people who have walked the trails you're interested in go way up if you're in a hiking or walking club at home. For more information on finding a group like that, check out Chapter 5, Find (the Right) Adventure Companions.

Speaking and/or reading the language of the place you want to walk makes the research process a lot easier—you'll be able to quickly access non-English, locals-only information. Don't speak the local language? Try copying and pasting trail descriptions and other information into Google Translate or install a browser add-on that translates websites automatically.

Specific Websites and Apps

Traildino: This website has a variety of resources for individual trails, including trail descriptions and links to guidebooks, maps and GPX tracks (see Chapter 16, Electronic Tools).

Wikiloc: If you're looking for downloadable GPX tracks (see Chapter 16, Electronic Tools), this free site is a great place to get them.

Wikipedia: For general trail descriptions and occasionally even information on daily stages, Wikipedia is a good resource.

Wikitravel: This website's trail selection isn't very good, but it has really helped me in the past with a couple of very off-the-beaten-path trails.

Google Maps and Google Earth: You can mine a lot of information from Google Maps and Google Earth, including the prevalence of towns, restaurants and accommodations on your intended route—and how much wilderness versus civilization you're getting yourself into. Want to see what your guesthouse or restaurant choices look like in real life? Check out the satellite view.

See Resources for all of the above.

CHOOSE A TRAIL

Once you've gathered all of the information you need to make your decision—you're certain that a trail matches your needs, and it meets the deal breaker criteria in the sidebar in Chapter 1, Understand What's Ideal for You—it's time to make it official. This is really exciting! It's also the step that everything else covered in this book hinges on, so choose wisely. The trail choice you make today will inform the memories you'll make in the not-so-distant future. Good luck!

If you're having trouble independently planning a walk that meets all of your needs, consider hiring a walking company to customize a trail experience for you. For a fee, they'll ask for all of your needs and preferences—and then present you with a trip plan that matches what you're looking for. Check out Chapter 6, Walk Independently or Hire Help, for more information.

PART 2
PLANNING

Many of the trails in Europe, especially those in Switzerland, are signed in time, not distance.

Once you've decided on the right trail, it's time to start tackling everything you'll need to do to make it happen. Planning a big trip can be intimidating—there are so many things to think about!—but Part 2 takes this topic nice and slow, going through everything step by step. Before you know it, you'll have your trip all planned. Chapter by chapter, Part 2 covers finding travel companions, hiring help, planning your transportation, finding a place to stay, training for the trail, being prepared for anything and making your walk a cultural experience.

But before we go any further, let's talk about timing. To some degree, the trail you choose will determine how far in advance you need to plan. Very popular trails like Iceland's Laugavegur Trek (Walk 14) book up far in advance, so you'll have the best chance of finding somewhere to stay if you reserve your space a year before you intend to walk. For other trails, you're fine to plan—and book—anywhere from a few months to a few weeks in advance.

I suggest giving yourself as much time to plan as possible, even if the trail you're going to walk doesn't demand it. Transportation and accommodations will be cheaper if they're reserved earlier, you'll have a better selection of everything from plane tickets to guesthouses, and there won't be stressful last-minute surprises (or fewer, anyway), such as finding out that all of the rooms on your route are already booked. Plus, planning is fun! It's said there are three phases to enjoying an experience—anticipating it, experiencing it and reminiscing about it—so don't miss out on this opportunity to anticipate your trip by planning it. You might be surprised how much you enjoy it. So dive in!

To keep you on track in the months leading up to your big trip, I've developed a couple of checklists of high-level tasks you'll need to accomplish and a timeline for getting them done. So without further ado, let's get started. It's time to plan that trip!

CHECKLISTS: PLANNING

✓ Six Months to a Year in Advance

- ☐ Decide on a trail.
- ☐ Order a passport if you don't already have one.
- ☐ Apply for a visa if you need one.
- ☐ Make sure your smartphone is unlocked and GSM-compatible (see Cell Phone Service in Chapter 16, Electronic Tools) if you plan to use it in Europe (some carriers may not unlock your phone if you haven't had their service for at least a year).
- ☐ Optional: Find a travel companion.
- ☐ Optional: Make a reservation with a tour company.
- ☐ Finalize your itinerary, taking into consideration ground transportation to and from the trailhead.
- ☐ Buy your plane tickets, including short domestic flights.
- ☐ Book your accommodations, if you're going on a popular trail or in high season.
- ☐ Optional: Purchase trip insurance.
- ☐ Start a training program.

TRIP INSURANCE

Trip insurance (also called travel insurance) is an excellent way to safeguard your expenses if you're planning a big trip. It can be especially important if you or anyone you'll be traveling with has a health condition that could change. It's also a good idea if you have other uncertainties in your life—potential changes in your work commitments or in any family members you provide care for—or in case any kind of emergency crops up.

I learned the hard way how important it can be to have trip insurance. When I was in Europe on one of my walking trips, my flight from Edinburgh to Paris was cancelled due to an air traffic controller strike. The airline couldn't rebook me for five days but I needed to get to Paris by the next morning for my flight back home to the United States. So as much as it hurt, I had to cough up $400 for a last-minute Eurostar ticket. I got a $50 refund for my cancelled flight, but when the dust settled, I was still out $350 that I hadn't counted on. Ouch! I wish I'd had trip insurance.

Some credit cards offer trip insurance as a standard cardholder benefit. If yours doesn't, compare insurance plans online, such as at an aggregator like InsureMyTrip (see Resources). At a minimum, the right policy will include the following:

- Trip cancellation insurance: Covers reimbursement of prepaid trip expenses (for example, flights and accommodations) if you have a covered reason for canceling your trip before it starts
- Missed departure insurance: Covers meals, lodging and/or additional transportation costs if you miss a connection to a flight, cruise, et cetera, for a covered reason
- Travel delay insurance: Covers meals, lodging and/or additional transportation costs if your travels (for example, a flight) are delayed for a covered reason
- Luggage insurance: Covers reimbursement of lost or stolen luggage

Beautiful Chamonix, France, is a great place to explore before embarking on the Tour du Mont Blanc. (Photo by Cheryl Nilson)

What if you don't have six months to plan your trip—you only have two months, or even just a few weeks? Don't worry! Depending on the trail you've chosen, your base level of fitness and the availability of accommodations, you may still be able to pull off your big trip. First things first: Check what accommodations are available. Once you've verified that there are available beds or rooms, next check for plane tickets and ground transportation. You may have to pay a premium for booking at the last minute, but as long as you can find somewhere to sleep and a way to get there, you should be able to make that trip happen, so start booking!

✔ Three Months in Advance

- ☐ Buy your train and/or bus tickets.
- ☐ Book your accommodations, if you're not going on a really popular trail or you're walking outside of the main season.
- ☐ Book any additional services, adventures and activities.
- ☐ Start studying up on the local culture.
- ☐ Purchase any remaining gear, including an international SIM card if that's how you're going to get cell phone service in Europe.

✔ One Month in Advance

- ☐ Verify that your health insurance company will cover you while you're in Europe, or purchase international health insurance for the time you'll be gone (see the International Health Insurance sidebar in Chapter 15, Trail and Travel Tools).

CHAPTER 5

FIND (THE RIGHT) ADVENTURE COMPANIONS

Once you have the perfect trail in mind, it's time to start thinking about who you want to share the experience with. The right travel partner can make or break your trip. That person can mean the difference between sharing a bottle of wine at the end of a rewarding day on trail—or needing something stronger to get you through another day. There are three main options when it comes to companionship: going with someone you know, adventuring by yourself and traveling with strangers.

GOING WITH SOMEONE YOU KNOW

Most people who explore Europe on foot travel with someone they know. There are real benefits to bringing along a friend or family member. To start with, there is safety in numbers—and often-times cost savings. (Two can often travel for the cost of one and a half.) It's also a great opportunity to spend more time with someone you already really enjoy, whether that's your partner, mother or best friend. And you won't just have fun together on trail. Think about the months and weeks leading up to your trip. When you travel with someone, you get to share the anticipation of the trip with that person. You have someone to accompany you on shopping excursions and to travel lectures, someone who's just as excited about what's coming up as you are.

When Mac and I were getting ready for our grand tour of Europe, we had a date night every week to plan our adventure. Some nights we'd get cozy on the couch to watch a travel show together, vigorously taking notes when we came across things we wanted to do. Other nights we'd do trial runs with our gear, putting everything on and walking to the gym a couple miles away, where we'd weigh the latest version of our kit. Those trip date nights were full of planning, dreaming and

Walking partners don't always have the same pace—and that's okay as long as you tackle the trail in a way that works for both of you. (Photo by Roger Ward/Flickr)

togetherness—and they're some of my fondest memories of the whole trip.

When you travel with someone you know, you don't just have someone to anticipate the trip with, you also have someone to help you celebrate the highs and weather the lows of the trip. And once it's over, you'll spend the next few years remembering it together. All of that can be really amazing.

But sometimes it's not, and that's where things get tricky. You see, not everyone travels well together. Just because you get along with your cousin or your coworker at home doesn't mean that you'll gel on the road. If you're an early riser who loves to jump out of bed and hit the ground running but your companion needs an hour to wake up and read the news before leisurely starting preparations for the day, you

could run into some issues. The gap between you and your adventure companion can widen even further when it comes to active travel. Not everyone likes the same amount of physical challenge. You might have no problem walking 10 miles a day, but maybe your spouse doesn't have any fun after 5 miles.

All of this is food for thought. Exploring on foot with someone you already know can make the experience that much better—as long as you're smart about who you go with.

Tips for Choosing an Adventure Companion

Here are my tips for choosing the right adventure companion:

Choose someone you travel well with. If you're not sure how the two of you would travel together, go away for a test weekend. While you're traveling, ask yourself: Do you both enjoy the same kinds of activities? Is it easy to compromise with this person? To what degree are each of you open to new experiences? Is your energy level about the same? Can you talk to this person for days on end? Is this someone you can have companionable silence with? At the end of the weekend, you should have your answer.

Choose someone you walk well with. To really enjoy exploring Europe on foot together, it helps if the two of you are at about the same fitness level and enjoy the same kinds of walks. Make sure you can agree on daily mileages and difficulty levels, but don't worry if you walk at slightly different paces; almost every pair I've encountered does. Just put the slower person up front so they can set the group pace and not fall behind. For other tips on walking well together, check out the When Your Walking Companions Are Slower Than You Are sidebar in Chapter 10, Be Prepared for Anything.

Stay on the same page. Although it's quite common for one person in every pair to be the planner, make sure you are both on the same page about your trip and the experiences you're seeking. Plan activities that both people will enjoy—and don't be afraid to try something new to accommodate the other person. You might just surprise yourself by liking something you didn't expect you would. When Mac and I were traveling together, he added to our list the Running of the Bulls in Pamplona, Spain. Truth be told, I wasn't excited about it. But it turned out to be an amazingly authentic cultural experience and celebration of the local people; I'm so glad I didn't miss it because of my preconceived notions. The same thing could happen to you.

Traveling with Young Children

Exploring Europe on foot with children isn't just possible—it's also completely doable (and totally fun), with a few key considerations and adjustments. The two biggest things you need to think about when you're walking with young children are the physical challenges and the mental challenges of the trail.

Walking for several hours can be really daunting for a child, especially a small one. Just think of their short little legs and how much harder they have to work to keep up with an adult! A conservative estimate is that a healthy, active kid is typically capable of walking the mileage of half of their age, assuming there's not a lot of elevation gain. That means you could reasonably expect a five-year-old to walk 2.5 miles (4 km) by themselves just fine; an eight-year-old should be able to cover 4 miles (6.4 km). Things start to change when a child reaches ten years of age—by that point, many kids' limbs have lengthened and strengthened to the point that they can walk much farther. Regardless of how old your child is and whether you're prepared to carry them and their belongings when they're tired (this is easy with a very small child but much harder when your kid no longer fits in a carrier), you'll need to adapt your chosen trail to what your child is physically capable of.

Also be mindful of the mental challenges your child will have on trail. Not all kids,

Avoid a meltdown on trail with a few key considerations and adjustments for small children. (Photo by Seth Stoll/Flickr)

CAN I BRING MY DOG?

I don't recommend bringing your dog. Fido may be your favorite walking companion, but there are a lot of bureaucratic hurdles to clear when it comes to getting your pet to Europe—getting your dog microchipped, getting a checkup from your vet exactly ten days before you travel and sending that info to the US Department of Agriculture, booking a cargo flight (which most airlines won't do in the summer) or packing your dog under your airline seat, enduring the questioning of annoyed customs officials. Even if you manage to do all that, you could still have a hard time finding accommodations that will welcome your four-legged friend. Your best bet: Take your dog on a big walk—or backpacking trip—closer to home.

especially young ones, have the attention span and patience to enjoy walking—or being in a carrier—for long periods of time. I like to recommend the Disneyland test: if your child can easily withstand a full day at Disneyland, they could be ready for a full day on trail—try a couple of long walks at home just to be sure. Regardless of how old or mature your child is, you'll still need to tweak your ideal trail experience for it to be interesting to them. After all, most kids just aren't interested in the same things adults are. They may not care about art, history or culture. What they want to see and experience is much more tactile: cool bugs, gigantic birds, furry critters—even other kids. So make sure to plan activities that they'll enjoy, whether it's geocaching, trail bingo, wildflower identification or playground time with local kiddos.

> One of the easiest ways to adapt your trail experience to match what your young child is physically and mentally capable of is to plan a trip that's flexible. Rather than walking a long trail that has concrete daily stages, consider home-basing in one town and doing a variety of half-day or daylong walks from there. Because you'll leave most of your belongings at your accommodations, you'll have extra capacity to carry your little one when necessary, as well as the flexibility to choose shorter or longer walks each day based on how things are going.

Traveling with Older Kids

While traveling with older children—those in middle school or high school—is considerably easier than traveling with young kids, you'll still need to make some adjustments to your trip to make sure everyone has a good time. One of the best things you can do early on to ensure a great trip is to give older kids some ownership of the trip and a role in the planning process. Each child who's old enough can help with a different aspect of the trip research, whether it's as simple as figuring out what local delicacies can't be missed or as complex as cherry-picking accommodations that fit everyone's needs—and the family budget. When traveling with older kids, the more you can plan—and decide on—together, the more successful your trip will be.

> Want even more tips on traveling internationally with kids? World Travel Family (see Resources) is a great resource that can help you plan the perfect trip. It has articles and personal recommendations from a family that has been backpacking around the world for several years.

ADVENTURING BY YOURSELF

While it's wonderful to travel with someone you know, sometimes the best adventure companion for you is, well, you.

WALK INDEPENDENTLY OR HIRE HELP

As you and your walking companion(s) start to plan your trip, you'll need to decide whether you want to plan and walk independently or if you'd like some help. Lucky for you, there are many companies eager to make your trip a little—or a lot—easier, whether that means something as simple as transporting your luggage or as complex as taking over all of the planning and logistics so you can just show up and walk. Depending on the amount of help you'd like, your trip will fall into one of four main categories: walking independently, walking independently using supplemental services, taking a self-guided walking tour of an established itinerary or going on a guided walking tour. I'll cover each of them in turn.

WALKING INDEPENDENTLY

Thanks to the availability of good trail information and well-signed nontechnical trails in Europe, it's entirely possible (for most routes) to plan your own trip and walk the trail without the help of a company or service. There are many benefits to walking independently.

The biggest is that it's the most affordable way to explore on foot. You'll pay the lowest amount possible for your accommodations and meals because they won't be marked up for the benefit of a middleman, you'll avoid additional fees for services such as guides and luggage transfer, and you'll even save on tips since you won't be hiring services that would require them.

There are other benefits beyond the economic ones. Walking independently is the most flexible way to travel—you won't be constrained by others' schedules or itineraries. And if you're on a trail that has plenty of places to stop, you don't have to be limited by your own itinerary either. Rather

If you are using a luggage transfer service or walking with a guided tour, you can pack a few extra creature comforts.

than having a fixed destination each day, you can take the trail as it comes and stop walking whenever it feels right.

All of these benefits can be pretty darn nice. There's just one caveat to walking independently: it does require a bit more work. You'll be in charge of everything from booking your airfare to reserving your accommodations to carrying all of your own belongings—pack light (see Part 3, Packing)! It's also your job to learn everything you need to know about the trail and be a good guide for yourself once you're walking.

All of that work is totally doable. And for those who like being the master of their own adventures, it's also fun. When I explore Europe on foot, I usually walk independently. This book is designed to teach you how to do the same. So if you're certain you want to walk independently and that you don't need any of the supplemental services covered in the next section (spoiler alert: they're pretty enticing!),

FREE INFORMATION FROM TOUR COMPANIES

Even if you're walking independently, tour companies are helpful resources for planning your trip. Most of them offer a wealth of information online for the walking trails they feature in their tours, from route descriptions to photos of what you'll see along the way. My favorite thing to use them for is itinerary planning: On trails that don't have a lot of information on daily stages, I look to see where tour companies stop for the night. I also pay attention to what sections of the trail, if any, tour companies skip over. They usually indicate road walking, undesirable scenery or daily stages that are too long for the average person—all information that comes in handy when you're planning your own time on trail.

skip ahead to Chapter 7, Get There, to continue building your dream trip.

WALKING INDEPENDENTLY USING SUPPLEMENTAL SERVICES

Even if you're determined to plan and walk on your own, there are a variety of supplemental services that you can add to your trip to make it easier, more fun or more comfortable. Four specific kinds of services will be most helpful for you on trail: luggage transfer, private transport (between your accommodations and the trailhead or other places you want to see), private guides and urban walking tours. Because these services are offered piecemeal, you can choose which of them to utilize.

But that's not all. You also have the flexibility of choosing how often you want to use each service. Maybe you want your luggage transferred every day but you only need a taxi once—you can do that. Want a private guide for two out of the six days you're walking? You can have that too. Because these supplemental services are also quite affordable, they're a prime example of how little money it can take to vastly improve your happiness on trail. This section covers each of these supplemental services in more depth.

Even if you don't think you'll need supplemental services, it's always good to know what's available on your chosen trail and keep those phone numbers in your back pocket. You never know when a particularly challenging stretch of trail or a change in circumstances might lead you to reconsider.

Luggage Transfer

For those who are staying somewhere new every day—and packing their belongings from one town to another—luggage transfer is a great service. When you hire someone to transfer your luggage, they drive your main bag containing all your clothes and nighttime supplies—toothbrush, pajamas, electrical chargers, et cetera—to your next accommodations while you're walking. That means all you have to carry on trail is a light day pack. This is an especially great option if (1) you have physical issues like a bad back or bad knees that prevent you from carrying much weight, (2) you're attempting particularly challenging daily stages, (3) you want to walk faster or farther than you could with a large pack or (4) you suddenly realize you did not actually pack as lightly as you'd thought (oops!).

How it works: My friend Mitzi and I had been walking Scotland's West Highland Way (Walk 13) for several days when we came upon a flyer in a pub advertising £5 luggage transfer. We decided it'd be perfect for our final and most challenging trail day, so that night we called the service provider to arrange pickup for the next day. It was quite easy—he told us to leave the bag we wanted shuttled (we combined all of our heavy things into one bag) in our guesthouse's luggage room with our names, the delivery address and £5 secured to it and promised that it would be at our next guesthouse by 4:00 p.m. When we got there after that very long day on trail, sweaty and tired, the first thing we saw was our bag—safely delivered and waiting for us. It was the best £5 we spent all trip.

With luggage transfer, you typically pay per bag, so you and your hiking companion(s) can save money by combining your heavy items into one big bag to be shuttled.

How to do it right:

- Bring a lightweight day pack for the things you'll carry on trail, as well as a

When it comes to Europe's many Caminos, all routes lead to the Cathedral of Santiago de Compostela. (Photo by Elentir/Flickr)

resealable plastic bag and twist tie for affixing your contact information, delivery address and the fee to your bag.

- Hire someone legitimate: look online for reviews by previous customers.
- If having your luggage transferred is a deal breaker for you, make sure to book it before you leave home.
- If you arrange the service last minute, do it no later than the night before you want your bag shuttled; earlier is better.
- Let your accommodations proprietor know that someone will be coming to get your bag.

How to find it:

- Do an Internet search for "luggage transfer" and the trail name.
- Ask the local tourist information office.
- Look for brochures at your accommodations, especially if you're staying where a

lot of other walkers stay, such as a guesthouse or hostel.

- Ask the proprietor of your accommodations for a recommendation.

How much it costs: Luggage transfer is usually not expensive. Count on between €7 and €20 per day, depending on how many bags you want transported and the distance they'll travel.

Private Transportation

You can hire someone, whether a guesthouse's shuttle vehicle, a taxi or private vehicle service, to drive you around, typically between where you're staying and the trailhead or other places in the region you want to see. These kinds of private transportation services can be really important if public transportation (bus or train) isn't available for that area or if it's too inconvenient to schedule around. Private transportation is especially good when you're modifying a trail's daily stages so you can walk shorter or longer distances, when you can't find available or affordable accommodations near the trail or when you want to skip sections of the route.

How it works: When Mac and I were researching Spain's English Way (Walk 2), one particular daily stage didn't sound enjoyable. It was really long, there was quite a bit of elevation gain and the last third of it was a giant hill. I had a feeling there would be a mutiny if we did it in one day, and we weren't in a rush anyway, so I broke the one megastage into two days of walking with the help of private transportation—a guesthouse owner who advertised a free pickup and drop-off service to entice walkers in the region to stay at his place. When we arrived at the base of the hill, we called him from a pub. He picked us up twenty minutes later, drove us up the hill to his establishment and then the next morning drove us back down to where we'd left off walking. It was perfect—we tackled that hill on fresh legs and even got to walk without our backpacks for a few hours, since we could leave them at the guesthouse and pick them up as we walked by later in the morning. Thanks to private transportation, we turned one potentially exhausting day into two completely enjoyable days on trail.

How to do it right and find it: Let's look at the three primary options for private transport.

Accommodations Vehicle

- Ask about the possibility of getting a ride—and any fees that you would incur—when you book your room.
- If your accommodations owner goes out of their way to give you a ride, show your gratitude with a "thank you" and a €1–€2 tip.

Taxi

- If you need a ride to or from a particularly small town or remote spot, arrange your taxi hours or even days in advance.
- Use a licensed taxi whenever possible; I always look for a big taxi-company logo and/or name and phone number clearly posted on the outside of the cab. Find a licensed cab at a taxi stand, through the local tourist information office or by asking your accommodations proprietor or concierge.
- Make sure your driver uses a meter. Rates should be clearly posted in the cab. There are usually different rates for weekdays, evenings and weekends.
- If your driver won't use a meter (sometimes there are set fees for standard trips), make sure you establish a price up front and be sure to ask about any additional costs such as tolls.
- If you call a taxi in Europe, the driver will often start the meter when they get the call and head in your direction, so don't be surprised when they pick you up and there's already a balance accruing.

Private Vehicle Services

- Uber isn't as prevalent in Europe as it is in North America—especially in small towns—so check online to see if it's available where you're traveling (see Resources).
- Check to see if similar private vehicle services are available in the country you want to visit, such as mytaxi in Germany and eight other European countries, HopOnn in the United Kingdom or Cabify in Spain and Portugal.

How much it costs: The cost of private transport can vary widely in Europe. In Portugal, the standard fare is €1 per kilometer (0.6 mile); in other countries, the rate can be double or triple that. There's typically a minimum charge. You should always be prepared to pay with cash. Know what to expect in advance with the help of World Taximeter (see Resources), which lists estimated taxi fares for larger cities. If Uber is available where you're traveling, plug your intended route into the app for a fare estimate.

Private Trail Guide

When you hire a private trail guide, you'll have someone to lead you on a walk and narrate the journey, either for one day or several days. If hired as a supplemental service (meaning you didn't book your trip through this guide service), your guide may pack a lunch for you and drive you to and from the trailhead on the day of your guided hike, but they won't handle the greater logistics of your trip (for instance, your accommodations). Private trail guides are especially great if you love learning the details of a trail as you walk (flora and fauna, history and geology, et cetera), as well as interesting tidbits about the local culture. They can also be an excellent choice if you want to do a day or two of walking without any trail research or planning, if you want to walk in a place that requires more technical knowledge or language skills than you possess or if you want to find hidden-gem trails that are known only to locals.

Want to find those hole-in-the-wall restaurants? You know, the ones with mouthwatering food that only the locals know about? Ask your guide!

How it works: When I was walking Germany's Moselsteig Trail (part of Walk 10, The Moselle), I was lucky enough to get a guided tour of the world's steepest vineyard from Andy Offinger, a local trail guide who is also the friend of a friend. During our time on trail, Andy explained so many things that I would've otherwise completely missed: from the meaning of the heart-shaped ties of the grapevines (a local tradition) to the practicalities of harvesting grapes in such steep conditions, to the challenges local farmers face when it comes to wild boars. It was fascinating! And when we finally made it to the top of the steep ridge we were walking, laddering and cabling our way up, Andy pulled out a chilled bottle of local wine to share. Huge props there! Andy's tour turned what would've been a good trail day into something extra cool and special—one of my all-time favorite days on trail.

How to do it right:
- Check out Finding a Good Tour Guide or Company later in this chapter for the baseline due diligence you should give every potential guide, as well as what you should additionally look for in a trail guide.
- When you book, be sure your private trail guide understands your level of fitness, how much of a physical challenge you're looking for and whether you have any health concerns that could be a problem on trail.
- Know exactly what's included in your tour: lunch, transportation, et cetera.
- Pack everything you need to be comfortable on trail for the day, including comfortable shoes, good layers (including a rain jacket), sunscreen and plenty of water.

How to find it:
- Search the Internet for "hiking guide" or "walking guide" and the name of your trail or destination.

Urban walking tours are a great way to learn more about the history of the cities you're passing through.

- Contact the mountain guide agency, alpine center or mountain guide office at your destination for a list of certified guides.
- Contact a local hiking or walking club for suggestions on prolific walkers who also guide.
- Ask the local tourist information office or your accommodations proprietor or concierge for a recommendation.

How much it costs: You can count on paying €150–€300 per day for a private trail guide for two people.

Urban Walking Tour

One of my favorite ways to supplement my time on trail is to take a guided urban walking tour that dives into the history and major sights of the towns I pass through along the way. Although not all towns have them (especially very small ones), a surprising number do. They're usually about two hours long and

include 1–2 miles (1.6–3.2 km) of walking; most have anywhere between five and fifty participants. Some of them include a sampler of information about a particular town, from history to current affairs to major sights, whereas others are themed. You might sign up for a ghost tour, a literary tour or even a foodie tour.

A really great category of urban walking tours has recently cropped up: free ones. In actuality, these tours are more pay-what-you-want than completely free, but they tend to be very good because the quality of the experience determines how big the participants' tips will be. Sometimes you can also find short self-guided urban tours, in which you follow a brochure's descriptions of the city's sights.

Urban walking tours are especially great for those who love stories and want to discover more about the towns they pass through. They're also amazing for those who prefer to spend the majority of their time exploring on foot in an urban environment, those who want to get some walking in even when they're not officially on trail and those who want to explore personal hobbies or interests while traveling.

How it works: One of the best urban walking tours I've ever been on was a Communist walking tour of Budapest, Hungary. Our guide was a man who'd grown up during Soviet rule, and as we walked around the city he spun an almost unbelievable story about what it was like to experience that era: forbidden to listen to American music, unable to drink a Coke, crammed into one of the unsightly and impersonal housing blocks that still dominate the city. It was fascinating—and a great way to spend a couple of hours.

How to do it right:
- Don't drink a lot of liquids beforehand, since you'll be walking around town for a couple of hours and there's typically just one bathroom break halfway through the tour.
- If you're part of a group that's first-come, first-served, make sure to arrive at least fifteen minutes early. Some tours allow reservations—check online.
- Especially in a large group, do your best to stay close to the guide so you can hear the commentary and ask questions when you're walking from one important spot to the next.
- Have cash handy; sometimes you can pay for walking tours online, but many of them (including all the free ones) accept payment or tips only in cash.

How to find it:
- Search for the city you're visiting at SANDEMANs New Europe Tours (see Resources).
- Do an Internet search for the city you're visiting and "free tour."
- Look at Lonely Planet or other city guidebooks for tour listings.

- Check the activity board at local hostels. Most also offer their own free walking tours throughout the week.
- Stop by the local tourist information office for a listing of staff-led free walking tours.

Want a private guide for your urban walking tour? Check out these specific companies that might be able to help: Tours by Locals, Vayable, Viator and Airbnb Experiences (see Resources).

How much it costs: Paid urban walking tours for groups generally cost anywhere from €5 to €50 per person for a two-hour tour. Private tours of the same length can range from €50 to €150 per person for the same amount of time. Free walking tours are gratuity-based, so consider what other local experiences and attractions cost and pay accordingly (see the How Much Should I Tip? sidebar at the end of this chapter). FYI, some free-walking-tour companies charge their guides a flat fee per tour participant, so if you don't tip, your guide may actually lose money.

TAKING A SELF-GUIDED WALKING TOUR OF AN ESTABLISHED ITINERARY

Unlike when you walk independently or with supplemental services, when you take a self-guided walking tour, you pay someone else to do your trip planning for you. You'll still walk on your own (that is, you won't have a guide on trail), but you'll be provided with an itinerary and the reservations you need to make your trip a reality, from transportation to the trailhead to accommodations to some or all of your meals. You'll also receive a packet of information about the trail that usually contains a map, route description and packing list. Depending on the self-guided walking tour you choose, the service may also include transportation from the airport, luggage transfer and/or travel insurance.

Most self-guided walking tours come with some degree of customization. You can let the company know how many days you want to walk versus rest, what you're most interested in seeing and what kinds of accommodations you prefer. Self-guided walking tours are an excellent choice if you want to walk a long trail without handling any of the logistics or if you really like the idea of having a point of contact for your trip, someone to support you if you have any questions or issues on trail.

There are a couple of different options for finding information online about self-guided-walking-tour companies in Europe. If you know the trail you want to walk, do an Internet search for "self-guided walking tour" and the name of the trail. If you don't have a trail preference yet but you know you'd like to do a self-guided walking tour, search for "self-guided walking tour in Europe" and drill down to the companies—and then experiences—that look good to you. These are some specific companies that might be able to help: Sherpa Expeditions, Macs Adventure, Inntravel, Country Walkers, SoloWalks, and Butterfield & Robinson (see Resources).

If you hire the services of a company that offers self-guided walking tours, it's less expensive than taking a guided tour, but you'll still pay more—sometimes several hundred euros more per person—than you would if you plan your trip on your own. For example, when Mac and I walked the Lycian Way (Walk 7), our week on trail cost us about €200 each. We ran into some walkers who were staying in our same accommodations but who'd gone with a self-guided-walking-tour company and found out they'd paid more than €600 each for essentially the same experience.

Over the years, I've met quite a few walkers who have been on self-guided walking tours of the same trails I've tackled alone. Some of these walkers have been really happy with the experience, and others have been pretty disappointed. I've learned that it's rarely the logistics (for instance, the accommodations) that make the difference between the happy and unhappy customers—it's usually the trail information. When you commit to a self-guided walking tour, you're outsourcing all your trail research, which means that if a company hasn't updated their walking directions to reflect changing trail conditions or provided you with a detailed map, you typically don't have your own knowledge to fall back on—you're just out of luck. Guarantee yourself a good self-guided-walking-tour experience by following these suggestions:

- Check out Finding a Good Tour Guide or Company later in this chapter. Many of those tips also apply to finding a good self-guided-walking-tour company.
- Search for reviews online, and check specifically for people's comments on the walking directions and maps provided by the company.
- Before you leave home, analyze the trail information the self-guided-walking-tour company has given you. Are the walking directions easy to understand? Is the map detailed enough to keep you on track? Even if the information looks good (but especially if it doesn't), look online for additional sources of trail information—a good guidebook, downloadable GPX tracks, et cetera. You can never have too much trail information.
- Keep the phone number of your company contact person in your phone so

A nice side benefit of adventuring with a guided walking tour is meeting like-minded travelers. (Photo by Carol Veach)

it's easy to access if you need it. (You'll need an international cell phone service plan or a local SIM card to make calls in Europe. For more information, check out Chapter 16, Electronic Tools.)

GOING ON A GUIDED WALKING TOUR

When it comes to making your trail experience as easy as possible, there's nothing better than going on a guided walking tour. In addition to handling all of the planning and logistics for your trip (outside of international flights), the tour company will also be responsible for guiding you on trail. That means you—and the eight to twenty other walkers who are in your group—will have someone to navigate the trail

for you and narrate all of the highlights along the way, from rare wildflowers to ancient ruins.

A variety of guided tours in Europe include walking. Some are adventure tours that feature a mix of everything from biking to kayaking to walking. Others combine walking with extensive sightseeing, visiting museums and historical landmarks that are nearby but not on trail. Yet other tours are devoted entirely to walking.

The tours that focus exclusively on walking vary a lot. On some tours, you can choose a different trail each day based on what you're able to walk. On other tours, the trip is graded for difficulty (easy, moderate or difficult) and everyone walks the same trail at the same time. Group demographics also vary widely. Some trips are designed with solo travelers in mind;

others are for couples, women, families, et cetera.

Guided walking tours can be an especially good choice if you want a full-service trail experience. It can be really nice knowing that you won't have to handle any of the trip logistics; you just show up and walk. This is especially good for all of you superplanners who need your vacation to be relaxing instead of more work. Guided walking tours are also great if you haven't done much international travel and want to build your confidence, if you'd like to hone your outdoor skills (for example, navigation) with the help of a professional, if you're not comfortable doing that technical a trail on your own (for instance, fording rivers) or if you are a solo traveler who wants to walk with other people.

> Want a guided walking tour that's just for you and your group—no strangers? That's an option too! Check the websites of tour companies you're interested in and ask for information on private tours, including pricing.

There are a couple of different options for finding information online about guided-walking-tour companies in Europe. If you know the trail you want to walk, do an Internet search for "guided walking tour" and the name of the trail. If you don't have a trail preference yet but you know you'd like to do a guided tour, search for "guided walking tour in Europe" and drill down to the companies—and then experiences—that look good to you. These specific companies might be able to help: REI Adventures, Backroads, The Wayfarers, Country Walkers, National Geographic Expeditions, and Butterfield & Robinson (see Resources).

Guided walking tours are the most expensive of the options presented in this chapter because they include so much. They vary, however, based on how budget oriented or luxurious they are. Expect to pay between €800 and €5,000 per person for a one-week trip.

When I was looking into walking Iceland's Laugavegur Trek (Walk 14) with my mom, joining a guided walking tour seemed like the very best option. The trail is really popular and the huts had been reserved for months, so our only guaranteed way of getting an indoor bed and avoiding camping in the infamously crazy Icelandic weather at night was by booking with a company. (Most tour companies reserve hut space as soon as it's available and release any unbooked beds at the last minute.)

I liked the idea of a guided tour for other reasons as well. I knew we'd have to ford several rivers on the route—an entirely new skill for me and my mom—and that Iceland is famous for its dense fog and heavy rain, which can make for dangerous trail conditions. The deciding factor was comfort—and not just creature comfort. I wanted the peace of mind of knowing that my mom and I would be safe on what was a challenging trail for both of us.

I booked the guided walking tour, and it turned out great. We had a fantastic Icelandic guide who had walked the trail many times and was familiar with all of its challenges (and taught us so much about Icelandic culture), we mastered some important new outdoor skills (fording those rivers) and we made incredible memories on—and off—trail with some amazing people in our group. Signing up for a guided walking tour was definitely the right call for us.

> I love the camaraderie you get with a good walking group. There's nothing like having people to chat with all day and laugh with all evening. Going on a guided walking tour is a great way to meet active, like-minded people who may just turn out to be friends—and travel companions—for life.

Here are my tips for getting the most out of taking a guided walking tour:

- When you're looking at companies and trail experiences, pay attention to what kind of people the trip is marketed to. If you're young and single, you probably don't want to be on a tour for senior citizens or families. Find a group you'll feel comfortable in.
- Pay attention to how physically challenging the trip will be and choose something that matches what you're capable of.
- Make sure you know what you're paying for in advance and what you're responsible for on the trip—meals, tips, et cetera.
- Most companies won't book international flights, so make your own reservation as soon as you have your tour confirmation, in order to get the best possible airfare.

FINDING A GOOD TOUR GUIDE OR COMPANY

When you're entrusting all or even just a part of your vacation planning to a tour guide or company, it pays to do your due diligence. Here are some of my favorite ways to vet the people and companies I walk with.

Look at Reviews

Built-in reviews on a company website: If you're booking your tour guide or company through a website that has built-in reviews, such as Airbnb Experiences or Viator, that should be your first stop for helpful information from past customers.

Reviews on other websites: If you can't find review information elsewhere, or you want to see more reviews, check out TripAdvisor, Yelp or Google Maps.

It can be a little unsettling to plan a trip—and put money down—so far in advance of when you'll be traveling. If you're feeling nervous, consider purchasing travel insurance (see the Trip Insurance sidebar in the introduction to Part 2, Planning), which can help you recoup your financial investment if something like an illness or a change in work or family commitments comes up and you have to cancel your trip.

Reviews of guides' abilities: When you're looking through reviews on trail guides, pay particular attention to what people have said about how confident they've felt in their guide's outdoor skills and abilities.

Reviews of trail information: When you're looking through reviews on self-guided walking tours, pay particular attention to what people have said about the quality of trail information provided. Do they bring up getting lost easily or being given outdated information?

Your opinion matters—both to the individuals and companies you've walked with and to other walkers who are contemplating the same kind of trip you took. So use your voice and leave a review, whether it's positive, negative or somewhere in between. It does make a difference. In Istanbul I went on a tour that was disappointingly cut short by the guide. When I said as much in my review, I was contacted by the tour company I'd booked through, which was very apologetic and offered to refund part of my money to make up for my bad experience with them.

Be discerning when it comes to reviews. Even TripAdvisor has been known to host false positive reviews (people either paying for entirely fake reviews or getting money discounted from their stay if they post "honest but positive" reviews), although it tries to crack down on that as much as possible. Some

If you're hiking in Ireland (see One-day Wander #6, Cliffs of Moher), venture to nearby Belfast for a black cab tour to learn about The Troubles.

"tells" that can signal a fake review: too much narrative about the vacation as opposed to the service, a focus on who the reviewer was with, the use of words like "very" and "really," and exclamation marks.

Look for Certifications and Industry Awards

Some countries have very rigorous standards for tour guides that include formal education in tourism and rigorous testing to make sure that knowledge sank in (for example, England has its Blue Badge program). If this is the case where you're traveling, support high-quality tourism by going with a certified guide.

Check certifications online: You can see online whether an individual tour guide is certified or whether a company hires certified guides—most promote that information wherever they can.

Check for certifications suitable for your type of tour: When choosing a trail guide, also look for someone who has certifications for the level of activity you're attempting—and the degree of remoteness you'll be experiencing. If you're walking in a very isolated area, the ideal guide will have wilderness first-aid experience. If you're mountaineering, choose someone who has been certified with the International Federation of Mountain Guides Associations (see Resources).

Check for environmental responsibility: It's good to make sure your tour guide or company is part of an organization or coalition that promotes environmental responsibility and sustainable tourism. This isn't a certification per se, but you want to be adventuring with people who will protect the environment and the experience in the long term.

Tipping in Europe can be quite confusing, especially for Americans and Canadians, who have been raised to think that tipping is absolutely essential. And it is in most of North America—in some industries, like the restaurant industry, wages can be based almost entirely on tips. So, not many tips, not much take-home. But that's not the case in Europe, where livable wages and good health care are prevalent and tips really function as extra little rewards for great service. (In some countries, such as Iceland, it's not common practice for locals to tip at all.)

That said, thanks to all of the Americans and Canadians who have overtipped in Europe in the last few decades, many European service workers and tourism professionals now expect North American–level tips. If you're part of a group tour, check your confirmation documents to see whether gratuities have been automatically included in the base fee—for some companies, they are. If not, how much should you tip? Below are some suggestions for when and how much to tip for supplemental services and guided walking tours:

Luggage transfer: This isn't required, but a tip of €1 per bag per day is always appreciated.

Taxi: You're fine if you round up to the nearest euro.

Private tour guides and guided tours: Most tour guides don't expect tips but do appreciate them. Guides working through a booking service or a tour company are more reliant on tips; in that case, 5–10 percent is appropriate (10 percent is considered a very generous tip). Private tour guides who are not part of a company, however, are getting the full amount of the paid service fee, so you don't need to tip as much.

If you're part of a group tour, don't feel pressured to tip individually—that can be really uncomfortable. It's better to pass a hat and have everyone tip what they want, then present the guide with an envelope of cash from the whole group. Read more about tipping in Europe, including in restaurants and bars, in the When You Get to Europe section of Chapter 18, Check Off Your Final To-Dos Before Walking.

Check for travel-industry awards or trade-organization endorsements: If your tour guide or company has any awards or endorsements to their name, these can be a good indicator of quality.

Look at Trip Information

Check out the guide-to-guest ratio: This ratio isn't necessarily important for a two-hour urban walking tour, but it becomes crucial when you're on a guided walking tour that's a week or more long, especially when you're walking a technical or challenging trail that might require some extra assistance. Aim for at least one guide for every eight guests.

Check for repeat customers: Look for information on how many guests on each trip are returning (have traveled with the guide or company before). A high percentage means people have enjoyed their previous trips so much that they're coming back for more, which is promising.

Make sure there's transparency when it comes to trip fees: There's nothing worse than thinking you've paid for everything up front and then being nickel-and-dimed your entire trip. There should be a breakdown in advance of exactly what you're paying for up front—and what you'll need to pay for later, including gratuities (see the How Much Should I Tip? sidebar).

CHAPTER

7

GET THERE

Once you know which trail you're walking, who you're going with and whether you're traveling independently or with a tour group, the next thing you need to figure out is the best way to get to Europe and then to and from the trail, so you can book your transportation. It's important to plan your transportation early because it has a tremendous impact on your itinerary—and, thus, all of your other trip plans. And it can take some creativity.

Even with the incredible public transportation options that Europe is known for, it's always more challenging to get to a small town (where most trailheads are located) than a large city. Not all planes, trains or buses run every day, so you may need to tweak your ideal itinerary based on what transportation is available—and when. This happens to me almost every time I plan a trip.

Figuring out the best way to get to and from the trail may require a little creativity and flexibility, but the process itself isn't difficult once you know your options for the three main distances you need to cover: getting to Europe, getting across Europe and getting to the trailhead. This chapter tackles them in that order. Just don't book anything—transportation or accommodations (see Chapter 8, Find a Place to Stay)—until you have a concrete plan for every step of the journey and you're certain everything fits together.

Even if you are traveling with the help of a self-guided or guided walking tour, you still need to plan and book your transportation to the established meeting point, which is generally (1) the closest airport to the trailhead if the tour company includes transportation from the airport or (2) the town nearest the trailhead if the company's services don't include transportation from the airport.

STEP ONE: GETTING TO EUROPE—TRANSCONTINENTAL FLIGHTS

The first step in getting to the trailhead is getting to Europe. There are two ways to go about this: the easy way and the cheap way.

Flying to the airport that's closest to the trail is the easy way. You can usually find out which airport this is with an Internet search for "closest airport to (insert the name of the town you're starting your walk in)." There are many airports in Europe, so there might be two or three with equally advantageous locations; choose one based on price or the convenience of flight schedules from your home airport. For the best pricing information, I recommend using a European flight aggregator like Skyscanner or momondo (see Resources), which pull fares from major carriers and budget carriers alike, because most US flight aggregators don't have access to budget carrier rates. If you find a flight you like, you're set; you can skip ahead to Step Three, Getting to the Trailhead, later in this chapter.

Flying to one of the major hubs in Europe and using regional transportation to get to the trailhead is the cheap way. This can save you a lot of money—sometimes even hundreds or thousands of euros—if you're on a budget and have a little time and patience. The reason? Mile for mile, regional transportation (budget airlines, trains, buses and rental cars) is often vastly more affordable than an extended multi-stop transcontinental flight.

Also, it's a lot easier to find screaming deals to these hubs than to smaller airports in Europe. Check out the Top Ten Air Hubs in Europe sidebar to choose a hub. A simple way to price your options from your home airport to one of these hubs is to search on Skyscanner for flights from your home airport to "Everywhere" (yep, this is a legitimate search term) and browse through the results for the best European deals.

> If you're walking a long trail, depending on how far you're planning on walking, you may want to consider flying out of a different airport to get back home than the one you flew into to get to Europe.

Saving Money on Transcontinental Flights

Regardless whether you choose the easy way or the cheap way of getting to Europe, here are a few additional ways you can save money on your transcontinental flight:

- Set up a fare alert on Skyscanner or Airfarewatchdog (see Resources) to be notified when prices drop.
- Look for deals with companies that offer free layovers at their major hub, such as Icelandair (Reykjavik), Turkish Airlines (Istanbul), Air France (Paris) and Finnair (Helsinki).
- Be flexible with your airport of origin. There's usually a box you can check on flight aggregators called "Add nearby airports" or something similar—checking that one box can yield significantly better deals if you're willing to travel to, say, Oakland's airport instead of flying out of San Francisco.
- Fly during less popular times—shoulder season, early morning, late night, midweek.
- If multiple people are traveling together, price one seat at a time instead of two

TOP TEN AIR HUBS IN EUROPE

- Amsterdam Airport Schiphol, the Netherlands
- Barcelona Airport, Spain
- Charles de Gaulle Airport, Paris, France
- Fiumicino Airport, Rome, Italy
- Frankfurt Airport, Germany
- Gatwick Airport, London, United Kingdom
- Heathrow Airport, London, United Kingdom
- Istanbul Atatürk Airport, Turkey
- Madrid-Barajas Airport, Spain
- Munich Airport, Germany

Thanks to the proliferation of budget airlines like RyanAir, getting across Europe can be fast—and cheap. (Photo by Paul Evans/Flickr)

or more—just make sure there are enough seats on the plane for everyone. When purchased individually, tickets are charged at the lowest available rate, but when seats are purchased together and there's a difference in fare, all of the tickets are usually charged at the higher rate.

When to Book Your Flight

- If you're paying with miles, book transcontinental flights twelve months in advance.
- If you're traveling during peak times, book your flight six to twelve months in advance.
- If you're traveling during shoulder seasons, book your flight three months in advance.

STEP TWO: GETTING ACROSS EUROPE—REGIONAL TRANSPORTATION

Once you know which airport you'll be flying into in Europe, it's time to plan the regional transportation you'll need to get across Europe to your trail. There are four main options for

doing this—budget airline, train, bus and rental car—although not all of them will apply to each and every trail.

To get a general idea of which options are available for the trail you're intending to walk, do a search on Rome2rio (see Resources). I am a huge fan of this free trip planner: It helps you find your way from Point A to Point B—anywhere in the world—using Rome2rio's network of more than 5,000 transportation operators. Your origin is the European airport you're flying into; your destination is the town that's closest to the trailhead. Once you hit "search," Rome2rio will display your regional transportation options with estimated travel times and fares. The search results aren't always perfect—occasionally a regional transportation option won't show up in your results even though it actually exists, because it isn't part of the Rome2rio network—but it's a really great place to start (and much better than similar services like Google Maps).

Once you know what your regional transportation options are for getting across

Europe—and generally how they compare with regard to travel time and cost—it's time to do a deeper dive into your top choices, especially if they're pretty similar in time and/or cost. The subsections below help you understand what each choice entails, what its benefits and drawbacks are, and how to find out what the actual schedule and cost look like for your intended day of travel. Only when you have all that information will you be able to make a good decision about which regional transportation option is the best choice.

> If you're walking a long trail instead of home-basing in one town and doing a series of daylong walks from there, you'll need to do the general search with Rome2rio and the deeper dive into your top choices twice: once between the airport you fly into and the town you're starting in, and again between the town you're ending in and the airport you're flying out of.

Budget Airlines

Thanks to the proliferation of budget airlines like RyanAir, EasyJet, Vueling and EuroWings, the conventional transportation adage of "slower is cheaper" has been turned on its head. Now, the fastest way to get across Europe—via airplane—is also often the cheapest.

There are some downsides when it comes to budget airlines: the short flight time becomes a much longer time commitment when you consider how long it will take you to get to and get through the airport; there are often sneaky charges that can increase the cost of your flight; and less popular routes typically aren't served every day.

Schedules and prices: Check a European flight aggregator like Skyscanner or momondo (see Resources). These sites will also show you the cheapest places to buy your ticket once

you're ready: it's usually the website for the winning airline.

What to know:

- Everything on a budget airline costs extra—checking bags, choosing a seat, checking in at the airport, et cetera.
- If you want to travel as cheaply as possible, bring only a carry-on (pay particular attention to the size of your backpack—read the fine print for how large it can be and how much it can weigh without incurring extra fees), let the airline automatically assign you a seat, and check in online.
- If you plan on checking a bag, pay for it when you buy your ticket to avoid an at-the-airport fee that's often double or even triple the original price.
- Double-check which airport your flight leaves from and where it touches down—there can be several airports in each of the larger European cities.
- Keep your flight information and boarding pass handy by downloading the airline's app and using it to check in and download an electronic version of your boarding pass.
- Check in for your flight as early as possible (some companies allow you to do it as soon as you book your ticket) to avoid having your seat given away if the flight is overbooked.

WHAT'S A HOPPER FLIGHT?

The short, cheap flights most budget airlines in Europe offer are often referred to as "hopper flights."

There's no more relaxing way to travel across Europe than by train. (Photo by Nelso Silva/Flickr)

When to book: Book your budget airline flights as soon as possible; because of flexible pricing, rates will only increase as the travel day gets closer.

European budget airlines measure baggage weight in kilos. Not sure how much a kilo weighs? It's just over 2 pounds (2.2 to be precise).

Trains

Traveling by train is definitely my favorite way to get across Europe. There's a lot to love about train travel: it's usually affordable, there's tons of availability (most European train routes are served several times a day, even those to small towns) and it's convenient—you usually depart from and arrive at the center of town instead of the outskirts (as with most buses and budget airlines). I also like the things trains don't have: an onerous check-in process, long security lines

or luggage limits. But the top reason that I love traveling by train is that it's so relaxing! There's nothing better than sitting in a comfy train seat and drinking wine as the landscape rolls on by.

There are a few drawbacks with trains. Thanks to on-demand pricing for intercity routes, last-minute tickets are usually very expensive, and if you're going to a particularly remote place that requires a lot of transfers, it can take a while to get there.

Schedules and prices: There are a couple of good resources. Check first with the German national rail company Deutsche Bahn (see Resources), which has a nice user interface and reliable schedules for all of the trains in Europe. However, Deutsche Bahn shows prices for trains only in Germany, so once you know what your train options are, look for pricing with the national rail company for the country where you're starting your trip (for example,

SNCF for France or Renfe for Spain). Most of these sites have English portals, but their user interfaces aren't always good.

You may have more luck finding pricing with Rail Europe (see Resources), which aggregates schedules and fares for more than fifty different train companies throughout Europe. I don't recommend starting your search with Rail Europe because its database of trains is not as comprehensive as that of Deutsche Bahn or the other national rail companies. When it's time to book a ticket, your cheapest option is usually directly with the national rail company instead of through middlemen like Rail Europe, which mark up fares by 20 percent or more.

Want to learn the ins and outs of taking trains in Europe and getting the best fares? Check out The Man in Seat Sixty-One (see Resources), the amazing pet project of a former British Rail employee and the most comprehensive resource out there on European train travel. I can't recommend this site enough—it offers an astounding wealth of helpful information!

What to know:
- Travel off-peak for the cheapest fares.
- First class is generally not worth the upgrade in price.
- Input your age and the age of your travel companion(s) for discounts. Kids under four usually travel free, ages four to eleven are typically 50 percent off, ages twelve to twenty-five are eligible for a discount card and reduced fare, and the senior discount starts at age sixty.
- Most national rail companies will allow you to buy your ticket abroad but won't ship a printed ticket internationally. This isn't an issue as long as you print your ticket from a self-service kiosk when you arrive. You'll need to retrieve the

booking with the same credit card you paid for the ticket with, so make sure you pack it.
- If you can't buy a given ticket abroad (this has happened to me with the TGV, or high-speed train, in France), check out The Man in Seat Sixty-One (see sidebar) for help. Get to the right information quickly by doing an Internet search for "buying a ticket abroad" and "(insert the name of the national rail company you're trying to buy from)" and "seat61."
- Most train tickets are nonrefundable, but if your train is delayed or cancelled, you'll be rebooked for free.

When to book: While most regional, local and suburban trains have fixed prices (you'll pay the same amount whether you buy in advance or on the day of travel), nearly all intercity and high-speed train lines (including the Eurostar) now have flexible prices. That means they're cheapest when the tickets are first offered for sale (between one and six months before the date of travel; six months in advance for Eurostar) and get more expensive as more seats are sold; book your ticket as soon as tickets are available.

For a good fare estimator for train travel across Europe, check out the fare maps that travel guru Rick Steves developed (see Resources).

Buses

Just as budget companies have taken over the flight world in Europe, they've also taken over the bus world, and there are now a lot of cheap long-distance buses just waiting to drive you across Europe, some of them for as little as €1. In addition to being light on the pocketbook, buses are heavy on options and can get you into towns that are too small for train service. It's

IS A RAIL PASS WORTH IT?

Eurail passes (see Resources) can give you some flexibility with your travel. You won't have to buy individual train tickets in advance or at the station—once you get your pass book, you simply hop on and off any included trains as often as you want for the amount of days you selected for your pass.

That flexibility comes at a price, though. Unless you're traveling long distances each day you use it, a rail pass usually isn't a good value: you're allowed to use only the slow regional trains for the price of the pass; for trains that require a seat reservation, you have to shell out extra money like everyone else; and don't even think about taking a high-speed train unless you buy a separate full-price ticket.

So does it make sense to get a Eurail pass? With a few easy calculations, you can figure it out:

1. Write down all of the journeys you want to take by train.
2. Look up the fares for all of those journeys (see the Trains section in this chapter); the earlier you look, the better chance you'll have of finding good deals on tickets.
3. Note any trains that require seat reservations or high-speed trains that aren't covered by the rail pass.
4. To see how much your trip would cost without a rail pass, add up all of the individual fares and seat reservations.
5. Count up how many days you'd need a rail pass for.
6. To see how much your trip would cost with a rail pass, combine the price of the rail pass for the number of days you'd need one with the price of any seat reservations and high-speed trains.
7. Compare the totals at steps 4 and 6 to see which is the better deal. If it's buying individual train tickets, order them as soon as possible to avoid an increase in fares. If it's buying a rail pass, order it at least six weeks before your trip to allow time for shipping; you'll need your rail pass in hand before you travel.

Love the idea of a bus pass instead of a train pass? Check out Busabout (see Resources), the bus version of the Eurail pass.

---

also a great way to see the countryside, especially in countries that don't have extensive rail networks.

There are some drawbacks when it comes to traveling by bus: Your timing is at the mercy of traffic, and it can be uncomfortable to sit for long periods of time without much opportunity to get up and walk around.

Schedules and prices: Check out the bus aggregator Busbud (see Resources), which also has links to the cheapest place to buy your ticket once you're ready.

What to know:
- You'll usually select your seat when you book your ticket.
- There typically won't be space inside the bus for your backpack, so you'll need to put it underneath in the bus's luggage compartment. Pack a smaller bag to keep any snacks, entertainment and valuables with you.
- Most bus companies say they have Wi-Fi, but in my experience it works only half of the time, so don't count on it.

There are lots of budget bus companies in Europe, many with fares as low as €1.

- Most buses have bathrooms (not all do, though, so go before you get on), and longer-distance ones also stop every two hours at a gas station where you can use the facilities and get food or something to drink. Your driver will tell you what time to be back on board; don't be late or the bus will leave without you.

When to book: Those amazing promo rates (€1!) usually apply to the first ticket sold on each bus, and the prices only go up from there, so book as soon as tickets are available; most tickets are released one to six months before the date of travel.

Rental Cars

Driving across Europe can be a dream—you can stop anywhere and everywhere you like, get to places where public transportation doesn't go (remote beaches, mountain passes, deep into natural parks) and be free from schedules.

But there are also downsides to traveling across Europe with a car. You won't be able to kick back and relax, you'll probably have to

drive a manual transmission and you might even have to drive on the opposite side of the road from what you're used to at home. And if you're walking a long trail, you'll have to pay

DO I NEED AN INTERNATIONAL DRIVERS LICENSE?

There are two entities to consider if you decide to drive in Europe: rental car companies and governments. Most rental companies don't require an international drivers license as long as you can provide proof that you have a drivers license at home—bring it to show them. In many countries, the foreign government will allow you to drive with a US or Canadian drivers license if you're staying in their country for less than ninety days. You can find more information by calling the local consulate for the country or countries you're planning on driving in. An Internet search may also be able to point you in the right direction. If you need an international drivers license, find one at an American Automobile Association (AAA) location near you (see Resources).

DO I NEED TO BUY EXTRA INSURANCE FOR MY RENTAL CAR?

All car rentals in Europe come with mandated basic liability insurance that applies to anything or anyone outside the car. So what you need to think about is how much risk you're willing to take on in case something happens to the rental car—or you—while you're driving. If you don't want to pay entirely out of pocket for the car and any injuries to those inside of it in the case of an accident that's your fault, consider a collision damage waiver (CDW), either through the rental company or your travel insurance provider.

There are different levels of CDWs, the most comprehensive of which is a "super" CDW with no deductible in case of accident or theft. These can be quite expensive, often between €10 and €30 a day. Depending on where you're driving, the peace of mind that comes with a super CDW may be worth the extra expense. (It was for Mac and me in Ireland!)

You may not need to pay anything for a CDW if you have comprehensive and collision insurance on your home auto policy or if you have a good travel credit card. If you're unsure about what rental car benefits are included with your home auto policy or your credit card, call them before you travel, make sure to find out the details and limits of the policy and ask for a letter of coverage to present to the European rental company when you pick up your car. Just understand that you can't double up on CDWs to use one policy to pay for the deductible on another if there's an accident.

for the car even on the days you're not using it, unless you can drop the car off before you start walking and get a new rental when you're done walking the trail.

Where to find rental cars and prices: Check out the consolidator Auto Europe, which also links to the companies where you can reserve your car (see Resources).

What to know:

- Larger car-rental companies like Europcar and Sixt (see Resources) have a wider selection of pickup and drop-off locations than smaller companies.
- Most European rental cars have manual transmissions—practice at home or pay up to 50 percent more for an automatic (if you can even find one).
- In some countries, it costs the same to pick up and drop off in different locations within that country, which might be more convenient for your travel plans. It almost always costs a lot more to pick up in one country and drop off in another country.
- Depending on where you are in Europe, color-coded fuel handles may be the opposite of what you're used to: for instance, regular gasoline may come out of a green handle instead of a black one. And the foreign words for regular gasoline and diesel can be almost identical (for example, in Spanish, regular gasoline is *gasolina* and diesel is *gasóleo*). Know what kind of fuel your rental car takes, and if you're unsure at the pump about what's what, ask an attendant.
- Many European highways have cameras to catch speeding drivers. If you go over the speed limit, your rental car company will track you down and send you the bill—along with a handling fee.

If you'd like to travel across Europe by car but you don't want to rent one, try carpooling with the help of BlaBlaCar (see Resources), a website that will match you with a car and driver on your route. To get to the English-language version of the site, select "United Kingdom" as the country you'll be traveling in, regardless of which European country you're actually going to, and then input your origin, destination and date of travel from there. If you're a woman and would rather ride with other women, select the ladies-only option (you have to create a free account and log in).

When to book: For the best rates, book your rental car before you leave home. For the best car selection, reserve at least a month before your trip.

Making Your Choice

Once you have all of the details on your top choices—you know their benefits and drawbacks, when they're available and how much they cost—it's time to make a decision. Sometimes there's a clear winner; other times, not so much. If the benefits and drawbacks of your choices are close, think about what matters the most to you. Is it money? Time? Comfort? The chart below illustrates how all of the options described in this section compare when it comes to those three criteria.

Remember, any and all of the four main regional transportation options can get you where you need to go. But you do need to decide on which one(s) to use before you move on to Step Three.

STEP THREE: GETTING TO THE TRAILHEAD—LOCAL TRANSPORTATION

Once you know which airport, train station, bus station and/or rental car drop-off you'll arrive at using regional transportation, it's time to plan the final part of your journey: getting to the trailhead using local transportation, everything from local buses to subways to taxis—even walking. Because you'll be covering a relatively short distance, it shouldn't be too complicated.

There are two main resources that can help you plan your route: Citymapper and Rome2rio (see Resources); occasionally Google Maps is also helpful. All three resources will show you local transportation options to get you those final few miles; Citymapper and Google Maps will also give you walking directions. It's sometimes challenging to find accurate timetables for local transportation, especially in very small towns. If you have trouble finding information,

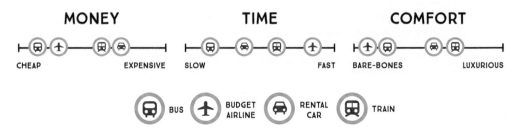

Compare the pros and cons of travel options to decide what is best for you.

In Europe, it's often possible to shorten your mountaintop hike with a variety of alternative transportation options, from funiculars to gondolas.

your best bet is to call the local tourist information office for assistance. Also check whether it's possible to hire private transportation (see that section in Chapter 6, Walk Independently or Hire Help) or whether your accommodations will provide local transportation.

In small towns, it's often easy enough to walk everywhere without the assistance of public transportation. But it does help to have a good map—and this is where a cell phone comes in handy. If you'll have service in Europe, you're in luck—you'll be able to use Google Maps on the go to fetch walking directions to wherever you're trying to go in town, whether that's from the train station to your accommodations or from your accommodations to the trailhead. If you won't have service in Europe (or you want a Plan B just in case your service doesn't work), I recommend using Google Maps to save offline maps of all the towns you'll visit on your trip. (Hint: It's best to do this at home and when connected to Wi-Fi.)

If you're coming up short on transportation options from an airport or bus station into town, check out the airport or bus station website or search online for what other travelers recommend; many travel forums cover local transportation.

FIND A PLACE TO STAY

The next step in your planning process is choosing the right accommodations for your trip. This matters more than you think it will, and not just because a sizable chunk of your travel budget will go to wherever you stay. It matters because your accommodations can make a significant difference in how much you enjoy exploring on foot and how well your body performs on trail.

You might not realize it until you're traveling, but accommodations are pretty amazing. If you're part of a group, they're your best chance of carving out some alone time so you don't go crazy being surrounded by people all the time. And if you're walking alone, they're your best chance of finding someone to talk to so you're not lonely. If it's rainy, they're a warm spot to hang your clothes and get dry. If it's hot, they're somewhere to wash the sweat off your body and out of your clothes. No matter who you are or what the conditions outside are like, your accommodations are a soft place to land after a long (and sometimes hard) day of walking. And they'll give you the things you need to keep going, day after day: a good night's sleep, food and hydration, and a place to take a load off and let your body rest.

All of that makes a tremendous difference to your happiness and your performance. I've seen it with my own walking firsthand. When I'm constantly around other people, anything and everything annoys me and I just don't enjoy myself as much as I do when I can recharge with alone time. And on days when I'm sleep deprived (I'm a light sleeper, so this happens every time I stay in a dormitory, unfortunately), my muscles are achier and I get winded a lot easier than on days when I'm well rested.

As much as you're looking forward to your time on trail, you're going to love rolling into your accommodations each night, so choose them wisely. It all starts with determining what accommodations are available on your chosen trail. Then you'll select your ideal type of accommodations. The last step is choosing your individual accommodations and booking them.

STEP ONE: DETERMINE WHAT ACCOMMODATIONS ARE AVAILABLE

The first step in choosing the right accommodations is knowing what's available. There are nine main options—luxury or specialty stay, hotel, bed-and-breakfast, guesthouse, private rental, hut, hostel, campground and free accommodations—although not all of them will apply to each and every trail.

To get a general idea of which options are available for the trail you're intending to walk, look at a variety of resources until you're confident that you've found all—or enough—options to choose from. If you're walking a long trail, you'll be staying in multiple small towns along the way, so you'll need to run a separate search for each town, making sure to change your travel dates accordingly.

Booking.com: I always start my accommodations search with this platform, which has up-to-date and detailed information, including pricing, photos and reviews, for a wide variety of European accommodations. The site allows you to filter and sort results by what's most important to you, whether that's a place that offers free Wi-Fi or includes breakfast in the room rate or is smack-dab in the center of town. You can also sort your results by lowest price first, which is a helpful way of finding the most affordable accommodations that match your criteria.

While Booking.com is a great place to start your accommodations search, it doesn't always include every option in a given location, so if you're having trouble finding places to stay on trail, it's time to expand your search. A couple of resources are especially helpful in this

Most accommodations proprietors, especially in areas that attract a lot of walkers, don't mind if you hang your laundry line outside.

regard: the local tourist information office and the guidebook for your trail.

Local tourist information office: Especially in small towns, the local tourist information office is usually a great source of information on accommodations, and it can lead you to a variety of small, family-owned businesses that aren't on the big booking websites. Most tourist information offices have a web presence and several pages devoted to local accommodations; to find the official site of the tourist information office in the town(s) you're traveling to, search online for "Visit (insert the name of the town or region you're visiting)." If the accommodation information you're looking for isn't on the website, there will usually be a phone number or email address of someone you can contact for assistance. (And most tourism professionals in Europe speak fluent English, so don't worry about communicating with them.)

Guidebook: Another really good source of accommodation information (especially for alpine huts and other remote options) is the guidebook for your trail, because in the course

THOSE QUIRKY EUROPEAN ROOMS

Some of the features that are standard in European rooms are quite a surprise to North American visitors. Here's what you can expect:

Shared bathrooms. Whereas in North America nearly all rented rooms come with an en suite bathroom, in Europe it's far more common for accommodations to have a few bathrooms on each floor that are shared by all of the guests. That means you'll typically have to walk down the hall to use the toilet or shower. Most places that have shared bathrooms also have a sink and mirror in each guest room so you can at least brush your teeth and get ready for bed without leaving your room. In some accommodations, en suite bathrooms are available—you'll just have to pay extra for them.

A bidet and a heated towel rack. There are two extra things that most European bathrooms have that North American ones don't: a bidet and a heated towel rack. The bidet looks like a urinal—but it's not one, so don't pee in it. It's actually there for more comprehensive cleaning of your undercarriage after you've used the toilet. (You can find more information online on the particulars of using the bidet; if you want a good laugh, check out some of the YouTube videos of confused travelers trying to figure out how it works.) The towel rack looks like a water heater or radiator that has a big temperature knob on one side, and it extends partway (or all the way) to the ceiling. It's used for drying wet towels. It's also perfect for getting your hand-washed clothes dry by morning. (For more laundry tips, check out Chapter 12, Clothing.)

Separate mattresses and comforters for couples. In North America, when you reserve a double room, you get either a queen- or king-size bed that has large bedding to match. In Europe, double rooms usually consist of two smaller beds pushed together, each with their own comforter. That's perfect if you're sharing a bed with a friend or your mate is a restless sleeper—you can just separate the beds. It's a little less convenient if you want to get cozy with your sweetheart. If bed choice is important to you, ask your preferred accommodations about what kind of beds their rooms are equipped with—and the likelihood of getting a different kind of bed. (For example, at one guesthouse in Spain, Mac and I splurged for what the accommodations termed a "matrimonial" bed—a queen-size bed with bedding large enough for two people.)

of researching and walking the trail (sometimes multiple times), the author has curated a lot of that information for you. I like guidebook recommendations because they often narrow things down to the top two or three accommodations in each cost category—budget, midrange and luxury—and they're peppered with personal observations and recommendations that are walker-specific. The one thing to be careful of with guidebook information is that it can go out of date relatively quickly because businesses open, close and change hands more often than guidebooks are updated. So verify any information you find in a guidebook by going online or checking with the local tourist information office.

Online: Once you've looked for accommodations on Booking.com, through the local tourist information office and/or in your guidebook, you can expand your search one last time with a general Internet search for "accommodations in (insert the name of the town you're visiting)." That should bring up any remaining accommodations you might have missed, including those on other booking platforms, those with independent websites or those that have a map entry on a service like Google Maps.

STEP TWO: SELECT YOUR IDEAL TYPE OF ACCOMMODATIONS

Once you know what your options are for accommodations, it's time to start narrowing things down. Rather than focusing on the tens or even hundreds of individual choices (those are covered later in this chapter), your best bet is to first choose the general category of accommodations that best fits the kind of experience you want.

If you're inclined to skip this step because you think the categories are the same as in North America, hold on—a lot of the time

they're not! Even in categories that go by the same name as back home, there are some significant differences—for example, in Europe, bed-and-breakfasts are actually a budget option rather than a luxury one. This section covers the basics of each category, so you'll know what to expect and can make the best decision possible.

Because European accommodations can be significantly cheaper than North American ones, you'll probably be able to afford something more luxurious than you'd typically choose at home. Just to make sure you don't accidentally rule out something that's within reach, the list in this section is organized from those having the most amenities to the least.

If you have your heart set on a specific kind of accommodations (castle lovers, I feel you) and your trail just doesn't offer it, you can always switch trails. Follow the search suggestions in each accommodations category's "Where they're most common" and "How to find them" to locate more of that kind of accommodations. If you can't find a long trail that features the accommodations you want, you can always use your ideal accommodations as a home base and piece together several daylong walks in the surrounding area.

Luxury and Specialty Stays

The luxury or specialty stay involves accommodations that aren't just a place to lay your head—they're designed to pamper you and often are paired with cool experiences that you'll remember for years: fly-fishing, falconry and beekeeping, to name a few. Most luxury and specialty accommodations are in gorgeous old buildings that are just as unique as the experiences they promote, from aristocratic estates and famous vineyards to repurposed monasteries and romantic castles.

What they're best for: A bucket-list adventure; a splurge night.

Where they're most common: You'll find luxury and specialty accommodations all over Europe, but castles are especially prevalent in the United Kingdom and Ireland, and large chateaus are more typical of France and Italy.

How to find them: While many luxury and/or specialty stays can be found on Booking.com, an Internet search for "luxury accommodations in (insert the town or region you're visiting)" or more specific searches for things like "castle accommodations in (insert the town or region you're visiting)" should also bring up some good options. Also, if you're open to designing a series of walks around your accommodations, there are occasionally some really interesting deals on Groupon Getaways (see Resources); I have a couple of friends who spent a week traveling between different luxury castles in Ireland for only €900 per person, including airfare!

How much they cost: €100–€500-plus per night for a double room.

Hotels

This category covers a wide range of accommodations, from quaint hotels to large chains, all of which focus on giving you a solid place to sleep more than an experience you'll remember for years. While there's a lot of variety in the amenities and rooms they offer, most hotels are more centrally located and have more in-room amenities, from a coffeemaker to an electric kettle, than guesthouses. Because hotels can be so different, it's helpful to look at their star ratings to see what kinds of rooms and amenities they are likely to offer (see the Decoding Hotel Star Ratings sidebar below for more information). Just remember that you don't always need a lot of stars for a good stay; I regularly sleep in comfortable hotels that have one or two stars because I don't mind sharing

DECODING HOTEL STAR RATINGS

While there's no international standard for hotel ratings and most hotels are self-rated, below is what you can generally expect based on the number of stars a hotel has:

- **One star:** Only basic rooms, shared bathrooms, no meals
- **Two stars:** Only basic rooms, shared bathrooms, television, on-site restaurant or bar
- **Three stars:** A variety of room options, television, on-site restaurant or bar, gym
- **Four stars:** A variety of room options, several on-site restaurants or bars, gym, swimming pool, concierge
- **Five stars:** Only luxury rooms, all of the amenities that are standard at a four-star hotel—and usually a lot more

a bathroom, I don't need a television and I like to eat my meals at hole-in-the-wall restaurants instead of at the hotel.

What they're best for: A good night's sleep that's just as luxurious—or not—as you want it to be.

Where they're most common: You'll find hotels all over Europe.

How to find them: Most hotels are listed on Booking.com.

How much they cost: €45–€350-plus per night for a double room.

If you decide to go with a hotel, try a local one rather than the chain you know from back at home. You'll have a much more memorable experience, I promise!

Bed-and-Breakfasts

While a bed-and-breakfast in North America is usually a luxury option, in Europe it's a budget choice—lucky you! While bed-and-breakfasts are similar to guesthouses in that they're typically run by families, they're much smaller: often only one or two rooms are rented out in the family's house, which is also often a really interesting building like a farmhouse or a historic home. The best part of staying in one is definitely the breakfast. Depending on what country you're in, that breakfast is almost guaranteed to be your biggest and best meal of the day (we're talking Ireland and the United Kingdom here!), with plenty of local ingredients and delicacies.

What they're best for: A tremendous breakfast (especially for foodies); the opportunity to interact with a local family.

Where they're most common: While you can find bed-and-breakfasts all over Europe, they're especially prevalent in Ireland and the United Kindgom.

The best part about staying in a bed-and-breakfast is definitely the breakfast; it's the perfect way to kick off a long day of walking.

How to find them: Some bed-and-breakfasts can be found on Booking.com, but most are too small to be listed on a major website and are more easily found by contacting the local tourist information office, consulting a regional bed-and-breakfast association that has a web presence or doing an Internet search for "bed-and-breakfast in (insert the town or region you're visiting)."

How much they cost: €40–€100 per night for a double room with breakfast.

There's no more welcome sight on a mountain trek like Switzerland's Alpine Pass Route than a cozy alpine hut.

Guesthouses

When it comes to accommodations on trail, guesthouses are the most prevalent. Their rooms are similar to hotel rooms, but the overall facilities are smaller and have fewer amenities—you'll rarely find a gym or a swimming pool in them, because oftentimes they're a wing in a larger house. While some guesthouses come with breakfast and others don't, they're almost always family owned and operated, which means that most of the time, you'll be dealing directly with the owner. Because of the personal touch, guesthouses tend to feel a lot cozier and more personal than hotels.

Because there are so many guesthouses in Europe, in your search they can all start to seem the same. Make sure you look carefully at the reviews online to differentiate them—and then leave a review yourself to help the next traveler.

What they're best for: A good room that's reasonably priced and has a personal touch; the opportunity to interact with a local family.

Where they're most common: You'll find guesthouses all over Europe but they're especially common in France and Germany.

How to find them: Most guesthouses will show up on Booking.com, although you can

I can't speak highly enough of guesthouses. Most of the owners are extremely kind and will go out of their way to help you have a comfortable stay. When I flew into Reykjavik, Iceland, to walk the Laugavegur Trek (Walk 14), I came down with the most terrible toothache of my life. The owner of the guesthouse where I was staying was so concerned when I told her I was having trouble finding a dentist that she called her own dentist for an emergency appointment and had her son drive me to the appointment—where I was diagnosed with an infected tooth. Especially because I was far from home, it was really nice to know that someone was looking out for me. And that's why I stay in guesthouses more than any other kind of accommodations.

also find them through the local tourist information office.

How much they cost: €40–€100 per night for a double room.

Private Rentals

Staying in a private rental like an Airbnb or a Vacation Rentals by Owner (VRBO) property is a great opportunity to experience local neighborhoods and see how real families actually live. There are several options for private rentals—anything from a room to a whole apartment or house. One of the benefits of renting an entire apartment or house is that it can be a lot cheaper per person if you're traveling with a group. And while breakfast won't usually be provided for you, you'll save money on food because you'll have a refrigerator and cooking facilities for preparing your own meals instead of eating out. You'll typically also have access to a washing machine and a drying rack so you can do laundry.

Trying to book an Airbnb without the back and forth with the owner and the wait time that involves? Look for lightning deals, which can be confirmed immediately. This is especially helpful for last-minute bookings. Having trouble finding accommodations? Zoom -way in to see spots that aren't listed on the main accommodations map because they are too new or don't have a lot of reviews yet—this can open up a lot of availability.

What they're best for: A group stay; the opportunity to live more like a local; the chance to cook your own food; the ability to do laundry.

TAKE A BREAK WITH A PRIVATE RENTAL

Long-term travelers who want to get off the tourism bandwagon and take a break can find that private rentals are great for that, as Mac and I discovered during our grand tour of Europe. After we'd been traveling for several months, we rented a cozy house in the countryside of Connemara, Ireland, for a week and did all of the completely ordinary things we'd started to miss: making our own coffee and cereal in the morning after working out, sitting on the couch in front of the fire while reading a book, hanging out with the neighbors at the local pub. The experience was so relaxing that we now regularly book private rentals as minivacations within our longer vacations.

Where they're most common: Private rentals are available all over Europe.

How to find them: While some rentals are available on Booking.com, a much better selection can be found by searching sites like Airbnb and Vacation Rentals by Owner (see Resources).

How much they cost: €25–€65 per night for a double room, €40–€150 per night for an apartment, €100–€350-plus per night for a house.

Huts

In more remote sections of wilderness, huts are the most common type of accommodations, used mainly by walkers and mountain bikers. These vary widely when it comes to the food and other amenities they provide but because there are typically plenty of other walkers around, the experience can be downright chummy.

In Sweden and Iceland, huts tend to be very bare-bones; it's like camping, except indoors. You're provided with a stove and basic things to cook and eat with (pots and pans, utensils, bowls and plates), as well as a kitchen sink with running water, a group table to eat at and a bunk bed with a mattress to sleep on—but that's about all. The bunk beds are usually in a big dormitory room with anywhere from ten to thirty bunks, and your personal space is the size of your bunk (your bag typically goes under the bed or along the wall). The bathroom facilities (toilets, showers and sinks) are often located in a separate outbuilding beside the hut. You need to pack in your own food, sleeping bag and everything else you'll need to stay the night.

The huts in France, Switzerland and Italy are downright luxurious by comparison. A warden oversees the property and cooks your meals. Many times, these huts also offer beer and wine for sale and—gasp—private rooms! Even if you stay in dormitories, they tend to be smaller (four to ten bunks) in these more luxurious huts, which often translates into fewer roommates snoring, a better night's sleep and a little more personal space. There are bathrooms in the huts, and bedding is

Mattress rooms, also called massenlagers *or* matratzenlagers *in German, are the most affordable accommodations in often-expensive Switzerland.*

almost always provided: a comforter and pillow, plus clean linens (sheet, pillowcase and comforter slip); it's your job to make your bed when you check in and then strip off the used linens in the morning. Many huts in Switzerland have mattress rooms, a great budget option for people who don't mind sleeping side by side on a long row of mattresses instead of in bunk beds.

What they're best for: A group stay; solo travelers; the opportunity to meet other walkers; a more remote trail experience.

Where they're most common: While there are huts all over Europe, they're most common in remote areas like mountain ranges or highlands.

How to find them: It's rare for huts to show up on Booking.com, although many of them do have a web presence via their own informational websites. Oftentimes the best way to find a hut is by contacting the local tourism information office or looking in a guidebook or on the trail website (if your chosen trail has one). To expand your search to find more hut systems in Europe, search online for "hut-to-hut hikes (or walks) in Europe."

How much they cost: €20–€60 per bed per night.

Tips on Staying in Huts

Booking: Because most huts are in remote regions that may not have Wi-Fi, it can be difficult to book them online. If you can book online, it'll be by email, so expect to go back and forth a couple of times. The best way to book a hut is often by phone; if you get a Skype account, the call will set you back only a few cents. And remember, there's a time change, so call in the morning to reach someone in Europe during their late afternoon or evening.

Myth: Dormitory accommodations aren't for couples. Truth: Dormitory accommodations are for everyone, even couples. While some huts have double bunk beds that are large enough for two people, it's pretty uncommon to find more than single bunks, so most couples who want to cuddle either book two bunks in the dormitory and cram into just one of the small bunks they've paid for, or they sleep side by side in mattress rooms (see Huts in this chapter).

Afterward: If you're going to stay in a hut dormitory for several days, do yourself a favor and also book yourself a private room with an en suite bathroom for the night following your hut stay. As much as you'll love being around other walkers, by the time it's all said and done, you'll probably be craving your own space—and a few extra comforts.

Hut Etiquette

Staying in a hut can be a really magical experience—there are so many walkers around to talk to and get to know! Make the experience as positive as possible by being a good roommate (especially if you're sleeping in the dormitory) and following hut etiquette:

Take your shoes off. Most huts have a boot room just inside the main door where you're expected to leave your hiking boots. Some have slippers you can borrow for the night—but you might want to bring a lightweight pair just in case.

Hang your wet gear. There's usually a specific drying room or area for wet raingear and pack covers—hang your wet things there.

Keep your mess contained. Out of respect for your fellow walkers—and your own ability to move around the dormitory with ease—keep your backpack on your bed until it's time to sleep. If there's not a drying room and you want

If you're staying in a dormitory, your fellow walkers will appreciate you keeping your mess contained to your own bed.

to string up a laundry line to hang your gear or freshly laundered clothes to dry, do it in the corner or wherever it's least obtrusive.

Keep your shower short. In some remote huts, water (especially hot water) is scarce. And because most walkers tend to get in around the same time and all want a shower before doing anything else, there will probably be a line of walkers behind you. Do your part to make sure everyone gets a hot shower—keep it short, and use as little hot water as possible.

Bring something to share. One of the best ways to get to know other walkers is to bring something to share, whether a travel cribbage set, a deck of playing cards or a flask of body-warming spirits.

Prep for your next day's walk before you go to sleep. Avoid making noise and turning on the light before your roommates are ready

to get up the next morning by taking care of as many tasks as possible before people go to bed. This means laying out your clothes, reorganizing your pack, filling up your water bottles—and anything else you can do in advance to be ready to walk the next morning.

Keep your voice down. Most walkers who stay in huts tend to go to bed pretty early, so if you want to stay up and visit, be quiet and do your socializing in the dining room or other common area—not the dormitory.

Use your headlamp. It's tough for people to sleep when the main room light is on, so be prepared with your own light if you want to read or do anything else that requires light after the lights have been turned off.

Clean up after yourself. Some huts ask that you completely strip your bed in the morning when it comes time to leave. Other places also want you to fold the comforter and place the pillow neatly on top so the bed is ready for the next walker. Wherever you stay, always throw away any trash and follow the cleanup instructions—and be sure to leave your sleeping area better than you found it.

Hostels

Just like huts, hostels provide a great opportunity to meet other travelers, but instead of being in the wilderness, hostels are found in towns—and mainly medium-size or large towns at that, unless you're walking the Camino de Santiago in Spain (Walk 2, English Way), in which case nearly every town, no matter how large or small it is, has an *albergue*. Hostels rent inexpensive individual beds in dormitory rooms; oftentimes, you can choose between staying in a male dorm, a female dorm or a coed dorm. Sometimes you can also rent a private room.

Most hostels offer shared kitchen facilities in case you want to cook your own food, laundry facilities and a common room with couches and tables—perfect for relaxing, journaling or chatting with other travelers. They also typically provide linens (or rent them, if they're not provided) and a cheap (or free) continental breakfast. The bathrooms are typically shared, so you can expect a short walk down the hall for a toilet, shower or sink. Hostels are especially good options for solo travelers, groups and the budget conscious. And they're not just for twenty-somethings—they're for people of all ages, including families.

What they're best for: A cheap bed; a group stay; solo travelers; the opportunity to meet other walkers.

Where they're most common: Hostels can be found all over Europe, although they're more common in medium-size and large towns.

How to find them: Most hostels are listed on Booking.com, as well as hostel-specific sites like Hostelworld (see Resources).

How much they cost: €5–€35 per bed per night.

GET A GOOD NIGHT'S SLEEP IN A DORMITORY

A hostel's sleeping dormitory can present a real challenge for light sleepers. Here are my top tips for getting some shut-eye.

Create a sleep routine: Even though you're traveling, do something to help you wind down for the day, whether that's journaling, meditating or listening to calming music in your bunk. This is also a good signal to your roommates that it's time to start quieting down.

Turn off the main room light when you're ready to go to bed: If you have trouble sleeping when it's not completely dark, be proactive about turning off the lights—other people can use the smaller lights on their beds or their headlamps. There's bound to be someone who comes to bed way later than everyone else and turns the light on because they forgot to unpack their headlamp, so wear an eye mask or drape a shirt over your eyes as well.

Bring some earplugs: If you need it to be perfectly quiet, use earplugs. I've also had luck using a white noise program on my cell phone with earbuds to block out the sounds of other people snoring or talking. Just be mindful that if your alarm is on your phone and your earbuds fall out overnight (like mine tend to do), you might not hear your alarm in the morning.

Campgrounds

If you really love sleeping outside, you can have that experience in Europe. There are two kinds of camping. The first is dispersed camping (known in Europe as wild camping), which involves putting a tent up in an area that's not an established campground, such as in the middle of a forest or in a big field. Wild camping is not as common or accepted in Europe as it is in North America, so I don't recommend it. The kind of camping that is widely accepted in Europe is campground camping, which is very popular. In fact, there are more than 10,000 campgrounds in Europe—that's more than in the United States! Campground camping can be a great way to meet and befriend middle-class Europeans, especially families, who also love spending time outside. And European campgrounds are typically a lot more luxurious than North American public campgrounds, with laundry and shower facilities, restaurants and even Wi-Fi!

If camping to you means a campfire, you're out of luck. Most campgrounds in Europe don't allow campfires.

What they're best for: Families; the budget conscious.

Where they're most common: Campgrounds are scattered all over Europe.

How to find them: It's rare to find campgrounds on Booking.com. If you're specifically looking for a campground on trail, you'll have better luck if you contact the local tourist information office or do a search for campgrounds on Google Maps. Another great resource is Eurocampings (see Resources), which allows you to search for more than 8,600 campgrounds by country or by zooming in on a map. Each

Because of the limited hut space along Iceland's Laugavegur Trek, if you don't secure a bed in advance, you'll have to camp.

Eurocampings listing has a rundown of campground facilities, approximate prices, dates of operation and traveler reviews. Its coolest feature, though, is its search engine, which allows you to look for campsites with Wi-Fi, disability accommodations, a view of the sea, et cetera. Another good resource for camping is Campinmygarden.com, which connects campers to people who will let them camp in their backyards for a small fee.

How much they cost: €10–20 per person per night.

Don't want to carry all of your camping gear through airport security? Rent it in Europe! See the Don't Pack It—Rent It! sidebar in Chapter 15, Trail and Travel Tools, for more details.

Free Accommodations

For the budget conscious or for those who are more interested in cultural exchange than comfort, a variety of organizations in Europe can connect you to locals who have a free place—a bed, a couch or a room—for travelers to stay. Some of these hosts are travelers themselves who are trying to give back while they're at home. Others just enjoy getting to know people from all over the world. Always be discerning about who you stay with, whether the accommodations are free or not. While there's no money exchanged, there is usually an expectation that you'll spend some time together talking or exploring the local area. This is a great chance to get to know the local culture from someone who's part of it. Your host might offer to make you a meal or take you along when they spend time with friends. And you'll usually be able to ask all of your burning questions about how everything functions, from politics to gender roles. You might even make a lifelong friend in the process.

Nervous about trying something like Couchsurfing? Try it at home first! My experiences with Couchsurfing have been nothing but positive—the people I've stayed with have been really interesting and generous folks who love to travel as much as I do. Some of my good friends from home are even hosts! But don't take it from me—experiment when you're on your own turf so that you feel safe when you're traveling.

What they're best for: The opportunity to spend time with locals; budget-conscious travelers; those who don't mind staying on a stranger's couch or in their spare room.

Where they're most common: Free accommodations are available all over Europe.

How to find them: Free accommodations won't show up on Booking.com. Instead, check out Couchsurfing and GlobalFreeloaders.com, which are both free to join (see Resources).

How much they cost: Free.

A few organizations that promote cultural exchange through free lodging charge an expensive membership fee to join their network. I tried one of these when Mac and I were touring Europe, and it was really disappointing. Not one person in the organization's host network emailed me back, and when I contacted the organization for a refund, they didn't respond either. The $200 I lost on a useless membership for the two of us taught me a valuable lesson: when it comes to homestaying organizations, sometimes totally free really is better.

STEP THREE: BOOK YOUR INDIVIDUAL ACCOMMODATIONS

Once you know what accommodations are available on your trail and specifically what category of accommodations you're most interested in, it's time to narrow things down to the individual accommodations you want to book and then make the reservations.

Guesthouses and other small, family-owned accommodations in Europe typically have very helpful proprietors who will go out of their way to assist you. (Photo by Kelsey Overby)

If you're an optimizer like me, it can be a little difficult to try to choose the very best option out of, say, six guesthouses that are priced the same and offer identical amenities. This is where reviews from other travelers come in really handy. (For more information on finding and utilizing independent reviews, check out Finding a Good Tour Guide or Company in Chapter 6, Walk Independently or Hire Help.) They'll usually speak to a deciding factor that will make all the difference—and make your choice apparent. For me, it's typically location: I love staying in the center of town. For you, it might be something entirely different. Maybe you're a stickler for cleanliness or it's really important to you that the staff goes the extra mile.

It can make your decision easier to know that you don't have to stay at one place—or even one kind of place—the whole time. If you're walking a long trail, each night is another opportunity to switch things up and have a totally different experience. You can even save up so you can splurge on something special. Maybe you want to stay in guesthouses all week

so that you can afford that superfancy castle on your last night. Go for it!

Once you're ready to book, you have a few options. If you found your accommodations on Booking.com, the easiest thing to do is make your reservation directly through the site. If you want to be sure you're getting a competitive rate, check out similar platforms online and choose the cheapest rate you can find for your accommodations. To be extra sure that you're getting the best rate out there, call or email the accommodations (they'll usually have a website you can search for) and ask how much a room of your specifications and on your chosen date would cost. Because they won't have to pay a commission on the sale (they often have to shell out 20 percent of the room rate or more to online listing companies), they may be able to give you a better deal. Here are a few other things you should know when you make your reservations:

The room rate includes tax. Whereas in North America you need to add an additional 10 percent or more to the advertised cost of a room for taxes, the price you see in Europe is the price you pay because the tax has already been rolled into the stated amount. Depending on where you make your reservation, the one exception may be city tax. If you book with Booking.com, you may still need to pay €0.40–€2.50 per person per night (typically in cash). If so, this will be clearly stated on your reservation.

You can typically order half board and packed lunches. One of my favorite things that European accommodations offer is food, specifically half board and packed lunches. Never heard of half board before? It means the accommodations will provide you with breakfast and dinner (you can look forward to a rotating set dinner menu that's two to three courses). Half board is usually a great deal—and cheaper than eating out at restaurants in town. The option of ordering packed lunches is also great when there aren't many restaurants on your chosen trail and you don't want to bother packing your own picnic. Many accommodations request that you order half board and packed lunches in advance of your stay, although you don't necessarily need to order them when you make your reservation.

Most accommodations aren't open every day. Although most accommodations in North America are open every day during the busy season, it's very common for small or family-owned accommodations in certain parts of Europe (such as Germany and Switzerland) to be closed one day a week, even in the summer. In German, this is called a *ruhetag* (rest day), and it's a way for a small staff to get a little time off. Accommodations try to stagger their closed days, so in any given town there should always be at least one place open, but if there's somewhere specific you want to stay, verify their closed day in advance by contacting the establishment.

You may need to pay in cash. If you're staying in a remote location such as a hut that doesn't have a credit card machine or Wi-Fi on-site and you haven't paid for your reservation in advance, you may need to pay in cash when you arrive. If you're unsure of what payment methods your accommodations accept, check their websites or contact them before you leave.

It's best to book as soon as possible, or at least three to six months before your trip. There usually isn't a downside to booking your accommodations early, especially if you have travel insurance in case your trip is cancelled for some reason (see the Trip Insurance sidebar in the Part 2, Planning, intro for more information). Booking early guarantees you the best selection of accommodations, especially ones that are budget friendly, so take advantage of it.

BUT I WANT TO BE FLEXIBLE!

If you're traveling during a shoulder season and in a location where there are plenty of accommodations to choose from, you probably could get away with showing up to your chosen trail without having your accommodations booked in advance. That said, would you want to? You might have more flexibility if you fly by the seat of your pants, but you'll also have more decisions to make each day of your trip, not to mention the stress of possibly not finding accommodations to suit your wishes or budget. Rather than just rolling into town and heading to your guesthouse for a hot shower after a long day on trail, you'll need to find a good place to stay first—which you might not have a lot of energy for. Something to think about.

TRAIN FOR THE TRAIL

It's time to start moving your preparations from the computer to the trail! Remember, you don't need to be a superathlete to explore on foot but, that said, you do still need to train.

Training is important to make sure you're as healthy and prepared as possible for your trip. It helps you prevent injuries that can make it difficult or painful to move or even cut your walk short entirely. It also guarantees that you'll enjoy your trip as much as possible. After all, it's hard to take in everything around you, from the wildflowers to the birds to the incredible views, when you're having a hard time making it up the trail. Training also gives you time to get to know your body and figure out where you might have issues—and then come up with solutions in advance.

But that's not all. Training can also help you get ready mentally as well as physically by building your confidence in your abilities. And there's an added bonus to all these benefits: the positive results from training your body will extend into other parts of your life as well. I never feel better or stronger than right before, during and after a long walk—I feel like I can take on anything. And I bet you'll feel the same way.

There's a difference between getting in shape and getting in shape for the trail. I'm reminded of this every time I bring people backpacking with me at home. Even if they're in good shape and they have regular activities, such as tennis or cycling, that require them to be fit, they all say the same thing about their time on trail: it was a challenge! That's why I've organized this chapter around the things you need to master in order to be not just generally fit but trail fit: going uphill, going downhill, wearing a backpack, being on your feet all day and walking for days on end. Once I've introduced you to all of the exercises, I'll help you put everything together with an actionable trail workout plan.

A couple of things to note: First, you can't start optimizing your body for the trail unless you're already relatively fit, so your initial challenge is to get relatively fit. What does that mean? For the purposes of exploring Europe on foot, it means you can walk 6 miles (9.7 km) with 500 feet (150 m)

If you're not already relatively fit, don't despair. Depending on where you're starting from, you can get relatively fit in as little as three to six months if you do a couple workouts each of cardio and strength training every week.

If you're not sure where to start, talk to your doctor or a professional trainer. They can design a training program for you based on your age, health and current fitness level. Most gym memberships come with a complimentary consultation. I also recommend checking out the variety of free couch-to-5k training programs available online, which can help you increase your base level of fitness slowly and safely.

Remember, getting fit doesn't need to be expensive or complicated. At the most basic level, all you need are just some activewear clothes, a pair of tennis shoes and the determination to keep yourself on track.

of elevation gain in three hours, no problem. If you're not able to do that yet, check out the Building Your Base Level of Fitness sidebar. If you're already relatively fit, great! Keep reading.

And the second thing—the fine print. I'm not a doctor or a personal trainer. The information in this chapter is based on what I've discovered during years of researching for and experimenting with optimizing my own body for walking—and my travel companions' experiences too. It should be a good starting point for you as well. Let the training commence!

Want to work out in the comfort of your own home? Check out free resources that will help you make it possible: exercise videos and fitness books from the library, fitness channels on YouTube and on-demand workouts through your cable provider.

GOING UPHILL

Obviously, walking uphill is a lot more challenging than walking on flat ground. It's safe to say everyone has had a familiar experience with inclines at some point—doubled over and gasping for breath, thighs burning, body sweating. Luckily, if you do a little training, going uphill doesn't have to be that painful. All you need to

do is train your lungs and heart to supply your body with good quantities of oxygen and your leg muscles to propel you up, up, up.

Strengthen Your Lungs and Heart

EXERCISE 1: **Cardiovascular Training**

INSTRUCTIONS: The activity you choose is up to you—swimming, running, biking, an elliptical machine. All you need to do is get your heart rate up and keep it there. Aim for a target heart rate of 60 to 70 percent of your maximum (which is 220 minus your age) if you're a beginner, and gradually increase the intensity as you're able. (For example, if you're forty, your maximum heart rate is 180, so your target heart rate would be 108 to 126.) To make the exercise harder, do it in water (swimming, water aerobics, et cetera) for added resistance.

TIME: Work up to 30 minutes per session.

Train to Walk at High Elevation

If you live at low altitude, there's not much you can do to prepare yourself for the elevation challenge (that is, thin air) of a mountain hike. But the one thing you can do is develop your lung capacity. You're already doing this when you get aerobic (cardiovascular) exercise. For a more intentional lung exercise:

TRAVELING LUNGES

TRAVELING LUNGES

EXERCISE 2: Holding Your Breath

INSTRUCTIONS: Take a deep breath. You want your lungs to be at 80–85 percent capacity and the air to be in your chest, not your cheeks. Hold your breath for at least 10 seconds (longer if you can, just not so long that you pass out), then slowly exhale. I recommend doing something to distract yourself while you're holding your breath, such as mentally going through the alphabet. It can also help to have someone else time you so you're not constantly watching the clock.

TIME: Work up to 1 minute per session. (The world record is more than 24 minutes!)

Strengthen Your Legs

EXERCISE 3: **Stair Climbing**

INSTRUCTIONS: If you have access to a stair-climber machine, work out on that. If not, climb the bleachers at your local high school or stadium or tackle a big staircase—the ones in very tall office buildings are great for this. For some variation, you can alternate between walking up stairs one at a time and taking them two at a time. To make the exercise harder, increase your speed.

TIME: Work up to 30 minutes per session.

EXERCISE 4: **Traveling Lunges**

INSTRUCTIONS: Start with your feet hip-width apart and your hands on your hips. Take a giant step forward with your right foot and sink into a lunge, so your right knee is bent at a 90-degree angle (your knee shouldn't extend out any farther than over the tips of your toes). Return to a standing position by bringing your left foot forward to meet your right foot. Repeat by lunging with your left leg. These are traveling lunges, not stationary ones, so you'll move forward with each lunge. To make the exercise harder, hold a dumbbell in each hand—choose whatever weight you're comfortable with. For some people, that may be 5 pounds (2.3 kg); for others, 20 pounds (9 kg).

REPETITIONS: Work up to 15 reps on each leg.

EXERCISE 5: **Squats**

INSTRUCTIONS: Start with your feet a little more than hip-width apart. With your spine as straight as possible, push your hips back as you bend your knees (they should not extend

SQUATS

SQUATS

EXERCISE 6: **Step-ups**

INSTRUCTIONS: This exercise is similar to stair climbing but you step up onto a bench instead of a stairstep—aim for a bench that's 18–24 inches (46–61 cm) high: step up with your right leg, then step back down, and repeat on your left leg. Parks are great for this since they usually have benches of some kind. To make the exercise harder, wear your pack loaded with some weight (see Exercise 13, Weighted Pack).

TIME: Work up to 10 minutes per session.

STEP-UPS

STEP-UPS

beyond your toes) and torso to drop toward the ground, squeezing your tush the whole time. Stop when the backs of your thighs are nearly parallel with the floor, then return to a standing position. It helps to look sideways in a mirror while you do this one, to maintain good form. To make the exercise harder, hold a dumbbell in each hand.

REPETITIONS: Work up to two sets of 25 reps each.

HEEL RAISES

HEEL RAISES

EXERCISE 7: Heel Raises
INSTRUCTIONS: Stand with your feet a few inches apart. Rest your hands on something that can help stabilize you (the back of a chair

works well) as you slowly raise your heels off the floor. Hold for 5 seconds, then slowly lower your heels back to the floor.
REPETITIONS: Work up to three sets of 15 reps each.

GOING DOWNHILL

For me, one of the most surprising parts of diving into the literature on trail training was learning that it takes more energy—some sources say three times more!—to walk downhill than uphill because your muscles are contracting while they're lengthening, a pretty complex task. Help your body become better and more efficient at walking downhill with the following leg exercises.

Strengthen Your Legs

EXERCISE 8: **Step-downs**
INSTRUCTIONS: Stand on a stool (or a stair-step, facing downhill) that's around 6 inches (15 cm) tall. Balancing on your right foot, bend your right leg and lower your left leg until your left heel lightly touches the floor. Straighten your right leg to return to a standing position as you bring your left foot back up to the stool or stairstep. Alternate legs. To make the exercise harder, wear your pack loaded with some weight (see Exercise 13, Weighted Pack).
REPETITIONS: Work up to two sets of 20 reps on each leg.

EXERCISE 9: **Downhill Lunges**
INSTRUCTIONS: Find a gentle downhill grade (a 30- to 45-degree hill works well) and do traveling lunges down it (see Exercise 4, Traveling Lunges) for 50 yards (46 m), then walk back up the hill for one set. To make the exercise harder, wear your pack loaded with some weight (see Exercise 13, Weighted Pack) and/or hold a dumbbell in each hand.
REPETITIONS: Work up to three sets.

STEP-DOWNS

STEP-DOWNS

your hip flexors and gradually build up to your intended pack weight. You'll also need to work on your balance, since wearing a loaded pack can make you tippier than normal, especially when you walk on uneven terrain.

Strengthen Your Core

EXERCISE 10: **Planks**

INSTRUCTIONS: On a yoga mat or carpet, get into starting push-up position with your elbows directly underneath your shoulders. Keep your spine as straight as possible as you tighten your core and hold for as long as you can—but keep breathing!

TIME AND REPETITIONS: Work up to three repetitions of 1 minute each.

Strengthen Your Back

EXERCISE 11: **Swimmers**

INSTRUCTIONS: Lie on your belly on a yoga mat or carpet, with your head up and eyes facing forward, then extend your arms out from your sides, flat on the ground, and bend them 90 degrees at the elbow. Lift your chest and arms off the mat a few inches and hold for 2 seconds. Lower yourself down and repeat.

REPETITIONS: Work up to two sets of 15 reps each.

WEARING A BACKPACK

If you're not used to wearing a backpack, you might be surprised to feel your hips, lower back and shoulders (all of which are where you carry most of the weight) groan in protest. To combat pack pain, strengthen your core (specifically your stomach and low-back muscles), stretch

PLANK

SWIMMERS

WARRIOR II

Stretch Your Hip Flexors

EXERCISE 12: Warrior II

INSTRUCTIONS: Stand with your feet farther than hip-width apart. Rotate your torso so it's in line with your right leg and rotate your right foot to point in the same direction as your torso. Lean into that forward leg and push your right foot forward, bending your right leg and keeping your right knee in line with your right ankle. Extend your arms straight out to your sides, palms open and facing down, and balance. Lean your torso slightly back until you feel your right hip open up. Repeat with your left leg.

TIME: Work up to 2 minutes per leg.

DID YOU KNOW . . . WHY YOUR HIPS ACHE?

When you wear a pack, your natural tendency is to lean forward to compensate for the extra weight. As your pelvis rotates forward, your hip is compressed and the muscles around it get tight—and sometimes achy. The solution? Keeping those hip flexor muscles stretched out with moves like Warrior II.

Build Up to Your Pack Weight

EXERCISE 13: Weighted Pack

INSTRUCTIONS: Start with carrying 5 pounds (2.3 kg) in your pack during your training walks (see Exercise 19) and increase the load by 2 pounds (0.9 kg) each week until you can comfortably carry 20 pounds (9 kg). Bundles of heavy clothes, bottles of wine (wrapped in clothes so they don't break) and family-size cans of soup work great as adjustable weight for your pack. You can also carry your weighted pack while doing Exercises 6, Step-ups; 8, Step-downs; and 9, Downhill Lunges.

TIME: Work up to carrying a full pack in nine weeks.

Work on Your Balance

EXERCISE 14: One-legged Stand

INSTRUCTIONS: Stand on one foot while staring at a fixed point in the distance. Hold for several minutes and switch feet. This works really great if you do it while you're brushing your teeth—in the morning, balance on your right foot. In the evening, balance on your left foot. Want to make the exercise harder? Try it with your eyes closed.

TIME: Work up to 5 minutes on each foot.

BEING ON YOUR FEET ALL DAY

Most people aren't used to being on their feet for hours at a time, let alone having their feet strike the ground thousands of times a day. The results can be sore feet, blisters and rolled ankles. Unless, that is, you toughen the bottoms of your feet, strengthen the muscles in your feet and ankles and build up to walking all day.

Toughen the Bottoms of Your Feet

EXERCISE 15: Barefoot Walking

INSTRUCTIONS: In an area that's safe to do so (free of glass, et cetera), walk around barefoot.

TIME: Work up to 30 minutes per session.

Strengthen Your Feet

EXERCISE 16: Barefoot Sand Walking

INSTRUCTIONS: Walk barefoot in the sand. To make the exercise harder, choose sand that's loose instead of hardpacked.

TIME: Work up to 30 minutes per session.

DID YOU KNOW . . . YOUR FEET HAVE MUSCLES?

Walking in sand requires a lot more effort than walking on a firm surface. You'll feel muscles in the bottoms of your feet that you never knew you had!

EXERCISE 17: Towel Grabs

INSTRUCTIONS: On a smooth surface such as a wood or linoleum floor, spread a bath towel out flat on the floor and stand at one of the ends of it. Standing on your left foot, use the toes of your right foot to slowly pull the towel under that foot until the towel is behind you. Repeat with the other foot.

REPETITIONS: Work up to 2 reps on each foot.

Want tougher feet? Stop babying them with pedicures—and definitely don't remove your calluses. As unsightly as they are, you need those calluses to protect your delicate skin from friction and blisters. Two foot-care tasks to keep in your routine: clipping your toenails short and filing down any nail snags that could grip your sock or impact your other toes. What should you do if you do get blisters? Check out Know How to Treat Blisters in Chapter 10, Be Prepared for Anything.

Strengthen Your Ankles

EXERCISE 18: Alphabets

INSTRUCTIONS: Sit down on a chair or couch and put your right foot out in front of you. Trace the alphabet with your big toe. Switch to your left foot.

REPETITIONS: Work up to 2 reps on each foot.

Besides toughening the bottoms of the feet and strengthening the muscles in your feet and ankles, the number one thing you can do to prevent foot pain is to walk in good socks and good shoes, even when you're training. For tips on choosing the perfect sock-shoe combination, check out Chapter 13, Footwear.

Build Up to Walking All Day

EXERCISE 19: Walks

INSTRUCTIONS: Nothing prepares you for being on your feet all day like walking, so lace up your boots and get outside. Start by walking for 30 minutes at a time and slowly work up to 6 hours, which is the length of a typical walking day when you're exploring on foot. Make it fun by listening to music or joining a walking group. Make it harder by increasing your elevation gain and/or wearing a weighted pack (see Exercise 13, Weighted Pack).

TIME: Work up to long walks of 6 hours per session.

WALKING FOR DAYS ON END

Once you've mastered daylong walks, it's time to start chaining them together. This is really important, because even though going on several daylong walks will help you work up to exploring on foot, it won't get you all the way to being trail fit. That's because there's an added element you'll need for walking for days on end: the ability to perform with only a night, rather than several days, of recovery time. The best way to train your body to do this is to actually get out and do it.

EXERCISE 20: Weekend Warrior

INSTRUCTIONS: Set aside a training weekend to do two long walks back-to-back (one on Saturday and one on Sunday). Each walk should have elevation gain that's typical of what you'll experience on trail in Europe. Make it

Tight muscles are prone to injury and can feel achy, so keep them loose and limber by learning stretches that you can do before, during and after your walks. Target muscles in both your upper body and your lower body, making sure you ease into each stretch to avoid injury. Want a book that can help you put together your own stretching routine? I highly recommend *Yoga for Hikers* by Nicole Tsong.

Sometimes it's hard to choose between drinking a cold beer and stretching at the end of a long hike. The solution: both. (Photo by Jerriann Sullivan)

harder by taking three- and four-day weekends, to chain even more training walks together.

TIME: Work up to a long training weekend that entails 75 percent of the total distance and elevation gain you'll walk on your trip to Europe.

Want even more exercises to get you trail fit? Check out these great resources: *Fit by Nature* by John Colver describes a twelve-week fitness program that you won't need a gym or any special equipment for. Instead, you'll hop over logs and use the outdoors to get in shape. *Backpacker* magazine and REI both have great online articles with fitness plans and specific exercises to get you in shape for walking and backpacking (see Resources).

BRINGING IT ALL TOGETHER

Once you know all of the exercises you can do to prepare your body for the trail, it's important to put them into an actionable plan that you'll start to follow six to twelve months before your trip. This plan will differ for everyone. After all, your training will look very different if you're walking a relatively flat trail for three days than if you're attempting the more challenging Tour du Mont Blanc (Walk 5). You'll also want to address any aches and pains that emerge while

you're getting trail fit, to avoid injury before or during your walking tour.

Have a Workout Plan

I suggest that you start with a training calendar that assigns one of the four types of trail-fit workouts to each day, regardless of which trail you're going to walk. The four types of workouts are cardiovascular training, strength training, flexibility and balance training, and walk training. Then adjust the time and intensity of your workout depending on what you're training for and how soon your trip is coming up. Here are the goals and guidelines for each type of training:

Cardiovascular training: Aim for a variety of aerobic activities for 30 minutes two times per week (see Exercises 1 and 2 earlier in this chapter). Your goal is to fatigue your body but not exhaust it.

Strength training: Do a variety of upper- and lower-body exercises (including Exercises 3–11 and 15–18) two times per week. Always give yourself forty-eight hours between strength training sessions to recover and build more muscle.

Flexibility and balance training: Work on stretching, yoga and balance twice a week (see Exercises 12 and 14).

Walking: Get outside for a long walk (building up to a daylong walk) at least once a week (see Exercises 13, 19 and 20).

In calendar format, your training plan could look like the following:

TRAINING PLAN

DAY OF WEEK	TYPE OF WORKOUT
Sunday	Flexibility and balance training
Monday	Cardiovascular training
Tuesday	Strength training
Wednesday	Cardiovascular training
Thursday	Flexibility and balance training
Friday	Strength training
Saturday	Walking

You'll notice that I've assigned a workout for every day of the week. I know some people recommend taking at least one day off each week, but I find it's a lot easier to do something every single day than sporadically. It seems to take less willpower to actually get yourself to work out when it becomes part of your daily routine—a habit. I don't recommend working out hard every day, however, and that's the beauty of the flexibility and balance training days; they are perfect for sitting on the grass in the park as you stretch and take the opportunity to physically and mentally recover.

Even if you're gung ho about starting your training program, make sure you ease into things. You don't need to jump into working out for an hour a day, especially if your body isn't at all used to it—you can actually do more harm than good that way, injuring yourself and burning out. You need to start slow. So if you haven't worked out in a while, warm up for the first week by aiming for only 15 minutes of activity each day. If you're in great shape and active as can be, 30–45 minutes is probably your sweet spot.

Want to make your workouts more fun? Set a training goal with your travel companion and either work out together or hold each other accountable. And don't forget to give yourself some variety; if your workouts look the same week in and week out, you're likely to get bored and give up. Also, your muscles could get used to the exercises, and the workouts could lose their effectiveness. Increase your chances of sticking with your training goals by mixing things up a bit.

If you work out consistently, you should start to see results within six weeks, although your base level of fitness will start to increase long before that. If you're anything like me, you'll love how healthy and toned your body starts to feel—and how much farther you can walk. Your performance should peak when you're on trail in Europe, as you walk farther than you probably ever have before.

Have Aches?

Below are the most common aches and pains people experience when training for the trail—and some remedies that can help. **Note:** If you suspect an actual injury, suspend your training and make an appointment with your doctor or see a sports medicine specialist. Your body may need professional attention.

IT (Iliotibial) Band Pain

Feels like this: Pain and sometimes inflammation on the outside of your upper leg.

Make it better with this:

- Wear an IT band strap while you walk.
- Massage the tissue by rolling on your side on a firm foam roller.
- Do stretches that target the IT band.

If you train well, a mountainous hike like the Tour du Mont Blanc can be more joy than struggle.

Knee Pain

Feels like this: Pain and sometimes swelling in and around the kneecap.

Make it better with this:

- Strengthen your legs, especially your inner thighs and hamstrings.
- Wear an elastic knee brace while you walk.
- Search out flatter walks with less elevation gain and loss for your training walks and European adventure.
- Tackle softer trails—dirt paths rather than pavement.
- Lighten your backpack.
- Use trekking poles.
- Take shorter steps and walk in a zigzag pattern (switchbacks) when going downhill.

General Muscle Aches and Pains

Make it better with this:

- Have an arsenal of stretches you do after you work out or walk.
- Make sure you drink enough water and consume enough electrolytes.
- Take a nonsteroidal anti-inflammatory such as ibuprofen for pain and inflammation (acetaminophen doesn't have an anti-inflammatory effect).
- Use an ice pack for 15–20 minutes on the affected area, especially if there's swelling.
- Don't rely on topical muscle-rub creams or gels: according to the Sports Medicine Center at the Mayo Clinic, there's no conclusive evidence that they actually work.

Stay Trail Fit After Your Trip

To keep yourself in top trail shape, especially for walking long trails when you're back at home, don't abandon your workout routine when you get back from your trip. Instead, just ratchet down the time and intensity of your workouts to more of a maintenance level—30 minutes a day should do it. Your body—and your trail performance—will thank you.

BE PREPARED FOR ANYTHING

When it comes to preparing yourself for the walking component of exploring Europe on foot, training your body is only half of the battle. The other half is mastering a few key outdoor skills that will keep you safe, confident and happy on trail. This isn't just important; it's essential—even if you're walking with a guided tour and especially if you're walking by yourself. So if there's one chapter of this book to commit to memory, it's this one. (If you want to take this chapter with you to refer to on trail, check out the e-version of the book.)

The most obvious reason for mastering these skills is safety; the very thing that seduces us about the outdoors—the remoteness, wildness and unpredictability of nature—can also be our undoing if we're not prepared for it. But being knowledgeable about the outdoors and the situations you could encounter on trail is essential for other reasons as well: It can help you protect the paths you fall in love with as well as have better interactions with those you meet on trail. And to the degree that you continue to build and improve on your outdoor skills, that knowledge will equip you to venture farther and farther off the beaten path.

Ultimately, the number and type of outdoor skills you should add to your tool belt will be determined by how technical and remote the walk is that you're attempting. (Any technical skills or special considerations that a trail requires should be spelled out in the guidebook or trail description.) But there are ten basics that you should learn no matter how challenging—or downright easy—your chosen trail is. They include knowing how to read a map, how to calibrate your pace, when to take a break, how to handle inclement weather, how to treat minor injuries and ailments, what to do if you need to help, how to survive a night outside, how to treat the land you're walking through, how to treat your fellow walkers, and where to go to improve your outdoor skills. I'll cover each of these skills in turn.

Even on trails like Scotland's West Highland Way that are very well signed, it's important to always carry a good paper map. (Photo by Mitzi Sugar)

1. KNOW HOW TO READ A MAP

One of the most important things to master before you explore on foot is how to read a map. While most people are semiproficient at reading road maps, topographic maps can take some getting used to, because they give graphic representations of features such as elevation gain and terrain.

But once you can use a topo map, you'll have a huge amount of really important information at your fingertips, including where you are, where the trail is and the easiest way to get back on trail if you've somehow gone astray. You'll also be able to tell how far you've walked, how far you still have to go and how much elevation gain or loss you can expect on your route. Depending on the level of detail on your map, you'll even be able to see where there are services such as towns or restaurants on your route.

Learning the basics of reading a topographic map is too complex a skill to cover in this book, so taking a map and compass class or an online tutorial for orienteering is your best bet. Just don't forget to practice your learning outside in the real world—reading a map gets a lot easier the more you do it on trail.

Try my favorite trick for cutting down on the time it takes to find your location on a paper map: continually "thumb" the map. When you take off from the trailhead, place your thumb at your location. Then every time you pass a feature that's recognizable on the map, move your thumb to that spot. You'll always have a general idea of where you are.

Other Navigation Tools

You should always have with you a compass and paper map (and know how to read them—otherwise they're pretty useless) when you're on trail, but a stand-alone Global Positioning System (GPS) unit or a GPS app can also be a really helpful tool to figure out where you are and which direction you're walking. (For more information on choosing the right GPS device, check out Chapter 16, Electronic Tools.) I primarily navigate with a GPS device these days, although I always carry a paper map for backup.

2. KNOW HOW TO CALIBRATE YOUR PACE

Learning how to calibrate your pace is important because it can give you a good prediction of whether or not you're on track to reach your destination when the trail information says you should. It's better to calibrate your pace earlier in the day, rather than later, so you have more options if you're running behind. This becomes really important in the shoulder seasons, when you have less wiggle room for your walk because the days are shorter. (You don't want to be walking in the dark.) And if you're walking with other people, it's not *your* individual pace that matters—it's the pace of the slowest person in your group. (See the When Your Walking Companions are Slower Than You Are sidebar for tips on managing your differences in pace.)

To know if you're on track, compare how far you've traveled and how long it took with how far the trail information says you should have traveled in a given amount of time. Because most trail information lists mileage and time to major milestones such as towns, lakes and viewpoints, these places provide the perfect opportunity to make your comparison. As you walk, time yourself between major milestones, and include not just walking time but breaks in your comparison of mileage and time.

If your time for a given mileage is close or faster than what's in the trail information, you should be fine. If you're significantly slower—enough

that you won't make it to your destination before dark—you need to consider your options:

- If it's possible, speed up your pace.
- If you're on a training walk or an out-and-back, consider turning around early.
- If you're on a loop walk or walking village to village, you may need to shorten your walking route by using chairlifts (common on alpine routes in Europe), public transportation or a taxi to bypass some of the trail.

3. KNOW WHEN TO TAKE A BREAK

When it comes to walking for several hours, the old adage usually applies: the tortoise is faster than the hare. So don't get caught up in walking as fast as you can and never take a break. You need to stop at regular intervals—at least once every two hours for ten to fifteen minutes at a minimum—to rest your body, stretch out any sore muscles, fuel up (even if you're not hungry), hydrate (even if you're not thirsty) and reapply sunscreen. And you should always stop if something hurts—this is the number one way to make sure that something small, like a

WHEN YOUR WALKING COMPANIONS ARE SLOWER THAN YOU ARE

In every group, small or large, there's bound to be a variety of paces. Some people are just naturally faster—or slower—than other people.

If you're walking with someone who's slower than you are, how you deal with the situation can make or break your walk. Rather than charge ahead and wait for that person at regular intervals, which can make you feel bored and the other person feel rushed, put the slower person in front to set the pace. Then avoid the temptation to walk right behind them—they'll feel you breathing down their neck. Relax. Take the opportunity to have an extra-long look at the plants and flowers you pass, stop to take pictures often and then catch back up.

And remember, when you're walking with others, you're only as happy as the least happy person in your group. So if your partner is struggling, put yourself in their shoes—and then do what you can to help them along, whether that's giving them a word of encouragement or taking some of the weight from their pack.

Take frequent breaks on trail. Eat, drink, rest, reapply sunscreen—and even air out your feet.

hot spot on your foot, doesn't turn into something big, like a blister that's so painful you can't keep walking. Put a layer on when you take a break, especially in a windy spot (or when you start down a big descent)—it'll keep you from getting chilled.

Avoid running out of energy while you walk by consuming enough calories. How much is enough? Probably more than you think. According to *Backpacker* magazine, a 160-pound (72 kg) person walking for several hours with a backpack can burn more than 4,000 calories per day.

---

4. KNOW HOW TO HANDLE INCLEMENT WEATHER

Avoid as many weather surprises on trail as possible by checking the forecast in advance. I like to look the night before and the morning of a big walk. A little rain never hurt anyone, but if a serious weather front is approaching, find something else to do that day. If you're at home, get your trail workout a different way—or head to

where there's better weather; if you're in Europe, take the day off and explore in town before traveling to your next town by public transportation.

If weather conditions change suddenly when you're on trail, you need to be able to handle anything that nature throws at you. Here's how to cope with the most common weather situations that can sneak up on you while you're walking:

Intense rain: Put on your raingear and pack cover as soon as possible and seek shelter until the worst of the storm has passed, even if it's just under a big tree. Watch your footing on rocks and other surfaces that could be slick. If you're in a canyon or another place that could be in danger of flash flooding, head for higher ground.

Lightning: Stay away from exposed ridges, rock faces, meadows and marshy areas. Whenever possible, seek shelter in uniform forests where the trees are all roughly the same height. Stay low to the ground while bringing your arms and legs in to give your body the

smallest footprint possible; a crouching position is best—don't lie down.

Fog: Slow down and take care to stay on the trail; if you get lost, stop and wait until visibility improves before trying to find your way. If you get chilled, do jumping jacks or squats to stay warm while you wait for the fog to lift.

Snow: Fight the cold by putting on extra layers. Watch your footing; trails can be very slick, especially if there's ice in addition to snow. If you have traction devices (such as YakTrax) with you, put them on. Don't proceed if the trail is unsafe to walk. (For information on calling for help, check out skill number 6, Know What to Do If You Need Help, later in this chapter.)

Intense sun: Make sure to stay hydrated—drink at least a liter of water an hour in warm climates—reapply your sunscreen at least once every two hours, and limit your exposure to the sun as much as possible; for example, take your breaks in the shade.

What should you do if your walking shoes get soaked on trail? As soon as you get to your accommodations for the night, stick as much newspaper in your shoes as will fit. It'll absorb the water better than pretty much anything else. Make sure to swap in dry paper every hour or so until you go to bed (or you run out of newsprint), and leave the newsprint in your shoes overnight. By morning, your shoes should be only damp, if not completely dry.

The best thing you can do when something small is bothering you is stop and fix it so it doesn't create a big problem.

5. KNOW HOW TO TREAT MINOR INJURIES AND AILMENTS

When you're away from civilization and far from a doctor, it's important to have a game plan—and supplies—for treating the most common injuries and ailments that can occur when you're on trail. (Recommendations for things to include in your trail first-aid kit are in Chapter 15, Trail and Travel Tools.) These include blisters, minor cuts and scrapes, turned and sprained ankles, and general aches and pains. To learn how to deal with these and other injuries and minor ailments, read up on basic first aid (or take a class) and create a cheat sheet with the most helpful information. For an even more extensive resource, you can download a wilderness first-aid app onto your smartphone.

Know How to Treat Blisters

Blisters are a long-distance walker's worst fear. The best thing you can do for blisters is to prevent them. If you're blister prone, try walking in toesocks like the ones made by Injinji. If you have a hot spot, treat it as soon as you feel any pain or notice any rubbing.

If it's too late for prevention and you already have a blister, drain it by piercing it with a clean

I THINK I NEED A DOCTOR

If you need medical attention in Europe for a minor ailment (for example, a fever) and you're in a town, it can save you quite a bit of time and money to head to the pharmacy before the doctor. European pharmacies have greater latitude on what they can prescribe than North American pharmacies, and oftentimes they'll have some medications available over the counter that you'd need a prescription for back home. If the pharmacy can't help you, they can refer you to a doctor or clinic.

If there's a more serious health issue and you need to see a doctor, the following resources can also refer you to the right kind of physician—even one who speaks English:

- The local tourist information office
- Your guesthouse proprietor or hotel concierge
- Your travel health insurance company, via their twenty-four-hour assistance number

needle—don't remove the skin, just deflate the bubble—and stick enough moleskin on top to cover and pad the general area. I like to aim for a margin of at least a half inch (1.25 cm) around the blister, if not more. Take the moleskin off at night while you sleep—airing your feet out (try sleeping with your feet out of the covers) will help everything dry out and heal.

Know How to Treat Traveler's Diarrhea

The most common ailment you'll likely face in Europe is traveler's diarrhea. It usually strikes about the third day after you arrive; it can be caused by a number of things (including too much rich food or caffeine) and is usually more annoying than serious. Drink a lot of fluids (but avoid alcohol, sugar and dairy), rest and eat bland and starchy foods. If there's any blood in your stool, or if your diarrhea lasts for more than a couple of days, get an appointment with a local doctor (see the I Think I Need a Doctor sidebar for how to find one).

6. KNOW WHAT TO DO IF YOU NEED HELP

You should always know how to call for help from the trail if you need it. If you have cell phone service, this can be as simple as dialing the local emergency number or the international emergency number: 112. (For service in Europe, see Cell Phone Service in Chapter 16, Electronic Tools.) This international emergency number works for most of the countries in the European Union and many other countries around the world. Before you travel, verify that it's valid in the country you're traveling to.

In most of continental Europe, the international emergency number is 112.

Things get a little trickier when you're walking in an area with no cell phone service. If it's really important to you to have the peace of mind that comes with being able to send an emergency signal no matter what, consider carrying a SPOT device, satellite communicator or personal locator beacon (see Chapter 16, Electronic Tools, for more on these devices).

If you're confident that there will be a decent number of other walkers on your route and that civilization (even a mildly popular road) is somewhat nearby, you could ask someone to help you by walking out to the road or a nearby town and alerting the proper authorities for you. Depending on how popular your route is, you may have to wait a while for someone who might help you to come by.

Have an Informed Contact Person Who Can Call for Help for You

When you're out for a long walk, especially if you're on a remote or challenging trail or by yourself, it's a standard practice to leave a detailed copy of your itinerary with a contact person—a close friend or family member. When you're a long way from home, it's also a good idea to check in with your contact person on a regular (and pre-established) schedule. Thus, if something should happen and you're unable to call for help, your contact person will call for help on your behalf.

Give your contact person clear instructions for what to do if you don't check in as scheduled. For example, "If I haven't checked in by 7:00 a.m. your time (keep in mind whatever time difference applies), call the local authorities at (insert the number)." That way, if you're in distress on trail and can't call for help, you don't have to wait for someone to come by to help you.

7. KNOW HOW TO SURVIVE A NIGHT OUTSIDE

In the event that something prevents you from reaching your destination during a walk—you get lost or hurt, for instance—you should know how to survive a night outside. That is much more important when you're walking a remote trail, such as the Lycian Way (Walk 7) or the Laugavegur Trek (Walk 14), than one near a road—and civilization. At the very minimum, you should have a basic understanding of survival skills such as building a shelter out of whatever's at hand, staying warm and signaling for help.

Taking a wilderness survival class is a very good idea; you can typically find these at your local sporting goods or outdoor store. At the very least, read through one of the many survival-tip roundups online or check out some of the really great books and tutorials that go into more detail (see Resources). Also see The Ten Essentials in Chapter 15, Trail and Travel Tools. And don't freak yourself out—the chances of anything like this happening are pretty darn remote. But regardless, it's better to be prepared.

8. KNOW HOW TO TREAT THE LAND YOU'RE WALKING THROUGH

The more you walk, the more you'll come to revere the land you're walking through. And that's a really good thing, because walkers can leave quite an impact on a landscape. En masse, we're like a continuous drop of water that eventually creates a canyon, except our impact isn't nearly that scenic. Instead, it's quite ugly: erosion, trash (toilet paper on trail is the worst!), aggressive wildlife that prefers human food. The list goes on.

Unless you're on an urban trail or you have a bladder of steel, you'll probably have to go to the bathroom while you're out on trail. Please don't try to avoid it by drinking less water than what your body needs! (I see this all the time with my female walking companions.) Instead, get comfortable with the idea of going to the bathroom while you're on trail (see the Leave No Trace list in this section for tips). Once you do, you may just find that it's kind of freeing and certainly much quicker (and more convenient) than finding an actual restroom.

Be a better kind of walker—this is a point of pride for most experienced walkers—by reducing your impact on the environment with

"Clean up the garbage from the land so it does not go to the sea! Do not ruin the world. Think about your future!"

the help of Leave No Trace, a collection of best practices that was developed by the US Forest Service in the 1960s and has since become the worldwide standard for how to behave when you're in nature. The LNT principles can be summed up pretty easily: minimize your impact and leave things the same as (or better than) you found them. The section below lists the most important points.

Leave No Trace
- Know and obey the rules where you're going.
- Whenever possible, travel in small groups.
- Stick to the trail.
- Don't cut switchbacks.
- Close all gates behind you.
- Pack out all trash, including leftover food.
- If you have to go to the bathroom while you're on trail, walk off trail to where

no one can see you, bury your waste in a cathole that's 6–8 inches (15–20 cm) deep, and pack out your toilet paper (yes, you must) and any feminine hygiene products.
- Don't take elements of the natural world (for example, pretty rocks) with you.
- Watch wildlife from a distance—don't try to get close.
- Don't feed wild animals, including birds and squirrels.
- Be especially considerate of wildlife during times when they're vulnerable: mating, nesting, raising young, winter.
- If you're camping, set your tent up at established sites that are at least 200 feet (60 m) away from lakes or streams, and have a fire only where it's permitted, keep it small and put it out completely when you're done.

9. KNOW HOW TO TREAT YOUR FELLOW WALKERS

Some of the best times you can have on trail are with your fellow walkers, so keep things as positive as possible by knowing how to treat them. There are two different types of walkers that you should think about: your walking companion(s) and the strangers you encounter on trail.

Your Walking Companion(s)

It's important to be proactive about keeping the peace with your walking companion(s). It's not such a big deal when you're just on a training walk back at home—after all, you'll probably get a break from each other in a few hours. But it does become a big deal when you're in Europe together, day in and day out without a decent-length break in sight. Your relationship with that person—and how happy or unhappy you both are—often really colors your trip, for good or for bad. So do your part to keep things going well.

Start by keeping yourself happy on trail. If you have pain, address it. If you're hungry, eat something. (Hungry people are angry people!) If you are exhausted, get a good night's sleep. If you don't take care of your needs, you run the risk of taking things out on your walking companion(s).

BE A CONSCIENTIOUS WALKER IN TOWN TOO

You'll get a much warmer reception from guesthouse owners, restaurateurs and shopkeepers if you're considerate with your walking gear when you're in town. Here are some things to remember:

- If requested, leave your backpack outside. (But be smart about where you leave it and keep an eye on it the whole time.)
- Be careful with your raingear—don't let it drip all over the floor. Instead, look for a coat hook and hang it up.
- Don't take your boots and socks off in establishments, especially bars or restaurants. It's a definite no-no to subject other people to your stinky feet, and in some cultures it's considered insulting.
- Don't track mud all over your accommodations' common areas or your room—remove your dirty shoes as soon as possible. Some places will make you leave them at the door.
- Don't dry wet clothes by draping them over wooden furniture—it can discolor the wood. Instead, use a laundry line and/or dry your clothes in the bathroom.
- When using public transportation, don't take up an extra seat with your backpack unless there is an abundance of open seats (and never make someone stand just so your bag can have a seat beside you). Instead, keep your backpack on your lap.
- When you're in a store or restaurant, be conscious of your backpack and its size, especially when you turn around or are in a tight space—you could easily knock something over. Have more control over your backpack by wearing it on the front of your body.

Apologize with more than words—offer your companion a fresh bun and slice of butter snagged from the breakfast buffet and some local jam.

Once you've looked to your own needs, do what you can to keep the other person happy as well. Be positive and encouraging. Compromise. Be patient. If disagreements or tensions do arise, calm your temper by counting to twenty before responding, or take some time apart. Just never get so far away from each other that you can't see the other person if the two of you are on trail. This is really important—you don't want to get separated.

If you do say something in anger, apologize as soon as you can. And do whatever you can to get your companionship back to a good place. The happiness of your walk depends on it.

Other Trail Users

On most trails, you'll encounter more people than just your walking companion(s) each day. You'll come across other walkers, as well as mountain bikers and sometimes even equestrians. You can increase your chances of having positive interactions with these other trail users if you keep a few things in mind:

- Say hi and be friendly. At the very least, nod to acknowledge the other person.
- Don't monopolize the best spots—share them, so everyone gets their turn for a look at wildlife, a photo of a great vista or a sit-down in the best rest spot.
- If you ask someone to take your photo, offer to take theirs as well.

- Use headphones or earbuds if you feel the need to listen to music or a podcast on trail.
- Keep your voice down so you don't disturb others.
- When walking in a group, walk single file so you don't make it hard for another walker to pass.
- If people are walking faster than you are, let them pass.
- If you're walking downhill, yield to someone who's going uphill.
- If you come across pack animals or horses, step to the downhill side of the trail and let them pass.
- If you come across mountain bikers, they should yield to you. But if they don't, step to the side of the trail and let them pass. (This is for your own safety!)

10. KNOW WHERE TO GO TO IMPROVE YOUR OUTDOOR SKILLS

Falling in love with exploring on foot means having a lifelong love affair with walking, so get familiar with the resources that can help you improve your skills. There are so many out there, from online tutorials to books to classes to walking groups! It's easy to learn more about anything and everything you're unfamiliar with in the outdoors.

Some of the best online walking and hiking tutorials you can find are through *Backpacker* magazine, which offers self-paced classes in things like thru-hiking, navigation and wilderness first aid. (They also publish a lot of free online articles that can help you do everything from getting in shape to building an emergency shelter.) For books, check out the outdoor section of your library or favorite bookstore—I like in-depth instructional guides such as Chris Townsend's *The Backpacker's Handbook* or Dave Canterbury's *Bushcraft 101*. Local outdoor stores typically have a variety of free classes that are great for beginners. I also recommend joining a walking group like the ones available on Meetup.com or through your local outdoor organization, so you can learn on trail and in the real world from people who are more experienced than you. (Plus, it's really fun!)

Even once you've mastered the basics, I encourage you to keep learning more-advanced outdoor skills. A couple of organizations that are great for this are the National Outdoor Leadership School and Outward Bound (see Resources), where you'll head into the wilderness with highly trained instructors to further your trail education.

Improving your outdoor skills isn't only fun, it'll also make you a better hiker—and expand the number of trails that are accessible to you.

CHAPTER

11

MAKE YOUR WALK A CULTURAL EXPERIENCE

When it comes to exploring Europe on foot, it's not a surprise to most people that it's important to train your body for the trail and be prepared for any situation that you could encounter in the outdoors. What does come as a surprise? My focus on preparing for the cultural element of the trip as well.

It can be a hard concept for people to grasp—most of us see exploring a foreign culture as something that happens when we're there, not still at home. It's those unexpected discovery moments that you seem to stumble into: having an enlightening conversation with a German farmer or finding a tiny restaurant that serves the very best French food you've ever tasted.

But I'm going to let you in on a little secret: more often than not, travel magic—and the deeper understanding of a culture that it gives you—happens to those who have prepared for it. It happens to the person who speaks enough German to say hello to the farmer or knows enough about French cuisine to order the local delicacy. And that travel magic can happen to you as well.

There are two aspects to being prepared for these incredible opportunities. The first is knowing enough about the local culture to know what to expect and have some appreciation for it. The second is being intentional about what cultural opportunities you pursue on trail. This chapter provides suggestions on how you can tackle both of these aspects, by learning before you leave and continuing to learn when you're traveling.

These tasks are organized around eight specific aspects of culture: history, politics and current events, customs, language, art and architecture, literature, music and food. By preparing for the cultural elements of the trip, you won't just encounter more travel magic—you'll make it.

HISTORY

Having some knowledge of a country's or region's history is really powerful—once you know what the local people have been through, it's a lot easier to understand why they are the way they are, what they value and hold dear, and where the future might take them. Knowing local history can also give you some context and patience about forming an opinion on issues—such as the United Kingdom voting to leave the European Union—that you might otherwise have thought were clearly black or white, right or wrong.

Learn Before You Leave

Take a history class. You don't need to officially go to school to take European and country-specific history classes. Many are available online, where you can learn from the comfort of your home and at your own pace. Here are some of my favorite free resources:

- Open Culture includes more than 1,200 classes, such as European Civilization, the Early Middle Ages, and Modern France from schools like Yale, Oxford and MIT.
- Khan Academy features short educational videos that you can chain together for longer courses on subjects like WWI and WWII.

Preparing in advance for a history hike by attending lectures and reading books can make your time on trail more enlightening.

- iTunes U has downloadable courses like Modern Europe and Medieval Europe that are broken down into short segments that you can listen to on your way to work, when you're running on the treadmill, et cetera.

A great resource that's not free but is well worth the money (and has a free one-month trial) is the Great Courses Plus, which offers more than 8,000 educational videos like "A History of Eastern Europe" and "The Black Death" that you can stream on your TV or mobile device. (See Resources for all of the above.)

Watch history movies and documentaries. One of the best ways to prepare for a trip is to watch history movies and documentaries that are set in the country you're visiting. For example, when Mac and I were getting ready to travel to Poland, we watched *Schindler's List* before we visited Oskar Schindler's factory and the nearby Auschwitz concentration camp, and the movie really gave us a better understanding of what conditions were like at both of those facilities in the early 1940s.

While we were able to find *Schindler's List* on YouTube (which also has a good selection of documentaries and educational history videos), you can find a big selection of similar movies on paid streaming apps like Netflix and Hulu. If you want to watch these movies while you're traveling, be sure to download them to your device—most streaming apps won't work when you're out of your home country because of licensing issues.

Learn When You're There

Take an urban walking tour. This is a great opportunity to not only learn about local history in the towns you're passing through but also ask any questions you may have about what you've learned. For more information

on finding an urban walking tour, check out Chapter 6, Walk Independently or Hire Help.

Visit an open-air or living-history museum. If you haven't been to one of these kinds of museums before, you're in for a treat. They are typically set in a specific time in history (for example, the late 1800s) and feature live actors who re-create what life was like back then. One of my favorite living-history museum experiences was in Ireland, where we got to wander through straw-thatched huts like the ones Irish farmers used to live in (complete with rough-hewn furniture and straw-stuffed mattresses from that era) and taste thick bread that was made over a fire by a woman dressed in period clothing. It was like traveling back in time.

POLITICS AND CURRENT EVENTS

Having a basic understanding of local politics and current events won't just open your eyes to the biggest issues your host country is experiencing. It can also give you a way to connect with local people over the things that matter most to them—the things they're talking about in the subway, in the pub and on the street corner. It can also give you some interesting perspective on how other countries are solving problems that we all share, from poverty to immigration.

Learn Before You Leave

Accumulate some background knowledge.

- The *CIA World Factbook* (see Resources) has brief write-ups on the government, economy, military and transnational issues of more than 267 governments around the world.
- Rick Steves's book *Travel as a Political Act* is another resource with good background information on how European governments are handling important political and social issues (oftentimes

much differently than North American governments).

Read up on current events. Many news sites can give you a better understanding of what's happening in Europe and in the specific country where you'll be traveling. Here are some ideas:

- British Broadcasting Network (see Resources): To get an overview of what's happening in Europe (in English, even), check out the Europe edition.
- *The Guardian* (see Resources): For another overview of what's happening in Europe (in English), check out both the international and UK editions.
- Local newspapers: To learn more about what's happening in the country you'll be visiting, set your browser to the homepage of a local newspaper and spend a few minutes each day skimming the headlines. If the information isn't in English, use the Google Translate Chrome Extension, which allows you to quickly translate foreign language websites.
- Another way to see what's happening where you'll travel—and what the locals have to say about it—is to follow a local newspaper on social media. Just remember, there are Internet trolls everywhere, so don't judge popular opinion based on a few strongly worded comments.

Reflect on the issues. If you'd like to gain a deeper understanding of what's happening in the country you'll visit, hear multiple viewpoints and debate issues back and forth, check out Meetup.com and browse the Internet for foreign language conversation groups in your area.

Learn When You're There

Visit government buildings. Some Europeans, such as Norwegians, are extremely proud of their local governments, so make sure to stop by the town hall to see what all the fuss is about. Occasionally local governments offer tours to help you do just that. Even if you can't find a tour, pay attention to the statues and paintings of political heroes that are sprinkled around the building and look up their stories—this can teach you a lot about what social and political challenges the local people have struggled through and what values they aspire to.

Ask a local. It's not hard to find a local who's eager to talk your ear off about politics and what's happening in their city and country. All you have to do is plant yourself in the right spot (the local pub is a good choice), show a genuine interest in your temporary home and ask questions in a respectful manner. People tend to clam up if they sense criticism, so keep an open mind and remember that you'll learn the most if you listen instead of speak.

If you're traveling to several countries within Europe, asking a variety of folks their opinions on matters concerning the European Union, from immigration to taxes, is a great way to get a corresponding variety of perspectives—and plenty of food for thought.

CUSTOMS

Learning local customs is a great way not only to recognize and start to appreciate how people do things where you're traveling but also to figure out how you can best blend in with the locals while you're there. And it can help you avoid misunderstandings or accidentally offending someone.

Learn Before You Leave

Read a good guide on the country. Various sites on the Internet that are dedicated to local customs and etiquette include information on nearly every country in the world. Many

THANK YOU
for adhering the rules.

✓ ✓

You'll have an easier time getting into cultural hotspots like churches and mosques if you follow the dress code.

At some point, it's just going to happen—you're going to commit a cultural faux pas. Typically when this happens, it's not a huge deal. Most locals are really understanding about travelers—they know you may do things a lot differently in your own country. The best thing you can do if you commit a faux pas is to show you're trying, have a sense of humor about the whole thing, be polite and apologize. And don't forget to show them a genuine smile—it's the very best thing for bridging cultural divides.

Learn When You're There

Be a good observer. If you want to know how people go about their daily lives—everything from how they interact with each other to what they wear—head to a local cafe or park and start people watching. And if you're thinking of doing something you're a little unsure of, such as buying produce from a market stall, watch to see how other people do it first (for example, are customers allowed to touch the produce, or does only the proprietor do that?) to save yourself some embarrassment.

Dress like the locals dress. This applies to both conservative and liberal travel destinations. If you're in a place where women traditionally cover their shoulders and knees (such as a Catholic church), show your respect for the culture and blend in by doing the same. If you're lounging at a nude beach in the south of France, follow the lead of the locals and take off your swimsuit.

Schedule your day like the locals do. Depending on where you are in Europe, the rhythm of daily life can be quite different. Learn the benefits of having a totally different schedule than you're used to by following what the locals do, even if that requires starting your

of these were initially designed for business travelers, who either invest in making a good first impression or risk losing a big deal. One such resource that's worth checking out is Commisceo Global (see Resources).

Attend a travel lecture. Bookstores, travel agencies, travel stores and community education programs in community colleges often have lectures that can enlighten you about the specifics of traveling in different European countries—and what local customs you should expect. Find these lectures with an Internet search or by looking up the lecture calendar for individual organizations near you.

day later than normal, taking a nap midday and eating dinner as the sun goes down.

Participate in the activities of daily life. In my experience, the best travel experiences are often things that feel very ordinary to locals but are quite extraordinary to someone who's just visiting.

Take the time to participate in local life by going to a church, synagogue or mosque—it's a great chance to learn about the local religion.

Seek out festivals, which can be a really fun way to learn about what's important to the local people, from agriculture to history to pop culture.

Socialize wherever locals socialize, whether that's the pub or the football ("soccer" to us) stadium, a hookah bar or a sidewalk cafe. If there's a gender divide, you'll have the best chance of getting to know people—and participating in local life—if you head to where your gender typically hangs out, whether that's the barbershop, beauty salon or public bath.

One of my very favorite souvenirs is a new custom or attitude. From France, I brought home a love of long, lingering dinners. From Italy, it was a greater focus on family. And from Germany, it was a whole new appreciation for being on time. Wherever you travel, think about something the local culture does really well that you'd like to bring home—it will probably be your longest-lasting souvenir of all.

LANGUAGE

Learning a foreign language—even a few key phrases—can open up opportunities for interacting with so many people while you're traveling, especially those who aren't in the tourism industry or didn't have the opportunity to learn English in school. I've found it especially handy for conversing with rural folks, older people and small children. And it can make your trip

a lot easier if you're traveling in a remote area and want to occasionally be able to ask for directions, et cetera.

But learning a bit of the local language won't just allow you to communicate with people—words everywhere will start to come alive for you, words that can help you understand the local culture, from signs on the side of the road to newspapers in your guesthouse lobby, graffiti on old buildings and song lyrics on the radio.

Learn Before You Leave

Take a class. It's easy to learn a foreign language with the help of the continuing-education division of your local community college. You'll

Outdoor food markets are the best place to enjoy a region's delicacies and dine elbow-to-elbow with locals.

Before you travel, write down on an index card the top ten phrases you'd like to use when you're traveling—then keep the card handy so it's there when you need to refer to it. Here are the words and phrases I always put on my cheat sheet:

- "Hello."
- "Do you speak English?"
- "Please."
- "Thank you."

- "Excuse me."
- "Where is the bathroom?"
- "Goodbye."

be able to choose from beginner, intermediate and advanced levels; most programs also offer a crash course for travelers. Because these non-credit classes are intended for people who work, they're held on nights and weekends—perfect for your busy schedule. They're a particularly good choice for those who like structured learning and want to build their foreign language proficiency methodically.

Learn on the go. If a structured class isn't for you, a resource that allows you to learn on your own might be just the thing.

- Duolingo (see Resources): This really great (and free!) program for learning foreign languages is available in both desktop and mobile versions.
- *10 Minutes a Day* book series for foreign languages: I also suggest these books (for instance, *French in 10 Minutes a Day*), which are organized around major tasks such as telling time or buying a train ticket—and plenty more things that are helpful while you travel.
- Foreign language books: For more books that can help you learn a foreign language at your own pace, check out your local library.

Join a conversation group. To make language learning fun and social, check out Meetup.com and the Internet for a group near

you. Most groups don't include formal instruction; rather, they give you a low-pressure and low-embarrassment way to practice carrying on a conversation in whatever language you're learning.

Learn When You're There

Sign up for a one-off language class. In many towns, you can find language schools that offer one-off language classes that will give you an introduction to the language and the words you most need to know, as well as the opportunity to practice with a native speaker. To find a one-off language class, search online or contact the local tourist information office.

One of the best language classes I've ever taken was a half-day language, cooking and culture class in Marrakesh, Morocco. In the span of only a few hours, I learned a handful of Arabic words and non-verbal gestures, cooked my own *tajine* (the most famous of Moroccan dishes) and had tea with a local. This class also gave me the opportunity to ask any and all of the questions I had about Morocco. It was a great experience that really deepened my understanding of Moroccan culture. And after the class, the learning wasn't done. I was sent home with a small dictionary of important Arabic phrases and even a cookbook so I could practice re-creating the *tajine* on my own.

Learning about religious art can make visiting churches and mosques a lot more interesting.

Practice talking to locals. Even if you're not fluent in the language, if everything you say comes out incomplete (for example, "Where grocery store?"), or if everyone around you speaks great English, take every opportunity to practice your language skills with the locals. It won't just improve your skills; it will also show those you meet that you're really trying, which they always seem to respect and appreciate. I promise it'll endear you to them, even if you think you sound silly.

ART AND ARCHITECTURE

Art and architecture are subtle back doors to really interesting cultural insights. Understanding them can help you dispense with your preconceived notions (for instance, Brutalist architecture, the naked-concrete-block style made famous by the Soviets, actually got its start in the United States) and see what was most important to people at different times in history (for example, cathedrals illustrate how significant religion was in the Middle Ages).

Knowing the stories behind art and architecture can also help you understand why things look the way they do, so instead of seeing something such as several paintings from the Biedermeier period and saying to yourself, "Gosh, how boring. These artists had no imagination—they just painted people in their homes," you instead say, "Wow, I really see how suffocating the political repression following the Napoleonic Wars was; it really did drive people to focus completely on their home lives!"

Learn Before You Leave
Take a class. Look online for classes such as How to Understand a Picasso Painting or History of Architecture. You should be able to drill down to specific courses by topic (for example, "art").

Look up—way up—and you'll often see vestiges of medieval life in European buildings, like winches for hauling goods to upper floors.

- Open Culture offers more than 1,200 free classes, including ones on art history, art appreciation and architecture, from schools like Yale, Oxford and MIT.
- iTunes U has free downloadable courses that are broken down into short segments that you can listen to on your way to work, when you're running on the treadmill, et cetera.

Read for background knowledge. If you like your information to come from books, a good one that's also relatively entertaining is Rick Steves's *Europe 101: History and Art for the Traveler*.

Check out a lecture. There are plenty of online lectures that will help you understand European art. One series that I recommend is Rick Steves's "Art for Travelers," which consists of four videos that are each about an hour in length and together introduce you to the major styles of European art.

(See Resources for all of the above.)

Learn When You're There

Sign up for museum tours. Whenever you're in a museum, don't just walk around looking at paintings. Even if you read the little placards next to them, you're still missing a lot of background information about the pieces and why they're special. Instead, sign up for a group tour (some of them are even included in the price of admission), or if you'd like to learn at your own pace, take a self-guided audio tour.

Search out nontraditional museums: In addition to visiting traditional multi-artist museums, look for artist-specific museums, which are often located in the building the artist lived or worked in. Seeing what the artist surrounded him- or herself with can give you fascinating insights into their work.

Go on an urban walking tour. This is a great way to learn more about fascinating urban architecture that you'd otherwise just pass by. For more information on finding a tour, check out Urban Walking Tour in Chapter 6, Walk Independently or Hire Help.

Head to the theater. To learn about European performance art, from plays to operas to musicals (and some of the most famous ones in history, at that), check out the local theater. For more information, look online or contact the local tourist information office.

LITERATURE

Literature holds many of the same backdoor cultural insights that art and architecture do but can be far easier to grasp because you get to be part of the story; indeed, you're immersed in it. You can see what the characters are thinking, why they do what they do, how it feels to be them at that moment in time. And because of that, literature is a great way to understand all kinds of things about a culture, from ordinary life to extraordinary moments in history.

Learn Before You Leave

Read a book that's set in the place you're visiting. A book doesn't have to be nonfiction for it to transport you to where you're going and give you a better understanding of the local culture—oftentimes fiction and historical fiction are also good. To find books that are set in the country or region you're visiting, check the Internet or ask your friendly bookseller or librarian for help.

When I read in preparation for my travels, I like to choose books that teach me about local history and why things—especially confounding things—happened the way they did. For example, in preparation for walking in Germany, I read Erik Larson's *In the Garden of Beasts* because I wanted to understand just how someone like Hitler could come to power while the rest of the world stood by and let it happen. As I read the based-on-a-true-story tale of the US ambassador

to Germany in 1933, everything started to make more sense. In the end, my reading gave me a better understanding of not only the country I was planning on walking through but the role my own country had played in shaping it.

Look for country-specific collections of writing. One of the best ways to learn the ins and outs of a country is by reading stories that have been written about the area by writers who were born and raised there. A great resource that brings many of these stories together by location is the Travelers Literary Companions series by Whereabouts Press (see Resources); they offer collections for several European cities as well as countries.

Join an author-specific book club. If you're traveling somewhere a famous author used to live or put on the map, it can be really fun to dive into their collected works with a book club of other enthusiasts. This type of book club is more common than you'd think—for example, there are Jane Austen book clubs all over the world. To find an author-specific book club, check out Meetup.com, ask around at your local library or do an Internet search for the author's name, "book club" and where you live. If you can't find an existing group, consider starting one!

Get some help understanding a complex author. If you're having trouble understanding a foreign author, even someone like Shakespeare whose work is in English (well, kind of), don't be afraid to get some help.

- Open Culture offers more than 1,200 free classes, including several on the language and collected works of high-profile authors like Shakespeare and Goethe, from schools like Yale, Oxford and MIT.
- The Great Courses Plus offers more than 8,000 educational videos, including many on Europe's renowned writers.

- The Cliff's Notes series of books is an oldie but goodie with one-off explanations instead of classes.

Learn When You're There

Browse local bookstores. If you want to find good books that are set in the area where you're traveling, check out local bookstores and ask the staff for their personal recommendations. Most of the folks who work for independent bookstores, especially, are there because they love books, so they should be able to point you in the right direction. Even if they don't have a large English-language section, they can suggest titles that you can look for online and in English—or send you to a bookstore that has a better selection than they do.

    Visit author-specific museums. Just as there are artist-specific museums, there are writer-specific museums where you can explore the house or office of a famous author—and perhaps glean additional insights into their work.

Read poetry. Because poetry has a cadence to it, much like walking, the two go together really well (especially when the poetry is read aloud). Download some local poetry that has been translated into English (unless you understand the local language—in that case, go with the original) and make it a goal to read a new poem every time you take a notable break on trail. This is especially fun when the poetry was written about or inspired by the land you're walking through, such as famous poet William Wordsworth and England's Lake District (Walk 12).

MUSIC

Local music can tell you a lot about a culture, from what's most important to people (such as freedom, love, God) to what musical traditions and instruments they hold dear. It is also really handy for learning a foreign language, because it helps you understand the cadence that native speakers use. But one of the best reasons for learning about and exposing yourself to local music is that it will

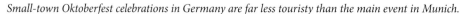

Small-town Oktoberfest celebrations in Germany are far less touristy than the main event in Munich.

increase your chances of actually liking what you discover—the more familiar you are with something, the more you tend to like it.

Learn Before You Leave

Take a music-appreciation class. If you've never been a music buff, or if your taste in music extends to a single genre, it can be worthwhile to invest some time in a music-appreciation class. In addition to expanding your musical comfort zone, a class can help you understand the different kinds of music that you'll likely encounter while traveling—and make you far more likely to appreciate, or at least enjoy, them.

- Open Culture offers more than 1,200 helpful free classes, including Music as a Mirror of History, from schools like Yale, Oxford and MIT.
- The Great Courses Plus offers more than 8,000 educational videos, including "How to Listen to and Understand Great Music" and "How to Listen to and Understand Opera".

Find out what's currently popular. If you want to know what locals are listening to, check out the charts on Shazam.com and Billboard. To find this information quickly, it's easiest to search online for "(Shazam or Billboard) top charts for (insert whichever country you're traveling to)." Just don't be surprised when a lot of it is American pop music—there's bound to be something local on the charts as well.

Search out folk and traditional music. If you really want to listen to music in the local language, especially music that has cultural significance, look online (iTunes and YouTube are great resources) for folk or traditional music from the country you're visiting.

Listen to anything you can get your hands on. You'll benefit from exposing yourself to all kinds of local music, not just the really popular or classical stuff. Create a channel (for example, "French music") on Pandora or Spotify. Or stream country- or language-specific compilations on YouTube and listen to anything and everything you can.

Because streaming won't work when you're out of your home country, create a playlist for your trip by downloading your favorite local songs and saving the playlist to your phone. (Don't forget to bring your headphones!) I love to listen to my playlist on the plane ride over, on the train—or even back at home when I want to reminisce about my trip.

Learn When You're There

Go to a live performance. You don't need to buy a ticket to an expensive show to hear local music when you're traveling; oftentimes, you can find amazing music in coffee shops or pubs. The local tourist information office should be able to point out which venues regularly have live music.

Learn a traditional dance. What goes perfectly with music? Dancing! Search out traditional forms of dance when you're traveling (like the *jota* if you're in Spain or the polka if you're in Germany) and kill two birds with one stone. Dance classes can often be found through the local tourist information office or by contacting venues that offer live music and asking if they offer free introductory dance lessons. Or just head to the local hot spot and, when the music and dancing are in full swing, ask a friendly local for some pointers. Chances are, they'll be really excited to help you learn.

FOOD

One of my favorite ways to learn about foreign cultures is through food. And that's because hiding behind those amazing tastes, just waiting to be discovered, is usually a good story about unique local products, interesting traditions and national or regional pride. Although it's fun to discover local food while you're traveling, I also suggest familiarizing yourself with a few main dishes or flavors before you leave home—just as with music, the more familiar you are with the food, the more you tend to like it.

Studies have shown that it can take up to fifteen times of trying a new food before you like it, but most people stop by five. If it's not love at first bite, keep trying!

Learn Before You Leave

Learn what the typical cuisine and local specialties are. A lot of this information is available online from various food blogs and websites and is only a simple Internet search away. But if you'd rather explore the best of local cuisine with a book, check out Lonely Planet's *Food Lover's Guide to the World*, which includes information on what you should eat in different parts of Europe, as well as fascinating details on local ingredients, cooking techniques and recipes.

Find out what the locals drink. The same food blogs and websites that give suggestions on typical cuisine also tend to offer up local drink specialties, from hard alcohol that will knock your socks off to a special variety of wine that shouldn't be missed.

If you want to be sure to hit all of the local specialties while you're traveling, write them down on an index card and keep them handy. I also like to look up photos of these dishes and drinks on the Internet and screen-shot them with my phone so that I can easily identify them when I'm at a restaurant.

BE THE KIND OF TRAVELER YOU WANT TO MEET

Like it or not, when you travel you're an ambassador, not just for your home country but also for travelers everywhere. Take care to be the best version of yourself that you can be—other people are watching and may form opinions about your countrymen or other travelers based on what you do. Here are some things to be especially mindful of:

Watch your voice. North Americans are some of the loudest people in the world. If you're in an enclosed area like a restaurant or a train, pay special attention to keeping your voice down.

Ask before you take photos of locals. No one likes to feel as though they're on display like an animal at the zoo, so if you want a picture of the old man sitting in the cafe or the young child toddling around in traditional clothing, be polite and ask first if it's OK. And if you have permission to snap a photo, do it quickly and move on.

Be polite—always. Things don't always go according to plan when you travel. That's one of the reasons it makes sense that the word *travel* is rooted in a similar word, *travail*. At some point, your flight might be cancelled, the bus driver might miss your stop or the guesthouse proprietor might accidentally give away your room. In those really frustrating moments, don't let your temper get the best of you. The best course of action is to be as polite as possible. This isn't just considerate; it's also your best chance of getting someone to help you correct the situation. (For more tips on dealing with challenging situations, check out Be Flexible When Faced with Challenges in Chapter 19, Make the Most of the Experience.)

Most bars in Spain offer a selection of tapas or pinchos *(small plates) in the evening—perfect for a post-trail appetizer or dinner.*

Learn When You're There

Go local. In my experience, the best restaurants are always the locally owned ones that utilize fresh ingredients from the surrounding region and change their menus depending on what's in season. These are typically hole-in-the-wall spots that don't have glossy photos of the food or an English menu—instead, they have three or four specialties written on a chalkboard out front. Eat at one of these places, and you'll typically get not just amazing food but also an education in local cuisine from an enthusiastic waiter or proprietor. When Mac and I were walking Cinque Terre (Walk 6), we found a spot just like this and ate there every night of our trip—that's how much we loved it.

Take a cooking class or participate in a food tour. Eating a meal once and loving it is one thing—knowing enough about local cuisine and its ingredients to be able to re-create it again and again, even when you're at home, is another. If you love the local cuisine, do a deeper dive. You can find many cooking classes and food tours online or through the local tourist information office. I also recommend checking websites that specialize in niche tours, such as Airbnb Experiences and Viator (see Resources). It can also help to do a broader Internet search for what you're looking for and where you're traveling or to look up local cooking schools and ask about half-day or day-long classes for travelers.

Let the proprietor take the lead. If you don't know what the best thing on the menu is, ask. And if you order it, trust that it'll come the way it's meant to be served. I learned this lesson the hard way in Florence when I ordered a local specialty, the Florentine steak, and asked for it to be cooked to medium well instead of medium rare. The proprietor didn't even blink before he responded, "No, madam. That would ruin it." Then he just turned on his heels and got to work on putting in the (unaltered) order. The steak came out as the house wanted it served—and I ate it. That night, I learned to appreciate undercooked meat a little more—and proprietors who love their food enough to stand up for it.

Try everything you can, even if it's out of your comfort zone. There's nothing worse than being really hungry and trying something new, only to figure out that you hate it. So if a dish is *really* outside of your comfort zone, don't order it as your main dish. Instead, order a small plate to share with your travel partner. If you end up loving it, you can always order more.

Don't let your curiosity outweigh your conscience. If you're presented with a food choice that's technically legal but also really unethical (such as eating whale or puffin or anything that's endangered), just say no.

When Mac and I travel, we love stretching our comfort zones with new food, everything from pigeon to haggis to insects. We don't like everything we try (steak tartare definitely wasn't a favorite for either of us), but we have discovered that most of the time, weird-sounding food isn't all that bad. And sometimes we really like it. It can be the same for you.

Want to turn great food into an even better experience? Slow down and treat your meal as an exercise in mindfulness. Chew without rush; taste everything. Focus on the subtle flavors and textures in your mouth. Only once you've thoroughly enjoyed that bite should you move on to the next.

Share a meal with a local. One of the best ways to experience local cuisine is in the company of a local, someone who can give you some perspective not just on what you're eating but the area you're traveling through. So be friendly and see what opportunities present themselves; you just might be invited to dine with a local family at their home (one of the best travel experiences ever) or to enjoy a post-walk meal at the local pub with a new friend.

If you'd rather not leave this to chance, a variety of websites will connect you with locals who'd love to share a meal or a drink with you. Check out Global Greeter Network, Eatwith and EatWithaLocal (see Resources).

PART 3
PACKING

He who would travel happily
must travel light.
—Antoine de Saint-Exupéry

En largo camino paja pesa. (On a long
journey, even a straw weighs heavy.)
—Spanish proverb

Once the broad strokes of your planning and logistics are taken care of and you've started to prepare your body and mind for the trip of a lifetime, it's time to embark on one of the most exciting parts of your preparations: figuring out what to take with you. I love getting my gear together for a big trip. It is my very favorite part of the planning process, because there's something completely energizing about imagining yourself in every scenario you could be a part of: hiking a gorgeous forest route, enjoying a chef's tasting menu at a hole-in-the-wall restaurant you find along the way, swimming in a sea-blue hidden lake. This will be you in a matter of months or weeks! This section will help you make sure you're ready for any and every adventure that awaits you.

However, that doesn't mean you will be packing a lot. In fact, I encourage you to pack as little as possible. Remember, unless you're splurging for luggage transfer, you'll be carrying everything you pack on your back—for days on end. Be kind to yourself and keep the weight down. If you follow each chapter's packing lists, you'll have everything you need for days (or weeks!) of enjoying both trail and town—all in one carry-on-size backpack that weighs no more than 18–20 pounds (8–9 kg).

PACKING STRATEGIES

The chapters in this section cover everything you'll need: clothing, footwear, toiletries and medication, tools for the trail and for travel, electronic tools, and packs to put everything in. But before you launch into the specifics of deciding what to bring in each of these categories, here are five general strategies that should govern all of your packing. Let the work—or should I say fun—begin!

HOW YOU PACK IS AS IMPORTANT AS WHAT YOU PACK!

How you pack your bag can make a tremendous difference, not only when you're trying to find something in your bag but when you have only minutes to repack after airport security turns your bag inside out. Make life easier by organizing all of your gear into subsystems, each with its own small organizer. Here's how to do it well:

- Organize your belongings into categories—clothing, toiletries, electronics—that make sense to you.
- Once you know what belongings each category contains (and, thus, what sizes of organizing containers you need), buy your storage solutions. I love packing in see-through mesh packing cubes and clear plastic bags so I can easily identify what's what.
- Give every subsystem a consistent home inside your bag. The best home will be determined by how heavy your items are (check out Chapter 17, Packs, for suggestions on packing your backpack) and how often you need to access them. If you create a routine for packing your bag—and do it the same way every time—packing and unpacking, even in a time crunch at the airport, will be a breeze.

Most walkers do a little laundry each night—just enough to refresh their walking clothes. (Photo by Cheryl Nilson)

My packing lists are designed for village-to-village walkers who will be sleeping in basic accommodations at night and have daily access to food and restaurants along the trail. If you're staying in hostels or bare-bones huts or camping in a tent, check out the information boxes in Chapter 15, Trail and Travel Tools, for things you might need to add to your gear.

1. Make sure everything is multifunctional. Almost everything in your pack, from clothing to toiletries, should be able to function in multiple ways. For example, to be worth its weight, a scarf should go with all of your tops and outfits. It should also be able to function as a shoulder cover in case you visit a church or a headscarf in case you're hoping to check out a mosque. If you pack sandals, they should be able to work as functional walkers, a dressy option for pairing with slacks and a sweater, or as shower shoes.

2. Keep everything as light as possible. Whenever you have a choice between lighter and heavier options, always choose the lighter option. It's worth spending a little more to keep your pack lean and mean. A great example is toiletries. Even if you're traveling for a couple of months (lucky you!) and you think you can use a full stick of deodorant, buying smaller and lighter travel sizes (even if it's more expensive over time) is a great way to reduce pack weight. As they say, to save pounds you have to shave ounces. Every little bit counts.

If you're traveling with a friend, shed some pack weight by divvying up things you'll share, from toothpaste to your guidebook.

3. To go big, keep things small. Whenever possible, opt for smaller, more compressible items over larger, bulkier ones. Think a puffy

In the perfect world, you would have all the money—and new gear—you could ever want. But don't de-spair if you're on a budget! Here are some other options for procuring the items you need for your trip—or refreshing something you already have:

Borrow it from friends and family who are the same size and/or from your local Buy Nothing group on Facebook.

Find it used from Goodwill or other thrift stores, from used-gear stores, and/or online at general buy-sell sites like Craigslist or gear-specific sites like GearTrade (see Resources).

Buy it cheap online at discount-gear sites like Steep&cheap, Backcountry, Moosejaw, Campmor, and the REI Garage (see Resources for all of the above).

Rehab your existing gear by washing it according to the label instructions, mending any holes or tears, and/or refreshing its durable water-repellent (DWR) layer.

---

down or synthetic coat instead of a fleece jacket or a small travel towel instead of a full-size one. This is a great opportunity to get creative—I'm always cutting back fabric I don't need (like my travel towel) or procuring tiny containers that hold exactly the amount of product I need for however long I'll be gone. (At this point, I have the amount of face lotion or toothpaste I use per day down to a science—and soon you will too.)

Think of your packing lists as a work in progress. I love perfecting mine over several months. To make your gear accessible, dedicate an area of your house to it for the months and weeks leading up to your trip—a closet or a spare bedroom. Spreading things out is better than keeping everything in a pile—the more you can see, the more you can work with it. It's also a great reminder that you have an adventure on the way.

---

4. Invest in high-quality items. Choosing multifunctional, light, small gear will go a long way toward guaranteeing you a good experience with your gear. But I suggest you take things one step further by investing in high-quality

items to the extent that you're able. What do I mean by high quality? I mean well made by a dependable manufacturer.

Remember, you'll use your gear a lot while you travel. You'll stress your clothes by wearing them every day, not to mention doing highly physical activities in them and then washing and drying them over and over again. You'll zip and unzip your backpack hundreds of times over the span of a week.

When you choose high-quality items, your gear is much more likely to put up with the beating you'll put it through—and that means that on your trip you won't have to deal with clothes that unravel or zippers that break. (I've been there and, trust me, it isn't pretty!) Choosing high-quality gear can seem like quite an investment up front, but it will pay divi-dends on trail.

5. When in doubt, leave it out. If you're like me, you love to be prepared for anything and everything. You don't feel at peace unless every situation is planned for—"I might need this" or "I might need that"—and suddenly you've added 10 pounds (4 kg) to your bag that you're probably not going to use. Tame those

A too-heavy pack can leave you feeling like an overturned turtle.

thoughts not by asking "Will I need this?" but "Will I need this enough to justify bringing it?" Remember, if you really need that bottle of conditioner or that extra town shirt when you're in Europe, you can always buy it there—and it'll be a good souvenir. If you're on the fence about something in your pack, don't bring it.

With these five guidelines in mind, you're ready to tackle the individual items you'll need, chapter by chapter.

Want suggestions on subsystems and packing? Check out my Pack It Away tips at the end of each chapter in this section.

CHAPTER

12

CLOTHING

When it comes to exploring on foot, one of the best things you can do for yourself is pack good clothing—the right items, and high-quality ones at that. This isn't just important—it's essential if you want to enjoy your trip. After all, it's hard to have a good time on trail if you get caught in an intense rain shower without a rain jacket—or with a low-quality one that soaks you to the bone. On the flip side, you'll pay no mind to challenging situations such as unexpectedly frosty mornings and muddy paths if you're properly attired for walking on trail.

Having the right clothing is just as important when you're in town as it is when you're on trail, but in a completely different way. In town, your clothing needs to help you blend in with the locals (not shout "hiker" or "tourist") and make you presentable for everything from a casual stroll through a museum to a fancy dinner at that famous restaurant you've been eyeing.

If packing to explore Europe on foot, with its trail and town considerations, sounds daunting, don't worry. I've got you covered with packing lists and suggestions for the individual items you should bring, as well as tips for washing your clothes while you're traveling and packing them away in your bag. But first I'll cover some general guidelines for what kind of clothing should—and shouldn't—be included in your trail-to-town wardrobe.

HOW TO SELECT YOUR CLOTHING

You'll pack a variety of very different clothes for exploring Europe on foot, from base layers to outer layers—and everything in between. But all of these items should have a few things in common. To go in your pack, they all need to be:

Lightweight. Even warm layers should be chosen in lightweight fabrics and designs.

Compact and packable. Bulkier items like vests and puffies can often be compressed into very small stuff sacks.

Comfortable. Choose clothes you will want to wear for days on end.

Thick and durable. Your trail outfit especially should consist of items that won't snag or rip.

Low maintenance. Select items that will always be ready to wear—won't wrinkle or lose their shape, for example. For clothes that won't retain odors, choose natural fibers rather than synthetics (see the next section). For clothes that won't easily show dirt, go for patterns and dark colors.

Washable. Select clothing that is easily washable and quick to dry; see How to Wash Your Clothes While Traveling later in this chapter.

Choose the Right Fabric

When it comes to clothing, fabric choice is incredibly important. It is the key determinant in guaranteeing that your clothes are lightweight, compact and functional. So what is the best fabric choice for a trail-to-town wardrobe?

Do: Use merino wool as your base fabric. Merino wool is generally light and thin, but it also keeps you warm even when it's wet, which is important if you sweat a lot or a surprise rain shower soaks you before you can put on your rain jacket. It also rolls easily for compact packability and doesn't wrinkle.

But the best property of wool is that it's antimicrobial. That means it resists bacteria, which is the culprit behind stinky clothes. Because of wool's antimicrobial nature, you can walk in your wool clothes for days on end without smelling like you've been on trail for a month. I use wool as my main fabric for traveling and recommend you do the same. Some good brands to choose from for outdoor-recreation-weight wool include Smartwool and Ibex.

Do: Accessorize with cotton and linen. Natural fabrics such as cotton and linen are very lightweight and can be a great addition to your trail-to-town wardrobe, especially when you use them for a skirt or a scarf. These fabrics aren't good for walking clothes, however. Cotton gets heavy and loses its warmth when wet; linen doesn't have enough insulation to keep you warm in cold weather, and it can be really delicate.

Don't: Rely on performance fabrics. Modern-day performance fabrics like polyester blends start to smell almost as soon as you put them on—and they need to be washed thoroughly in a washing machine for the odors to go away. Even though they're marketed to runners and outdoor enthusiasts, they're practical only if you have a washing machine nearby—and what traveler does? I use performance fabrics only for layers that don't get exposed to many body odors, such as walking pants rather than shirts.

Don't: Pack rayon clothing. Many flashy travel garments, especially convertible clothes (see Wardrobe Extension Ideas later in this chapter), are made from rayon. The fabric does drape well and cuts a nice shape, but unfortunately, it's incredibly heavy—better for the suitcase crowd than the backpack crowd. I suggest you leave rayon at home.

ONLY TWO OUTFITS? NO WAY!

Now, you may be thinking, "There's no way two outfits are all I need in Europe!" But it's completely possible. And not just possible—it's awesome! Think of all the time you'll save getting dressed and how great your back will feel without a superheavy backpack! All you have to do is choose clothing that's easily mixed and matched and easily layered—and then do a little laundry each night.

If you're worried about people noticing that you're wearing the same thing every day, think about Steve Jobs—he was famous for wearing the same black turtleneck, blue jeans and sneakers day in and day out. And no one cared! Even if you see the exact same people every day (walkers who are in your "walking bubble," traveling in the same direction at the same pace), no one will care if you're wearing your clothes over and over—because they'll be doing the same thing. That's just the nature of travel.

My favorite trail base layer for cool weather is a black, merino wool, short-sleeve shirt and matching long underwear bottoms. (Photo by Carol Veach)

WHAT TO BRING

Now that you know the general guidelines for what kind of clothing works best for exploring on foot, it's time to get more specific about your trail-to-town wardrobe. Because your trail and town clothing needs are so different, I recommend two base outfits—one for the trail and one for town—along with a handful of crossover layers that will keep you warm regardless of which outfit you're wearing and a few add-ons for other situations you'll encounter, from sleeping to swimming. The following sections describe the individual items you'll need, as well as my suggestions for choosing the best options possible.

My clothing suggestions are intended for three-season walking (spring, summer and fall) in continental Europe. If you're walking during the winter, or if you're going to a place with extreme weather (such as Iceland or Morocco), check out Wardrobe Extension Ideas later in this chapter.

Trail Outfit

Socks: Ankle-height socks, such as quarter-height crew socks that hit just above the ankle bone, save weight and space in your pack if you're trekking in low-top walking shoes like the European walking shoes I recommend in Chapter 13, Footwear. Merino wool socks that sport at least a medium cushion are your best bet. (I love Darn Tough socks, which have a lifetime guarantee.)

If you're blister prone, try wool toesocks like the ones offered by Injinji. Because the fabric goes in between each of your toes, kind of like gloves for your toes, they're a little awkward to put on and they look goofy, but they do their job extremely well—they completely eliminated all of my problems with toe blisters.

Underwear: Merino wool undies (trust me, they're way less scratchy than they sound) with flat-lock seams are the way to go—they're really comfortable, they resist odors and they dry quicker than anything else on the market. They're expensive but worth it—you'll launder your undies more than any other piece of clothing, and low-quality ones tend to fall apart when you scrub them. If you can't wrap your mind around wool undies, ExOfficio also has some good synthetic travel underwear options. For women, I also recommend a quick-dry sports bra.

Walking pants: If you'll be walking on a brushy trail, long pants are a better option than shorts or capris, because they guard your ankles and calves against scratches. Choose pants (or shorts or capris if weather and trail conditions permit) large and stretchy enough not to hinder your movement on trail—you should be able to climb onto a bench or rock, no problem. (Convertible long pants that zip off into shorts are a great single-item option for leg coverage in a wide range of weather conditions.) Choose a quick-dry fabric that's really comfortable and has a durable water-repellent (DWR) coating—if there's a sprinkle, your pants are less likely to soak through.

Short-sleeve shirt: The best base layer on trail is a short-sleeve shirt because, unlike a tank top, the fabric in the shoulders is wide enough to prevent chafing from backpack straps. (It's also a more modest choice for women walking in conservative countries like Turkey.) And unlike a long-sleeve shirt, it's the layer you'll want to strip down to if it's hot. I suggest merino wool because it's equally comfortable in the cold and in the heat. It's also odor resistant, so you can wear your shirt for multiple days without having to wash it because it's gotten stinky.

Long-sleeve full-zip shirt: For those chilly mornings or windy days, you'll need something to wear over your base layer; a merino wool long-sleeve top that zips up is perfect—it will give you a little more control over your temperature than a normal long-sleeve shirt because you can zip or unzip the shirt to your liking. Also, it's highly breathable and will keep you warm even if you're damp with rain or sweat.

Just because you buy something for your trail-to-town wardrobe doesn't mean it has to go on your trip with you. Give it a trial period by training in your trail clothes and wearing your town clothes all over your hometown. If something doesn't feel good during its trial period, take it out of the lineup—and start looking for a replacement. Eventually, you'll find the perfect item.

Crossover Layers

These items can be added to either your trail outfit or town outfit whenever you need a little extra warmth.

Down vest: A vest is an amazing layer. It's really versatile—you can wear it over everything from a short-sleeve shirt to a long-sleeve full-zip shirt. It'll give you some extra warmth (in your core, where you need it), and it'll add pockets to any outfit. Just make sure that the pockets secure with a zip or button (you can add these yourself), so you don't lose something. For the most warmth for the weight, choose a down vest; if the area you'll be visiting gets a lot of rain, choose a synthetic fill. And for the most outfit options, choose a relatively plain design and a neutral color that matches the rest of your trail-to-town wardrobe.

Puffy jacket: If you're traveling in summer, a light puffy jacket—sometimes marketed as a down or synthetic "sweater" because it's so lightweight—is your best bet for your warmest layer. If you're traveling in the shoulder seasons, look for something a little heavier; you might also consider a puffy with a hood for a built-in hat. Keep your eyes out for a puffy that compresses into its own stuff sack or pocket, which makes it easy to pack as well as double as a travel pillow.

Long-underwear bottoms: A good pair of long-underwear bottoms aren't just for wearing under your walking pants on cold days; they're also great as pajama pants, and women can wear them as leggings under a travel skirt or dress in town. Merino wool works best because it resists odors and will keep you warm even when it's wet; black is a versatile neutral color that works well for layering and as part of a larger trail or town wardrobe.

Lightweight rain shell: If you're traveling in summer, a basic lightweight rain shell or

You don't need to pack a lot of clothes to be covered for all occasions—a nice dinner out, walking on trail and exploring town.

waterproof windbreaker will be just fine; make sure it has a hood. If you're traveling in the shoulder seasons, look for something that can withstand more rain and wind. Good features for any season include armpit zippers, helpful for when you need some venting and rain protection at the same time, and adjustable elastic cord around the face, wrists and waist, perfect for when the wind kicks up and you don't want excess fabric blowing in the breeze. If you bring a rain shell that you've used a lot at home instead of buying a new one, make sure to rewaterproof it—durable water-repellent (DWR) coatings are only dependable for seven to ten rains before they need to be refreshed.

Thin gloves: It can get cold at higher elevations, and sprinkles happen even in summer, so keep a pair of lightweight gloves in your pack regardless of the season. Look for a pair with a DWR coating; merino wool will keep your fingers warm even if they're wet.

Lightweight hat: For the same reason that lightweight gloves are a good idea, bring a thin hat for chilly mornings and evenings. Choose a fabric like merino wool that will let your skin breathe and wash your hat often to avoid scalp breakouts.

Thin scarf: A good scarf is worth its weight in gold—it can be used as an ascot with a man's town outfit, and women can use it as a shirt, skirt, swimsuit coverup or head cover. It can dress up a boring outfit, function as a blanket on cold trains or planes, and double as a pillow. Nearly any scarf will do, as long as it's not too large or heavy. Pashminas work well for the shoulder seasons; linen is great for summer.

Town Outfit

Socks: For town socks, I recommend choosing the same style of sock that you wear on trail—quarter-height merino wool crew socks with at least a medium cushion (see Trail Outfit earlier in this chapter). Just be sure to get them in a different color from your trail socks so you can easily tell them apart. Since I recommend that you wear slip-ons as your town shoes (see Chapter 13, Footwear), you'll mainly use your town socks in lieu of slippers to keep your feet warm on the plane or as you pad around your guesthouse; they're also a great backup in case both pairs of your trail socks get wet and you need to sub in a dry pair.

Underwear: You can use the same kind of undies in town as on trail, but I suggest having a different color for town than for the trail so you can tell them apart (and know which pair is dirty versus clean). For maximum flexibility in women's town outfits—including with clothing that may be bought abroad as souvenirs—a nude-colored convertible bra (with straps that come off, can be crossed, et cetera) is a great choice.

Lightweight pants or skirt: Because your town outfit will need to cover all occasions, from casual to fancy, I suggest choices that can easily be dressed up or down, such as straight-leg pants in black or dark blue. For women, khaki capris, a travel skirt (paired with those long-underwear bottoms if it's cold) or jeggings are also good options.

Short-sleeve shirt: To guarantee you'll be ready for a nice restaurant, men should opt for a button-down short-sleeve shirt. For women,

DRESS FOR THE WEATHER

Stay warm: It's an old wives' tale that we lose a disproportionate amount of heat through our heads. We lose heat through any and all exposed skin, so if you're cold, cover everything up that you can, including fingers, neck and head—and layer up too. If you're walking during the winter, pack a heavier puffy jacket, thicker socks and a warmer hat and gloves. It can also help to pack an extra layer, such as a long-sleeve long-underwear top.

Stay dry: If you're walking during the rainy season—or if you're going someplace where the weather is always dicey, such as Iceland—pack rain pants and a heavier raincoat.

Stay cool: One of the ways your body gets hot is by absorbing heat from your environment, so if you're in a hot climate, reduce that absorption by (as counterintuitive as it seems) covering up; to maximize coverage and minimize sun exposure, I recommend packing a superlightweight long-sleeve base layer that has additional SPF applied to the fabric. Other ways to stay cool include wearing clothes that are light in color, loose-fitting and made of breathable fabrics: you should be able to hold your mouth up to the fabric and breathe through it. If you're walking when it's really hot and sunny out, pack a sun hat.

If you get too warm while you're walking in the cold, such as when you're trekking up a steep section of trail, it can help to cool your body off by removing your hat, scarf and gloves and unzipping the top part of your coat. Oftentimes, exposing a limited amount of skin to the cold air can counteract the extra heat your body's producing as it exerts itself—and help you avoid getting sweaty.

something on the dressier end of short-sleeve shirts, such as a top that drapes and/or has an interesting neckline (scoop neck, boat neck, et cetera), works the best.

Lightweight sweater: For those chilly nights, you'll want something to put over your short-sleeve shirt. A lightweight sweater that can be tied around your neck, prep school style, is perfect. Avoid the traditional bulkiness of sweaters by choosing a really thin and light fabric like cashmere or merino wool.

Wardrobe Extension Ideas

- If you know you'll be attending a fancy event (for instance, a wedding, the opera, et cetera) during your trip, pack something a little dressier. For women, a lightweight travel dress is a great option if you can wear it with your town shoes. Men can consider packing a long-sleeve button-down shirt and a tie.
- If you really can't live without a few more pieces of clothing than my bare-bones packing list, add another short-sleeve walking shirt and another short-sleeve town shirt; this expands your wardrobe options without adding too much weight or bulk.
- If you want to look different every day, consider using reversible clothing. It can double your wardrobe without adding any items or weight to your pack.

Accessories

Pajama top: I recommend packing a pajama top or any lightweight shirt that can be paired with your long-underwear bottoms for sleeping, walking around your room or hut/hostel and wearing while your washed clothes are drying.

Lightweight swimwear: Because there usually aren't a lot of opportunities to swim on trail (depending on where you go), it's hard to justify the weight and drying time of a traditional swimsuit—so get creative! For men, speedos are perfect—small and lightweight and ideal for blending in with those speedo-sporting Europeans. For women, I suggest packing a lightweight black bra and panty set (just make sure they're plain and not see-through) to save a few ounces in your pack and a few hours of drying time on the rack. No one will be able to tell the difference, and you'll even have backup undergarments in case you need them. That said, if you know you'll have an opportunity for swimming and want more modest swimwear, by all means pack a standard swimsuit that's lightweight and compact.

Watch: A basic wristwatch is great for all of those times when you don't want to pull your cell phone out of your pocket to check the time. It can also help you beat jet lag quicker (see Chapter 18, Check Off Your Final To-Dos Before Walking). Don't pack a fancy watch, or you could be a target for pickpockets. Basic and inexpensive is best.

The trail is no place for expensive personal items such as jewelry. If women want to pair a town outfit with something nice, bring along simple silver- or gold-colored hoop earrings (not actual silver or gold, but nice-looking, inexpensive hoops). They go with everything and look dressy, but you won't have to worry about losing them. (I have a pair that live exclusively in my travel toiletry bag—that's how much I swear by them.)

HOW TO WASH YOUR CLOTHES WHILE TRAVELING

When you don't bring very many clothes with you, you need to do laundry a little more often. But that doesn't mean everything has to be washed every day. I typically wash my

- Pack similar clothes together—for example, I have a trail subsystem, a town subsystem and a cross-over and accessories subsystem—so you can always find what you're looking for.
- To avoid wrinkles and save space, roll your clothes—don't fold them.
- Use compression sacks to shrink your clothing down even more. (Compression sacks are stuff sacks with straps you cinch down to compact everything as much as possible; they work really well with down clothing, such as vests and puffies, and can be found at outdoor-gear stores.)
- Use waterproof stuff sacks or compression sacks, or plastic bags, to store clothing if you'll be walking in rainy weather.
- Bring an extra stuff sack or plastic bag for dirty clothes.
- Wear your bulkiest clothes on travel days to save space in your pack.

underclothes nightly, my trail shirt and socks every other night, and my trail pants (and town outfit) every three or four days.

Get Your Clothes Clean on Trail

Because most accommodations on trail won't have guest laundry facilities, you'll typically hand-wash your clothes. Here are my tips for washing your clothes by hand:

- Do your laundry as soon as you get to your accommodations each night so it has as much time as possible to dry.
- Rather than wash your underclothes in the sink, jump into the shower with them on and wash them there; your shampoo or body soap will get them plenty clean.
- If you want to refresh your clothes without doing a full-on wash, just rinse them out or wash only the parts that really need it, like the armpits of your shirts.
- If your clothes are really dirty, plug the sink, fill it with warm, soapy water and let your clothes soak for fifteen to twenty minutes before you wash them.

Dry Your Clothes Fast

The hardest part of doing laundry on trail isn't the washing—it's getting your clothes dry before you need to wear them again. Here's how to speed things along:

1. First, hand-wring as much water out of your clothes as possible.
2. Next, roll your wet clothes in your travel towel (see Chapter 14, Toiletries and Medication) and wring everything out again. It helps to step on the bundle a few times too. The towel will absorb more of the water.
3. Then hang your clothes to dry. If you have a towel rack in your bathroom, place them there—and if it's a heated towel rack, turn it on, making sure as much of your clothing as possible comes in contact with the surface of the heater. If there's no towel rack or other place to hang your clothes, string a laundry line (see Chapter 15, Trail and Travel Tools) and drape your clothes over it. It's a good idea to put up the clothesline where it won't do any damage to have wet clothes dripping, such as over the bathtub or shower.

Want dry clothes by morning? It can help to hang them near an open window, especially one with warm sunlight streaming in.

4. Move items around as they dry, putting the wettest clothes in closest contact with the heated towel rack. If your clothes are hanging on a laundry line, train a hair dryer or fan on them to help them dry faster.

5. To dry clothes that are still a little damp in the morning, tie the ones you won't be wearing onto the back of your pack using a small length of thin cord (see Chapter 15, Trail and Travel Tools) so they can dry in the sun as you walk. The damp clothes you will be wearing will dry with the help of your body heat. This works only if you're wearing wool, which will keep you warm even if it's wet. Avoid wearing any cotton that's wet—it will chill you as it dries (and it takes a long, long time to dry). Wearing

damp clothes is a little uncomfortable at first, but as you walk they'll warm up in no time and dry quickly.

To test how quickly your chosen travel clothes dry, at home hand-wash them and wring them out as much as possible as described in this section. Then hang them up indoors. If they're not dry by the next morning, they fail—don't take them on your trip. (Note: The more cotton a piece of clothing has, the longer it takes to dry.)

Take Advantage of Laundry Facilities

If you're traveling long enough, you'll notice that eventually washing your clothes by hand just doesn't get them as clean and fresh as washing them in a washing machine. So every once in a while, find a way to take advantage of laundry facilities:

- Use the laundry service at your hotel or guesthouse.
- Find a laundromat and do your laundry like a local.
- Rent an Airbnb or VRBO property and use the laundry machine in the unit.

CHECKLISTS: CLOTHING

✓ Trail Outfit
- ☐ 2 pairs trail socks
- ☐ 1 pair trail underwear
- ☐ 1 pair walking pants, shorts or capris
- ☐ 1 short-sleeve trail shirt
- ☐ 1 long-sleeve full-zip trail shirt

✓ Crossover Layers
- ☐ 1 down vest
- ☐ 1 puffy jacket
- ☐ 1 pair long-underwear bottoms
- ☐ 1 lightweight rain shell
- ☐ 1 pair thin gloves

Rain shells aren't just good as coats; they also make excellent barriers against wet ground during snack breaks.

☐ 1 lightweight hat
☐ 1 thin scarf

✅ Town Outfit

☐ 1 pair town socks
☐ 1 pair town underwear
☐ 1 pair lightweight town pants or skirt
☐ 1 short-sleeve town shirt or top
☐ 1 lightweight sweater

✅ Accessories

☐ 1 pajama top or lightweight shirt
☐ 1 lightweight swimsuit
☐ 1 watch
☐ Small packing cubes, stuff sacks, compression sacks, plastic bags or other organizers

✅ Options

☐ Sports bra for the trail
☐ Convertible bra for town
☐ Lightweight travel dress
☐ Silver- or gold-colored hoops
☐ Long-sleeve button-down shirt and tie
☐ Heavier puffy jacket
☐ Thicker socks
☐ Warmer hat
☐ Warmer gloves
☐ Long-sleeve long-underwear top
☐ Rain pants
☐ Heavier rain jacket
☐ Long-sleeve sun shirt
☐ Sun hat

CHAPTER

13

FOOTWEAR

Once you have your trail-to-town wardrobe set, it's time to accessorize with footwear. The word "accessorize" makes it sound like shoes are just an addition to an already-complete outfit, but the truth is, your shoes can make or break your walking trip. If you've ever suffered through ill-fitting shoes or blisters, you know what I'm talking about.

You really need only two pairs of shoes for your trip: a pair of good walking shoes that are functional enough to carry you through everything from slick mud to deep puddles and comfortable enough to tromp around in all day long, and a pair of slip-ons that are nice enough to wear to dinner or a museum and cozy enough to give your tired feet the rest they deserve.

The trail and town shoes I recommend in this chapter are intended for three-season walking. If you plan on traveling in the winter, check out my tips in the Winter Walking sidebar. Here are my recommendations for finding the perfect shoes for exploring Europe on foot.

TRAIL SHOES

In my experience, the best shoes for exploring Europe on foot aren't hiking boots; they're European-style walking shoes, which have the traction, padding and waterproof qualities that you need for the trail without the very athletic look of hiking boots—or the weight: most walking shoes are incredibly light. My favorite thing about European-style walking shoes, though, is that they're not one-trick ponies, good only for the trail. They're nice enough to pair with your town pants for travel days or meandering around a museum as well.

If there's a chance you could encounter ice or snow on your walk (think shoulder seasons, alpine adventures or winter), be sure to pack traction devices such as Yaktrax.

If you have weak ankles or other body issues, are walking a more strenuous trail or are adventuring in adverse weather conditions, high-top hiking boots might work better for you than European-style walking shoes, because they offer more stability, support and grip. Lightweight options have Gore-Tex panels instead of leather, and hybrids look like walking shoes but have the higher top and ankle support of a lightweight hiking boot. Narrow down your choices and find what you like best at your local outdoor store.

What to Look for in Walking Shoes

- Look for shoes that have a definite raised rubber pattern on the sole, for the best grip. You don't want uniform and flat soles (like Keds).
- Choose only waterproof shoes to avoid wet feet on trail.
- Make sure the main material isn't really porous or matte, like suede, otherwise you'll have a difficult time cleaning and/ or waterproofing your shoes (leather works well, for shoes that are easy to wipe down on the go).
- Choose shoes that are as light as possible, to keep your load light and reduce strain on your knees.
- Go for a high-quality brand, for shoes that will last a long time; I really like Naturalizer, Aravon and Merrell.

If you plan on taking your time-tested and well-loved walking shoes or hiking boots to Europe, make sure to refresh the durable water-repellent (DWR) coating before you leave, for maximum protection against rain and puddles on trail.

How to Get the Best Fit

When shopping for walking shoes, follow these tips to get a good fit:

- Try them on with the socks you'll wear on trail so you don't have any last-minute surprises such as extra room or too-tight shoes (both of which can cause blisters).
- Shop for shoes at the end of the day, when your feet are slightly swollen from standing and walking, to simulate how your shoes will fit on trail.

European walking shoes are typically lighter and more stylish than traditional hiking boots.

In Portugal, trail shoes do double duty as beverage holders for post-walk beach time.

If you plan on walking a trail that requires fording rivers, like Iceland's Laugavegur Trek, it can help to pack neoprene socks and all-terrain sandals.

- Make sure there's plenty of room in the toebox to prevent your toes from hitting the front of your boot when you walk downhill (this is a recipe for losing a toenail—or several).
- Make sure that your heels don't slip inside the shoes; friction causes blisters.

With both your trail shoes and your town shoes, give yourself plenty of time to break them in and identify any hot spots. I like to wear mine every day in the month leading up to my trip; that way when I get to Europe, there are no shoe surprises.

TOWN SHOES

For town shoes that are as comfortable, versatile, low profile and lightweight as possible, slip-ons such as loafers, boat shoes and TOMS work really well. They're easy to get into and out of when you're traveling, such as through airport security, they look good with everything from shorts to pants and they can be worn without socks. It's also easy to find them in a color that will match your town outfit.

Depending on what the weather is like where you'll be traveling, lightweight sandals can make great town shoes as well. Just make

WINTER WALKING

If you're traveling in winter, you'll likely need warmer town shoes than slip-ons. I recommend letting your European walking shoes do double duty. You can pair them with traction devices like Yaktrax if the ground is slippery. Depending on where you're traveling, lightweight winter boots can also be a good option—just look for the least bulky pair you can find and aim for a neutral color that pairs well with your town outfit.

- My favorite way to store shoes in my backpack is in plastic produce bags from the grocery store. They're perfect—lightweight, see-through and free. This is a great way to keep the inside of your bag clean, even if your shoes are wet or muddy.
- Wear your bulkiest shoes (that should be your walking shoes) on travel days.
- If your town shoes are stinky, use a carabiner to attach them to the outside of your pack so they can breathe (and not stink up your other belongings) while you're on trail.

sure they're dressy enough to be paired with your town outfit and comfortable enough for walking around town, such as on an urban walking tour or in a museum.

A BETTER WAY TO BUY SHOES

Online retailers like Zappos.com and Shoes.com are great for finding a large selection of shoes, especially if they're currently out of season at your local retailer. Because these sites offer free shipping and free returns (including return shipping), it's easy to have a deluxe shopping experience with multiple brands, styles and sizes—all in the comfort of your own home and on your own schedule.

I recommend ordering at least three different styles of the kind of shoe you're trying to buy, as well as multiple sizes of each style if you're on the fence about what might fit. Try all of the shoes on and compare them to each other; there will usually be a clear winner. Send everything else back—it's that easy!

CHECKLISTS: FOOTWEAR

✓ The Basics
- ☐ Trail shoes
- ☐ Town shoes
- ☐ Plastic produce bags

✓ Options
- ☐ Lightweight sandals
- ☐ Traction devices
- ☐ Warmer town shoes

CHAPTER

14

TOILETRIES AND MEDICATION

Your toiletries matter more than you think—in fact, a heavy toiletry kit is one of the leading causes of a heavy backpack. It's all those darn liquids and gels! But the opposite is also true: honing your toiletry kit is a great opportunity to cut weight and make a big difference in your pack. This chapter covers my suggestions for individual items and the different types of products you might consider bringing along on your trip, as well as tips on lightening your load, bringing personal medications and packing it all in a way that will get you through airport security quickly and easily.

TIPS FOR LIGHTENING YOUR TOILETRY KIT

A well-packed toiletry bag has everything you absolutely need to get ready each morning, clean up after a walk and get ready for bed—and nothing more (check out What to Bring, below). Here are some overall strategies for creating a superlightweight toiletry kit:

Check what will be provided. Look to see what your accommodations offer in the way of free toiletries—you might not need to bring shampoo, conditioner or soap at all.

Bring only the amount you need for the time you'll be gone. To find out exactly how much toothpaste, face lotion and other toiletries you use and need to pack, put some into your travel containers at home and track how long it takes you to go through each container.

Choose products that do double duty. For example, Dr. Bronner's soap can be used as toothpaste, laundry detergent, body soap, dish soap, shampoo . . . the list goes on. You can also find shampoo-conditioner combos and face moisturizer that has foundation and sunscreen in it.

Eliminate liquids entirely. Liquids are really heavy, so minimize them as much as possible. Many products—shampoo, sunblock, lotion, toothpaste—are also available in powder or bar form.

When you fly, each container of liquid, aerosol, gel, cream and paste must be no larger than 3.4 ounces (100 mL) and must be packed together in one see-through quart-size plastic bag. Unless you have TSA Pre-Check, you will need to remove this toiletry bag from your carry-on at airport security. Don't lose that plastic bag once you're in Europe—you'll need it for your flight home.

WHAT TO BRING

The best way to discover what you absolutely need in your toiletry bag is to experiment in the weeks leading up to your trip. I like to put everything I think I'll need on the bathroom counter. Then, as I use products, I add them to a basket. I'll do this for a week or so (once a product has been used, it stays in the basket).

At the end of the week, I go through the basket. If I used something only once—and I figure I could get away without bringing it—or it was a luxury item, I take it out of circulation. Everything that remains in the basket—the things I really, really need—I package in smaller containers and add to my travel toiletry kit. This section covers the categories of products you will really, really need on a European walking tour.

Dental Care

Pack a travel toothbrush, travel-size toothpaste and dental floss. Travel toothbrushes have some type of cover; the simplest kind is a small plastic cover you put over the bristles of your regular home toothbrush. Other models are lighter and more compact, usually folding up for travel; some have a small plastic case instead of a cover.

Dental floss is pretty amazing, so definitely don't leave it at home—it can double as heavy-duty thread if you need to repair something on your trip, an emergency shoelace, a cheese cutter. It can even stop a dripping faucet from keeping you up at night: tie one end of it around the spout, put the other end in the drain and arrange it so the water can flow smoothly down it.

Hair Care

At the bare minimum, you'll need shampoo for basic hair care (if you're walking a remote trail or camping without regular access to showers, you may want to consider dry shampoo); some travelers may choose to pack conditioner and/or a lightweight small comb or brush as well. If you have long hair, keep it out of your face and eyes when you're on trail or sleeping by using bobby pins, elastics and/or a headband—but try to minimize your hair accessories.

Think of your walking tour as a great opportunity to go au naturel and style your hair in an easier way—leave gels and hair sprays at home. It helps to have a plan. In the days and weeks before my trip, I like to play around with a couple of hairstyles that can go from trail to town. One style I like is a high ponytail; another is wearing my hair down with a headband. My third go-to is usually twin braids or a single French braid. Find what looks good and feels good for you, and bring only the accessories you need for those two or three styles.

Exploring Europe on foot isn't the time to bring along power tools such as hair straighteners, curling irons and hair dryers. If need be, you can usually borrow a hair dryer from your accommodations.

Body lotion works great for smoothing flyaway hair, and talcum powder doubles as dry shampoo—sprinkle it on, brush it out and you might be able to go another day before washing your hair.

Body Care

You'll need basic maintenance items, such as soap and deodorant, as well as hygiene tools such as tweezers and nail clippers (both of which come in really handy when you're traveling for things like removing slivers, fixing zippers and clipping strings). You might want body lotion if you have dry skin. And don't forget plenty of sunscreen.

Bar soap has so many purposes—body soap, face soap, shampoo (in a pinch), laundry soap . . . (Photo by Dvortygirl/Flickr)

Regardless of whether or not your accommodations provide towels, you'll also need a travel towel; it'll come in handy for doing laundry (see Chapter 12, Clothing). You can bring a small terry cloth towel from home, but specialized travel towels have great features such as compactness, quick drying time, hanging loops and incredible absorbency (microfiber absorbs seven times its weight in liquid!) that can make them a better choice.

> Bring only as much bar soap as you'll need—travel sizes from hotels work great; you can also use a knife to carve your favorite bar from home into a smaller size.

Facial Care

If you don't have sensitive skin, I recommend using body soap to clean your face—in a pinch (or just for a week), it works just fine. If you do have sensitive skin, or if you have a skin-care routine at home that you want to keep up while you're traveling, you'll probably need face wash and face lotion as well. Another handy addition to your toiletry kit can be acne cream. It's really helpful for fighting sweat-induced breakouts while you're walking (toothpaste also does the trick).

Gentlemen, as you know, electric razors are heavy, especially when you consider the charging cord, attachments and converter (yep, not just an adaptor—you'll need a converter as well) you'll also need to bring along. If you need to shave while you're traveling, pack a basic non-powered razor instead. (Ladies, this goes for you too if you want to keep your legs and/or under-arms clean-shaven while you're traveling.)

You can skip bringing even a small travel mirror by using your smartphone in selfie mode.

Ladies, makeup can add a lot of weight and bulk to your toiletry kit, so bring as little as you can comfortably live with while traveling. When I travel, that means just lipstick, mascara and face powder. If you can't part with more of your makeup than that, at least pack only what you'll need for the length of your trip and store everything in the smallest containers possible. Investing in travel-size makeup brushes will also trim your toiletry kit.

Medication

Leave any nonessential supplements at home, but be sure to bring all of your medication—whether over-the-counter or prescription; see the Getting Through Airport Security: Medication sidebar for packing tips. Bring an extra three days' worth of medication, in case your flight is delayed or something else post-pones your trip home.

Feminine Hygiene Products

To women travelers, it can seem like Murphy's Law: although your period comes only once a month, it seems to show up for every trip you take. But never fear—your period doesn't have to interfere with your travels if you know what

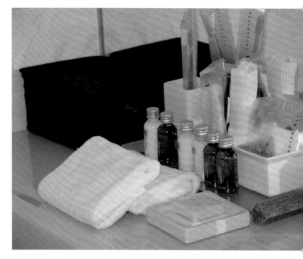

Check with your accommodations about what free toiletries they offer before you travel; you may be able to leave many of your products at home. (Photo by einalem/Flickr)

to bring with you to minimize the impact: a reusable feminine hygiene product.

A reusable product has a lot of benefits, including minimizing bulk in your toiletry kit (you won't need to pack a week's worth of tampons or pads) and eliminating the need to pack out used products from the trail.

There are several types and brands to choose from, including natural sponges and washable reusable cotton pads. I recommend an insert-able cup, such as the DivaCup, which is made from surgical-grade silicone that's completely safe for your body and as reliable as can be. Whatever you choose, bring along a waterproof bag to carry it in.

GETTING THROUGH AIRPORT SECURITY: MEDICATION

Although I regularly pack my pills in a small pill holder, I've never had a problem getting them through airport security. However, to be completely sure that your medication (especially any liquids) won't get confiscated at the airport, bring a written copy of your prescriptions (see Chapter 15, Trail and Travel Tools) and keep your medication in its original bottle.

- Get creative with your containers. Old pill containers work great for organizing cotton swabs; Tic Tac containers work well for bobby pins. I also suggest Altoids tins, contact-lens holders (for foundation, lotion, et cetera), small plastic envelopes (available from craft stores) or tiny earring organizers.
- However, for liquids and gels, don't be tempted by cheap containers—you don't want them leaking into your backpack, so it's worth it to invest in high-quality containers such as GoToobs.
- When packing liquids, squeeze the bottle a little before putting the top on, so the container will suck air in instead of letting product out.
- All of your toiletries should fit in one small bag—I really like the ones Outdoor Research makes for camping. (Just know that you'll have to temporarily move any liquids or gels to a separate plastic bag when you fly; see the Getting Through Airport Security: Toiletries sidebar.)
- Use a compact reusable grocery bag to keep your toiletries, clean clothing and travel towel together when you head to that shared shower down the hall. (I also use mine as a day pack or purse.)

If you switch to using a reusable feminine hygiene product, make sure you learn how to use it at home in the months leading up to your trip. You won't want to experiment with this on trail.

CHECKLISTS: TOILETRIES AND MEDICATION

✓ The Basics
- ☐ Travel toothbrush and cover
- ☐ Travel-size toothpaste
- ☐ Dental floss
- ☐ Shampoo
- ☐ Soap
- ☐ Deodorant
- ☐ Tweezers
- ☐ Nail clippers
- ☐ Sunscreen
- ☐ Travel towel
- ☐ Medication

- ☐ Small container for individual toiletries
- ☐ Toiletry bag
- ☐ See-through quart-size plastic bag
- ☐ Compact, reusable grocery bag

✓ Options
- ☐ Dry shampoo
- ☐ Conditioner
- ☐ Small lightweight comb and/or hairbrush
- ☐ Bobby pins
- ☐ Elastic hair bands
- ☐ Headband
- ☐ Body lotion
- ☐ Talcum powder
- ☐ Face wash
- ☐ Face lotion
- ☐ Acne cream
- ☐ Razor
- ☐ Makeup
- ☐ Feminine hygiene products

CHAPTER
15

TRAIL AND TRAVEL TOOLS

Exploring Europe on foot means getting out on trail and in nature—and because of that, you should add some extra things to your backpack that you wouldn't if you were just sightseeing or seeing Europe with a train, car or bus. You'll also need a few travel tools, from documents to currency to supplies for eating on the go. Keep reading for a detailed list of the individual items that should make it in your pack, as well as my recommendations for the very best options for the trail tools and travel tools that will make exploring Europe on foot as easy as possible (for electronics, see Chapter 16, Electronic Tools).

TRAIL TOOLS

Even though you'll be walking through regions of relative civilization in Europe (especially compared to North America), it's still important to carry the basics for recreating safely outdoors.

The Ten Essentials

This section's packing list is based on The Mountaineers' Ten Essentials, although I've modified it to be more relevant to exploring Europe on foot.

1. **Map, compass and guidebook:** A paper map of the trail—preferably a topographic one with a lot of detail—is essential, even if you'll be navigating primarily with a GPS device (for more on that, see Chapter 16, Electronic Tools): a paper map won't die on you because it doesn't have any batteries, and it won't lose service when you're far from town.

    In an emergency, especially if you're lost, a compass (paired with that paper map) is important. For this reason, I suggest packing a small manual compass in addition to downloading a good compass onto your smartphone. You can get tiny compasses that are the size of a nickel— they really won't take up any space and won't contribute any weight to your gear. You can just put it on the outside of your backpack and forget about it.

On an often-drizzly trail like Scotland's West Highland Way, a thermos with hot tea can be the ultimate trail luxury.

The third navigation tool you need is a guidebook or printout of the route details. Because books are so heavy, I usually either purchase them electronically and download them onto my smartphone or tear the necessary physical book pages out and carry those with me, tossing them when I'm done with each day's section.

2. **Sunglasses and sunscreen:** Especially if you're walking in bright sunlight or on snow or a glacier, it's important to have sunglasses that block ultraviolet (UV)

light. Don't forget to also bring a hard case for them, so they don't break when they're tossed around your backpack. Sunscreen is also vital; an SPF of at least 30 is the standard recommendation. Pack your sunscreen with your toiletries (see Chapter 14, Toiletries and Medication).

3. **Extra clothing:** It's important to always carry extra clothing with you in case there's a sudden change in the weather or you have to spend the night outside. If you're exploring Europe on foot in the summer or shoulder seasons, the items I recommend in Chapter 12, Clothing, should be more than adequate. If you're traveling in the winter, or if there's any indication that you might encounter more extreme weather on your trip, follow my suggestions in the Dress for the Weather sidebar in Chapter 12.

4. **Headlamp:** A headlamp is a great addition to your trail gear and not just as a survival tool. It lets you read in bed without disturbing your bed companion or the other people in your room; it lights your way to the bathroom if you need to walk outside to the toilets; and it can help illuminate dark corners of your backpack if you're searching for something. It's also handy in places like alpine farms that don't have electricity. I recommend putting fresh batteries in your headlamp before you leave for Europe, so you won't have to worry about finding replacements and swapping them out while you're traveling.

5. **First-aid kit:** It's important to have a small medical kit for when you're walking, in case you cut your knee, turn your ankle, have an upset stomach, et cetera. The most common thing you'll probably use it for? Blister care. In addition to carrying a first-aid kit, you should also know how to use its

contents, especially if your walk will take you into remote areas that are hours away from the nearest town.

Some people purchase a pre-assembled kit from an outdoor store and then modify it from there. If you assemble one on your own, store it in a compact waterproof container, and make sure it includes plenty of bandages, a packaged cleanser such as alcohol wipes, blister-care items such as moleskin, collapsible scissors and a needle. You might also want some sterile gauze pads and adhesive tape.

It's a good idea to include a variety of over-the-counter (OTC) potions and pills to cover any situations that might make you uncomfortable while you travel. In addition, you might want to include antibiotic pills—you'll have to ask your doctor to prescribe these. Here are the specific OTC first-aid remedies I recommend you have in your kit, at a minimum:

- ibuprofen (anti-inflammatory)
- acetaminophen (analgesic)
- anti-diarrhea pills
- antacid pills
- melatonin or natural sleep pills
- antibacterial cream
- cortisone cream

Because you'll likely be passing through towns as you walk, you should have ample opportunity to restock your first-aid kit if you start running low, so don't worry about packing a lot of each item initially—three or four days' worth should be enough.

---

6. **Matches:** In case of an emergency in which you get stuck sleeping outside, it's helpful to have a way to make a fire and stay warm. Your best option is to pack a normal book of safety matches (not "strike anywhere"

ones—they won't make it through airport security) or a lighter in your backpack—this has to be in a carry-on, not a checked bag. If you'd rather purchase your matches or a lighter in Europe, you can do so at any *tabac* (tobacco stand).

7. **Repair kit:** A few simple tools can come in handy in case you need to repair something on trail, from a tear in your jacket to a broken strap on your backpack. Below are the specific items I recommend for a fix-it kit—you can fix pretty much anything with this lineup:
   - a few strips of duct tape
   - a small sewing kit
   - 12 inches (30 cm) of thin cord (good for hanging damp laundry from your pack)
   - safety pins
   - rubber bands
   - twist ties
   - superglue

8. **Food:** It's always smart to have some food with you when you're walking—and a bit extra in case something goes wrong and you have to spend the night outside. Since most accommodations on trail will offer breakfast and dinner—and there are typically places to stop for lunch—you should only need to pack snacks such as dried fruit, nuts and jerky, but check what's available on your specific trail to be sure. I recommend purchasing these snacks from a grocery store once you arrive in Europe, unless you're traveling to an area that's really expensive, such as Scandinavia.

9. **Water:** Regardless whether you're walking in the heat or not, you'll need plenty of water and something to put it in. For water storage, I recommend several smaller containers—either water-bladder devices or water bottles—over one large one: having

You can't fly with trekking poles in your carry-on because of their sharp and pointy tips. Either check them (you'll need a separate bag for them, or you can check them in your backpack along with everything else you don't need on the flight) or buy them at an outdoor store in Europe and check them on the way home.

several smaller containers is more flexible when you want to take a small amount of water around town with you. The amount of water you need to carry depends on how many water sources there are for refilling on your route and how hot it will be, but you should always have at least a quart

If you have knee problems, trekking poles can make steep trails a lot less painful.

(liter) on you at all times. The majority of trails in Europe have potable water, so you won't need to bring along a water purification device, but check what's available on your specific trail to be sure.

10. **Space blanket:** In case you need to spend the night outside or you need to warm up—say you're extremely cold after getting drenched in a thunderstorm—you should carry an emergency space blanket in your pack.

Additional Items You May Need On Trail

Bug protection: Even if you're not anticipating a lot of bugs where you're going, I recommend packing a few insect repellent wipes just in case. There's nothing worse than being stuck on a trail with something as nasty as biting flies or midges and not having anything to ward them off. (This happened to me in Switzerland and it was awful!)

Trail comfort items: If you need braces or bands to support aching muscles and joints, or trekking poles for navigating intense inclines and declines, make sure they're in your pack and that you know how to use them.

What You Need Depends on Where You Stay

Depending on where you're planning on laying your head down at night, you may need to add a few extra supplies to your backpack.

Huts and refuges: Even within Europe, there is a lot of variation when it comes to how many amenities are offered at huts and refuges. In some countries (Iceland and Sweden),

DO I NEED A SLEEP SACK?

Most hostels in Europe now provide linens (because of the bedbug epidemic several years ago) and won't allow you to bring your own sleep sack (sleeping-bag-like bedsheets). That said, the occasional hostel will provide a comforter and a pillow but ask you to bring your own sleep sack—or pay to rent one from the hostel (this has happened to me in the United Kingdom and Switzerland). Check the hostel's website to find this information. Because it's quite rare now for hostels to ask you to bring your own sleep sack, and because you can always rent if you didn't bring one (think of the weight and bulk you'll save), I suggest leaving your sleep sack at home.

the huts are very basic—it's like camping, except indoors (see Chapter 8, Find a Place to Stay, and Camping, below). In other countries (France, Italy and Switzerland), the huts are much more luxurious, so you don't need to bring anything different than if you're staying at guesthouses and inns. If you're planning on staying in huts as you explore Europe on foot, do your research online to figure out specifically what you need to pack.

Camping: If you want to camp while you're in Europe, you'll need to pack a lot more gear than if you're staying in other kinds of accommodations, even basic huts.

Below are two camping scenarios and what gear they require.

Situation 1: Stay in a developed campground and eat at restaurants.

Take: Tent, sleeping pad, sleeping bag (rated for two or three seasons, depending on how cold it will be where you're going), camp pillow (optional)

Note: If you're bringing a tent from home, make sure it's well suited for wherever you plan on camping in Europe. A two-season or three-season tent should be fine in most of continental Europe during the spring,

GETTING THROUGH AIRPORT SECURITY: BACKPACKING STOVE AND FUEL CANISTER

At first blush, it might seem easy to pack your existing camp kitchen for a European jaunt. After all, backpacking stoves are allowed on airplanes—unless you fall victim to an ill-informed employee of the Transportation Security Administration (TSA), which has been known to happen. However, stove fuel is not allowed on airplanes, even in your checked baggage, so plan on purchasing it in Europe.

What about an empty refillable fuel canister that you plan on filling once you get to Europe? Not so fast. If it smells even a *little* like fuel, airport security will toss it out quicker than they can say "bomb." As if that doesn't complicate things enough, most fuel canisters you can purchase abroad aren't compatible with most US-brand backpacking stoves.

What to do? There are two solutions. One is to pack a stove that's meant for international use (such as the MSR WhisperLite International backpacking stove) with a brand-new or squeaky-clean empty refillable canister, which you can fill at most outdoor stores or gas stations in Europe. The other solution is to simply rent a camp stove and the accompanying fuel canisters in Europe. Either way, you'll be cooking in no time.

- A cloth jewelry organizer is perfect for organizing small trail tools.
- For water storage, I recommend purchasing disposable water bottles in Europe that you can use during your trip and recycle at the end.
- Store trail tools that you'll need frequently on trail in the convenient outer pockets of your backpack.
- Carry a few small plastic bags for packing out trash (including toilet paper) while you're on trail.

summer and fall. But if you're headed to Iceland at any time of the year, you'll need an all-weather, windproof, waterproof superstar of a tent, not just something that you pick up from a big-box store. Not all tents are created equal!

Situation 2: Stay in a developed campsite and prepare your own food.

Take: Everything listed above for Situation 1, plus a backpacking stove, fuel and canister, cooking pot or pan, cooking utensils, plate, bowl, cup, eating utensils, food

CHECKLISTS: TRAIL TOOLS

✓ The Ten Essentials
- ☐ Map, compass and guidebook
- ☐ Sunglasses (and case) and sunscreen
- ☐ Extra clothing
- ☐ Headlamp (with fresh batteries)
- ☐ First-aid kit (see separate list below)

- ☐ Safety matches or a lighter
- ☐ Repair kit (see separate list below)
- ☐ Food—trail snacks
- ☐ Water (in water bottles or bladders)
- ☐ Space blanket
- ☐ Plus, organizers for trail tools

✓ First-Aid Kit
- ☐ Bandages
- ☐ Packaged cleanser such as alcohol wipes
- ☐ Moleskin
- ☐ Collapsible scissors
- ☐ Needle
- ☐ Sterile gauze pads
- ☐ Adhesive tape
- ☐ Antibiotic pills (prescribed by your doctor)
- ☐ Ibuprofen (anti-inflammatory)
- ☐ Acetaminophen (analgesic)
- ☐ Anti-diarrhea pills
- ☐ Antacid pills

DON'T PACK IT–RENT IT!

Want to camp for some or all of your trip but don't want to lug everything through the airport and airport security? A great alternative can be renting camping gear when you're in Europe. Many European outdoor stores rent everything from tents to sleeping bags to backpacking stoves (and the fuel to go with them). You just order what you need online or in person, and they'll get everything together for you to pick up whenever you're ready.

☐ Melatonin or natural sleep pills
☐ Antibacterial cream
☐ Cortisone cream

✓ Repair Kit
☐ A few strips of duct tape
☐ Small sewing kit
☐ 12 inches (30 cm) of thin cord
☐ Safety pins
☐ Rubber bands
☐ Twist ties
☐ Superglue

✓ Options
☐ Water purification device
☐ Insect repellent wipes
☐ Support braces or bands
☐ Trekking poles
☐ Sleep sack
☐ Tent
☐ Sleeping pad
☐ Sleeping bag
☐ Camp pillow
☐ Backpacking stove
☐ Refillable fuel canister (add fuel to your kit in Europe)
☐ Cooking pot or pan
☐ Cooking utensils
☐ Plate
☐ Bowl
☐ Cup
☐ Eating utensils
☐ Food—camping meals

TRAVEL TOOLS

Just as there are a variety of trail tools that can help make the walking part of your trip safe and enjoyable, your town and travel days will benefit from a few travel-specific items and tools as well.

Travel Documents

You'll need to gather a variety of paperwork and pack it up before your trip, including your identification documents, itinerary and confirmation numbers, and trip insurance.

Identification documents: Most countries in Europe require that your **passport** be valid for at least six months after you fly back home (not to Europe!), so make sure that yours falls into that time frame—or renew your passport well in advance. Also, be sure you have enough blank spaces in your passport for entry and exit stamps while you're in Europe.

If you plan on renting a car and driving in Europe, you'll also need your **drivers license** and perhaps an **international drivers license** (see Rental Cars in Chapter 7, Get There). Also check whether the country you're visiting requires an entry and/or exit **visa** (for example, Turkey), and apply for and bring these documents if required.

Itinerary and confirmation numbers: Make sure your itinerary and all your confirmation numbers (flights, accommodations, rentals, et cetera) are organized and easy to find. I like programs on my smartphone that are simple to use, available offline, backed up in the cloud and easy to share—you'll want to give a copy to someone at home in case of emergency. If you have an iPhone, the Notes application (similar programs are available for Androids) does the job well.

Trip insurance: I recommend you purchase trip insurance (check out the Trip Insurance sidebar in the introduction to Part 2, Planning, for more information). This covers your financial investment in your trip and will pay out a claim if your luggage is lost or stolen, your trip has to be cancelled because of an illness, or in case of other similar disruptions. Make sure to

INTERNATIONAL HEALTH INSURANCE

Purchasing international health insurance is an easy way to guarantee that you'll be covered in case you need to seek medical attention while you're in Europe—and it's really cheap, oftentimes only a couple dollars a day. Here are a few things that are helpful to know:

Rates: These are based on your age, amount of coverage and deductible; I suggest going with a $0 deductible—it's not that much more expensive (it's paid off in spades for me).

Duration: You can activate the policy for anywhere from a few days to two years.

Location: The policy's coverage is good only while you're traveling (not in your home country).

Coverage: The policy covers only emergency medical and sometimes dental visits—no routine exams or pre-existing conditions are covered unless you purchase an additional waiver. At a minimum, the right policy will cover:

- assistance 24/7
- the activities you'll do on your trip
- local ambulance charges
- emergency medical evacuation
- hospital room and board
- an intensive-care unit
- repatriation of remains

A variety of international health insurance companies and plans are available; it's worth the time to find a good one. Major companies include International Medical Group (I use their Patriot International plan when I travel), HCC Medical Insurance, GeoBlue and AIG Travel. Compare prices online—and make sure to read all the fine print!

bring a copy of your trip insurance policy with you, including information on who to contact if you need to file a claim.

Health-Related Documents

Other paperwork that you'll need to have in order and get packed before your trip includes a written copy of your prescriptions, a doctor's note if you have a pre-existing health condition, and international health insurance.

Prescriptions: If you are bringing prescription medication with you on your trip (see Chapter 14, Toiletries and Medication), make sure you have a copy of the written prescription(s). This is helpful in case your bag is searched at airport security; it can also come in handy if you run out of or lose your medication and need to get it refilled abroad. In this latter case, you will probably still need to get a local doctor to rewrite the

prescription, but it will be good proof that this is something your primary-care doctor regularly prescribes for you, which can make the process a lot easier. Make sure your doctor includes the chemical name or common name of the drug, not just the brand name (which can vary by country), and if a therapeutic substitution (another drug that does the same thing) is OK.

Proof of pre-existing conditions: If you have a pre-existing condition that could present an issue while you're traveling or on trail, have your doctor write a short letter describing your condition and its treatment, including any prescription medication being used to treat your condition. This doctor's note is a requirement for taking many guided walking trips; it can also be helpful, even if you're traveling independently, in case you need to seek medical treatment abroad.

Health insurance: Before going abroad, it's important to check with your health insurance provider and make sure your policy will cover you when you're overseas. (Some policies will, but you're usually required to pay up front for services and then file a claim for reimbursement later.) If your health insurance provider won't cover you when you're overseas, make sure to purchase international health insurance for your trip (check out the International Health Insurance sidebar in this section for more information). Some health insurance policies won't cover injuries you get from participating in adventure sports such as paragliding, kayaking or mountain climbing, so consider purchasing a separate adventure sports rider if you need one.

Currency

Most of the countries in Europe are part of the European Union, whose common basic monetary unit is the euro (€). You can purchase **euros** (or other currencies) from a currency-conversion agency back home or in Europe, withdraw euros from an ATM once you're in Europe (this is your best option and how you'll get the most euros for your dollars; see Cash in Chapter 18, Check Off Your Final To-Dos Before Walking), and/or use **debit and/or credit cards** as you go. I recommend bringing one debit card and two different credit cards—I travel with both a Mastercard and a Visa because occasionally a merchant will accept one but not the other (and it's rare to find a merchant that will accept Discover or American Express); it's also good to have a backup in case one card doesn't work or gets lost. (For more information on paying for things in Europe, check out Paying for Your Purchases in Chapter 18, Check Off Your Final To-Dos Before Walking.) Besides the actual cash and cards, you'll need to bring something to carry them in.

Travel wallet: I travel with an RFID-blocking wallet containing a limited amount of cash and keep the rest of my cash locked deep in my backpack. The European monetary system relies a lot more on coins than we do in North America, so pack a travel wallet that has a good coin purse in it. I recommend storing your travel wallet in a money belt or travel scarf or deep in your day pack or purse—never in your pants pocket, where it can make you an obvious target for pickpockets.

Money belt or travel scarf: It's been a long time since I've traveled with a money belt; I don't like how scratchy they are, how they impede my movement or how I end up having to dig through them in public anyway. If you don't want to carry a money belt either, but you want your valuables safe and accessible, consider a travel scarf. These have a secret compartment for your passport and money, and they're made for both men and women.

Currency-conversion cheat sheet: Another really helpful item for your travel wallet is a cheat sheet for currency conversion. It is one of the best things you can carry to keep track of your money and understand how much you're spending, especially if you're traveling somewhere where the denominations differ wildly from what you're used to (such as Iceland). Here's how to make one that lists conversions both from and to your home currency:

1. Trim an index card to the size of a credit card so it will fit in your travel wallet.
2. On one side, write the currency units of your home currency (such as the US dollar) in the denominations you'll use often (for example, $1, $10, $20, $50, $100) and add the conversion to the euro or whatever currency is used where you'll be traveling.

Want to enjoy a nice wine break on trail? Pack a dedicated wine bladder and a TSA-approved wine opener.

3. On the other side, list the major denominations of the currency where you'll be traveling, and add the conversions to your home currency.

Town Tools

For your time in town—in the evenings after you walk as well as on rest days—I recommend packing a few items for impromptu meals, laundry and journaling.

Picnic tools: Nothing goes better with traveling than feasting on the go—think of all those local markets that you'll hit up!—so make sure you're prepared for putting together your lunch on trail, making a simple meal in a hostel or enjoying a healthy snack on the train

GETTING THROUGH AIRPORT SECURITY: PICNIC TOOLS

Make sure the travel flatware you pack is sturdy plastic instead of metal, and avoid anything that looks too much like a knife—sporks work great. Interestingly, pocketknives with blades shorter than 2 inches (5 cm) are typically allowed through security but larger, duller knives you would use for eating are not. If you'd rather purchase an eating knife or pocketknife in Europe, you can buy them at most supermarkets or *tabacs* (tobacco shops) once you've landed. If you bring a wine opener on the plane, make sure it's TSA-approved or it will likely be confiscated.

- Make electronic copies of all of your important paperwork and travel documents (including your passport and the front and back of all of your credit cards) and store them in a secure email account or cloud vault (such as Dropbox) that you can access from abroad if needed.
- Clean your picnic tools before you pack them—a touch of water from your water bottle and a little rub on the grass will keep them clean and fresh for the next time you use them.
- Pack town tools you use less frequently (such as laundry supplies) in a lightweight toiletry bag or jewelry organizer (one with a few medium-size zippered pockets works best) to keep everything together and organized in your pack.
- Store town tools that you'll need frequently on trail (such as your picnic and wine tools) in the convenient outer pockets of your backpack (just like you do with your trail tools).

by packing basic picnic tools. I suggest bringing these:

- small travel flatware
- small pocketknife (which doubles as a trail tool; see the Getting Through Airport Security: Picnic Tools sidebar in this section)
- small bottle of hand sanitizer

Wine tools: My favorite town tool of all time is a 1-quart (1-liter) **hydration bag** (I recommend one with a screw-off top, not a drinking tube) dedicated to carrying wine. Especially when I'm traveling in Italy or France (but honestly, wherever I go in Europe), I love finding local wine and carrying it with me for impromptu wine hours. Yes, it's extra weight, but it's totally worth it!

With a soft wine container, it's a lot easier to enjoy wine on the go because you don't have the weight (or breakability) of a glass bottle, and when you're not using the container, it folds up very compactly and weighs almost nothing. It feels so decadent to have a sip of Chianti on the train as you're watching the world go by or to put your feet up in your guesthouse after a long day on trail and unwind with a glass of Bordeaux and a bit of cheese. Try it—I guarantee you're going to love it!

Complete your wine kit with a TSA-approved **wine opener** (see the Getting Through Airport Security: Picnic Tools sidebar in this section), then decant a bottle of wine into your dedicated wine bag. You can drink the wine straight out of the hydration pack or pour it into cheap paper or plastic cups you find along the way (most supermarkets and delis carry them).

Laundry supplies: Pack a travel laundry line to hang-dry your clothes (for my tips on doing laundry on the go and getting it dry overnight, see How to Wash Your Clothes While Traveling in Chapter 12, Clothing). The other things you'll need are two items already on your toiletries packing list—some sort of soap to get things clean and a travel towel for wringing out as much water as possible (see Chapter 14, Toiletries and Medication)—plus a small cord for hang-drying things on the outside of your pack (see Repair Kit under Trail Tools earlier in this chapter).

Small notebook and pen: It's really helpful to have something to scribble notes on while you're traveling, whether it's to verify the amount you're being charged by a merchant, remember key phrases in another language or leave a note for your napping travel companion that you ventured out for some food and will be back soon. Keep your pad of paper small and light; I recommend something no bigger than an index card.

Journal: Travel brings you so many intense memories that you think you'll remember all your life, but even incredible experiences that you cherish can fade with time. I recommend packing a small journal to jot notes and impressions about your trip so that nothing slips away. The pocket notebooks that Cavallini Papers (see Resources) sells are the best I've found for traveling—they're small and lightweight.

CHECKLISTS: TRAVEL TOOLS

✓ The Basics: Travel Tools
- ☐ Passport
- ☐ Drivers license
- ☐ Itinerary and confirmation numbers
- ☐ Trip insurance paperwork
- ☐ Health insurance paperwork
- ☐ Cash

- ☐ Debit card
- ☐ Credit cards
- ☐ Travel wallet
- ☐ Currency-conversion cheat sheet

✓ The Basics: Town Tools
- ☐ Travel flatware
- ☐ Pocketknife
- ☐ Hand sanitizer
- ☐ Extra hydration bag for wine
- ☐ TSA-approved wine opener
- ☐ Travel laundry line
- ☐ Small notebook
- ☐ Pen
- ☐ Journal
- ☐ Organizers for travel tools

✓ Options
- ☐ International drivers license
- ☐ Visa
- ☐ Written copy of your prescriptions
- ☐ Letter from your doctor about any pre-existing conditions
- ☐ Money belt or travel scarf

CHAPTER

16

ELECTRONIC TOOLS

All of the trail and travel tools I cover in the preceding chapter are important, but there's another category of tools that is so useful and important that it deserves its own chapter: electronic tools. In the next few sections, I detail all of the individual items you need to consider and have in your pack, from that now-essential tool, your smartphone, to other electronic devices such as GPS units and digital cameras—and what you'll need to plug them in, charge them and connect to the Internet as you explore Europe on foot. I also give you recommendations on specific items that are so useful you won't want to leave home without them.

SMARTPHONE

A smartphone is one of the best things you can pack when you explore Europe on foot. It can help you check in for your flight, give you turn-by-turn directions to your next guesthouse, give you a way to stay in touch with family and friends back home and even take the place of several other devices, including a digital camera and a GPS unit. Oh, and it'll do about a billion other great things too. But bringing a smartphone to Europe isn't quite as simple as just throwing it in your backpack. You'll need a handful of apps and accessories to make your smartphone the best trail and travel tool it can be (see the Cell Phone Service section for tips on connecting in Europe).

Recommended Trail and Travel Apps

A variety of online roundup articles can help you find the latest and greatest travel apps, but these change all the time as technology improves, so I won't offer too many specific app suggestions here, in case they're out of date by the time you try to use them. That said, don't forget to download apps that contain confirmation numbers and booking information, such as those for Booking.com or the train company or airline you're traveling with. You'll also want to download any apps that relate to your trail. Besides those basics, here are four of my time-tested favorites:

GPX tracks are a GPS route similar to what Google Maps gives you for driving directions, but for walking on trails. They're widely available for free for many of the trails featured in this book (see Chapter 3, Get a Recommendation). If you download the GPX tracks for your route, you can see exactly the path you should be on as well as the path you have been walking—the two lines are shown with different colors on your device. Keeping the two sets of lines one over the other means you're walking exactly where you want to be: on the trail.

It wasn't until a few years ago that I started walking with GPX tracks in addition to my paper map—and it was one of the best upgrades to my trail tools that I ever made. There's something really reassuring about knowing where, exactly, you are on the map and which direction you're traveling in. More than once, I've missed an important junction that was poorly signed and needed the GPX tracks to get back on route.

You can use GPX tracks on a variety of devices, and it can be a little overwhelming to choose which device you'll use for creating and following them. I've walked in Europe with both a stand-alone GPS unit as well as a variety of apps on my smartphone, and this is what I recommend:

- Use a stand-alone GPS unit if you're planning on walking a remote trail through mostly wilderness and you're heavily reliant on your device—and its dependability—for navigation (see Other Electronic Devices below for more on GPS units).
- For walking anywhere else, use the Gaia app (described below) on your smartphone, which will be significantly cheaper, lighter (you won't need a separate device, batteries or charger) and easier to use. (Tip: The Gaia app works offline but is at its most dependable when you have cell service so you can regularly refresh the maps.)

Kindle app: This free app can help you eliminate the weight of books and papers in your pack, because not only can you download e-books, you can email PDFs of your documents (for example, packets of information that your tour company sends you) to the app too.

WhatsApp: This free app is a more global alternative to Skype that can help you communicate both with locals and with people back home for free.

Google Maps: This free app is really helpful when you need turn-by-turn walking directions.

Gaia: This GPS app isn't free but it's well worth the cost. It can help you navigate on trail by allowing you to upload and follow GPX tracks (see the Should I Walk with GPX Tracks? sidebar for more information) for your route.

Optimizing Your Trail and Travel Apps

One of the best things you can do before you leave home is to optimize the apps on your smartphone. I like to temporarily hide the apps that I use only at home (for example, my local bus app) by putting them in a folder on the last screen that I can swipe through. This gives me the space to put front and center the apps I use when I'm traveling. Regardless which apps you prefer, here are a few suggestions for using them:

Download, set up and test all of your apps while you're still at home: This is really important if the app tries to verify your identity by sending you a text—you'll need to have cell phone service with your home SIM card to receive it.

Protect all of your sensitive information: Password-protect your phone to keep your bank apps and other apps with sensitive information secure.

Organize your apps into folders: It is a lot easier to find the specific app you're looking for if it's in a folder of similar apps (for example, transportation apps) than if it's on an unorganized page of unrelated apps (trust me, the icons all start to look the same).

Smartphone Accessories

Smartphone case: Bring a sturdy, weatherproof case to protect your smartphone in your backpack or on trail.

Lens cloth: Smartphone touch screens won't unlock or function if they're wet, and your camera app won't take good pictures if the lens is dirty, so bring a small lens cloth to wipe everything down.

Earbuds: Choose earbuds that also sport a microphone so they do double duty: you can listen to music on the go and talk to your family back home. Opt for earbuds with a tangle-free design to keep yourself from going crazy.

Want to listen to music out loud in your guesthouse, but don't want to bring a speaker? Place your smartphone, speaker side down, in a drinking glass (there's usually one in the bathroom) for a little extra oomph.

Cell Phone Service

I've traveled in Europe with and without cell phone service, and I can honestly say that having service is worth the extra cost. It can give you peace of mind, and it lets you do a lot of things that are important on trail:

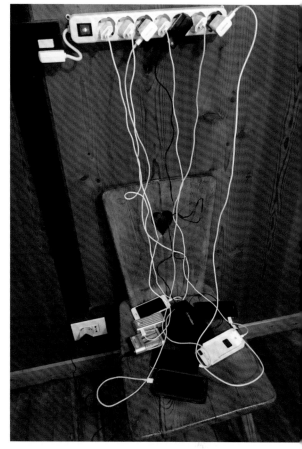

Electrical outlets in huts and hostels can fill up quickly—stake your claim as soon as you get in.

You'll be able to place an emergency call if need be. If anything unexpected happens on trail, you're just a phone call away from help.

You can connect to the Internet. Your GPX tracks and map will update regularly, you can get those turn-by-turn walking directions when you roll into town and can't seem to find your guesthouse, and you can even make spontaneous reservations from anywhere there's service if you decide to change your travel plans at the last minute.

You won't depend on Wi-Fi. For some reason, European Wi-Fi is a lot less dependable than North American Wi-Fi—half the

There are three main ways you can get cell phone service—you'll want both calling and data service—while you're in Europe:

Global plan: If you're traveling for a short amount of time (two weeks or less), the global plan through your existing cell phone service provider is probably your best option. Although it's usually expensive, it's also easy and convenient—you'll typically experience a seamless transition to international coverage once you've contacted your service provider. (No swapping out SIM cards for you!)

Foreign SIM card: If you're traveling for longer or if you're planning on using your phone quite a bit, it's cheaper to buy a foreign SIM card.

There are a couple of drawbacks with foreign SIM cards: (1) You have to have an unlocked phone, which means you either have to purchase a phone that's already unlocked (most times if you buy a used phone from a third party on a site like Amazon or pay for your phone in full at the time of purchase rather than having it subsidized by your service provider, it'll be unlocked) or ask your US carrier to unlock your phone, which they might not do if they've subsidized it and you've had it for less than a year. (2) Foreign SIM cards are usually good for only one country, so you'll have to purchase multiples if you're traveling to several countries.

Otherwise, the process is relatively straightforward. You can find cheap SIM cards at most *tabac* (tobacco) shops in Europe—look for them at or near train and subway stations. They're simple to install and activate. (Tip: Store your home SIM card in a small plastic bag once you've put the foreign SIM in your phone, so it doesn't get lost.)

International SIM card: If you're traveling to several countries, a good alternative to a foreign SIM card is an international SIM card, such as KnowRoaming (see Resources); these have higher rates but can be used all over Europe (or the world, depending on the package you buy). Purchase and install an international SIM card while you're still at home; your phone needs to be unlocked for the service to work.

time when I'm staying somewhere, the Wi-Fi doesn't work. If you have cell phone service, your smartphone will be a backup in case the Wi-Fi at your accommodations isn't working and you really need to do something online. (See Connect to Wi-Fi in Chapter 18, Check Off Your Final To-Dos Before Walking.)

That said, getting cell phone service in Europe isn't always simple: North America and Europe use different networks and frequencies for cell phones. For your phone to work in Europe, it has to be compatible with the GSM 900/1800 network. Find out your phone's compatibility by searching online for "world-capable" or "tri-band" and the brand and model you're using. If your phone isn't GSM-compatible, you'll have to change phones to have cell phone service in Europe. Check out the Three Options for Cell Phone Service in Europe sidebar for more information.

OTHER ELECTRONIC DEVICES

You might want other options for communicating or taking photos, and you might want a stand-alone GPS unit. Here are my tips on these other devices:

Alternative Communication Tools

If you won't have cell phone service while you're in Europe but you want to be able to call for help if need be, consider purchasing a SPOT device, satellite communicator (such as the DeLorme inReach Explorer) or personal locator beacon (PLB), all of which have a panic button of sorts that you can hit if you're in trouble on trail. Once you hit the button, the device sends an emergency signal with your location to local search and rescue (often via a central dispatch that determines the right people to respond), which will then come to your aid.

These devices can all be set up to work internationally; many two-way satellite communicators allow you to communicate directly with your rescuers before they arrive (simple devices like PLBs can only send an emergency signal, not communicate back and forth). An added bonus with a SPOT device or satellite communicator is that people at home can follow along with your adventure by seeing your location on a map (you just provide them with a web link)—and you can send periodic check-in messages to let them know that you're alright. For more information on choosing between a SPOT device, satellite communicator and PLB, I recommend diving into the plethora of more detailed research and comparison articles that are available online.

Stand-Alone GPS Unit

If you're planning on walking a remote trail through mostly wilderness and you're heavily reliant on your device—and its dependability—for navigation, it's better to use a stand-alone GPS unit than your smartphone. I highly recommend the Garmin GPSMAP S-series for walking the trails of Europe; I've used mine everywhere from Iceland to France without issue.

If you plan on bringing a stand-alone GPS unit, don't forget to pack everything that goes along with it: a case, a wrist strap or tether, a charger and a spare set of batteries—this last item is very important (my batteries lasted only three-quarters of a day on average).

Dedicated Camera vs. Smartphone Camera

When it comes to capturing and preserving your trip memories, cameras are wonderful. However, they can also be pretty heavy. Luckily, thanks to huge advancements in image technology, you don't have to actually carry a dedicated camera anymore to take amazing photos. Even some professional photographers I know no longer pack a dedicated camera when they travel because they use a smartphone instead.

There are many benefits to traveling with only the camera on your smartphone. You'll have a lighter pack, you'll be less of a target for theft and all of your photos will be automatically backed up to the cloud. Don't be concerned about image quality, either; smartphone cameras are now outperforming point-and-shoots. And thanks to high megapixel count, you'll have no problem enlarging your favorite photos and decorating your walls with images from your trip.

That said, there are some benefits to carrying a dedicated camera. They give you greater control over depth of field, they shoot even larger image sizes, and many—especially digital single-lens reflex (DSLR) cameras—have the ability to shoot in raw image format (also called a digital negative). If these are things that really matter to you and you're set on carrying a separate camera, stick with something small like a point-and-shoot or a mirrorless camera. Several in this category have much of the manual control and functionality of DSLRs without being huge and heavy. Your local camera store is an excellent place to sort through all the options. Also be sure to check consumer reviews online.

No matter whether you carry a dedicated camera or just use your smartphone camera, be sure to learn everything you can about your camera in the months and weeks leading up to your trip. Think about all of the scenes you'll want to capture—star trails, the northern lights, incredible landscapes, colorful crowds, tiny flower petals. Your list will be extensive, and so are the camera techniques. Read everything you can find on photography and your specific camera, go out on practice shoots and download a PDF of the camera's user manual to your Kindle app in case you have questions while you're traveling. Covering all of your bases now will mean gorgeous photos while you're traveling.

If you plan on bringing a dedicated camera, don't forget to pack everything that goes along with it: a case, a wrist strap or tether, batteries and a charger.

CHARGING YOUR DEVICES

Europe has a different electrical standard than North America, and you'll also encounter four different styles of wall outlets, so charging your devices might entail bringing more than just their chargers.

European Voltage Converters

If you're traveling with a device like a hair dryer or an electric shaver that needs to be plugged into an electrical socket, check the cord for information on what voltage the device accepts. North America uses 110 volts and Europe uses 220 volts. A device that says "110–220 volts" is fine to be used in both North America and Europe, but to use an appliance in Europe that says only "110 volts," you need to purchase and bring along a separate converter. Because converters are bulky and heavy, it's better to leave

them—along with your North America–only devices—at home whenever possible.

European Wall Outlet Adaptors

There are four main outlet shapes in Europe; check out Power Plugs and Sockets of the World (see Resources) to see which adaptor you'll need for the specific country you're traveling to. An adaptor doesn't regulate the flow of electricity from the socket to your electronic device like a converter does. Instead, it just adapts your device charging plug to physically fit into a European outlet.

If you're going to charge several devices each night, consider buying an adaptor that has more than one input.

Smartphone Charging Components and Power Bank

Most smartphones these days are dual voltage, meaning they can accept both North American (110 volts) and European (220 volts) voltage. However, you'll need a European adaptor, in addition to your typical charging components, to charge your phone (see European Wall Outlet Adaptors, above, to find out what adaptor you'll need).

Your smartphone is likely to die before the day is over if you're using a battery-draining GPS app like Gaia, and if you're walking in a remote area that doesn't have electricity, you'll need a way to charge your phone at night. Solve these problems easily by carrying a power bank; mine holds five full charges for my smartphone. (And don't forget the charging components!)

Your power bank may also be able to charge your other electronic devices, from a stand-alone GPS unit to a dedicated camera (if they can charge by USB, like a smartphone).

PACK IT AWAY: ELECTRONIC TOOLS

- Keep your smartphone within reach on trail (especially if you're using a GPS app) with the help of a chest or belt holster.
- Store your earbuds in a small bag separately so they don't tangle or break. (Small clear plastic bags typically used for beads are perfect for this—find them at craft stores.)
- Save weight and bulk by cutting your lens cloth even smaller—you don't need anything larger than the palm of your hand.
- Pack your other electronic devices and components in a plastic bag or waterproof container in case it rains.

CHECKLISTS: ELECTRONIC TOOLS

The Basics

- ☐ Smartphone
- ☐ Trail and travel apps
- ☐ Smartphone case
- ☐ Lens cloth
- ☐ Earbuds
- ☐ Cell phone service
- ☐ Adaptor
- ☐ Smartphone charging components
- ☐ Power bank
- ☐ Power bank charging components
- ☐ Smartphone chest or belt holster
- ☐ Small plastic bag for earbuds
- ☐ Waterproof electronics organizer

Options

- ☐ Foreign or international SIM card
- ☐ Small plastic bag for home SIM card
- ☐ SPOT device, satellite communicator or PLB
- ☐ Stand-alone GPS unit
- ☐ GPS case
- ☐ GPS wrist strap or tether
- ☐ GPS charger
- ☐ Spare set of GPS batteries
- ☐ Point-and-shoot or mirrorless camera
- ☐ Camera case
- ☐ Camera wrist strap or tether
- ☐ Camera batteries
- ☐ Camera charger
- ☐ Converter

CHAPTER

17

PACKS

The last chapter of Part 3, Packing, covers one item that won't just bring the rest of your gear together—it can make or break your trip as you explore Europe on foot: what you pack everything into. You'll need a backpack to contain everything, as well as a day pack for short walks or more lengthy excursions around town.

BACKPACK

Your backpack will be your constant companion during your travels, an extension of your body. It's important when you pack it to keep it compact, light and comfortable.

Backpack Features to Look For

Because exploring on foot involves both walking on trail and in town and traveling by airplane, train, bus and/or car, choosing the right backpack can be difficult. A backpack that's designed purely for hiking isn't ideal, because it doesn't have the functionality you need for traveling, such as the ability to open all the way when a Transportation Security Administration (TSA) employee wants a closer look at something inside, or zip-off straps that tuck into the pack so you can check your bag on a flight. And the average travel backpack isn't ideal either, because it doesn't have the functionality you need while walking on trail, such as holsters for water bottles or a variety of external pockets for stashing everything from snacks to maps that you want close at hand.

The perfect backpack for exploring on foot is a mix of these two types of bags, and fortunately it is becoming more commonly available as walking-based travel gains in popularity. In particular, the backpack features you should look for include these:

- A rectangular shape to maximize storage capacity
- A size that's compatible with airline carry-on regulations to facilitate flying with your pack (check the websites of all the airlines you'll fly on during your trip for their exact size limitations; they often differ)—if you're staying in indoor accommodations each night, aim for 35–45 cubic liters; if you're camping, I recommend 45–65 liters

- An opening that spans the entire bag, not just the top, so you don't have to unpack your bag every time you need something deep down inside it
- Double zippers for the main opening so you can lock them together to secure the main compartment of your bag
- A padded waistbelt to keep the weight of the pack on your hips instead of your shoulders
- A sternum strap to keep your shoulder straps from slipping down your shoulders while you walk
- Mesh next to your back to vent heat while you're walking, especially on challenging sections
- A lot of pockets and compartments to organize your gear, including a variety of external pockets for items you'll need to access frequently on trail
- Two side compartments to hold your water bottles
- A large waistbelt pocket to store your cell phone or camera
- Internal tie-down straps to hold the load firmly against your back and stop things from shifting inside the bag
- External compression straps to minimize the size of the bag

---

If you find a pack that's nearly perfect—but not quite—get creative and see what you can modify yourself. I wouldn't recommend trying to add something substantial like a waistbelt or a new zipper, but you can certainly sew on simpler things like additional pockets or water-bottle holsters.

Backpack Shopping Tips

Shop at a physical store where you can try on all of your options. Get an idea of what's available by looking in the store's hiking backpack

Convertible backpacks like Tom Bihn's Hero's Journey typically have zip-off lids that become day packs.

section and travel backpack section—they're usually in different spots.

Have a sales associate help you find the right size for your body. Backpacks are usually sold in different sizes based on your torso length, not your overall height, and can be designed with men-specific or women-specific shapes and features in mind.

Make sure the sales associate fits each backpack to you. These are the features that should be tweaked until the pack is comfortable:

- waistbelt
- shoulder straps
- sternum strap
- load-lifter straps

If luggage transfer is an option on the trail you want to walk, all you need to carry is a light day pack. Score! (Photo by Caroline Calaway)

Test your top choices by walking around the store. The packs should be fully loaded with weight—I recommend around 20 pounds (9 kg) to simulate the load you'll carry around Europe (most outdoors stores have a selection of weighted bean bags for this). Keep fine-tuning all the adjustments until everything feels good.

Be picky. You don't want any pressure spots, especially pain between your shoulder blades or in your upper back; the majority of

the pack's weight should be on your hips, not your shoulders. Ladies, watch that the sternum strap doesn't ride too high (hitting you in the neck) or too low (at an uncomfortable spot on your breasts).

Try your top selection on trail. If your favorite outdoor retailer has a money-back guarantee, take your backpack home and test it out some more—this time with a full trial run on trail—before you fully commit to removing those tags that make the sale final.

Just as you wouldn't go on a long walk in brand-new boots, don't go exploring on foot without breaking in your backpack, even if it seems comfortable right out of the package. Take a short walk with your loaded backpack, then try a longer daylong walk, working up to your maximum pack load and number of walking hours for your trip (see Chapter 9, Train for the Trail).

Backpack Accessories

In addition to your backpack, you'll need to bring a few other items:

Pack cover: Surprise sprinkles happen even in summer, so make sure you have a pack cover to keep your belongings dry. Some backpacks come with a pack cover; for others, you'll need to buy a separate one. You can find a selection of generic pack covers at your favorite outdoor store.

Combination lock: If you plan on staying in hostels or huts, bring a backpack that has double zippers and a lock that fits those zippers, for peace of mind. I recommend a combination lock so you don't have a key to worry about.

Resealable plastic bag and zip ties: If you're hiring luggage transport, stow your money and delivery address in this bag and zip-tie it to your backpack.

DAY PACK

I recommend bringing along a day pack too; it's necessary if you're hiring luggage transport but can also be helpful if you want to explore town without your main backpack. I also use my day pack as my "one extra personal carry-on item" on flights or trains so that I'm not constantly searching through my big pack for small things I like to have on hand in such moments, like snacks or a notebook and pen; I stash my main backpack overhead in a luggage rack and leave it there for the duration of the flight or train ride.

If you'll be using your day pack on trail, for one-day wanders from a home-base town or accommodations, choose one that has most of the features outlined above for your main backpack, but smaller—I recommend 20–35 liters. You'll definitely need a padded waistbelt, wide and comfortable shoulder straps, good pockets and holsters for your water bottles.

If you'll be using your day pack only in town and for a travel carry-on, you can use something more casual. For instance, I like to bring a reusable cloth grocery bag, which I pack as part of my toiletry kit; it's really light, compact and a neutral color, and it looks like a shoulder bag (and it is already part of my gear). Sometimes I also bring a lightweight cross-body travel purse. Gentlemen, if you want to use something that's similar but more manly, consider a drawstring backpack; the straps are too narrow to be comfortable on trail, but it's a great option for exploring in town.

There are some really cool backpacks available— the Transformers of the travel world. Like Tom Bihn's The Hero's Journey travel backpack, these packs zip, fold, et cetera, to reveal all sorts of great features, such as removable day packs and different kinds of straps. These transforming backpacks are more expensive than basic ones, but they can eliminate the need for multiple packs—and they're really fun.

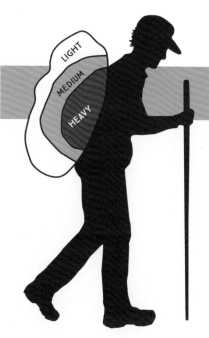

THE BEST WAY TO PACK A BACKPACK

- Pack heavy things next to your back and in the middle (core zone) of your backpack; place light things on top and down below.
- Pack big things first, then small things.
- Attach your trekking poles or town shoes to the tool loops or lash-on points on the outside of your pack when you're on trail; tuck them inside when you're traveling.
- If you're walking with someone else, store your trail essentials in the outside pockets of *their* pack—and have them do the same with yours—so it's easier to get to your things without taking off your backpack.

- If you have to check your backpack for a plane or train ride, tuck any loose straps into the backpack—this is a cool feature of many travel bags.
- If your backpack's straps don't tuck in, remove any straps that can get caught on the conveyer belt or the inside of the plane and stash them inside the pack.
- If you can't tuck in or remove any loose straps, most airlines will provide you with a large plastic bag to put your backpack in so it will travel safely as a checked bag. Make sure your pack stays in the bag by tying a big knot in the top of the plastic—most of these bags are huge.
- If you try to carry on both your main backpack and your day pack (loaded with the things you want on hand for the flight) and the airline says you're only allowed one carry-on (this happens a lot with budget airlines), tuck your day pack into your main pack until you get inside the plane—then unpack it again.

CHECKLIST: PACKS

✔ The Basics
- ☐ Backpack
- ☐ Pack cover
- ☐ Day pack

✔ Options
- ☐ Combination lock
- ☐ Resealable plastic bag
- ☐ Zip ties

PART 4
TRAVELING

One of the most colorful places to walk is Greece, where bright white and sunset-painted homes make for gorgeous photos.

You've done all the dreaming and planning. You've made your reservations, trained your body and prepped your mind. You've purchased and assembled your gear. Only one thing remains: living out this incredible trip you've planned.

Although this book is drawing to a close, I do have some final advice for you on doing it well. This last section covers the important tasks you need to check off your to-do list before you travel, as well as the big things I urge you to keep in mind as you finally embark on exploring Europe on foot.

But first, I want to share one of my favorite memories with you as proof that the best part of this process—the thing that makes all of the work worth it—is just around the corner:

I could tell there was a problem the moment I asked Frau Müller (not her real name) about a restaurant for dinner. The kindly older German woman—a farmer's wife and the owner of the private room Mac and I had rented for the night—smiled regretfully.

"We do have one restaurant in town, but it's closed for the night," she said. "Everyone is headed to the annual village festival. We're so small—it's the biggest thing that happens here all year."

My stomach growled in protest. We had just walked more than a dozen spectacular miles along King Ludwig's Way (Walk 9) and we were hungry. Very hungry.

Frau Müller put her hands on her hips and thought for a moment.

"I can find you a restaurant in a nearby town, if you'd like," she offered, "or . . . you could come with us to the festival." She continued, her voice almost apologetic: "It'll be simple—just beer and sausages—but there's always food."

Twenty minutes later, we arrived at a large beer hall packed with all two hundred inhabitants of the town, most of them farmers and all of them dressed in dirndls and lederhosen, the traditional clothing of Bavaria. Waitresses passed through the crowd with mugs of foaming beer, massive sausages and steaming pretzels.

Everyone seemed to look up in unison when Mac and I entered the room, curious about the only two strangers in attendance. And with shy smiles, they went back to doing what they had been before. Small girls with plaited hair chased each other in circles around the tables; a big group of old men with white beards chuckled and slapped their knees over something one of them had said. A ragtag band played loud polkas that swirled around the room and made even the grandmothers tap their feet. The air buzzed with excitement—something was coming; we just didn't know what.

Almost as soon as our food arrived, the lights dimmed and a group of young men gathered on stage. With beer, axes and wood as props, they chopped, danced and sang their way through a German folk song about life as a woodcutter that brought the house down. The performance was so good and the applause so loud that I thought the entertainment was over. But it was just starting. For more than an hour, various groups from the audience performed elaborate, choreographed acts that highlighted important and historical aspects of local village life. They were some of the best performances I'd ever seen.

As we drove back to Frau Müller's farm that night, I said as much to her. And although she was clearly amused that we were such fans of the "simple" food and the show, she couldn't hide the pride in her voice as she summed up the whole magical evening in just a few words: "That's small-town life for you."

On that car ride, my feet and legs were tired from walking all day, my stomach was contentedly full and I was getting very sleepy. But what I felt, more than anything else, was a sudden realization that everything I'd been through with my experiences of traveling—being so disappointed with it I gave it up, taking that leap of faith with Mac and trying it again, stumbling around until I found a better way to do it—all of that was worth it for nights like this. I knew that this was what travel was really about, and there was nowhere else on earth I'd rather be.

That's exactly the kind of experience you have to look forward to—and you're almost there.

CHECK OFF YOUR FINAL TO-DOS BEFORE WALKING

As your trip gets close, I'm sure you'll be able to almost taste the *wienerschnitzel* and *bockbier* that you'll search out the moment your plane touches down. But as hard as it might be, don't let your mind take off for vacation quite yet. There's just a little more work to do to get yourself ready for your European walking tour.

Now I know how crazy things can get in the days before you leave on a big trip. There's so much to do: big projects to finish up or temporarily transition to coworkers, in-boxes to clean out, fridges to purge, mail to pause. It's tempting to spend all your time doing these things that feel like they *have* to get done—and then madly tackle your last-minute trip chores the night before you leave. There's just one problem with this approach: in addition to it making you feel completely frazzled by the time you set out on your walk, something is bound to fall through the cracks.

But it doesn't have to be like that. You can set out on the trail feeling relaxed and uberconfident that every *i* has been dotted and each *t* crossed. All you have to do is carve out a little extra time to accomplish a few key tasks in those final few hours that stand between you and exploring Europe on foot.

THREE DAYS BEFORE YOUR FLIGHT

When there are seventy-two hours left before you fly to Europe, it's time to start tackling your final to-dos with gusto. Here are the most important things you need to accomplish.

Get Your Banking in Order

Make sure that your credit cards and debit card are authorized for use in Europe by calling your bank(s) and letting them know where and when you'll be traveling. Also verify your debit card and credit card personal identification numbers (PINs) if you don't know them already. (In Europe, you'll usually sign for purchases, but occasionally you will be asked to input your PIN when paying for something with your credit card.)

Plan Your Pre-Trail Errands

You'll usually have a few errands to run once you're in Europe and before you hit the trail— getting cash out of an ATM; picking up any last-minute supplies like maps, food and rental gear; purchasing a foreign SIM card if that's how you're going to get cell phone service—so make the process as easy for yourself as possible by listing everywhere you'll need to go and everything you'll need to pick up once you're there.

Figure out how you'll get to each spot and when you'll go. This last part is especially important because European shops aren't open all the time like North American ones; the places you'll need to visit may close early or not even be open certain days of the week. So factor their hours of operation into your plan. Two errands that are probably on your to-do list are getting cash from an ATM and stocking up on snacks for the trail. It's worth talking about each one of these in greater detail.

Cash: One of the most important things you'll do before you hit the trail, especially if you're walking somewhere that doesn't have banks along the route, is withdraw enough cash from an ATM for your trip. Because it's generally cheaper to make one big withdrawal than several small ones, it's helpful to know exactly how much cash you'll need.

Add up all of the things you haven't paid for in advance, taking into consideration which places accept credit cards and which don't—you can find this information online or by calling the service or establishment. Then

Dining outside at charming cafes is one of the simple pleasures of exploring Europe on foot.

add in a cushion for the random cash-only restaurant, bakery or street vendor that you'll happen upon each day and for the establishments that won't take debit or credit cards for purchases under €10. (My cushion is usually €20–€30 per day.)

Whenever possible, avoid private ATMs (stick to the ATMs of major banks) and those that dispense money only if you agree to their exchange rate instead of your bank's: this is a sneaky way to assess fees— you'll get a much better deal from your own bank.

Tired of the same old hiking food? Wait until you're in Europe to buy your trail snacks—you'll find all sorts of new and interesting things to try.

Once you know how much cash you'll need, research online to find out your bank's European partner banks and plan on withdrawing your cash from these ATMs. You'll get the best deal on currency exchange and your ATM fee will be waived, which can save you €5–€10 every time you withdraw money.

Food: How much food you'll need to stock your backpack with will depend on what's available on your chosen route. Even if your accommodations provide breakfast and dinner and there's somewhere to stop for lunch midday, always have snacks with you in case you get hungry. This isn't just for your comfort—it's also for your safety. Even when I know there are grocery stores near my accommodations each night, I always like to carry a reserve of at least two or three days' worth of snacks in my backpack, just in case I don't feel like going to the grocery store one night—or (more commonly) in case it's closed. So figure out where you'll purchase trail snacks once you arrive in Europe.

Pack Your Bag

By now, all of your gear should be finalized, so it's time to pack it away. To make sure you don't forget anything, print out your packing list: a downloadable one is available free on my website (explore-on-foot.com) and you'll also find all of this book's checklists in the appendix at the back of the book. Check off each item as you put it in your pack. Highlight anything on your checklists that's still outstanding—those items that you'll pack the morning you head to the airport or that you plan on getting in Europe—so there are no accidental omissions.

While the majority of your gear can be packed away in the smaller organizers you'll use when you're on trail, pay special attention to where you stow anything that airport security screeners might be interested in taking a closer look at, such as toiletries, electronics or a pocketknife. Keep these items as accessible as possible until you're in Europe.

Get Enough Rest

One of the best things you can do before you leave for your trip is get enough rest. This is beneficial for your body and your mind. Stop training and give your muscles a break so you can hit the trail hard in a few days. And get a full eight hours of sleep each night—if you aren't operating with a sleep debt when you arrive, you'll have an easier time staying awake (and you'll be less grumpy!) that first day in Europe as you adjust to your new time zone.

ONE DAY BEFORE YOUR FLIGHT

Once you've tackled your initial to-dos, you're a lot closer to a stress-free departure to Europe. In all of the pretrip excitement of the final twenty-four hours, don't forget the most important thing that's still left to do.

Check In for Your Flight

Most airlines allow you to check in for an international flight from twenty-four hours to ninety minutes before your scheduled departure time. Do yourself a favor and check in as soon as possible so your seat isn't given away if the flight is overbooked. (This happened to my friend Mitzi when she was flying to meet me in Scotland for the West Highland Way, Walk 13, and it was a real bummer.) You can save yourself some time at the airport by printing your boarding pass at home or saving it to your smartphone.

THE MORNING OF YOUR FLIGHT

There's nothing more exciting than waking up and knowing that you're only hours away from an incredible adventure. Here's what you need to do before you leave home as the clock ticks down.

Add Any Final Items to Your Pack

If there's anything that still needs to go in your pack before you leave (such as your glasses or toothbrush), now's the time to add it. Check any items off your checklists and stow your lists in your backpack so they're accessible once you're in Europe and running your pre-trail errands.

DURING YOUR FLIGHT

You'll have several hours on the plane as you fly to Europe (typically anywhere between six and fifteen), so make use of your downtime and accomplish a few more key tasks—a little effort en route will go a long way toward guaranteeing yourself a great trip.

Put Your Phone on Airplane Mode

Airlines require that you have your phone on airplane mode for the length of the flight, for safety reasons. However, I also mention it because if you'll be using your smartphone offline in Europe—grabbing free Wi-Fi wherever you go instead of paying for cell phone service—you'll want to keep your phone on airplane mode for the duration of your trip to avoid accidental roaming charges. You can still use Wi-Fi while airplane mode is on.

Be Proactive About Jet Lag

Doing what you can to fight jet lag while you're on your way to Europe instead of simply dealing with it once you get there can be a game changer for you—it has been for me. My favorite trick: As soon as you get settled on the plane, set your watch to Europe time and then treat that time as your "real" time for the duration of your flight. Sleep, eat, drink caffeine only when

Your body clock governs pretty much everything inside your body, from when you're hungry to when you're tired to what your body temperature should be. Jet lag, also known as circadian rhythm disorder, occurs when you travel across the earth's east–west rotation so quickly that your body clock is out of sync with your environment.

Because your circadian rhythm is influenced to a large degree by environmental factors, such as exposure to light, during jet lag your body systems are thrown into chaos: Your body's "remembering" its normal rhythm from back home is telling them to do one thing ("Sleep now! It's nighttime!"), but the environmental signals your body "reads," such as light and temperature, are telling them something entirely different ("Actually, it's noon here in Europe!"). The result is that until you adjust to the new time zone, you want to eat and sleep at your "home" times, which are all the wrong times in Europe—and you probably feel really out of it.

Unfortunately, you can't avoid jet lag (unless you're a fan of slow travel and cross the ocean on a ship instead of a plane), and some people—typically, older people—feel it more than others. You can minimize its effects by following my suggestions for getting your body clock to reset and sync with your new time zone as quickly as possible.

the clock says it's time to in Europe. If you're having trouble napping on the plane, shut off your screens (entertainment system, smartphone, et cetera)—they emit blue light that can stimulate your brain to stay awake.

Stay Hydrated

Being well hydrated reduces fatigue (which can be caused by dehydration) and the symptoms of jet lag, and it is also great for your muscles: they'll perform better when you're finally ready to hit the trail. While you're flying to Europe, drink plenty of water and avoid the booze. If you're embarrassed about climbing over your seatmates all the time to use the restroom, ask if they'd like to switch seats with you. They may say no, but at least they won't be able to complain when you're getting up and down to use the loo.

WHEN YOU GET TO EUROPE

Once you get off the plane, you can finally tackle the to-dos that can only be done once you're in Europe. Here are the most important ones to focus on.

Be Easy on Yourself

Touching down in Europe is super exciting. Your trip is really happening! You're here! Unfortunately, you're also probably jet-lagged and exhausted—and, if you're anything like me, grumpy. So be easy on yourself.

The truth is, your first day in Europe—when you're doing battle with jet lag and

Caffeine is a stimulant that has a half-life of six hours—meaning that half of it is still in your bloodstream six hours after you drink it—so avoiding it the morning of your departure and not drinking it after noon (in Europe time) can help you adjust to the new time zone and sleep well your first night in Europe.

One of the local specialties along Germany's Moselsteig Trail is tresterfleisch, *pork marinated in wine spirits.*

sleep debt—will often be the toughest day of your trip. It can feel like a huge letdown in the moment, because you've been looking forward to your trip for *forever*, but things will get better. You'll get a good night's sleep, your body clock will begin to reset and you'll start to feel awesome again—in just a matter of hours.

Keep Fighting Jet Lag

The best thing you can do on your first day in Europe is help your body adjust to the new time zone. What that really means is working hard *against* what your body naturally wants to do—such as eat and sleep on its "home" schedule. It usually takes a little tough love to get your circadian rhythm aligned with Europe's time zone.

Let yourself get a little hungry, so that when it's mealtime in Europe, you're ready to eat. And definitely don't give in to how tired you feel—stay awake (no naps!) until your new European bedtime. Sleep is one of the most powerful resets your body clock gets, so it's really important to not sleep too soon!

The most helpful thing I've found for staying awake that first day in Europe is to stay upright and outdoors. If you sit down, you'll feel extra sleepy. But if you're up, walking around and exposing yourself to a lot of natural light outside, you're far more likely to stay awake until your new European bedtime.

Do Your Pre-Trail Errands

Because you want to be up and walking around anyway, to fight jet lag, your first day in Europe is the perfect time to tackle your pre-trail errands. You'll have the best experience if you do this without your backpack.

If you're spending a night in the city you flew into, either check in to your accommodations early (some places allow early check-in—ask in advance) or leave your backpack at your accommodations' front desk until your room is ready. Most places will store it in a secure spot, such as behind the front desk or in a locked luggage room, for free.

If you're not staying a night in this city, you might be able to check your bag at the train or bus station or tourist information office until it's time to take local transportation to the trailhead.

Once you've stashed your backpack, you're ready to find the ATM, a supermarket or any other shop on your list.

Communicating with the Locals

Although most people in Europe speak English (and hopefully you've learned some of their language as well), occasionally you'll happen upon a spot where there is a language barrier, so you'll need to get creative with your communication to understand and be understood. Here are my top tips for overcoming a significant language barrier:

Use your smartphone's tools. Download a language app or dictionary, use Google Translate (you can have it read the translation out loud if you're having trouble with pronunciation), or bring up a picture on your smartphone if you don't know the word for something.

Pantomime or use hand gestures. Sometimes acting something out is the best way to communicate. For example, if you're trying to find a shop with bananas, act out peeling and eating a banana and then jingle a couple of coins to indicate you want to buy something. Just be aware that hand gestures can mean different things in different countries.

Use props. If you're asking directions, have your map handy, and point to places on it. Carry a notebook and pen in case you need to draw a picture or write down numbers, such as the price of something.

Say things as simply as possible. If you're speaking to someone with a limited understanding of English, use basic vocabulary and simple sentence structures. Instead of saying "How much do I owe you?," say "How much?"

Ask open-ended questions. If you ask yes-or-no questions and someone doesn't understand you, they're likely to just nod their head "yes" in agreement—whether or not that's the right answer. Instead of asking "Do I take this right turn to get to the supermarket?," ask "Where is the supermarket?"

Get information written down. If there's something you really want to be able to communicate over and over again, such as "I'm a strict vegetarian," have a local (for example, your hotel concierge or guesthouse owner) write that phrase down on a piece of paper that you can pull out and show whenever you need to.

Go where people speak English. If you really need help—in English—go to a four- or five-star hotel or resort, even if you're not staying there; the concierges likely speak English. You're also likely to find English speakers at tourist information offices, pharmacies, banks and local universities.

Paying for Your Purchases

Beware the difference that punctuation makes! In Europe, commas and periods play opposite roles in monetary amounts. For example, a couture handbag that costs €7.000 in Europe isn't €7; it's €7,000. A sandwich that costs €7,30 isn't €7,300, it's €7.30.

Factor in fees. Many banks (with the exception of companies such as Capitol One's travel-specific cards) charge international transaction fees—typically 1–3 percent of the amount of a purchase—when you buy something with your credit or debit card in Europe or when you make an ATM withdrawal.

Always ask to see an itemized bill. Before you pay for your purchases, take time to make sure the bill is correct and that no previously undisclosed charges or fees are added.

Always ask for the amount to be charged in the local currency. Don't ever agree to be charged in your home currency—this is just a ploy by the merchant to charge hidden fees by giving you a worse currency conversion rate than your bank would.

Tip an appropriate amount. Self-service bars and restaurants, no tip; bad service, no tip; bellhops, porters and coat checkers, €1 per bag; casual restaurants, €1–€3; nicer restaurants, 5–10 percent of the bill (a 5 percent tip is good, a 10 percent tip is generous). Also see the How Much Should I Tip? sidebar in Chapter 6, Walk Independently or Hire Help.

Keep your payment card with you at all times. When you pay with a credit or debit card in Europe, the merchant is required to bring the card machine to you—your card should never leave your sight.

An old man at a bar in Scotland once gave me a passionate lecture on how unsafe it is for your credit or debit card to leave your sight—oh, the incredible opportunity for fraud! He simply couldn't believe that in North America, waiters regularly disappear with customers' credit cards—sometimes for ten or fifteen minutes when the restaurant is busy—to run them through the card machine in the back of the restaurant.

Connect to Wi-Fi

Whether you're using your smartphone to help you run your pre-trail errands or you need to check in with the folks at home, it's in your best interest to connect to free Wi-Fi whenever it's available—it'll help you keep your data costs down—or simply use your phone if you've opted to go without cell service in Europe. Many hotels, restaurants and train stations offer Wi-Fi (and most for free); if you need help locating free networks around you, an app such as Free WiFi Finder can help.

Tips for Connecting to European Wi-Fi
Although Wi-Fi is widely available in Europe, it's not as dependable as in North America. It's been my experience that much of the time the networks are slow or just plain down. Part of the problem is a lack of sufficient towers to cover demand in more-rural areas; another problem is an overload of individual networks—think a hundred hotel guests all trying to get online at the same time on the same network. Luckily, there are things you can do to improve your chances of connecting to European Wi-Fi:

Say it like a local. When you ask for directions on connecting to a Wi-Fi network, ask for "wee-fee." That's how the Europeans pronounce it—not "why-fi" like we do in North America.

Ask before ordering. Before you purchase anything at a cafe or restaurant, ask if the Wi-Fi network is working; if the network is down, you'll need to go elsewhere to connect.

Find the reliable spots. If you're in desperate need of Wi-Fi, head to the closest McDonald's, train station or airport. Most of these offer free—and reliable—Wi-Fi.

Make audio-only calls. Stick to audio calls with family and friends—there usually isn't enough Wi-Fi bandwidth for video calls.

Try texting. If the Internet connection keeps dropping out during your phone call, try switching to text messaging.

Change your phone settings. If your phone disconnects from the Internet as soon as its

In Europe, the twenty-four-hour clock, rather than the twelve-hour clock, is the standard (as it also is for military time). Midnight is 0:00 on the twenty-four-hour clock, and the times between that and 12:59 p.m. are the same on both clocks. To figure out what time you're looking at on the twenty-four-hour clock for any time between 1:00 p.m. and 11:59 p.m., subtract twelve. For example, to convert 19:30 to the twelve-hour clock, subtract twelve, which means it's 7:30 p.m.

screen shuts off but you have other tasks you're trying to accomplish online, such as continuing your Whatsapp call with your family back at home, go into your settings; your screen saver and auto lock are probably set to "2 minutes." Switch them to "30 minutes" or "never." This will drain your battery quicker than normal but should keep you connected.

Your first day in Europe shouldn't be all work and no play! Once your pre-trail errands are taken care of, it's time to have some fun. Go for a long walk or bike ride in a beautiful park, wander into an old cathedral that smells like incense and the fifteenth century, treat yourself to a fragrant glass of wine. This is what all of your hard work has been for. Let it pay off!

THE DAY BEFORE YOUR WALK

The countdown is on—there are only a few hours left before you start your walk. This is the perfect time to check off one of your last prewalk to-dos.

Take Local Transportation to Your Trailhead Accommodations

If you haven't already, you should take whatever local transportation you've arranged for traveling from the city you arrived in to the town or accommodations nearest to the trailhead so that you can get an early start on trail tomorrow.

THE NIGHT BEFORE YOUR WALK

Finish your prewalk to-dos the night before you start your walk. These key tasks will make your first day on trail a lot easier.

Figure Out What Time Breakfast Is

If you're staying somewhere that offers breakfast, the time it's offered will usually determine the time you can hit the trail: Aim to eat as early as you can. It's always better to start walking earlier in the day rather than later because you never know what cool things you'll see during your walk that will prolong your exploration. Set your alarm early enough that you can get completely ready for the day by breakfast time, then take your backpack to the dining room with you when you eat so you can hit the trail from there.

Reorganize Your Bag

Yes, you've already packed your backpack—but for the airport, not the trail. Now's the time to make sure everything is just where you want it

IT'S *HOW* HOT?

To know what to wear for your walk, it helps to know what the temperature forecast is. In Europe, that's measured in Celsius, not Fahrenheit. But don't despair, fellow Americans. It's not that hard to figure out what temperature to expect: Multiply the number in Celsius by two and add thirty. For example, 10 degrees Celsius is approximately 50 degrees Fahrenheit (10 x 2 = 20, 20 + 30 = 50). Or just remember this cute rhyme: "Zero's freezing, ten is not; twenty is warm and thirty hot."

for your walk. You won't be able to add absolutely everything just yet—for instance, those pajamas you're probably wearing right now—but you can get close. Doing these big things tonight will save you a lot of time—and stress—in the morning:

- Integrate the things you picked up on your pre-trail errands.
- Take your toiletries out of their TSA-approved plastic bag and stow them in your toiletry bag.
- Fill your water bottles.

- Put a day's worth of snacks in your pack's outside pockets.
- Lay out your trail clothes for the morning.

Get a Good Night's Sleep

Especially if this is your first night in Europe, you need good sleep to get your body and mind ready for the trail tomorrow. I always have trouble sleeping the night before a big walk, even when I'm really tired, because I'm so darn excited. (I also get the pre-trail jitters every

IT'S *HOW* FAR?

Most European countries use the metric system, which means that most of the distances you'll see—from walking directions to trail signs—will be in kilometers. If that's not the standard measurement at home (that's you, Americans), practice converting kilometers to miles. Multiply the number of kilometers by six and then move the decimal point one spot to the left. For example, 10 kilometers is approximately 6 miles (10 x 6 = 60, then move the decimal one spot to the left to yield 6.0).

In Italy's Cinque Terre, you can enjoy local limoncino *that's sourced from the verdant land you walk through.*

time I explore on foot, even after all this time, so don't worry if you're also a little anxious.)

If that's you, too, consider taking a natural sleep aid, such as melatonin; I usually take one for the first two nights I'm in Europe, until my body has switched over to the new time zone and my mind has calmed down enough to make going to sleep a breeze. Trust me, you have some of the best sleep of your life coming up—there's nothing like a good day on trail to make you sleep like a baby. Tonight as you drift off, remember: tomorrow your grand adventure begins!

CHECKLISTS: FINAL TASKS

 Three Days Before Your Flight

Get Your Banking in Order

- ☐ Authorize debit and credit cards for use in Europe
- ☐ Verify debit and credit card PINs

- ☐ Figure out how much cash you'll need when you arrive in Europe
- ☐ Look online for your bank's European partner banks
- ☐ Find out where those ATMs are

Plan Your Pre-Trail Errands

- ☐ List everything you need to get or do when you arrive in Europe
- ☐ Figure out how you'll get to each spot
- ☐ Figure out what time each spot is open

Pack Your Bag

- ☐ Use your checklists
- ☐ Highlight any missing items
- ☐ Keep items accessible for airport screening

Get Plenty of Rest

- ☐ Stop training and give your muscles a break
- ☐ Get a full eight hours of sleep each night

✓ One Day Before Your Flight
- ☐ Check in for your flight
- ☐ Print your boarding pass or save it to your smartphone

✓ The Morning of Your Flight
- ☐ Add final items to your backpack
- ☐ Check everything off your packing checklists
- ☐ Stow any uncompleted checklists (such as your pre-trail errands) in your backpack

✓ During Your Flight
- ☐ Put your phone in airplane mode
- ☐ Set your watch to European time
- ☐ Sleep, eat and drink caffeine on European time
- ☐ Shut off screens if you have trouble napping
- ☐ Stay hydrated

✓ When You Get to Europe
- ☐ Let yourself get a little hungry
- ☐ Stay awake until European bedtime
- ☐ Do your pre-trail errands
- ☐ Connect to Wi-Fi

✓ The Day Before Your Walk
- ☐ Take local transportation to your trailhead accommodations

✓ The Night Before Your Walk

Figure Out What Time Breakfast Is
- ☐ Set your alarm for an early start
- ☐ Plan to take your backpack to the dining room

Reorganize Your Backpack
- ☐ Integrate things you picked up on your pretrail errands
- ☐ Take your toiletries out of their TSA-approved plastic bag and stow them in your toiletry bag
- ☐ Fill your water bottles
- ☐ Put a day's worth of snacks in your pack's outside pockets
- ☐ Lay out your trail clothes for the morning

Get a Good Night's Sleep
- ☐ Consider taking a natural sleep aid

MAKE THE MOST OF THE EXPERIENCE

This is the moment you've been looking forward to and preparing for these past months. It's time for you to lace up your walking shoes, heft your backpack onto your shoulders and start your journey. It's finally time to explore Europe on foot.

I wish I could be there with you, to give you my famous pre-trail talk; it's a rite of passage for anyone I'm traveling with who's about to explore on foot for the first time. I get really excited about this moment, because it's my chance to pass on some of the biggest lessons I've learned over tens of trips and thousands of miles. Over a steaming-hot cup of coffee, our backpacks propped up on the other side of the breakfast room and ready to go, I'd love to encourage you in person.

However, I'm not there with you, so now I'll share my message with you in this chapter: keep your priorities in order, lighten your load if your pack is too heavy, be flexible when faced with challenges, give yourself some downtime each day, be a visitor rather than a tourist, allow your travels to change you, and when your time on trail starts coming to a close, don't get sad, get planning—for your next trip.

I know I'm not really there to give you this speech in person, share in your excitement at hitting the trail or see the look of exhilaration and satisfaction you'll be wearing when you roll into town for your first night on trail. But I hope my final words of wisdom resonate with you as you step out into the bright morning and take your first few steps on a European trail. And I hope you turn these thoughts around in your mind as you walk confidently into your own incredible adventure.

In Europe, a long and lingering lunch starts with plenty of wine and bread.

KEEP YOUR PRIORITIES IN ORDER

Even if you and your travel companion(s) start your walk alone, at some point on trail you'll come across other people. And once you do, you'll have to fight your urge to measure your journey against theirs.

This becomes especially challenging when you encounter folks who are intent on making their trail experience less about exploring and more about athletic achievement. On a steep section that has you gasping for breath, they'll politely charge past you without missing a beat or even breaking a sweat; to add insult to injury, some of them will even be running while they do it! In comparison to these cheetahs of the trail world, you may feel slow. And truth be told, I hope it's more than a feeling. If you have your priorities in order, you will actually *be* slow. And that's fantastic!

Remember, exploring Europe on foot isn't just about walking. It's about using the trail to discover some of the world's loveliest natural beauty and most intriguing foreign culture. Stop to photograph the morning dew on the flowers; make lunch a two-hour affair at a beautiful restaurant overlooking the next quaint town; never miss an opportunity to soak your feet when you pass a gorgeous cool stream—this is the perfect time to get out that wine hydration bag! When you explore on foot, the journey is the destination—you're exactly where you need to be. So don't rush it.

> Even though I encourage you to be poky on trail, you still need to get your destination by dark, so don't forget to calibrate your pace: check out Chapter 10, Be Prepared for Anything, for a refresher on how to do that, and modify your plans if need be.

LIGHTEN YOUR LOAD IF YOUR PACK IS TOO HEAVY

It's one thing to be slow because you're being intentional about enjoying the trail. It's another to be slow because you accidentally packed too much (I warned you!) and now your bag is so . . . darn . . . heavy. If this happens to you, you have a couple of options for lightening your load:

Abandon some things. You may have thought you'd need that extra plastic water bottle and tank top, but now that you're on trail, you haven't used them at all. If they're not expensive or you're just not that attached to them, abandon them. Many hostels have a free box you can drop them in, or you can just leave them on your hotel bed with a little note that says "free"—they're sure to find a new home on their own.

Send things home. If there's something you really love or think is too expensive to simply abandon (or if it's a brand-new souvenir), send it home. See the Sending Things Home sidebar for tips on how to do this.

BE FLEXIBLE WHEN FACED WITH CHALLENGES

At some point during your trip, you'll be faced with a challenging situation—or a few. In those moments, your ability to bend rather than break will mean the difference between bouncing back quickly from a setback or letting it ruin your trip. For example, on one of my trips, all of the flights into Paris were cancelled because of an air traffic controller strike, and I had to scramble to find another way to get there from Scotland in time for my flight home.

SENDING THINGS HOME

- Find the nearest post office by asking a local or searching on Google Maps.
- Make your first trip a reconnaissance mission. Pick up the customs forms you'll need to fill out (complete as much as you can before you return, to save yourself time and anxiety) and find out whether or not the post office sells boxes. (If they don't, you'll have to find one elsewhere.) Also find out when the post office is open, for your return visit.
- When you fill out the customs forms, estimate the value of your shipment, keeping in mind your duty regulations at home. (You can look this up online.) If you're sending home your own used items (items that were purchased in your home country), make sure to let the post office know—you shouldn't be charged duty on those items.
- When you return to the post office, bring your completed customs forms, your passport and your unsealed package. Make sure you have plenty of time and patience reserved for the errand.
- If you don't need your package to arrive right away, or if you'd like the shipment to be as cheap as possible, ask for ground transportation rather than air.

Marrakesh, Morocco's Jemaa el-Fnaa square is a fascinating place to explore, day or night.

Whenever I'm traveling and encounter a really challenging situation like that, I try to remember one of my favorite quotes: "An inconvenience is only an adventure wrongly considered; an adventure is an inconvenience rightly considered," wrote G. K. Chesterton in "All Things Considered" (*On Running After One's Hat*, 1908). Over time (and definitely thanks to the shenanigans of that cancelled flight), I also came to rely on a little game plan I developed for challenging situations. I hope it can help you too:

Stay calm: Be intentional about your breathing. Getting all worked up won't help anything.

Put things in perspective: Are you going to remember this in a year? Five years?

Get creative: Brainstorm all of the possible solutions out there that could solve your problem, not just the most obvious one that comes to mind.

Don't beat yourself up about extra costs: If there's nothing you can do about the situation, just throw money at it if you have the luxury of a credit card.

Be polite: Remember, you can catch more flies with honey than with vinegar.

Make sure your requests are actionable: If you need help from a customer service agent, for instance, ask them to do something specific.

Have an action orientation: It's often best to get going in some direction, any direction, rather than just sitting around mulling over the absolute best thing you could do. You can always adjust your plan once you have set it in motion.

Be nice to yourself: Do whatever you need to do in the moment to make yourself a little happier and improve your mood, especially if it's treating yourself to a small luxury like a hot cup of coffee.

Avoid getting "hangry": If you're hungry and angry, beware of taking your frustrations out on your travel companion(s) and anyone else who's in your path.

Look for a lesson: Once the situation has been resolved, look for a silver lining. If nothing else, perk yourself up by practicing how you're going to tell this story someday at a cocktail party. After all, it's always the most challenging situations that make the best stories.

GIVE YOURSELF SOME DOWNTIME EACH DAY

You'll have the best chance of making the most of the amazing opportunities you have on your trip and staying positive when challenging situations come up if you give yourself some downtime each day. If you're anything like me, that's a hard task. When I travel, I have a tendency to go, go, go because I don't want to miss out on anything. But traveling at that pace can really catch up with you, and ultimately you crash—or you go home more exhausted than when you left.

The solution is to build some downtime into your travel routine. I like to take an hour or two of downtime each day as I'm transitioning from trail to town. I've found that that's the perfect time for me to relax. I have a little routine that includes showering, changing into clean clothes and then diving into some light reading while enjoying a glass of wine and a predinner snack.

I really recommend stretching during your downtime—it will help your body transition to a resting state and decrease any soreness you're feeling. You can also help your body recover by eating a snack well-balanced with protein within thirty to forty-five minutes of finishing your walk. Also drink 16 ounces (half a liter) of water per hour for the next two or three hours.

When you're exploring on foot, you're mainly engaged in solitary activities with just your travel companion, so your downtime is also perfect for something else: taking a break from your adventure companion. No matter how much you love this person and being around them, it's smart to take some time apart each day, even if you don't think you need it.

Take it from someone who's been there—your chances of a drama-free trip are much higher if you're proactive, rather than reactive, about your time apart.

One of the best ways to combat soreness and muscle fatigue is a good night's sleep. If you want to feel your best, don't settle for your normal seven hours of sleep—give yourself at least eight or nine hours to recharge. Trust me, you'll feel much better in the morning.

BE A VISITOR RATHER THAN A TOURIST

Even with downtime and a good night's sleep, you'll still have hours and hours each day to explore Europe on foot, both on trail and in town. But you not only have time, you also have sheer opportunity: you're off the beaten path, deep in the heart of a place where you'll find real locals, not hordes of tourists. Don't pass this by.

Make the most of this opportunity by approaching your travels not as a tourist—someone who comes into a community, looks around, takes a few pictures and then moves on—but, rather, as a visitor, someone who's there to actively learn about and participate in a different way of life. Don't just admire local cuisine—learn how to make it. Rather than sit in a pub as people blow off steam after work, join in the conversation with your fledgling language skills. These are the moments you'll really remember.

Go Deeper with Your Explorations

When it comes to truly experiencing a foreign culture, sometimes your five senses are your very best guide.

Sight

- Instead of looking for extraordinary sights, look for ordinary ones that are

Locals and travelers alike take in the sunset on one of Florence's many scenic bridges.

just as interesting: the variations in "walk" signs or symbols at intersections, different styles of telephone booths, how people dress.

- Don't give things your normal cursory look—give them a deep, long look to take in the details that you're so used to missing. Look at things the way an artist does, as if you were going to paint them. Contemplate how you would describe those things to someone at home.
- Look at things from interesting angles: lying down on the ground and looking up, standing on a chair or a rock and gazing down from up high.

Smell

- Especially when you're in a new place, take time to notice and categorize scents. You'll become accustomed to new smells in a few days, so the perfect time to explore aromas is when they're completely fresh. Smell the ocean, fresh-cut grass, the scent of ripening grapes on the vine.

- Let your nose take you on a tour as you walk around the streets. Follow your nose to new bakeries or restaurants. Search out particularly fragrant places like gardens or spice markets.

Hearing

- Listen to the sounds of ordinary life that are so different from your home: the ring of a phone, a wailing police-car siren, the "walk" tone at an intersection, the announcement tune of a train that's preparing to stop at a new station.
- Tune in to the melody and cadence of the foreign language conversations around you.

Taste

- Try to identify individual ingredients in the foods you eat and the drinks you imbibe.
- Pay attention to how the tap water tastes and compare it to your water from home.

Touch

- Run your hands over all of the different textures you encounter: smooth grapes, gnarly grapevines, smooth beach rocks, grainy sand, rough coffee bags at the market.
- Explore the feel of traditional textiles: French table linens, Icelandic wool sweaters, Scottish plaid.

ALLOW YOUR TRAVELS TO CHANGE YOU

Even if you take in those memorable times and really savor them, you still won't get the most out of your travels until you allow them to change you. And for that change to happen, you need to be prepared to ask some big questions about the culture you're experiencing and how it applies to your own life.

Exploring on foot is perfectly suited to this exercise because there's no better time to ponder than when you're walking for hours at a time. As your feet methodically hit the trail, something magical happens to your brain. Even things you've been wrestling with for a while can suddenly become clear. It's no surprise to me that some of the greatest thinkers of all time were walkers. Put your walking mind to work by letting it chew on questions like these:

- *What do these people do better than me?* For instance, cook, make time for their family, et cetera.
- *What do they have that I want?* Maybe it's more time off or a stronger sense of community.
- *What can our differences teach me?* Perhaps to be slower to judge, to be more accepting of other people, and so on.
- *What steps could I take to bring that value, skill, trait or lesson into my own life?* Don't forget to ask yourself this perhaps most important question of all.

BRING YOUR TRAVELS HOME WITH YOU

I'm sure you love collecting meaningful reminders of your travels, just like I do. Avoid tchotchkes and things you'll throw away a year from now by getting creative with your souvenirs. Here are some of my favorite souvenirs—and they won't add a lot of weight to your backpack, either:

- Collect postcards that are representative of something you did or where you stayed and every day, write your favorite moments on them. Bundle them into a fun flip book when you're back home.
- Buy local music that you fall in love with on your trip.
- Jot down your favorite dishes and look up the recipes online once you're home. Pair them with photos from your trip for a foodie scrapbook that you can cook from for years.
- Collect everything you need to re-create your favorite sensory experiences (see Go Deeper with Your Explorations in this chapter). An essential oil can remind you of the lemon trees at your Italian bed-and-breakfast. A recording of the ocean crashing against the shore can remind you of your beachside hut in Greece.
- Save your train tickets and low-denomination paper money; they make great bookmarks that bring back favorite memories.

Along Germany's King Ludwig's Way, you'll see a variety of old-fashioned little signs with rhymes about the joy—and pain—of walking.

Want even more help sifting through your thoughts or remembering your favorite moments from your trip? Take the time to write in a journal as you explore on foot—it doubles as one of the best souvenirs you can bring home.

DON'T GET SAD, GET PLANNING

Eventually the day comes when thoughts will come crashing into your consciousness about your flight home, what's going on at work and how much you'll need to catch up on. That's when you'll know your trip is almost over.

The prospect of heading home to real life after such an intense travel experience—the highs, the lows, the crazy adventures, the magic of it all—can be daunting, especially if your world was rocked by falling in love with exploring on foot. It was certainly daunting for me—until I learned a secret: the best cure for

post-trip sadness is to start dreaming about another trip.

And don't wait until you're home to start planning, because while you're still in Europe is the perfect time to set yourself up for future travels. You're surrounded by Europeans and well-traveled fellow walkers who can help you build your bucket list. Ask them where they've walked and what trails they recommend. This is a great way to get insider information on trails that you might otherwise never hear about in North America. Write these ideas down.

While you're at it, jot down notes on things you want to remember for next time. I debrief after every trip, which is why my method, my gear and my experience get better every time I explore on foot. It can be the same for you—ask yourself these questions:

A good reminder from one hiker to many others along Scotland's West Highland Way.

- What were you super happy about on this trip?
- What would you do differently next time?
- Are there any gear changes you want to make in the future?

As you head home, take heart: when it comes down to it, you don't have to be in Europe to explore on foot. You don't even have to be traveling. You can explore on foot wherever you are—even at home. If you're ever in Seattle and you see me out and about, you'll probably also see my day pack. That's because I walk pretty much everywhere, even to the grocery store. It's my way of exploring on foot every single day, and the practice has shown me the truth of the famous quote by Marcel Proust from *The Prisoner* (1923): "The real voyage of discovery consists not in seeking new landscapes, but in having new eyes."

I hope this book shows you not only a better way to travel but a better way to see the world around you, and I hope that exploring on foot adds as much value to your life as it has to mine. Thank you so much for inviting me to be part of your journey; it is an honor, and I can't wait until we connect again, whether we meet in person at an author event or virtually in another of my books. Until then, happy trails!

CREATE MORE OPPORTUNITIES TO EXPLORE ON FOOT

If you'd like more places to explore on foot, whether at home or abroad, help encourage the development of walking-based travel:

- Participate in walking activities and vote with your feet and your dollars.
- Tell tourist information offices and tour companies that you want even more opportunities to explore on foot.
- Go into business for yourself to expand the network of village-to-village or hut-to-hut walking trails.
- Become a member of a trail organization that lobbies for funding for trails and helps maintain them.
- Volunteer to help on trail maintenance projects.
- Tell your city's elected officials that you want more sidewalks, urban trails and parks.

CHECKLISTS

PLANNING

✓ Six Months to a Year in Advance

- ☐ Decide on a trail.
- ☐ Order a passport if you don't already have one.
- ☐ Apply for a visa if you need one.
- ☐ Make sure your smartphone is unlocked and GSM-compatible (see Cell Phone Service in Chapter 16, Electronic Tools) if you plan to use it in Europe (some carriers may not unlock your phone if you haven't had their service for at least a year).
- ☐ Optional: Find a travel companion.
- ☐ Optional: Make a reservation with a tour company.
- ☐ Finalize your itinerary, taking into consideration ground transportation to and from the trailhead.
- ☐ Buy your plane tickets, including short domestic flights.
- ☐ Book your accommodations, if you're going on a popular trail or in high season.
- ☐ Optional: Purchase trip insurance.
- ☐ Start a training program.

✓ Three Months in Advance

- ☐ Buy your train and/or bus tickets.
- ☐ Book your accommodations, if you're not going on a really popular trail or you're walking outside of the main season.
- ☐ Book any additional services, adventures and activities.
- ☐ Start studying up on the local culture.
- ☐ Purchase any remaining gear, including an international SIM card if that's how you're going to get cell phone service in Europe.

✓ One Month in Advance

- ☐ Verify that your health insurance company will cover you while you're in Europe, or purchase international health insurance for the time you'll be gone (see the International Health Insurance sidebar in Chapter 15, Trail and Travel Tools).

PACKING

✓ Clothing

Trail Outfit

- ☐ 2 pairs trail socks
- ☐ 1 pair trail underwear
- ☐ 1 pair walking pants, shorts or capris
- ☐ 1 short-sleeve trail shirt
- ☐ 1 long-sleeve full-zip trail shirt

Crossover Layers

- ☐ 1 down vest
- ☐ 1 puffy jacket
- ☐ 1 pair long-underwear bottoms
- ☐ 1 lightweight rain shell

- ☐ 1 pair thin gloves
- ☐ 1 lightweight hat
- ☐ 1 thin scarf

Town Outfit
- ☐ 1 pair town socks
- ☐ 1 pair town underwear
- ☐ 1 pair lightweight town pants or skirt
- ☐ 1 short-sleeve town shirt or top
- ☐ 1 lightweight sweater

Accessories
- ☐ 1 pajama top or lightweight shirt
- ☐ 1 lightweight swimsuit
- ☐ 1 watch
- ☐ Small packing cubes, stuff sacks, compression sacks, plastic bags or other organizers

Options
- ☐ Sports bra for the trail
- ☐ Convertible bra for town
- ☐ Lightweight travel dress
- ☐ Silver- or gold-colored hoops
- ☐ Long-sleeve button-down shirt and tie
- ☐ Heavier puffy jacket
- ☐ Thicker socks
- ☐ Warmer hat
- ☐ Warmer gloves
- ☐ Long-sleeve long-underwear top
- ☐ Rain pants
- ☐ Heavier rain jacket
- ☐ Long-sleeve sun shirt
- ☐ Sun hat

✔ Footwear

The Basics
- ☐ Trail shoes
- ☐ Town shoes
- ☐ Plastic produce bags

Options
- ☐ Lightweight sandals
- ☐ Traction devices
- ☐ Warmer town shoes

✔ Toiletries and Medications

The Basics
- ☐ Travel toothbrush and cover
- ☐ Travel-size toothpaste
- ☐ Dental floss
- ☐ Shampoo
- ☐ Soap
- ☐ Deodorant
- ☐ Tweezers
- ☐ Nail clippers
- ☐ Sunscreen
- ☐ Travel towel
- ☐ Medication
- ☐ Small container for individual toiletries
- ☐ Toiletry bag
- ☐ See-through quart-size plastic bag
- ☐ Compact, reusable grocery bag

Options
- ☐ Dry shampoo
- ☐ Conditioner
- ☐ Small lightweight comb and/or hairbrush
- ☐ Bobby pins
- ☐ Elastic hair bands
- ☐ Headband
- ☐ Body lotion
- ☐ Talcum powder
- ☐ Face wash
- ☐ Face lotion
- ☐ Acne cream
- ☐ Razor
- ☐ Makeup
- ☐ Feminine hygiene products

✔ Trail Tools

The Ten Essentials

- ☐ Map, compass and guidebook
- ☐ Sunglasses (and case) and sunscreen
- ☐ Extra clothing
- ☐ Headlamp (with fresh batteries)
- ☐ First-aid kit (see separate list below)
- ☐ Safety matches or a lighter
- ☐ Repair kit (see separate list below)
- ☐ Food—trail snacks
- ☐ Water (in water bottles or bladders)
- ☐ Space blanket
- ☐ Plus, organizers for trail tools

First-Aid Kit

- ☐ Bandages
- ☐ Packaged cleanser such as alcohol wipes
- ☐ Moleskin
- ☐ Collapsible scissors
- ☐ Needle
- ☐ Sterile gauze pads
- ☐ Adhesive tape
- ☐ Antibiotic pills (prescribed by doctor)
- ☐ Ibuprofen (anti-inflammatory)
- ☐ Acetaminophen (analgesic)
- ☐ Anti-diarrhea pills
- ☐ Antacid pills
- ☐ Melatonin or natural sleep pills
- ☐ Antibacterial cream
- ☐ Cortisone cream

Repair Kit

- ☐ A few strips of duct tape
- ☐ Small sewing kit
- ☐ 12 inches (30 cm) of thin cord
- ☐ Safety pins
- ☐ Rubber bands
- ☐ Twist ties
- ☐ Superglue
- ☐ Small plastic bags for packing out trash

Options

- ☐ Water purification device
- ☐ Insect repellent wipes
- ☐ Support braces or bands
- ☐ Trekking poles
- ☐ Sleep sack
- ☐ Tent
- ☐ Sleeping pad
- ☐ Sleeping bag
- ☐ Camp pillow
- ☐ Backpacking stove
- ☐ Refillable fuel canister (add fuel to your kit in Europe)
- ☐ Cooking pot or pan
- ☐ Cooking utensils
- ☐ Plate
- ☐ Bowl
- ☐ Cup
- ☐ Eating utensils
- ☐ Food—camping meals

✔ Travel Tools

The Basics: Travel Tools

- ☐ Passport
- ☐ Drivers license
- ☐ Itinerary and confirmation numbers
- ☐ Trip insurance paperwork
- ☐ Health insurance paperwork
- ☐ Cash
- ☐ Debit card
- ☐ Credit cards
- ☐ Travel wallet
- ☐ Currency-conversion cheat sheet

The Basics: Town Tools

- ☐ Travel flatware
- ☐ Pocketknife
- ☐ Hand sanitizer
- ☐ Extra hydration bag for wine
- ☐ TSA-approved wine opener

- ☐ Travel laundry line
- ☐ Small notebook
- ☐ Pen
- ☐ Journal
- ☐ Organizers for travel tools

Options
- ☐ International drivers license
- ☐ Visa
- ☐ Written copy of your prescriptions
- ☐ Letter from your doctor about any pre-existing conditions
- ☐ Money belt or travel scarf

✔ Electronic Tools

The Basics
- ☐ Smartphone
- ☐ Trail and travel apps
- ☐ Smartphone case
- ☐ Lens cloth
- ☐ Earbuds
- ☐ Cell phone service
- ☐ Adaptor
- ☐ Smartphone charging components
- ☐ Power bank
- ☐ Power bank charging components
- ☐ Smartphone chest or belt holster
- ☐ Small plastic bag for earbuds
- ☐ Waterproof electronics organizer

Options
- ☐ Foreign or international SIM card
- ☐ Small plastic bag for home SIM card
- ☐ SPOT device, satellite communicator or PLB
- ☐ Stand-alone GPS unit
- ☐ GPS case
- ☐ GPS wrist strap or tether
- ☐ GPS charger

- ☐ Spare set of GPS batteries
- ☐ Point-and-shoot or mirrorless camera
- ☐ Camera case
- ☐ Camera wrist strap or tether
- ☐ Camera batteries
- ☐ Camera charger
- ☐ Converter

✔ Packs

The Basics
- ☐ Backpack
- ☐ Pack cover
- ☐ Day pack

Options
- ☐ Combination lock
- ☐ Resealable plastic bag
- ☐ Zip ties

FINAL TASKS

✔ Three Days Before Your Flight

Get Your Banking in Order
- ☐ Authorize debit and credit cards for use in Europe
- ☐ Verify debit and credit card PINs
- ☐ Figure out how much cash you'll need when you arrive in Europe
- ☐ Look online for your bank's European partner banks
- ☐ Find out where those ATMs are

Plan Your Pre-Trail Errands
- ☐ List everything you need to get or do when you arrive in Europe
- ☐ Figure out how you'll get to each spot
- ☐ Figure out what time each spot is open

Pack Your Bag
- ☐ Use your checklists
- ☐ Highlight any missing items
- ☐ Keep items accessible for airport screening

Get Plenty of Rest
- ☐ Stop training and give your muscles a break
- ☐ Get a full eight hours of sleep each night

✔ One Day before Your Flight
- ☐ Check in for your flight
- ☐ Print your boarding pass or save it to your smartphone

✔ The Morning of Your Flight
- ☐ Add final items to your backpack
- ☐ Check everything off your packing checklists
- ☐ Stow any uncompleted checklists (such as your pre-trail errands) in your backpack

✔ During Your Flight
- ☐ Put your phone in airplane mode
- ☐ Set your watch to European time
- ☐ Sleep, eat and drink caffeine on European time
- ☐ Shut off screens if you have trouble napping
- ☐ Stay hydrated

✔ When You Get to Europe
- ☐ Let yourself get a little hungry
- ☐ Stay awake until European bedtime
- ☐ Do your pre-trail errands
- ☐ Connect to Wi-Fi

✔ The Day Before Your Walk
- ☐ Take local transportation to your trail-head accommodations

✔ The Night Before Your Walk

Figure Out What Time Breakfast Is
- ☐ Set your alarm for an early start
- ☐ Plan to take your backpack to the dining room

Reorganize Your Backpack
- ☐ Integrate things you picked up on your pretrail errands
- ☐ Take your toiletries out of their TSA-approved plastic bag and stow them in your toiletry bag
- ☐ Fill your water bottles
- ☐ Put a day's worth of snacks in your pack's outside pockets
- ☐ Lay out your trail clothes for the morning

Get a Good Night's Sleep
- ☐ Consider taking a natural sleep aid

ACKNOWLEDGMENTS

From the time I was seven years old, I knew I wanted to be a writer. And not just any writer—a book author. At family events, I'd hide away in my grandpa's study, dreamily penning chapters and picturing the towering stack of books that would someday bear my name and decorate my coffee table.

Back then, it all seemed so easy. It took many years—and more than a few false starts—for my dream to become a reality, but the book you're holding is evidence that childhood wishes can come true. It's also evidence that it takes much more than just a dream—or your own blood, sweat and tears—to create something meaningful. It takes a community. And throughout the development of this book, I had an incredible one, filled with supportive family, friends and colleagues who didn't just encourage me to pursue my dream but did whatever they could to help make it happen.

My husband, Mac, was one of those people. This book wouldn't exist without him. He generously invited me into his own big dream, the grand tour of Europe that you'll read about in the Introduction and that led to the idea for *Explore Europe on Foot*. But he did more than share his trip—and the money he'd worked long and hard to save for it. He also encouraged me in the sweetest ways. When we were in Ireland and I was inspired to start writing, he temporarily dismantled a chest in our rental house to make me a desk and spent a week tending the peat fire I wrote in front of. His support has continued back at home as well. Each day he goes to an office job so I don't have to. What a tremendous gift—if only every author could be so lucky.

This book might never have gotten out of the idea stage if it hadn't been for my good friend and editor at *Washington Trails* magazine, Eli Boschetto, who offered to pitch it to his publisher. I'm so glad he introduced me to Mountaineers Books and editor in chief Kate Rogers. It's hard giving up total control of such a personal project, but from the beginning Kate made the publishing process a collaborative endeavor, one where I always felt valued and included. The book is better for her contributions and our partnership.

Writing *Explore Europe on Foot* required a lot of research. In addition to drawing on several extended trips I'd already taken, I spent an additional ten weeks in Europe with my boots on the ground, hiking, researching and narrowing down my selection of handpicked walks. I'm grateful for the friends and family who joined me on trail: Carol Veach, Cheryl Nilson, Mitzi Sugar, Caroline Calaway, Kelsey Overby, Mackenzie Mendoza, Sofia Gaiaschi, Quentin Pierre and Jerriann Sullivan. I'll never forget our adventures—and misadventures.

Once the research was over, it was time for the writing to begin. The process was made a little less

Opposite: *Day or night, the sights of Europe are a dream that you'll long to return to time and time again.*

challenging—and a little more fun—thanks to my coworking space, Office Nomads, and the support of our monthly writers' lunch, which I often describe as group therapy for writers. Being able to talk through my struggles with the manuscript and the writing process with such bright and generous colleagues was incredibly helpful.

Of course, there were still tough days, days when I thought I could never finish a project of this magnitude or do it justice. And on those days, I called my favorite cheerleader and number one fan: my mom. She never failed to lift me up and encourage me to keep writing, and she never missed a chance to help me celebrate a victory—big or small—along the way.

One of those victories was finally turning in my draft manuscript to Mountaineers Books, where it morphed into a real book with the help of several talented individuals, including copyeditor Kris Fulsaas, project editor Janet Kimball and designer Jen Grable. I'm grateful for their many skills, from fact-checking to production schedule tweaking to illustration drawing. It's because of them that this book came together at all—and that it looks as beautiful as it does.

Thanks to everyone who has helped me along the way, *Explore Europe on Foot* has become something I'm really proud of, a book deserving of display—and not just on my own coffee table. Thank you!

Traveling for weeks at a time is wonderful—and exhausting. The following tourism organizations, guides and local businesses made my research trips so much more comfortable and enjoyable with their hospitality and support:

Icelandic Mountain Guides (Reykjavik, Iceland)
The Tourism Office of Chamonix (Chamonix, France)
Hotel Oustalet (Chamonix, France)
The Tourism Office of Courmayeur (Courmayeur, Italy)
Hotel Gran Baita (Courmayeur, Italy)
Glasgow City Marketing Bureau (Glasgow, Scotland)
Glencoe Youth Hostel (Glencoe, Scotland)
The Moselland Tourism Office (Bernkastel-Kues, Germany)
Weinberghotel Nalbach (Reil, Germany)
Hotel Zum Grünen Kranz (Zell, Germany)
Landhaus Hübner (Neef, Germany)

Guide Andy Offinger (Bernkastel-Kues, Germany)
The Ardenne-Luxembourg Regional Office of Tourism (Vianden, Luxembourg)
Natural Park of the Two Ourthes (Houffalize, Belgium)
Tourism Office "Heart of the Ardenne" (La Roche-en-Ardenne, Belgium)
Hotel Huberty (Kautenbach, Luxembourg)
Hotel du Commerce (Clervaux, Luxembourg)
Hotel Moulin d'Asselborn (Asselborn, Luxembourg)
Hotel Vayamundo (Houffalize, Belgium)
Hotel Floreal (La Roche-en-Ardenne, Belgium)
Rota Vicentina (Odemira, Portugal)
Guesthouse Três Marias (Vila Nova de Milfontes, Portugal)
Herdade do Freixial (Vila Nova des Milfontes, Portugal)
Restaurant Porto das Barcas (Vila Nova des Milfontes, Portugal)
Monte Novo da Longueira (Almograve, Portugal)

Restaurant O Josué (Almograve, Portugal)

Monte das Alpenduradas (Zambujeira do Mar, Portugal)

Restaurant O Sacas (Zambujeira do Mar, Portugal)

The Tourism Office of Saint-Malo (Saint-Malo, France)

Hôtel Les Charmettes (Saint-Malo, France)

Hôtel La Voilerie (Cancale, France)

Restaurant A Contre-Courant (Cancale, France)

Chemins de la Baie du Mont Saint-Michel (Genêts, France)

The Tourism Office of Bavaria (Munich, Germany)

The Starnberg Five-Lake-Region Tourism Office (Starnberg, Germany)

Tourism Association Pfaffenwinkel (Schongau, Germany)

Tourist Information Schwangau (Schwangau, Germany)

Angelo Design Hotel (Munich, Germany)

Andechs Monastery (Andechs, Germany)

Gasthof Unterbräu (Dießen, Germany)

Ferienwohnung Alpenpanorama Familie Eva-Maria Rössle (Hohenpeißenberg, Germany)

Landhotel Moosbeck-Alm (Rottenbuch, Germany)

Gasthof "Zur Alten Tenne" (Prem, Germany)

Gästehaus Groß (Prem, Germany)

Guide Erih Gößler (Füssen, Germany)

Gästehaus Sankt Ulrich (Füssen, Germany)

RESOURCES

PART 1: DREAMING

Alsace Wine Route, France (Walk 4).
www.alsace-wine-route.com

American Pilgrims on the Camino, offers free
credentials to pilgrims in North America.
www.americanpilgrims.org
/credential-request

Aosta Valley Wine Route.
www.routedesvinsvda.it/en/

Arthur's Seat and Holyrood Park, Scotland
(One-Day Wander #7).
www.walkhighlands.co.uk/lothian
/arthurs-seat.shtml

Bastogne War Museum.
www.bastognewarmuseum.be/home.html

Bike Air, bike rental in Colmar, France.
www.bikeair.fr

Britain on Foot, has a great routefinder tool
called OS Maps. www.britainonfoot.co.uk

Calmont Klettersteig (part of Walk 10).
www.calmont-klettersteig.com, available
only in German.

Cathedral of Santiago de Compostela,
for schedule of masses.
www.catedraldesantiago.es/en/

Cinque Terre National Park.
www.parconazionale5terre.it

Cinque Terre sanctuaries. www.cinqueterre
.a-turist.com/the_sanctuaries_path

Cinque Terre tourist information.
www.cinqueterre.com

Cliffs of Moher Coastal Walk
(One-Day Wander #6).
www.cliffsofmohercoastalwalk.ie

Cliffs of Moher, Ireland. www.cliffsofmoher.ie

Clow, Kate. *The Lycian Way* (and companion
app of the same name). Upcountry
(Turkey) Ltd., 2005.

Confraternity of Saint James, publishes
detailed guidebooks on several Camino de
Santiago routes, including the English Way
(Walk 2). www.csj.org.uk

Country Walking, a UK publication. www
.livefortheoutdoors.com/countrywalking/

Cycling Europe, has official websites, blogs,
books, forums and maps for each EuroVelo
route. www.cyclingeurope.org

Deutsche Bahn, German national rail carrier.
www.bahn.de

Escapardenne Eisleck Trail (Walk 11).
www. blog.escapardenne.eu/?lang=en

European Ramblers' Association, administers
certification process for Leading Quality
Trails (LQT); has local chapters you can
walk with. www.era-ewv-ferp.com

EuroVelo.com, has information on EuroVelo
routes. www.eurovelo.com

Explore on Foot, author Cassandra Overby's
travel brand. exploreonfoot@gmail.com;
www.explore-on-foot.com

Ferrol, Spain, *Semana Santa* calendar of
events. www.semanasantaferrol.org

Opposite: *When it comes to jaw-dropping scenery, it's hard to top the Tour du Mont Blanc.*

Footprint Maps, map for West Highland Way (Walk 13) is under "Long Distance Paths." www.footprintmaps.co.uk

Freilichtmuseum Hessenpark, historical park in Germany. www.hessenpark.de/en/

Gardner, Nicky. "A Manifesto for Slow Travel." *hidden europe* magazine. www.hiddeneurope.co.uk /a-manifesto-for-slow-travel

Grand Route (GR) footpaths in France. www.gr-infos.com

Hohenschwangau castle, Germany, tour tickets. www.hohenschwangau.de/1392.0.html

Icelandic Mountain Guides, professional guide company for Laugavegur Trek (Walk 14). www.mountainguides.is

Iceland Touring Association, information on Laugavegur Trek (Walk 14). www.fi.is/en

Internationaler Volkssportverband, has local chapters you can walk with. www.ivv-web.org

Jardin Majorelle, Marrakesh, Morocco, botanical garden. www.jardinmajorelle.com/ang/

Juliff, Lauren. "An Incredible Experience in the Sahara Desert," helpful article with suggestions on how to book a good tour, from her blog. www.neverendingfootsteps .com/2012/08/31/an-incredible -experience-in-the-sahara-desert

Kinderdijk, the Netherlands (One-day Wander 5). www.kinderdijk.com

Lake Bled, Slovenia (One-day Wander 3). www.bled.si/en

The Lake District, England (Walk 12). www.golakes.co.uk

Lake District National Park. www.lakedistrict.gov.uk

La Roche Museum of the Battle of the Ardennes. www.batarden.be/site/en.html

Laugardalslaug, Iceland, geothermal baths. www.visitreykjavik.is/laugardalslaug

Lonely Planet travel forum. www.lonelyplanet.com/thorntree

Loram, Charlie. *West Highland Way.* Trailblazer Publications, 2016.

Manning, Robert and Martha. *Walking Distance.* University of Oregon Press, 2013.

Meetup.com, online community of local interest-based groups that have in-person gatherings. www.meetup.com

Moda Camp, Merzouga, Morocco, luxury camp. www.modacampmerzouga.com/en/

Mont Saint-Michel, France (Walk 3). www.ot-montsaintmichel.com and us.france.fr/en/mont-saint-michel-3

Moselle Tours, daylong boat cruises leaving from Cochem, Germany. www.mosel rundfahrten.de/en/cochem/home

Moselsteig, Germany (part of Walk 10). www.moselsteig.de

Mount Vesuvius National Park, Italy (One-day Wander 2). www.parconazionaledelvesuvio.it

National Cycle Network, network of national cycle routes in the United Kingdom. www.sustrans.org.uk/ncn /map/national-cycle-network

National Trust, information on the Lake District. www.nationaltrust.org.uk /days-out/regionnorthwest/lake-district

Naturpark Öewersauer, Luxembourg. www .naturpark-sure.lu/index.php?id=1;lang=en.

Overby, Cassandra. *Explore France's Alsace Wine Route on Foot: Kientzheim to Molsheim.* Cassandra Overby, 2018.

———. *Explore France's GR 34 on Foot: Saint-Malo to Mont Saint-Michel.* Cassandra Overby, 2018.

———. *Explore Germany's King Ludwig's Way on Foot.* Cassandra Overby, 2018.

Plitvice Lakes National Park, Croatia (One-day Wander 4). www.np-plitvicka-jezera.hr/en

Rede Expressos, buses in Portugal. www.rede-expressos.pt/default.aspx

Reynolds, Kev. *Tour of Mont Blanc*. Cicerone Press, 2012.

———. *Trekking the Swiss Alpine Pass Route—Via Alpina Route 1*. Cicerone Press, 2017.

Rick Steves travel forum. www.ricksteves.com/travel-forum

Romantic Road, Bavaria. www.romantischestrasse.de

Rota Vicentina trail system, Portugal (Walk 1). www.rotavicentina.com

Route Notes, online adventure magazine of tour company Macs Adventure. www.macsadventure.com/us /about-us/adventure-inspiration /route-notes-travel-magazine/

Santella, Chris. *Fifty Places to Hike before You Die*. Stewart, Tabori and Chang, 2012.

Santiago de Compostela Pilgrim's Office. www. oficinadelperegrino.com/en/

Southwest Alentejo and Vicentine Coast Natural Park. www.natural.pt/portal/en /AreaProtegida/PontosInteresse/12

Sterna, buses for travel to start point of Laugavegur Trek (Walk 14). www.sternatravel.com

Theatre by the Lake, Keswick, England. www.theatrebythelake.com

Tour du Mont Blanc (Walk 5). www.autourdumontblanc.com/en

Tourism in Alsace, France. www.tourisme-alsace.com

Tourism in France. us.france.fr/en/

Tourism in Germany. www.germany.travel/en

Tourism in Moselle region. www.mosellandtouristik.de/en/

Tourism in Normandy. en.normandie-tourisme.fr

Traildino, offers trail descriptions and links to other resources. www.traildino.com

Trekopedia, offers TrailSmart app, with digital maps and comprehensive walking directions for each stage of the Lycian Way (Walk 7) and other trails as well. https://trekopedia.com/trailsmart/

TripAdvisor travel forum. www.tripadvisor.com/ForumHome

UNESCO World Heritage Sites. www.whc.unesco.org

Vesturbæjarlaug, Iceland, geothermal baths. www.visitreykjavik.is/vesturbaejarlaug

Via Alpina (part of Walk 8). www.via-alpina.org

Wanderbares Deutschland, a German magazine. www.wanderbares-deutschland.de

West Highland Way, Scotland (Walk 13). www.west-highland-way.co.uk

Wikiloc, free source for downloadable GPX tracks. www.wikiloc.com

Wikipedia, Camino de Santiago page. www.en.wikipedia.org/wiki /Camino_de_Santiago

Wikitravel, offers information on very off-the-beaten-path trails. www.wikitravel.com

PART 2: PLANNING

Airbnb Experiences, offers urban walking tours and other travel experiences. www.airbnb.com/experiences

Airfarewatchdog, provides alerts on fare drops. www.airfarewatchdog.com

Alpine Club of Canada, offers social events, outdoor adventures and skills courses. www.alpineclubofcanada.ca

American Alpine Club, offers benefit dinners and athlete tours. www.americanalpineclub.org

American Automobile Association (AAA), offers international drivers licenses. www.aaa.com

American Hiking Society, leads volunteer trail maintenance. www.americanhiking.org

American Long Distance Hiking Association—West, western chapter of long-distance hikers, including thru-hikers and section-hikers. www.aldhawest.org

American Volkssport Association, local chapters offer organized walks. www.ava.org

Appalachian Mountain Club, organizes 7,000 trips yearly. www.outdoors.org

Auto Europe, rental car consolidator. www.autoeurope.com

Backpacker magazine, offers online articles on fitness and outdoor skills. www.backpacker.com

Backroads, offers guided walking tours. www.backroads.com

BlaBlaCar, carpooling website. www.blablacar.com

Booking.com, offers up-to-date and detailed information for a variety of accommodations. www.booking.com

British Broadcasting Network, Europe edition for politics and current events. www.bbc.com/news/world/europe

Busabout, bus version of the Eurail pass. www.busabout.com

Busbud, bus schedule aggregator. www.busbud.com

Butterfield & Robinson, offers guided and self-guided walking tours. www.butterfield.com

CAMIGAS, a Facebook group's buddy system for women traveling alone on the Camino de Santiago (Walk 2). www.facebook.com/groups/CaminoBuddySystemForWomen

Campinmygarden.com, lists people who allow camping in their backyard for a small fee. www.campinmygarden.com

Canterbury, Dave. *Bushcraft 101.* Adams Media, 2014.

CIA World Factbook, information about governments around the world. www.cia.gov/library/publications/resources/the-world-factbook

Citymapper, shows local transportation options. www.citymapper.com

Colver, John. *Fit by Nature.* Mountaineers Books, 2011.

Commisceo Global, information on local customs. www.commisceo-global.com/country-guides

Couchsurfing, free membership organization for finding free accommodations. www.couchsurfing.com

Country Walkers, offers guided and self-guided walking tours. www.countrywalkers.com

Deutsche Bahn, German national rail company; offers train schedules for all of Europe but prices only for Germany. www.bahn.de/en

Duolingo, free program for learning foreign languages. www.duolingo.com

Eatwith, connects travelers with locals to share a meal. www.eatwith.com

EatWithaLocal, connects travelers with locals to share a meal. www.eatwithalocal.com

Eurail, offers train passes. www.eurail.com

Eurocampings, has listings for more than 8,600 campgrounds. www.eurocampings.co.uk

Europcar, larger car-rental company. www.europcar.com

GlobalFreeloaders.com, free membership organization for finding free accommodations. www.globalfreeloaders.com

Global Greeter Network, connects travelers with locals to share a meal. www.globalgreeternetwork.info

Great Courses Plus, offers more than 8,000 educational history videos. www.thegreatcoursesplus.com

Groupon Getaways, offers interesting travel and accommodations deals. www.groupon.com/getaways

The Guardian, international and UK editions on politics and current events. www.theguardian.com

Hike It Baby, kid-friendly walks. www.hikeitbaby.com

Hostelworld, hostel aggregator. www.hostelworld.com

Inntravel, offers self-guided walking tours. www.inntravel.co.uk

InsureMyTrip, aggregator of travel insurance options. www.insuremytrip.com

International Federation of Mountain Guides Associations, certifies mountaineering guides. www.ivbv.info/en/home.html

iTunes U, has free downloadable courses, including history courses. www.itunesu.itunes.apple.com

Journeywoman, for solo women travelers. www.journeywoman.com

Khan Academy, offers free short educational videos. www.khanacademy.org

Lonely Planet. *Food Lover's Guide to the World.* Lonely Planet, 2014.

Macs Adventure, offers self-guided walking tours. www.macsadventure.com

The Man in Seat Sixty-One, comprehensive resource on European train travel by former British Rail employee. www.seat61.com

Meetup.com, offers resources for meeting with discussion groups and book clubs. www.meetup.com

momondo, European flight aggregator. www.momondo.com

The Mountaineers, membership organization that offers classes and outings in the Pacific Northwest. www.mountaineers.org

National Geographic Expeditions, offers guided walking tours. www.nationalgeographicexpeditions.com

National Outdoor Leadership School, offers outdoor education courses. www.nols.edu

National Rail, aggregator of more than twenty different rail companies in Britain. www.nationalrail.co.uk (best place to buy tickets is www.virgintrains.co.uk)

Open Culture, offers more than 1,200 free classes, including history courses. www.openculture.com

Outward Bound, offers outdoor education courses. www.outwardbound.org

Rail Europe, offers train schedules and prices for all of Europe. www.raileurope.com

REI, offers classes on outdoor skills and online articles on fitness. www.rei.com

REI Adventures, offers guided walking tours. www.rei.com/adventures

Renfe, Spain's national train company. www.renfe.com/EN/viajeros/

RickSteves.com, has a good fare estimator for European train travel. www.ricksteves.com/travel-tips/transportation/trains/cost-maps

Rome2rio, offers a free trip planner. www.rome2rio.com

SANDEMANs New Europe Tours, guides urban walking tours. www.neweuropetours.eu

Sherpa Expeditions, offers self-guided walking tours. www.sherpaexpeditions.com

Sierra Club, offers local walks and camping, backpacking and international trips. www.sierraclub.org

Sixt, larger car-rental company. www.sixt.com

Skyscanner, European flight aggregator.
www.skyscanner.com

SNCF, France's national rail company.
www.sncf.com/en/passengers

Solo Traveler, free resource for traveling solo.
www.solotravelerworld.com

Solo Travel Society, free resource for traveling
solo. www.facebook.com/solotravelsociety

SoloWalks, offers self-guided walking tours.
www.solowalks.com

Steves, Rick. "Art for Travelers" online lectures.
www.ricksteves.com/watch-read-listen
/video/travel-talks#art

———. *Europe 101: History and Art for the
Traveler.* Rick Steves, 2007.

———. *Travel as a Political Act.* Rick Steves,
2014.

10 Minutes a Day book series, for learning a
foreign language. Bilingual Books.

Tours by Locals, guides urban walking tours.
www.toursbylocals.com

Townsend, Chris. *The Backpacker's Handbook.*
Fourth edition. International Marine/
Ragged Mountain Press, 2011.

TravBuddy, has more than 650,000 members
all over the world. www.travbuddy.com

Travelers Literary Companions series by
Whereabouts Press, books that gather
stories from specific areas.
www.whereaboutspress.com/category
/traveler-literary-companions

TripAdvisor, for reviews on tours and much
more. www.tripadvisor.com

Tsong, Nicole. *Yoga for Hikers.* Mountaineers
Books, 2016.

Uber, provides ride-share services.
www.uber.com/cities

Vacation Rentals by Owner, for private
accommodations. www.vrbo.com

Vayable, guides urban walking tours.
www.vayable.com

Viator, guides urban walking tours.
www.viator.com

Wanderlust and Lipstick, site for solo women
travelers. www.wanderlustandlipstick.com

The Wayfarers, offers guided walking tours.
www.thewayfarers.com

Women on the Road, site for solo women
travelers. www.women-on-the-road.com

World Taximeter, lists estimated taxi fares for
larger cities. www.worldtaximeter.com

World Travel Family, offers articles and
personal recommendations from a family
who has backpacked around the world.
www.worldtravelfamily.com

PART 3: PACKING

Backcountry, for finding discount gear online.
www.backcountry.com

Campmor, for finding discount gear online.
www.campmor.com

Cavallini Papers, offers small, lightweight
pocket notebooks. www.cavallini.com

Craigslist, for finding used gear online.
www.craigslist.org

GearTrade, for finding used gear online.
www.geartrade.com

KnowRoaming, offers international SIM cards.
www.knowroaming.com

Moosejaw, for finding discount gear online.
www.moosejaw.com

Power Plugs and Sockets of the World,
information on Europe's four main outlet
shapes. www.power-plugs-sockets.com

REI Garage, for finding discount gear online.
www.rei.com/rei-garage

Shoes.com, offers shoes for sale online.
www.shoes.com

Steep&cheap, for finding discount gear online.
www.steepandcheap.com

Zappos.com, offers shoes for sale online.
www.zappos.com

INDEX

Tour du Mont Blanc, France & Italy, 86–90
tour groups, 160
tour guides, finding good, 172–174
Tour of Mont Blanc (Reynold), 89
tourism trails, 39
tourist information services, 59
tours
guided walking, 170–174
niche, 237
taking self-guided walking, 168–170
towel grabs (exercise), 209
towel racks, heated, 188
towns, walking through, 221
Townsend, Chris, 223
trail shoes, 254–256
trail tools, 263–269, 313
Traildino, 41–42, 57
trails
See also hiking, walks
bathrooms and, 220
categories, 39–43
chaining together, 34
choosing, 149
cycling routes, 43–45
different types of, 36–37
in Europe, 15–16, 38–43
Grand Route Footpaths, 42
identifying good, 55–59
mileage, 31
national, regional, local, 42–43
one-day wanders, 45–55
tipping, 174
training for, 202–212
urban walking, 167–168
walking. *See* walking tours
training for the trail, 202–212
trains, 179–180
transcontinental flights, 175–177
transportation
local, 298
private, 164–166
regional, 177–185
transcontinental flights, 175–177
trash, 220–221
travel insurance, 151
Travel as a Political Act (Steves), 226–227

travel blogs, 57
travel guides, 227–228
travel research, 145–148
travel tools, 269–274, 313–314
travelers, being a good, 236
Travelers Literary Companions series, 233
traveling
with children, 155–156
with companions, 153–160
solo, for single ladies, 158
tour groups, 160
as visitor instead of tourist, 306–308
traveling lunges (exercise), 204
Trekking the Swiss Alpine Pass Route . . . (Reynold), 107
Trip Advisor, 172
trip insurance, 151, 269–270
Turkey's Lycian Way, 96–100
Twain, Mark, 225

U
Uber, 165
UK (United Kingdom)
the Lake District, 123–128
West Highland Way, 128–133
UNESCO designation for cultural, geographical importance, 46
UNESCO World Heritage Sites, 40–41
Unterhäusern, Germany, 108
urban walking tours, 167–168

V
Vernazza, Italy, 92, 94
Via Alpina, 39
visas, 269

W
walking
breaks, taking, 215–216
calibrating your pace, 214–215
faster than your companions, 215
final to-dos before, 290–301
independently, 161–168
shoes, footwear, 254–257
tours. *See* walking tours

training for the trail, 202–212
treating fellow walkers well, 221–222
Walking Distance (Manning), 13, 58–59
walking tours
taking self-guided, 168–170
urban, 167–168
walks
See also specific walk
culture, 37, 224–235
fifteen handpicked at a glance (table), 61, 63
history, 36, 225–226
walks (exercise), 209
wallets, 271
Wanderbares Deutschland magazine, 58
Warrior II (exercise), 208
washing your clothes, 250–252
water, drinking, 264–265, 294
weather
dressing for, 249
handling inclement, 216–217
websites
travel companies', 56–57
travel research, 149
weekend warrior (exercise), 209–210
weighted pack (exercise), 208
West Highland Way, England & UK, 128–133
West Highland Way (Loram), 133
Wi-Fi, 14, 277–278, 297
Wikiloc, 57
wildlife, 17
Windermere, England, 124, 126
wine and food walks, 36–37
wine tools, 273
women, single ladies travel tips, 158
Wordsworth, William, 124
World Heritage Sites (UNESCO), 40–41
World Travel Family, 156
writing materials, 273–274

Y
Yelp, 172
Yoga for Hikers (Tsong), 210

ABOUT THE AUTHOR

Cassandra Overby grew up hiking and camping in the beautiful Pacific Northwest. She started adventuring internationally in college, when study abroad programs in Germany and Austria got her firmly hooked on travel. Her adventures have taken her all over the world, from Central America to Southeast Asia, but she loves exploring Europe more than anywhere else.

Both hiking and traveling continue to shape her life—and her career. She's a travel and outdoor writer by trade, regularly contributing active travel stories to magazines like *Washington Trails* and *Northwest Travel & Life* when she's not working on developing her travel brand, Explore on Foot.

Much of what Cassandra does for work—exploring and writing—she also does for fun. But when she's not on trail or in a foreign country, you can usually find her in her other happy place: a country bar, sporting well-loved leather cowboy boots and dancing to live music.

Unless, that is, she's at home with her family. Cassandra and her favorite travel companion/husband, Mac, recently became parents for the first time. They love exploring Seattle with their baby and are currently planning their first kid-friendly international trip.

To read more of Cassandra's active travel writing, visit cassandraoverby.com. Learn more about Explore on Foot, and discover the other books in the series, at explore-on-foot.com.

MOUNTAINEERS BOOKS is a leading publisher of mountaineering literature and guides—including our flagship title, *Mountaineering: The Freedom of the Hills*—as well as adventure narratives, natural history, and general outdoor recreation. Through our two imprints, Skipstone and Braided River, we also publish titles on sustainability and conservation. We are committed to supporting the environmental and educational goals of our organization by providing expert information on human-powered adventure, sustainable practices at home and on the trail, and preservation of wilderness.

The Mountaineers, founded in 1906, is a 501(c)(3) nonprofit outdoor recreation and conservation organization whose mission is to enrich lives and communities by helping people "explore, conserve, learn about, and enjoy the lands and waters of the Pacific Northwest and beyond." One of the largest such organizations in the United States, it sponsors classes and year-round outdoor activities throughout the Pacific Northwest, including climbing, hiking, backcountry skiing, snowshoeing, camping, kayaking, sailing, and more. The Mountaineers also supports its mission through its publishing division, Mountaineers Books, and promotes environmental education and citizen engagement. For more information, visit The Mountaineers Program Center, 7700 Sand Point Way NE, Seattle, WA 98115-3996; phone 206-521-6001; www.mountaineers.org; or email info@mountaineers.org.

Our publications are made possible through the generosity of donors and through sales of more than 800 titles on outdoor recreation, sustainable lifestyle, and conservation. To donate, purchase books, or learn more, visit us online.

MOUNTAINEERS BOOKS
1001 SW Klickitat Way, Suite 201 • Seattle, WA 98134
800-553-4453 • mbooks@mountaineersbooks.org • www.mountaineersbooks.org

Mountaineers Books is proud to be a corporate sponsor of the Leave No Trace Center for Outdoor Ethics, whose mission is to promote and inspire responsible outdoor recreation through education, research, and partnerships. · The Leave No Trace program is focused specifically on human-powered (nonmotorized) recreation. · Leave No Trace strives to educate visitors about the nature of their recreational impacts and offers techniques to prevent and minimize such impacts. · Leave No Trace is best understood as an educational and ethical program, not as a set of rules and regulations. · For more information, visit www.lnt.org or call 800-332-4100.